The Handbook for Reluctant Database Administrators

JOSEF FINSEL

Apress™

The Handbook for Reluctant Database Administrators
Copyright ©2001 by Josef Finsel

ISBN (pbk): 1-893115-90-9

Printed and bound in the United States of America 12345678910

Editorial Directors: Dan Appleman, Gary Cornell, Karen Watterson, Jason Gilmore
Technical Reviewers: Francis Stanisci, Tom Schraer
Managing Editor: Grace Wong
Marketing Manager: Stephanie Rodriguez
Project Manager: Alexa Stuart
Developmental Editor: Marty Minner
Editor: Kim Wimpsett
Production Editor: Kari Brooks
Page Composition: Impressions Book and Journal Services, Inc.
Indexer: Carol Burbo
Cover Design: Tom Debolski

Distributed to the book trade in the United States by Springer-Verlag New York, Inc., 175 Fifth Avenue, New York, NY, 10010
and outside the United States by Springer-Verlag GmbH & Co. KG, Tiergartenstr. 17, 69112 Heidelberg, Germany

In the United States, phone 1-800-SPRINGER; orders@springer-ny.com; http://www.springer-ny.com
Outside the United States, contact orders@springer.de; http://www.springer.de; fax +49 6221 345229

For information on translations, please contact Apress directly at 901 Grayson Street, Suite 204, Berkeley, CA, 94710
Phone: 510-549-5938; Fax: 510-549-5939; info@apress.com; http://www.apress.com

Contents at a Glance

Contents

Chapter 15   Should I Bother to Learn SQL Profiler?   . . .433

Chapter 16   What Are System Monitor and Performance Monitor? 461

Chapter 17   What a Reluctant DBA Needs to Know about .NET 493

Last Words: Does Reading This Book Make Me a DBA? 501

Bios

Josef Finsel is a software consultant with G.A. Sullivan, a global software development company, but that doesn't come close to telling the whole story. He started playing with computers as a teenager, using his school's Apple IIe. Then he got the opportunity to work on a real live IBM personal computer, with 640KB of memory, two 360KB 5¼-inch disk drives and an RGB monitor. Working his way through college as a computer consultant, he reached the end of his college career and realized he was making more money programming than he could make with this political science degree, so he was off and programming.

In 1999, after years of programming, he decided what he really wanted to do was to share his expertise and experience, so he started trying to disprove the old theory that says, "When you create a programming language in English you'll find programmers can't write in English." Since that time he's been writing articles that cover his two programming loves: Visual Basic and SQL Server. Currently, Josef is eagerly looking toward blazing a trail through the Yukon wilderness from the comfort of his Cincinnati home, which he shares with his wife Celia, his son Benjamin, his father-in-law Carl, and his assorted cats. You can reach him through `http://www.ReluctantDBA.com`.

Francis Stanisci is currently an independent contractor. He was baptized in computers by way of punch cards in the language of FORTRAN and COBOL. Needless to say, COBOL is tough; COBOL with punch cards is something else—best left in the past. There was light at the end of the tunnel, and it came in the form of the Tandy Color Computer (affectionately known as the "CoCo"). This led to more grown-up systems in the Radio Shack line, including the various flavors of compatibles, almost compatibles, and non-compatibles. Part of this experience included working extensively with hardware, which would later pay off in skills for building corporate servers running Windows NT. Francis learned VBA using Microsoft Access and at the same time learned SQL Server 4.21 on OS/2. When Microsoft introduced version 4.21a, there was no turning back.

He has worked with many companies, small to large, which have included such titans as Boeing and Microsoft. His work has included end-to-end application and database development, database design, and re-engineering, and he excels in SQL Server and database optimization.

His hobbies include restoring classic cars (namely El Caminos), building models, and photography. He has a wonderful wife and three super children, though having teenagers has taught him what a wonderfully easy thing learning SQL Server really is.

Tom Schraer has been a consultant with G.A. Sullivan for more than three years and working in the information technology field for more than ten.

Tom first started working with FoxBASE many years ago while in college at the University of Toledo (yes, he did graduate!). Once in the real world, Tom migrated quickly to Visual Basic and then to SQL Server, Informix, and Oracle. Now he is starting all over again, like everyone else, and learning .NET.

Tom is also the co-founder and co-president of the Cincinnati SQL Server User's Group in Cincinnati. Tom presents several times a year along with supporting the user's group Web site and discussion groups.

Tom has been married for more than six years and has two wonderful children that take up any spare time remaining.

Acknowledgments

EVERY PUBLISHED BOOK is the result of the hard work of many individuals. I can't possibly thank them all individually, but I would like to thank John DeGiglio for getting this project started; Karen Watterson for believing in it; Bill Vaughn and Kimberly Tripp-Simonnet for providing focus; Grace Wong, Alexa Stuart, and the incredible Apress staff for guiding me through the process; Marty Minner and Kim Wimpsett for polishing the words; and Francis Stanisci and Tom Schraer for keeping me in line. Last, though far from least, thanks to my loving wife Celia and son Benjamin for giving me up long enough to get this book written.

Foreword

IT HAS HAPPENED to so many of us: One day you get a call from someone in your company. They need a "simple program" to handle some data with which they are working. Being the nice person you are, you agree to set aside some time to build the solution, design the data tables, and help them install and use the application. Sure, little things come up: a change here, an added feature there, and so on. Although it took a bit more time than you had planned, the project is a success. You get thanks from your coworkers and recognition from your superiors. All in all, it is a good experience for all involved.

Now fast forward several months. Somehow, this simple program has turned into a much more serious beast. As all growing children do, this creature requires constant attention, continues to consume more resources, and threatens to misbehave and embarrass you at the least opportune times. Like a good parent, you are equally proud and annoyed by your "offspring." Now, instead of a small bit of code and some data, you are responsible for multiple databases, server management, backup operations, and more. You find yourself handling queries from other departments asking for access to the data, too. Suddenly there are issues of concurrency, optimization, and security. There is even a rumor that the head office wants to use your work to provide new services and features to key customers by giving them direct access to the data! This is no longer a simple program; this is an important mission-critical database. And your colleagues are looking to you for answers.

There's no question about it: You are now numbered among the ranks of reluctant database administrators (RDBAs)!

Thankfully, the book you have in your hands can go a long way toward easing your burden. Josef Finsel has taken the time to pull together a wealth of valuable information, presenting it in a way that is easily accessible to RDBAs. Eschewing complicated jargon and theoretical discussions, Josef has written clear and direct prose while also supporting it with numerous screen shots and succinct examples that help focus readers on the task at hand. Additionally, frequent notes, cautions, and sidebars all help highlight key issues that might otherwise have gotten lost in the mix.

As a veteran RDBA, I found this book not only valuable but also enjoyable to read. I certainly wish I had this book at my side all those times I found myself staring blankly at the SQL Server Enterprise Manager screen wondering just how I was going to find the proper menu and dialog options to help me solve my current dilemma.

So, thanks to Josef, RDBAs everywhere have an ally in the effort to manage the growing databases under their care. To quote the bard: "Rest, rest, perturbed spirit!"

Mike Amundsen
Trainer/Programmer/RDBA, EraServer.NET
August 2001

Introduction

*HAS ANYONE NOTICED that all the letters of the word database are typed
with the left hand? Now, the layout of the QWERTYUIOP typewriter
keyboard was designed, among other things, to impair the speed that
typists could type in order to prevent the keys from jamming. It follows, therefore, that writing about databases is unnatural.*

—Anonymous

How Do You Define a Reluctant Database Administrator?

SOME PEOPLE ARE natural-born database administrators (DBAs), some achieve DBA
skills through training and mentoring, and some have DBA tasks thrust upon
them. Whether you are a programmer who is now responsible for creating and
maintaining a SQL Server database or someone who wants to understand the
basics of database administration, this book is for you. Reluctant DBAs are those
of us who haven't had formal training in administering a database and are
surviving on a combination of our wits, Books Online (BOL), and technical manuals. The biggest problem associated with BOL and technical manuals is the
assumption of prior knowledge or experience. Though, truthfully, they are still
regarded as the best source of information for SQL Server. This book is designed
for the programmer, or casual user, who has to handle database administration
in addition to normal programming duties. I'm not going to go into all of the
technical details that books like Kalen Delaney's *Inside SQL Server 2000* do.
Instead, I'm going to give you the knowledge you need to do your job and point
you to where you can get more information if you're interested. In addition,
many of the headings in the book are in the form of questions, so you can easily
skim the table of contents to find solutions.

If we are Reluctant DBAs, it's probably a good idea to define what a database
administrator does and take a look at why there are so many of us having to
assume that role.

There isn't really a set definition of DBA duties, and the skills required usually
vary from company to company. In some cases, a single DBA may be responsible
for not only SQL Server and all its related databases but also for the server hardware and operating system as well. Large companies might have numerous
databases where each database is maintained by a separate DBA. In almost all
cases, however, there are some common tasks for which the DBA is responsible:
security, backups and restores (and testing those), design and implementation of

changes, user management, performance tuning and monitoring, capacity monitoring and planning, even documentation of the database!

And the number of databases has quickly outstripped the number of trained DBAs, leaving more and more programmers with the task of designing and maintaining databases. This often means that many programmers who show the slightest knowledge of what the difference is between a table and a view are being called upon to perform tasks normally associated with database administration. This is often in addition to their full-time programming jobs and usually without the benefit of additional compensation or training. Although many companies view having one employee perform multiple tasks as a "magic bullet" to help the bottom line, you can think of it as an opportunity to make yourself more marketable with new skills.

The good news is that it is much easier today than at any other time to perform DBA tasks. SQL Server 7 and 2000 have taken many traditional DBA tasks, such as memory and disk management, and automated them. This doesn't negate the need for DBAs, but it does allow a non-DBA to hit the ground running. I know first-hand how a true DBA can take SQL Server and tweak an index here, some memory there, and a stored procedure somewhere else until the whole system spins like a finely balanced gyroscope, even under the most demanding of environments. Although this book may not take the place of formal training, it should certainly help you deal with the tasks at hand more knowledgeably.

What Will This Book Accomplish?

I'm going to walk you through understanding the tools that come with SQL Server, showing you how to build databases that will scale up to more than a couple of users, and teaching you how to manipulate your data to make it easier for yourself and other programmers to use. Along the way, I'll share tips and shortcuts I've learned (often the hard way) that will make your job easier. There is always the chance that a full-time DBA will be hired to take over your DBA-related tasks, so it's important to document your work as best you can, as time permits. This way you won't have a DBA breathing down your neck asking why something was done the way it was. You may not like taking over from "someone else's work," so show the same consideration for your successor.

To make this learning process easier to relate to, I'm going to use a fictional veterinary practice that wants to move from its current paper system to one stored in a database. All of the examples in this book will revolve around that project so you can see how SQL Server's tools, good database design, and database programming work together. And, while the project will grow throughout the book, each chapter will have a copy of the database that you can easily install and use to walk through the examples.

Now, without any further delay, let's dive into learning more about SQL Server and databases!

CHAPTER 1

Where Did Databases Come From?

LET'S COVER THE BASICS FIRST. Databases did not come from a turnip patch nor did a stork deliver them under a full moon. In fact, even though many people consider the database a recent invention, people have been organizing data into databases at least as long as recorded history. After all, what is recorded history except an attempt to organize the data of events? With the advent of the computer, it became easier to manipulate data, which then led people to formally define databases, which led to simplifying the gathering and manipulating of even large amounts of data. In this chapter, we'll take a whirlwind look at the history of databases, including how they evolved from paper to electronic, and define some database terms in easily understood terms.

A History of Databases from Rolodex to Relational

Merriam-Webster's Collegiate dictionary defined databases in terms of computers as early as 1962:

> *A usually large collection of data organized especially for rapid search and retrieval (as by a computer).*

Even though the term *database* may only have been coined three decades ago, the concept of a database has been around for much longer. Step back almost a century before the word was created, and you'll find a man by the name of Melvil Dewey. In 1873 he codified a system for organizing the books in a library. Although the system itself is not a database, one could easily argue that a library is a large collection of data organized for rapid storage, search, and retrieval. Computers may make that organization, search, and retrieval much faster, but all of the functions of a database have been around for decades before computers, as evidenced by the long history of the Dewey Decimal system.

Figure 1-1. Thanks in part to the Dewey Decimal system, it is now easier to locate books in a library, particularly by topic. Photo by Celia Finsel.

Step back further in time and you'll find businesses have always needed to track data. Though the methods of organizing data and the means of storing it have changed over the centuries, the basic building blocks of a database haven't. Let's take a veterinarian's practice. On the receptionist's desk there might be a Rolodex containing address cards with names, addresses, and phone numbers of all the people who have brought their pets in for treatment. The information in the Rolodex isn't limited to pet owners—it might also contain contact information for people who sell the various supplies the practice uses.

In addition to the Rolodex, there is also a filing cabinet with a folder for each pet, filed away by owner's last name, first name, and then the pet's name. Finally there is a third filing cabinet with more information about each owner, including a history of bills and payments. This combination of Rolodex, file folders, and filing cabinet is a database.

> *Reluctant DBA* definition of a *database*:
> A database is any system that lets you store and retrieve information.

In the realm of database theory, there are many definitions for a database. SQL Server's Books On Line (BOL) takes almost an entire printed page to define a database, but the core definition of a database is "a system that allows you to store and retrieve data." Whether it is the catalog in the library, a receptionist's Rolodex, or a beefed-up computer running SQL Server, each is a system for storing and retrieving data. One of the most significant differences between the database in a computer and other databases is that the data in a computer can't be touched. In other words, when data is stored in an electronic format, you can't handle it the way you can a physical folder or file, but you can still use the physical objects as analogies of what makes up a database.

What Are Tables and How Do They Relate?

Though there are many different parts to a database, the most important is the *table*. Tables are where data is stored, and data is the core reason for having a database. Although Microsoft markets SQL Server as a Relational Database Management System (RDBMS), it isn't limited to that role. A perfect example of a non-RDBMS role would be using SQL Server as a Data Warehouse. Unfortunately, I have seen a number of databases on SQL Server that were not relational but should have been. Remember, just because SQL Server supports relational databases doesn't mean all of the databases that use SQL Server are relational. A good relational database needs to be designed that way, and in order to design a good relational database you must begin by understanding tables, columns, rows, and what is meant by the term *relational*.

> *Reluctant DBA* definition of *relational*:
> Relational databases are composed of tables where logically related pieces of information are stored. Relational databases logically break data up so that each table stores all of the data "related" to that information. This is different from "relating" data in two or more tables by joining them together, which is how *I* understood the term relational for a long time.

NOTE *Although database design often focuses on tables and indices and columns and rows, there is another aspect that is generally overlooked:* business rules. *It is true that many n-tier applications are designed to put the business rules in a tier that is not the database but those business rules will still influence the design of the database. In addition, by defining the business rules for a database (in other words, it must be able to do some specific tasks), you can quantify the success of the database implementation.*

A table should represent one type of thing. Our receptionist's Rolodex of owners is a good example of a table. It represents one thing, an owner, and has several attributes such as name, address, and phone number for each one. All of the data should be fairly uniform for each owner: Last Name, First Name, Address, City, State, Zip, and Phone Number. These are all things you'd expect to find in such a Rolodex. The card for each owner would represent one row of data in a table. A column in the table represents each of the attributes.

A row *should* represent a unique instance of a well-defined object. In a perfect world, each card represents one owner, and each address would contain the same type of data for each contact. This is the *relational* in relational databases. All of the data *related* together belongs together. In other words, data describing owners would be recorded in one table and all of the data about their pets would be in another table. In a relational database, this type of segregation occurs because the database server defines what columns and types of data make up a row of data in a table (looking for uniqueness in information, as well as integrity of information). In addition, there might be data within the table that defines the pet to join the pet to the owner.

In the real world, however, paper databases often break this rule. The receptionist, when filling out an address card for an owner, probably adds a list of the owner's pets to prevent having to look up that information when someone calls in to make an appointment. There may not be a spot on the card to put pet names, so extra information gets written in the margins of the card. Or perhaps there are cards for people who aren't pet owners, say salespeople who supply materials to the office.

This is discussed in more detail in Chapter 5, "How Do I Define and Structure a Database?" For now, however, just keep in mind that paper documents don't have the same stringent requirements for data integrity that computers have.[1]

But personal computers haven't always supported relational databases; they have evolved to that level.

---

[1]   Of course, programs and databases are frequently used for things they shouldn't be. I had a boss once who had a stated goal of not allowing a comment field *anywhere* in the database because it would allow people to enter orders outside of what the system allowed.

How Computer Databases Evolved

It never hurts to know the history behind the tool with which you are working. In some cases it may cause you to view your tool differently or you may understand, though not agree with, the reason something was done in a certain way. Following is a brief history of data on the computer, culminating in Microsoft's SQL Server 2000.

In the Beginning There Were Text Files

The simplest way to store data on a computer is in a text file. Apart from the lack of structure, data typing and indices, storing data in a text file is simple. The text files are System Data Format (SDF) files. They are files of fixed-length rows with each line typically ending with a carriage return and line feed. Each column has a defined length that never varies from row to row and is padded with spaces for character fields and zeros for numeric fields. There are advantages and disadvantages to this type of data file. An example of this approach came with earlier versions of Windows, a "Card Filer," which allowed new users to Windows to transfer their old paper-based card filling systems to electronic form in the computer. For many users, this application was an introduction to the world of electronic databases.

 NOTE *As proof that all things come back to their beginnings, eXtensible Markup Language (XML) is a text-file database but a much different beast than we began with. XML support in SQL Server 2000 will be covered in detail in Chapter 13, "If SQL Server 2000 Is a .NET Server, Where's the XML?"*

One advantage to a text file is that it can be edited with a standard text editor, making it easy to view and modify the data. Unfortunately, that means it is also easy to modify data incorrectly, throwing the data columns out of alignment. Take the following example: You have a data file with a six-character record ID, a 15-character last name, and a 10-character first name. Because the data is in a text file, it can easily be edited with any text editor. But if you find a last name is missing a letter, say "SMIH" instead of "SMITH," then you have to remember to add the "T" *and* remove the "padded" space after the last name. If you don't remove the space after SMITH, the first name will start in the wrong position (out of alignment with entries above and below it).

R	E	C	.	I	D	L	A	S	T	N	A	M	E						F	I	R	S	T	N	A	M	E		
0	0	0	0	0	1	S	M	I	H										R	O	B	E	R	T					
0	0	0	0	0	1	S	M	I	T	H									R	O	B	E	R	T					

Figure 1-2. Sample System Data Format with misaligned columns

Another way to approach data in a text file is by using Comma Separated Value (CSV) files. In a CSV file, commas, tabs, or some other character like the pipe (|) separate the columns, and character fields are usually enclosed in quotes (commonly referred to as *double-quotes*). This is often easier to modify in a text editor because you don't have to worry about column lengths, but it is somewhat harder, visually, for a person to read because the data isn't lined up neatly the way it is in an SDF file. Also, columns may contain commas as part of the data, thus making it more difficult to read the file in a text editor because you may end up asking yourself: "Is this comma part of the data or is it the end of a column?"

One large disadvantage to using a text file to store your data is the sheer complexity it adds to your program. Any program that uses these types of files needs to know how they are defined. Use of object-oriented programming or simple code reuse can make this an easier task, but there is no reason that a phone number originally stored as a numeric field couldn't be changed to a formatted string. When that happens, any program or subroutine that isn't updated to reflect this change can start corrupting your data by replacing the formatted string with numbers. Worse, since it may be expecting a 10-digit number, it might turn (510) 549-5930 into 5105495 when it translates the string to a number. This problem of interpreting the string as a number doesn't even take into consideration display issues in the application. It's quite possible that the original program was designed to add the ()- to the phone number. Now, with the change in the data it is conceivable that the program could display ((51)0)5-49-5930!

Another problem with text data files lies in the lack of any way to link the files to each other without using additional programming. If you have customers in one text file and orders in another, the only way to join them together is by either writing or buying a program to pull the data together. The inability to join them together also means there is no data integrity. Using a text editor you can add an order to the Order file very simply. However, because there is no *explicit* relationship between the Order file and the Customer file, you could enter a Customer number that is incorrect, is for the wrong customer, is a number that doesn't even exist, or not enter a number at all! If there is no corresponding customer, you'll have an order record that you'll probably never see under normal circumstances.

Text files are also larger than they need to be. Take the size of a person's age. Storing the age as a string requires three spaces to handle the maximum age of a person. An unsigned one-byte integer will store numbers from 0 to 256, a large enough range to handle someone's age but a single byte isn't easy to read, and few text editors will allow you to easily enter the data as bytes.

The final problem with text files lies in the lack of indexing. Text files are sequential files and finding data generally means walking through the file, processing each record to find the data you need. Although it is easy enough to write B-tree routines to build and maintain an index, every program that touches the data needs to maintain that index. If just one program writes data to the text file without updating the database, then the index is no good.

When Text Files Needed Tweaking, Then There Was COBOL

In 1952, Grace Cooper started developing a series of programming languages that became more and more like natural language. These were the forerunners to the COmmon Business Oriented Language (COBOL). A COBOL data file is really a text file but with the advantage that the programming language has all of the data processing built in. In COBOL you no longer need to write separate functionality to deal with data, you just define your data structures in the code. COBOL's strength was that it took a number of data definition languages and put the best of them together. However, the data file used was still a text file with many of the drawbacks inherent in it.[2]

Then, Lo, There Were Database Files

The next big step in databases, particularly for computers, came with the creation of database files. Database files addressed several of the major drawbacks of text files. This is where companies like Ashton-Tate came into play with databases like dBase in the early 1980s. These early databases were better than using text files in several ways.

First, the data was stored compactly where possible. Numbers were stored as compact bytes instead of characters, and so were dates. This could easily reduce the size of a file, allowing more data to reside in less room. Another big gain was the introduction of an index to speed up data access. In many ways, using a database made it easier to program. Less time was spent in building the interface to the database, and more time was spent in developing programs to manipulate data. Finally, the programming language used simple, easy-to-understand syntax for manipulating data, and the database engine took care of all of the indexing automatically.

---

[2]   COBOL gets a lot of bad press these days, but it has been around for a long time and is very adaptable. There is a .NET version available, and COBOL can access databases through the same tools (ODBC, ADO, etc.) that other .NET languages can.

NOTE *Of course, while the data might take up less space because it's stored more compactly, the database would take up more space because the addition of indices could cause the overall database to be larger than comparable flat files. However, you could get 20MB disks if you were willing to shell out the money.*

Progress in databases didn't stop here, though. These early databases required you use their product to manipulate the data, making it hard to distribute anything you developed. Along came Clipper, a compiler for dBase code and with it came the entire universe of xBase programming (writing programs for dBase and its derivatives). This made it easier to distribute programs, but people wanted more flexibility. They wanted to access their data with programs that would allow them to manipulate the data, such as Lotus 1-2-3 or Microsoft Excel. It was time for the next advance in databases on computers.

Then There Was Open Database Connectivity

ODBC isn't a database, but it was an important step on the path to SQL Server. Open Database Connectivity (ODBC) was the simple way to access your data from any piece of software as long as the data had an ODBC driver and the software was built to utilize ODBC. This was good, but it created newer problems. About this time, more and more people were beginning to build networks, linking computers together to share printers and resources. People also wanted to share databases. They wanted to write a program to run on a bunch of machines concurrently and hit a common database file at the same time another user was accessing that database file to create a spreadsheet.

Many database programs had the ability to connect multiple users to a single set of database files, but all of the concurrency issues needed to be resolved by the copy of the database software residing on the user's machine. If the program you were using opened a table to insert rows and opened up five of the six indices that existed for the table, you could quickly run into issues where an index became corrupt.

Not only that, but networks for computers were in their infancy. Too many people would try to access the same database file at the same time and not everyone would be able to because the number of locks on the machine where the database was physically situated were in use. Both users and programmers were getting frustrated with the limitations of using ODBC to access database files. If only there were a system built to be a data engine to multiple users with full transaction capability.

And on the Sixth Day There Were Database Systems

Perhaps this section heading should read, "And on the sixth day, PCs and networks matured to the point that computer database technology caught up with what was available on other computer systems," but that would have been too long and not as dramatic. Part of the problem with database files is that they were really designed for single-user systems. But the theory for database systems had been around for years on other computer systems. In the late 60s and early 70s, a mathematician at IBM named E.F. Codd came up with the theory of relational databases. Unfortunately, IBM had a database called IMS, though it was a variation on the COBOL model. The history of how relational databases almost didn't come to exist is an interesting one.

 NOTE   *The National Research Council put out a really good book called* Funding a Revolution. *If you are interested in the twists and turns that led to what we see as the obvious solution of SQL, check out the book online at* `http://stills.nap.edu/html/far`. *Chapter 6 is about relational databases, but the book also covers the foundation of the Internet and is a good read.*

Eventually, relational databases were created and widely used on large computers and the stage was being set for such a database server on the personal computer. One of the things that indirectly helped with the development of SQL Server was a program called Ingres. A competitor to IBM's SQL developed Ingres but, unlike IBM's SQL, the source code for Ingres was readily available and made its way into several different commercial versions.

How Has Microsoft's Version of SQL Server Evolved?

Ashton-Tate (of dBase fame) and Sybase had developed a version of a SQL product that ran under Unix based on the Ingres code. In 1988, Microsoft teamed up with them to produce Microsoft's first version of SQL Server, this one to run under OS/2 with the name *Ashton-Tate/Microsoft SQL Server*. Although SQL Server running on OS/2 was released, Microsoft ended up switching the product from OS/2 to Windows NT, a decision that required a major rewrite of the core product. Nonetheless, they did indeed deliver a powerful database management system for NT. Over the next four years, Microsoft and Sybase came to realize they were headed in different directions, and Microsoft took over the role of developing SQL Server on NT while Sybase continued work on their OS/2 and Unix versions.[3]

SQL Server in its original Unix form had to supply significant systems-level functionality that was eventually replaced in Microsoft SQL Server by the operating system. For example, a SQL Server in Unix must support its own disk allocation and IO, as well as its own memory management and threading. Because Microsoft's SQL Server was designed to work solely within the Microsoft operating systems, SQL Server was designed to let the operating system handle those functions. Once the operating system started to take over those roles in the Microsoft versions, performance improved.

The first version of SQL Server that was composed of code written completely by Microsoft was SQL Server 7, released in 1998. Version 7 was a radical departure from its predecessors and included such new features as:

- Was scaleable from the laptop to Enterprise Servers using the same code base, while at the same time offered 100-percent code compatibility whether on NT or Windows 95

- Supported auto-configuration and self-tuning (which is key to making Database Administration easier)

- Offered the first database with integrated Data Transformation Services

- Integrated with Windows NT Server, Microsoft Office, and the BackOffice family

- Enabled high-performance access to a variety of information sources through Universal Data Access

- Supported clustering and failover support, making for improved reliability and high availability

- Advanced data analysis and highly scalable OnLine Analytical Processing (OLAP)

In 2000, Microsoft released SQL Server 2000 as the first of its .NET servers. Most of the new features in SQL Server 2000 are related to performance. In fact, in August of 2001, Microsoft's SQL Server held the first and third positions on the

---

[3] I'm vastly compressing this story. If you want to learn all of the details behind SQL Server's creation, read Kalen Delaney's *Inside Microsoft SQL Server 2000.*

TPC-C benchmark overall at a cost of less than $23 per transaction and holds a clean sweep of the Price/Perf category.[4]

But there were other enhancements, not just speed:

- Many tools were revamped and made easier to use.

- XML was integrated seamlessly into the database engine.

- Additional self-management and tuning were added.

- The data transformation tools were improved.

Which SQL Server Is Best for Me?

All in all, SQL Server 2000 is a powerful product that's easy to use and comes in multiple sizes. After all, not everyone needs to process hundreds of thousands of transactions a second. And you don't necessarily want to buy a copy of Enterprise Edition if all you're interested in is learning how to use SQL Server. I was surprised to find there are seven different flavors of SQL Server 2000, so you should be able to find the one that works best for you.

One key thing to remember about each of these different editions is they all work the same, more or less. The applications you develop on the Developer Edition will work everywhere from the Desktop Engine up to the Enterprise Edition.

Enterprise Edition (and Enterprise Evaluation Edition)

We'll start with the biggest of them all, Enterprise Edition. If you were at the Windows 2000 rollout or saw it from one of the many video feeds that were at every Microsoft office, you probably remember Bill Gates and crew demonstrating Windows 2000. They showed its scalability by having several massive walls of computers generating huge hit counts to the Web and database servers. The servers that were handling that load were Enterprise Servers. While it's important to remember that everything you write on one edition you can run on another, it is also important to remember that the different editions serve purposes.

Enterprise Edition is designed to work with anywhere from one user to the largest Web sites or data warehousing projects that are available. The Enterprise Evaluation Edition is the exact same thing with two differences. First, you can download it from the Web. Second, it only works for 120 days. SQL Server 2000 Enterprise Edition requires Windows NT Server 4 Enterprise Edition 4, Windows 2000 Advanced Server (AS), or Windows 2000 Data Center Server (DCS).

---

[4] TPC-C is an industry-standard benchmark. For more information, go to http://www.tpc.org, where you can find the most current statistics.

One of the nice features of the Enterprise Edition is the Symmetric Multi-Processor (SMP) support. This means SQL Server can take advantage of systems with multiple CPUs. With increased SMP support, you can take full advantage of new Microsoft Windows 2000 capacity. If you have the money and the need, SQL Server 2000 supports up to 32 CPUs and 64 gigabytes (GB) of RAM (Windows 2000 Data Center Edition and OEM installation, but it doesn't appear that any manufacturer is supporting the 32 CPU box).

Standard Edition

A step down from the Enterprise Edition is the Standard Edition. The big difference between editions is that the lower ones are not built to handle high-transaction loads. In other words, if you are trying to run a well designed, high-use data warehousing project using Standard Edition, it might not work too well, but upgrading your database to Enterprise Edition and your operating system to an Enterprise version would probably help matters (and it doesn't hurt to have a really big machine to handle the load either).

One of the reasons that Standard Edition doesn't scale as well as the Enterprise Edition is that it is supported on operating systems not designed to handle high-volume transactions. The Enterprise Edition is more tightly integrated with the Enterprise Server operating systems. Since SQL Server 2000 Standard Edition will install on Microsoft Windows NT Server 4 with Service Pack 5 (SP5) or Windows 2000 Server, it doesn't have the hooks into the Enterprise operating system features that the Enterprise Edition of SQL Server does. That means it can't take advantage of the same level of CPU sharing and RAM access that the Enterprise Edition does. Apart from that, it will do everything that the Enterprise Edition will do. An evaluation edition of SQL Server Standard Edition is available with the Office XP Developer Edition.

Developer Edition

Developer Edition is one step further down from Standard Edition. It really is Enterprise Edition but not licensed for use as a real SQL Server. It exists so that Reluctant DBAs can install it on their machines and not have to disrupt the server while they get the next release of the database ready. Not only that, it's easier to ask, "What happens when I do. . .?" Knowing that you can test modifications to a real database server without endangering the production server makes it easier to develop the database. SQL Server 2000 Developer Edition requires (at least) Windows NT Workstation 4 or Windows 2000—but it can be installed on AS and DCS versions of Windows.

Personal Edition

This version will run on Windows 98 (but no longer on Windows 95). Granted, there are some down sides to the Personal Edition. Because it was written to the lowest common denominator, it will not run as well as the other editions will when they are running on NT or 2000. One of the main targets for this version was the mobile user who needs some database storage or for stand-alone applications that need a database.

Microsoft Data Engine

What is Microsoft Data Engine (MSDE) other than the full-fledged SQL Server with no front end? Well, that depends on what you are looking for. If you want a fully redistributable database engine that you can package with your software so that you can write killer applications like the ultimate financial package, this is for you. Granted, it doesn't have the Enterprise Manager or Query Analyzer, but you don't really need those when you redistribute the database engine.

Although MSDE is the full SQL Data Engine, there are a number of differences in terms of installing it and what it can handle. In general, most of what you'll read in this book applies to designing and implementing and using databases with MSDE, but you should check out the "Resources" section at the end of this book to get more information on the differences between MSDE and the other editions.

SQL Server CE Edition

This edition is used as the data store on Windows CE devices. You can have CE connect to the local database and do data manipulation and then synch up with SQL Server 2000 to download data and upload changes. See "Resources" at the end of the chapter for more information on how Windows CE works.

Last Words

This chapter has included a brief history lesson leading up to Microsoft SQL Server, some database terms, and the various editions of SQL Server available. In the next chapter, you'll learn how to install and configure SQL Server. Unless you're installing it on Windows 98, you should be able to have SQL Server installed and ready to go in about 20 minutes. If you're installing on Windows 98, it might take longer because you have to install some prerequisite updates to the operating system first.

Even if your employer has a full-time DBA to manage the SQL Server and their responsibility is doing such installations, you should know how to install the Developer Edition on your own machine for development and testing purposes.

Resources

- Find out when to use MSDE:
  `http://msdn.microsoft.com/library/officedev/odeopg`
  `/deovrwhentousemsde.htm`

- Discover which version of SQL Server is for you:
  `http://www.microsoft.com/sql/techinfo/planning/SQLResKChooseEd.asp`

- Bill Vaughn's site includes white papers on MSDE:
  `http://www.betav.com/Content/whitepapers.htm`

- Learn more about SQL Server CE:
  `http://www.microsoft.com/sql/productinfo/ceoverview.htm`

- Read up on SQL Server:
  `http://msdn.microsoft.com/sqlserver/Default.asp`

- Learn about the history of SQL Server:
  Inside Microsoft SQL Server 2000 by Kalen Delaney (Microsoft Press)

- Find out more about the Windows operating systems:
  `http://www.microsoft.com/windows/default.asp`

CHAPTER 2

How Do I Install SQL Server?

He who chooses the beginning of a road chooses the place it leads to. It is the means that determines the end. —Harry Emerson Fosdick

THE EASIEST WAY TO START installing SQL Server 2000 is to slip the CD into your drive and close the door. That should automatically start the installation and display the SQL Server Installation screen (see Figure 2-1). If you haven't done so already, then you will need to install the prerequisites. To install the prerequisites or just view what they are, select SQL Server 2000 Prerequisites. If you need to install them, you'll probably have to reboot your computer. If you do have to reboot and the SQL Server Installation screen doesn't reappear, just open and close the CD drive to restart the installation process.

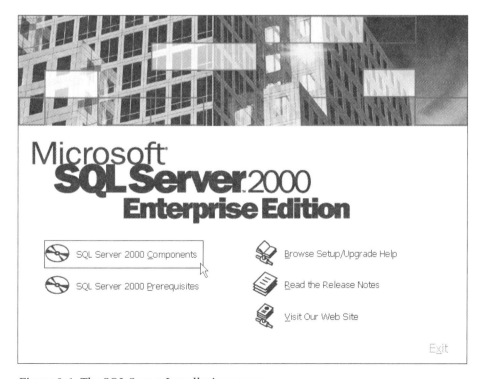

Figure 2-1. The SQL Server Installation screen

Once you're ready, click on SQL Server 2000 Components. This takes you to the next screen where you can install the Database Server, Analysis Services, or English Query (see Figure 2-2). Analysis Services lets you do some really neat things with data warehousing. English Query, much improved in this version, provides access to the data in almost natural language, and configuring it for use in a database is much easier than it used to be. (See the "Resources" section at the end of this chapter for more information on these two options.) Right now, we're going to install the Database Server, which is the heart of SQL Server 2000.

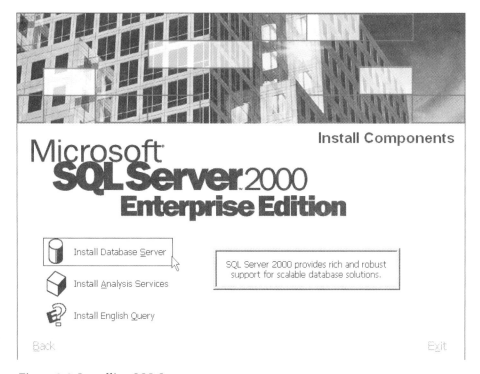

Figure 2-2. Installing SQL Server components

If you are trying to install the wrong version of the database for your operating system—for instance, you tried to install SQL Server 2000 Enterprise Edition onto Windows 2000 Professional—you'll get a polite error telling you that what you are trying to install isn't supported on this operating system. At this point, the installation process will offer to install the client components only.

Assuming you have all of the prerequisites installed, you'll get a Welcome dialog box saying you are about to run the Installation Wizard. Click on Next, and you'll come to your first set of options asking if you want to install this locally or remotely. A remote installation means you are using your computer to install the program on another computer. In this chapter, we'll show how to perform a local installation because it's the most common type of installation.

NOTE *SQL Server takes longer to install on a FAT partition than NTFS. With FAT, SQL Server must test the integrity of the file system before installing any databases.*

The next screen provides new options in SQL Server 2000 (see Figure 2-3). Here you can create a new instance of SQL Server, upgrade or change an existing SQL Server, or go on to advanced options. The advanced options let you create an installation script so you can perform unattended installations, which is handy if you are installing multiple copies of SQL Server on a lot of computers. This is rather pricey as well, given the costs for licensing SQL Server, even if it isn't as expensive as some other Relational Database Management Systems (RDBMS). You can also attempt to rebuild the SQL Server Registry hive in the advanced options. In this example, we're going to install a new instance of SQL Server. Select this option, and click Next.

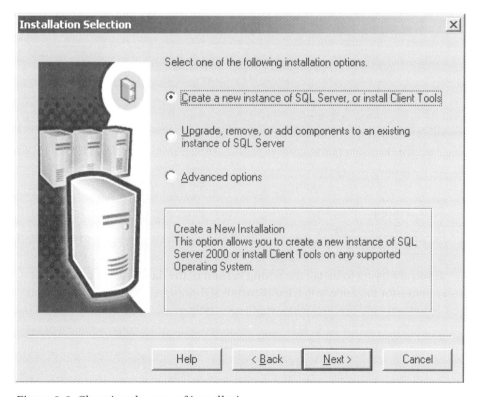

Figure 2-3. Choosing the type of installation

What's an Instance of SQL Server?

New in SQL Server 2000 is the ability to run multiple SQL Servers on one computer, with completely different system databases, login accounts, and everything else. You can create as many as you want *as* allowed by your license. According to Microsoft's Web site
(http://www.Microsoft.com/SQL/productinfo/pricing.htm):

> *Licensing SQL Server 2000 Enterprise Edition enables customers to run multiple instances on a single server or processor and only license once. This is not the case for SQL Server 2000 Standard Edition: each instance of SQL Server 2000 Standard Edition on a computer must be licensed separately.*

So, if you have Standard Edition, you must pay a licensing fee for each instance you install. If you have the Enterprise Edition, you can install as many instances as you want. There are additional licensing issues for Personal Edition, Developer Edition, and Microsoft Data Engine (MSDE), so check the fine print before deciding how to implement what you're doing.

Now comes the standard fill-in-the-blank (FITB) time. Enter your name and company name, and go to the next screen, your Software Licensing Agreement. *Read this screen!* Nobody ever does, but you might find some important information. For instance, you can use MSDE in a replication scenario, but the main SQL Server must be a fully licensed version. If you are planning on replication, you need a full-blown, licensed SQL Server, and you'll find that information in the licensing agreement.

Another FITB screen, this time the licensing key from the back of the CD case needs to be entered. Enter the combination of numbers and characters, and go on. (If you're like me, you may have to enter it twice; I always seem to transpose a digit somewhere.) Now, you can select to install either the client tools, the server and client tools, or connectivity only. In this example, we're going to install the server and client tools.

⚠️ **CAUTION** *SQL Server 2000 will install the newest version of ActiveX Data Objects (ADO) on the box. If you choose to install connectivity only, then that is all it will install. If you are using Visual Basic and writing programs, you will need to make sure you select the correct ADO (2.5 or 2.6) for the project at hand. Switching over to ADO 2.6 shouldn't present a problem, but if you have an installed base of programs, you might want to think about how that will affect them. One thing to consider is that using ADO 2.6 will require having users install that version of ADO, bloating your installations on simple updates of existing software.*

Now you're ready to install SQL Server. In this example, we're going to install a new instance of SQL Server called ReluctantDBA (see Figure 2-4). As you can see, my Default checkbox has been disabled. That's because the machine I'm installing on already has a default SQL Server, in this case SQL Server 7. Unlike prior versions of SQL Server, SQL Server 2000 can peacefully co-exist with SQL Server 7 and even other instances of itself.

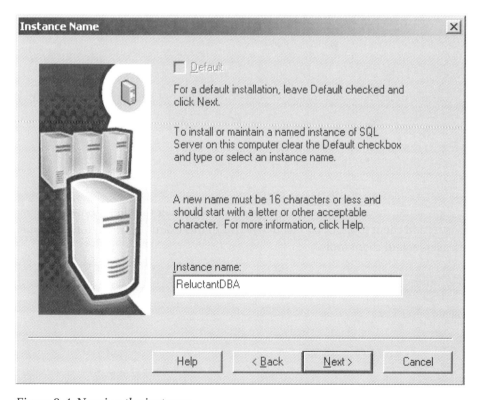

Figure 2-4. Naming the instance

Where Does SQL Server 2000 Install?

In SQL Server 7, the installation process wanted to create a directory off the root called "MSSQL7." In SQL Server 2000, however, Microsoft is playing by the rules they have requested everyone else to follow. The default directory for installation is a directory called "Microsoft SQL Server" in your Program Files directory. You can, however, change that if you want (see Figure 2-5). For this installation, the files will be going in "D:\Program Files\Microsoft SQL Server," but this is only half the story.

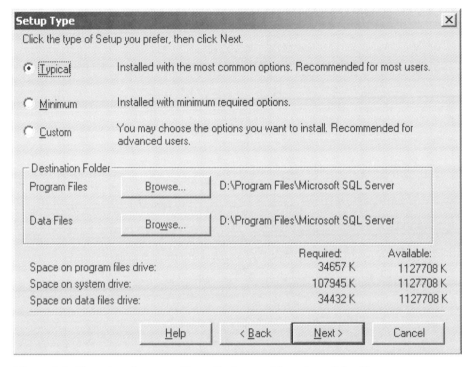

Figure 2-5. Choosing the type of installation and location of the files

The "Microsoft SQL Server" directory will actually be nothing more than a holding directory for two other directories. The first one is "80," which is where all of the client tools are located. (It's called this because SQL Server 2000 is actually version 8.) The more interesting piece of the puzzle is where the install will put the data. The data will actually go into a second directory under "Microsoft SQL Server." It will be called "MSSQL$*instancename*" (the default just goes in the directory "MSSQL"). This instance will contain *everything* for SQL Server. There's a "binn" directory with all of the DLLs that make up SQL Server, a "Data" directory to store the system databases, and so on. Each instance is a completely separate installation.

Although you can select Typical and have a fully functioning database server installed, there are a couple of pieces that don't get installed in the typical installation. For this example, select the Custom installation and click on Next.

When you get to the Custom installation, you'll see many of the checkboxes are already selected. This shows what is installed during a Typical install. You may also want to select the Full-Text Search capability (see Figure 2-6). You may never use it and you could always install it later if you want, but installing it now avoids the hassle of installing it separately later. The other options you may want to install are the Code Samples, including ADO, DBLib, Desktop Engine usage, Replication, MSDTC, SQL Namespace . . . the list goes on. You won't even see this option unless you scroll down to the bottom of the Components side. These all install in the "80\Tools\DevTools\Samples" directory.

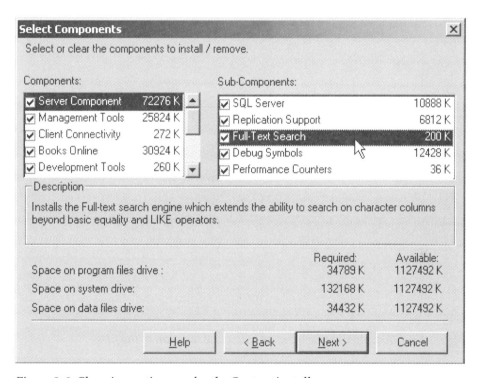

Figure 2-6. Choosing options under the Custom install

You might think SQL Server is now ready to install, but there are a couple of important dialog boxes that still need to be filled in. The first one is to tell the installation process what account SQL Server is supposed to run under. This will be discussed in Chapter 11, "How Do I Secure My Data?" For now, select Use the Same Account for Each Service and Use the Local System Account (see Figure 2-7).

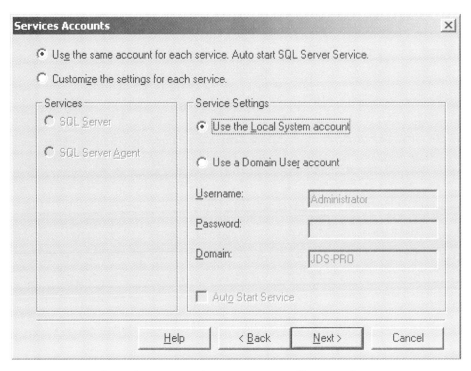

Figure 2-7. Specifying the account that SQL Server will run under

What Is the Difference between Windows Authentication and SQL Server Authentication?

One of the goals of SQL Server is to provide data only to people who are author-
ized to see it. If anyone who could connect to the server could get all of the data
in any database, it could never be used for any sensitive data storage. Therefore it
is necessary to have some level of security to limit what users can do. SQL Server
provides two means of doing this: through NT Authentication or through SQL
Server Authentication.

NT authentication is exactly what it sounds like. When a connection is made
to the server, it takes that user's ID and the token that represents that login and
validates it against the NT or Windows 2000 server that is acting as the domain
controller. Once it has authenticated the Windows login, SQL Server then checks
the appropriate system tables to determine to which database the user has
access. Database security is handled quite differently between 6.*x* compared to
7 and later. With SQL Authentication, an account and password are created in
SQL and are good only on that server. Unlike Windows, the SQL Authentication is
not encrypted in any way.

NOTE *Why use SQL authentication at all? One reason is to give a program a login to the database so it can run from a non-Windows machine. Another reason is to provide support for Web applications. By providing a user ID and password to SQL Server you don't have to worry about where the program is running, which is particularly useful when running over a global TCP/IP network like the Web. This will be discussed in more detail in Chapter 11, "How Do I Secure My Data?"*

In older versions of SQL Server, there were three authentication modes. You could have Windows Authentication, SQL Authentication, or a combination of the two that was called Mixed Mode. This is no longer the case. SQL Authentication is really Mixed Mode, and you can no longer choose SQL Authentication only. Unless, that is, you are running SQL Server under Windows 98. Windows 98 doesn't support the Windows Authentication for SQL Server so even though it runs in Mixed Mode, it is really using SQL Authentication only.

Does the Systems Administrator *Really* Need a Password?

Before we wrap up the discussion of security, we need to talk about the systems administrator (sa) and the password associated with it. For many versions, the default, unless specified otherwise, was no password for sa. That is not a good thing. The running joke at conferences, as people would demonstrate something using SQL Server, was: "As you can see, I'm using standard Microsoft Security: no password for sa."

The sa login is the most powerful login. It can do anything on the SQL Server that can be done. Not only does an sa have unlimited control of SQL Server, it can also do things within the operating system! Given all that, do you really need to use sa to login anyway? Besides, Windows logins that are members of Administrator on the server are automatically granted sa rights when connecting using Windows authentication. Although Chapter 11 covers this in more detail, suffice it to say that sa should *always* have a password and *never* be used for connecting to the database from a program. OK, *never* may be a little strong, but you should use a great deal of caution before designing a program to connect to a database because you are opening up a potential security breach.

You can still have a blank password for sa, but you have to go out of your way to do so (see Figure 2-8). You must check a box that specifically says, "I want to open my server up to the world as a security risk." OK, actually it says, "Blank Password (Not Recommended)," but you get the general idea.

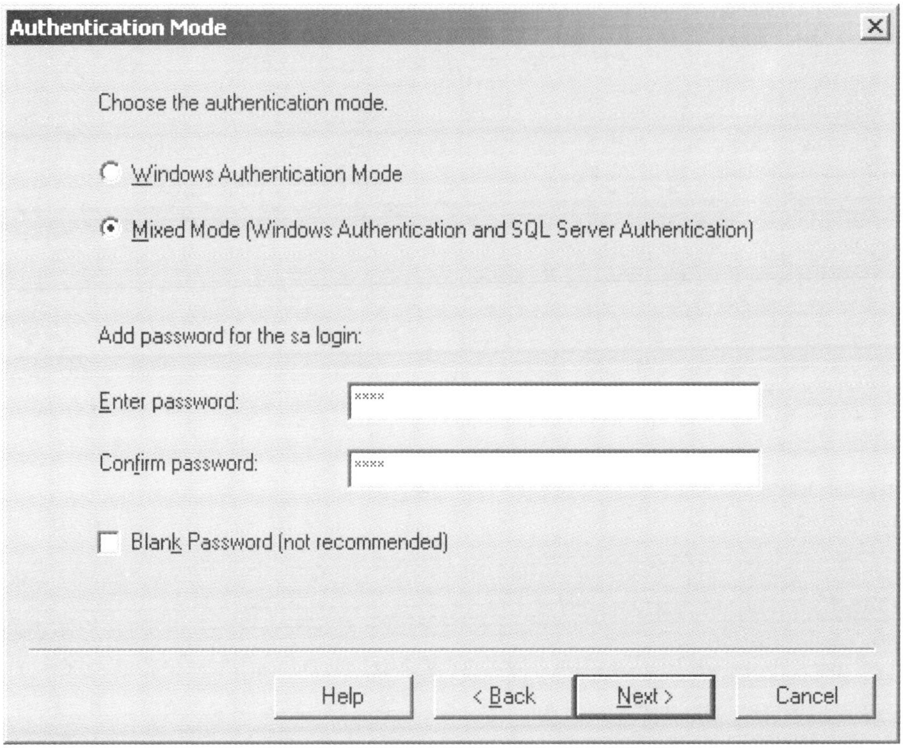

Figure 2-8. Defining your security model

If you had selected to do a Typical install, SQL Server would be installing right now, but there are a couple of questions that still need to be answered in a Custom installation. The first is the collation order (see Figure 2-9). In earlier versions of SQL Server, this was a really big deal. In fact, if you needed to change the collation order, you would have to uninstall and reinstall SQL Server! Fortunately, that's no longer an issue, and you can change the collation order easily enough later, so select the default (dictionary order, case insensitive) and go on.

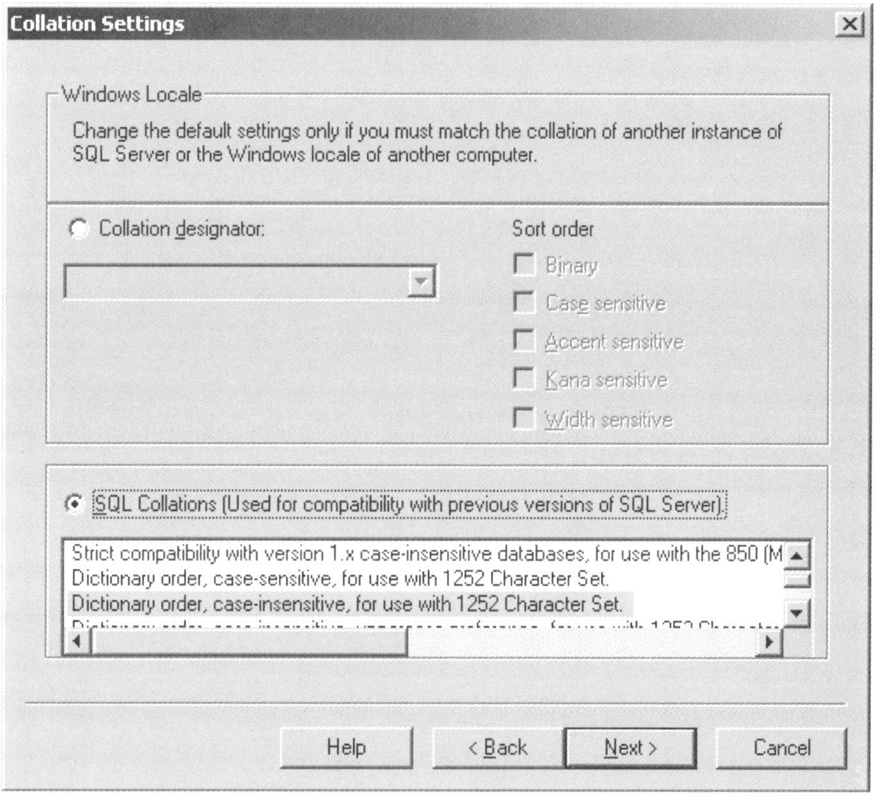

Figure 2-9. Defining the sort order

This last set of questions has to do with what libraries SQL Server is going to use to listen for requests on. The default is a combination of Named Pipes and TCP/IP Sockets. These will be covered in more detail in Chapter 11, "How Do I Secure My Data?" For now, unless you have some valid network problem that requires you to select NWLink/IPX/SPX or some other protocol, click the Next button.

Which Licensing Option Should I Use?

If you are installing on a machine that has not had a version of SQL Server installed previously, you will see the Choose Licensing Mode dialog box (see Figure 2-10). You have two options here for how you *license* the server you are installing. This is a legal issue and is dependent on what you have purchased. For more information on licensing, see the Microsoft site (http://www.microsoft.com/sql/howtobuy/pricing/default/asp).

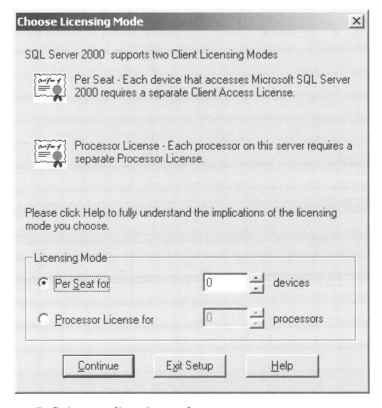

Figure 2-10. Defining your licensing mode

OK, now that we've finished filling in the blanks, away we go. Well, almost. SQL Server has to tell you it has enough information to move forward and *then* it will start actually installing SQL Server.

Were You Using That App?

By the way, you should close all of your applications before installing. Because SQL Server will be installing connectivity, ODBC upgrades, and all manner of other things, it will politely mention that you have programs (like Outlook) running and ask you to shut them down so it can go about its business.

Umm . . . My Install Didn't Work, What Now?

It just so happens that Microsoft has an answer to that question. In Knowledge Base article Q257716, it tells you the steps to take if you have a problem.[1]

The first and most important thing to do is to check in the "sqlstp.log" file in your "Windows" directory. This file has information for *every* setup you have done of SQL Server. If, like me, you have set up and removed multiple instances of the server, this log can be quite large. The information you want is toward the bottom. It is time stamped (but not date stamped), and it lists every detail of the installation.

The second thing to do is to check the error log for SQL Server. If you installed in a standard directory it will be in "\Program Files\Microsoft SQL Server\MSSQL\Log" directory and should be named ERRORLOG with no extension. If you were installing an instance of SQL Server, don't forget to add that to MSSQL to find the right directory.

Read through the error log carefully and see if you can find any obvious problems. Because each new instance is a complete set of SQL Server files, one of the common problems is running out of disk space. If you can't find anything in the log files, save the files and get ready to contact Microsoft Product Support (http://support.microsoft.com).

SQL Error Logs

Assuming you are installing SQL Server, there should be only one error log. It is possible, however, that you may see multiple error log files, so this is a good time to explain the naming convention SQL Server uses for logs.

If more than one error log exists, you'll see a number in the extension that represents how many times removed the file is, with "1" being the most recent, and larger numbers being the older. Generally, SQL Server maintains only six archive files automatically. These logs are closed and archived each time SQL is stopped, either intentionally or due to system failure. An install failing would constitute a system failure.

Last Words

There you have it. If you've been following along on your computer and the installation process has finished, then you have just installed a copy of SQL

---

[1]   In Internet Explorer 5 or later you can access Knowledge Base "Q" articles by simply typing in MSKB Q*xxxxxx*. In this example, you would enter MSKB Q257716.

Server on your machine. In the next chapter we're going to look at the Enterprise Manager, learn how to start and stop SQL Server using that tool, and much, much more.

Resources

- Find out what's wrong if your installation didn't work:
  `http://support.microsoft.com/support/kb/articles/Q257/7/16.ASP`

- Check the cost of SQL Server 2000:
  `http://www.microsoft.com/SQL/productinfo/pricing.htm`

- Find more information about ADO 2.6:
  ADO Best Practices by Bill Vaughn (Apress)

- Learn more about English Query:
  `http://www.microsoft.com/sql/productinfo/english.htm`

- Read a good introduction to English Query:
  `http://msdn.microsoft.com/library/periodic/period00/EnglishQuery.htm`

- Learn about Analysis Services:
  `http://www.microsoft.com/sql/productinfo/analysisservicesWP.htm`

CHAPTER 3

How Do I Visually Manage Objects?

A snap-in is a Component Object Model (COM) in-process server dynamic-link library (DLL). This COM interface is situated between MMC and the snap-in. MMC does not care how the snap-in communicates with the managed service. Snap-ins can communicate with the managed service through any data protocol that the managed service supports. MMC has no knowledge of the mechanism used for this communication. —From Microsoft's explanation of snap-ins for the Microsoft Management Console

ONE OF THE BEAUTIES of Microsoft SQL Server has always been that many of the tasks of a traditional database administrator (DBA) can easily be handled from the Enterprise Manager (EM). In this chapter we'll focus on using parts of the EM to manipulate the database. In subsequent chapters we will be focusing heavily on using the EM to work with the server and the databases, but bear in mind that just about everything we're going to cover can also be done through Transact SQL statements. In fact, many of the functions presented through the EM are just Transact SQL commands behind the scenes. So, let's start by answering a fairly obvious question.

What Is Enterprise Manager?

The EM is actually a Microsoft Management Console (MMC) snap in. The MMC is a container designed to hold tools that perform specific tasks, but all of the tools have the same look and feel. The concept is that if you can learn how to use the tool to do one thing, you'll be able to adapt easily to doing another. Microsoft uses the MMC for a variety of things, from Web server management to SQL Server management. Figure 3-1 shows an MMC with several snap-ins added, including SQL Server.

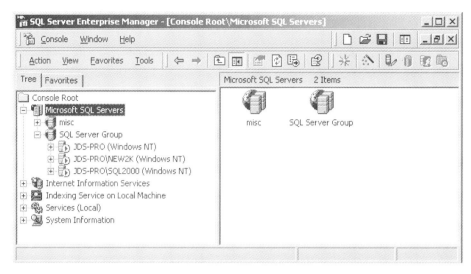

Figure 3-1. Microsoft Management Console with SQL Server and other snap-ins loaded

There are four major parts to the MMC:

- MMC's menu appears across the top of the screen and contains Console, Window, and Help. This menu doesn't change.

- Beneath the MMC's menu is another menu, this one showing Action, View, Favorites, and Tools. This menu changes to display menu options for whatever snap-in happens to be in control. (The menu in Figure 3-1 is for the SQL Server Enterprise Manager snap-in.)

- The left-hand pane displays a tree view that you can use to drill down into the parts of the snap-in.

- The right-hand pane is used by the snap-in to display and interact with the user. (In Figure 3-1, the Microsoft SQL Server's snap-in is selected, and the pane is displaying the groups of SQL Servers that have been defined on the server.)

Adding Snap-ins to the MMC

If you are working on Windows 2000 with Web Services and SQL Server running, then you can make your life a lot easier by creating an MMC view that contains the most often used components. As you can see in Figure 3-1, I've got several different snap-ins in this view that I use frequently. Accomplishing this is simple. From the Start button, select Run and enter MMC. That should start the console.

Next, select Add/Remove Snap-in (Ctrl-M). Follow the prompts from there to add or remove the snap-ins you want in this view. Then select Console Save As to save the file containing the view you want. If you save it to your desktop with the name of the machine you're working on, then you've got a tool you can always find with the snap-ins you usually use.

CAUTION *If you are using SQL Server 6.5 or earlier, you cannot use the EM that comes with SQL Server 2000. You will be able to register the servers; however, you will not be able to administer the servers at all with the EM. Instead, the EM will launch 6.5 utilities for this. So, do not remove the 6.5 utilities if you are upgrading a 6.5 environment or managing servers running 6.5.*

Where Is the Enterprise Manager?

If you are in the Add/Remove Snap-in menu of the MMC, you'll find the EM listed as Microsoft SQL Servers *if it is installed.* The truth of the matter is that SQL Enterprise Manager is *not* included with some version of SQL Server. You won't find it in the Microsoft Data Engine (MSDE) or Personal Edition. Don't despair, however, because you can do everything you can do in the EM another way, it's just not as easy. Once the database is created (using the command-line interface to SQL Server and Transact SQL Statements, for instance), you can then use Visual Basic's data tools to create tables and indices. But you are really going to want at least the Developer Edition of SQL Server so you can use the Enterprise Manager for a whole host of the tasks that you're going to learn about.

Once you've found the EM you'll find you can do almost anything you want to SQL Server with it. You can start and stop the server, create and delete databases, tables, indices, and more. You can do backups of database, schedule jobs to run, even have the server perform routine maintenance for you! If your appetite is whetted, let's dig in.

Which Server Am I Connecting To?

In previous versions of SQL Server you could manage multiple servers from the EM. In SQL Server 2000, where you can have multiple instances of SQL Server running on your server, it can get a little more confusing. Referring back to Figure 3-1 you can see that three servers are listed under SQL Server Group, and they all begin with JDS-PRO. That's because my Windows 2000 machine is named JDS-PRO. The first one is the default instance and NEW2K and SQL2000 are other instances of SQL Server.

Another nice thing about the EM is it tells you the state of your server at a glance. (Well, it appears to anyway.) Each server can be in one of four states:

- A green triangle indicates the server is running.

- A green circle with a white triangle indicates you are connected to that server and it is running.

- A red square indicates that it is stopped.

- An empty circle indicates that the EM doesn't know that status of the server.

Why wouldn't it know? Well, the snap-ins are all COM objects and they pop up inside the MMC immediately and then start querying their server to see if it's up. That takes time and while they are waiting, they don't show anything. It is also possible, particularly if the EM is connecting to a server via IP, that it will not get a response. In that case it will sit with an empty circle until you try to connect to the server. Then you'll see a message box informing you that the EM doesn't know if the server is running and asking if you want to try to connect to it.

Another interesting side effect of all this is that *you* might see that the server is up and running, but the EM doesn't know it yet. If you have a lot of servers registered in the EM, you can click on a server that has just been turned green but before the EM has been officially notified that the server is available and the EM will tell you that it doesn't know if the server is running or not. It's not really a problem; you're just typing and clicking faster than it is processing the information. Another quirk appears when you start and stop SQL Server from the EM, but we'll cover that *after* we've registered a server.

How Do I Add Servers to the Enterprise Manager?

Adding servers is a fairly simple task. You can use the pop-up menu and select New SQL Server Registration, or you can use Action ➤ New SQL Server Registration. Like many tasks in the EM, this will start a wizard; in this case, it will start the Register SQL Server Wizard.

Before registering servers, now would be a good time to mention groups. Depending on your operation (work environment), naming of servers can be generic, cryptic, or just plain out of this world. I've made a practice of creating groups for "Development," "Test," "QA," and "Production." Then I register the servers under the appropriate group. This not only helps in visually identifying the purpose of the server, it also aids in identifying how many are in a particular group and can help when you need to work with a specific group of servers or specific server. One way this helps is that only the group being used needs to be expanded. If you're working with just development servers, only that group needs to be expanded, thus less clutter on the screen. Refreshes will also occur quicker because few "active" objects are being refreshed.

CAUTION *If you check the little box that says "From now on I want to perform this task without using a wizard" you will get a different dialog box for registering, much like the one used for connecting to a server in Query Analyzer (covered in Chapter 8, "Introduction to Query Analyzer"). It is not, however, obvious how to turn the wizard back on when you want it again, but it really is simple. From within the EM use Tools ➤ Wizards. This will bring up a list of the wizards installed. Double-click on Register Server Wizard. When it comes up, uncheck the box. This procedure is simple but not covered in the Books On Line (BOL).*

After you have pressed the Next button on the first screen of the wizard, you'll be presented with a list of SQL Servers that your computer knows about that are not already registered within the EM (see Figure 3-2). This list would contain any servers on your domain but not servers on another domain. That doesn't mean you can't get to those servers, they just won't be in this box. If you happen to have Windows 98, your computer doesn't know how to poll the network for servers, so this list is always blank.

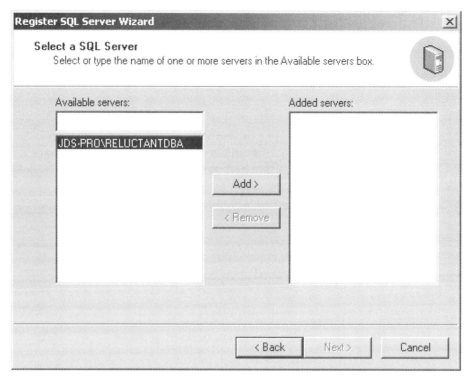

Figure 3-2. Adding servers to the EM through the Register Server Wizard

Select the server(s) that you want to add. If you don't see it but know the name, you can enter it in the box below Available Servers. Make sure you press the Add button to move it to the Added Servers column; otherwise you won't be able to go on.

The next screen asks you which security model you want to use to connect to the server. If you have specified multiple servers, then you will have to go through this page multiple times, once for each server. You can use Windows login or you can specify a login and password (for more information, see Chapter 11, "How Do I Secure My Data?"). The last question that needs an answer before the Server will show up in the EM is the group to which you want to add it. The default is to add it to an existing group. When you first install SQL Server, the SQL Server Group is created. You may want to group your servers based on a project or whether they are development or production servers. Adding a new group is as easy as specifying a new group name on this last wizard page.

Now that you're finished with the wizard, SQL Server will take the data you've given it and attempt to actually register the servers. You'll see a screen listing all of the servers that you have attempted to register along with a Finish button. If only it was really that simple. What the EM is really going to do is attempt to connect to each of the servers you're attempting to register using the authentication method and information provided. If it is successful then you will see a Registered Successfully message. If it is not able to connect, you'll get a cryptic message back: Either the server does not exist or access was denied. This message is less than helpful in diagnosing what the problem is because it could be a problem with authentication (you entered the wrong login/password), or it could be that it can't really connect to the server. It is, however, just as frustrating to a hacker trying to get into the system. Another possibility is security changes, such as passwords. It may be necessary to Exit the EM and restart so that the EM can get your most current "credentials."

Perhaps the most interesting thing about using the Registration Wizard is that you get two chances to register a server and if you fail both times you can *still* add the server to the Manager. Not only that, but if you tell the EM that you're fine with the fact that it can't connect, it displays that the server was successfully registered. Not that you can do anything with it until you resolve the problem of either access or security, but it is registered in the EM.

How Do I Change SQL Server's Registration Properties?

There are two sets of data you can configure about any SQL Server registered in the EM: SQL Server Registration properties and the Properties of the Server itself. The first defines how the EM interacts with the server and the second defines how the server runs.

One of the first things you can do whenever you register a server in the EM is to modify the registration properties. When you right-click and select Edit SQL Server Registration properties you'll get a dialog box like the one in Figure 3-3. This is where you can define how the EM interacts with the selected server. The first thing you can do is to modify the login being used to connect to the server. (I'm using Windows Authentication but I could easily change to use a login and password defined within SQL Server, which will be described in Chapter 11, "How Do I Secure My Data?")

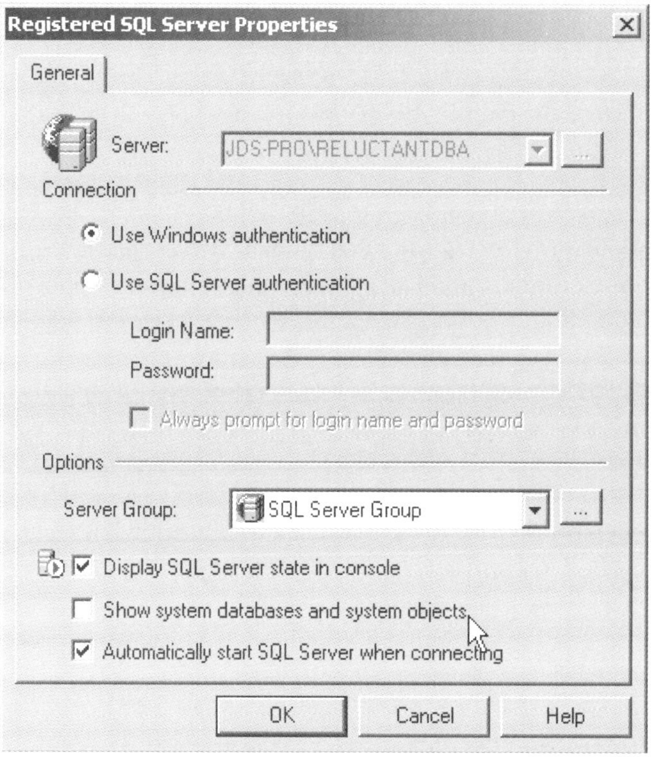

Figure 3-3. Modifying the registration of a SQL Server within the EM

The other important action to take here is to uncheck the checkbox at the bottom of the screen labeled Show System Databases and System Objects. By default, the EM displays System databases and system objects. System databases and objects will be discussed throughout the book, but for the time being, trust me that messing with them can be bad. Modifying tables or stored procedures that belong to the server can lead to loss of data or even the total destruction of your SQL Server. You do not want to have to rebuild your server because you accidentally deleted a system table. So the first thing you should do after registering a server is to uncheck this box. There are times that it is necessary to view these objects in the EM, so when you need to, go to the Registration properties and change it. Then, when you've finished with whatever you need to do you set it *back*. In general, if you can see the **master**, **msdb**, **model**, or **tempdb** databases, then you know you need to go uncheck this box.

How Do I Configure SQL Server?

OK, now that you know how to change how the EM *interacts* with a server, let's look at how you can *configure* the server. Configuring the server is as easy as right-clicking on the server and selecting Properties. You should see a box like the one in Figure 3-4. If you didn't, then you probably got a message telling you that only members of sysadmin can access this feature. Go back to the SQL Server Registration and make sure you are connecting as sa or a member of the systems administration group.[1]

There are a number of tabs in the SQL Server Properties dialog box, but we're only going to cover three of them in depth: General, Security, and Server Settings. You can explore the other tabs, but you probably won't need them because SQL Server's built-in administration and monitoring take care of things like memory management well.

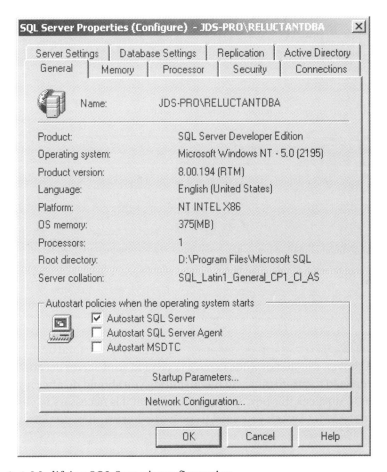

Figure 3-4. Modifying SQL Server's configuration

---

[1]   For more information on sysadmin and how to put logins into the sysadmin group, see Chapter 11, "How Do I Secure My Data?"

The General Tab

The General tab displays several pieces of information related to both SQL Server and the machine it is running on. As you can see in Figure 3-4, the Developer Edition is running on a Windows 2000 operating system (OK, so it says NT 5, but that's what Microsoft labeled Windows 2000 internally). You can also see what type and number of processors, the amount of memory, and the root directory for the server.

The three checkboxes under the heading Autostart Policies When the Operating System Starts are front ends to the NT Services for SQL Server, SQL Server Agent, and the Distributed Transaction Coordinator (DTC). You can chose to have any or all of these started automatically. Well, if you decide to auto-start the Agent or DTC, then it will automatically start the SQL Server engine. This doesn't work in reverse, however. If you manually stop SQL Server, the system will automatically stop Agent and DTC if they are running. What the system *won't* do is to restart them when you restart SQL Server. You will need to restart them separately when you manually start SQL Server.

The Security Tab

The Security tab enables you to set several security options. First is whether SQL Server will authenticate based on Windows only or Windows and SQL Server. So if you aren't happy with what you selected when you installed the server, you can change it here. You can also set the Audit level from this tab. Although the default is to not track logins, if you set the Audit level to Failure, then failed login attempts are registered in the Event Log. (This is almost a sure way of catching a hack attempt; though it's not guaranteed, you should still consider it).

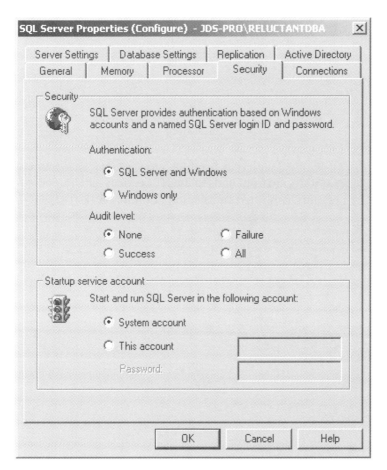

Figure 3-5. Setting Security parameters for an installed SQL Server

The Server Settings Tab

There is one important thing to point out on this screen: the two-digit year support. SQL Server is Y2K compliant, and it stores dates with four-digit years.
However, if SQL Server is passed a two-digit year it will interpret it through the
sliding scale that is set up here. It will then store that year as a four-digit year.
Because this is a Server setting it will be applied to all databases on the server.

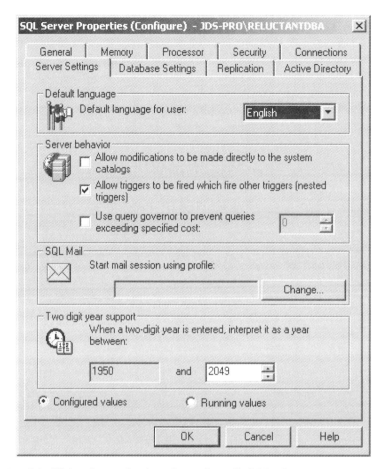

Figure 3-6. Modifying Server Settings for an installed SQL Server

The middle three checkboxes, in the Server Behavior section, determine how the server handles certain situations. They let you

- Allow modifications to be made directly to the system catalogs. This is a dangerous option.

- Allow triggers to be fired which fire other triggers (nested triggers). A trigger is like an event on a table in the database. We'll discuss both triggers and nested triggers in Chapter 10 when we talk about Advanced Stored Procedures.

- Use query governor to prevent queries exceeding specified cost. This can be used to have the system prevent "costly" queries from running. Cost is a number that is made up of disk reads and writes, processing time, and the number of rows involved. We'll cover cost more in Chapter 8, "Introduction to Query Analyzer."

We need to take a moment to discuss how dangerous the first option can be. SQL Server stores information related to the layout and configuration of a database in tables. When Allow Modifications to be Made Directly to the System Catalogs is *not* checked (the default) then changes to the server can only be made through system stored procedures. This is a *very* good thing. Changing data in a system table can lead to corrupted databases or even a corrupted server!

> **CAUTION**   *Microsoft says: Updating fields in system tables can prevent an instance of Microsoft SQL Server from running or can cause data loss. If you create stored procedures while the allow updates option is enabled, those stored procedures always have the ability to update system tables even after you disable allow updates. On production systems, you should not enable allow updates except under the direction of Microsoft Product Support Services.*

In other words, *don't check that box!*

How Do I Start and Stop SQL Server?

There are several ways to start and stop SQL Server, and we're going to look at four of them: the EM, the SQL Server Service Manager utility, the Services panel, and the command line.

> **CAUTION**   *During this section we will be talking about SQL Server running as a service, which it does under Windows 2000 and Windows NT. If you are running SQL Server under Windows 98 or ME, the easiest way to start and stop SQL Server is through the SQL Server Service Manager tool.*

The Enterprise Manager

Because this chapter is focused on the EM, we'll start there. Right-click on the server and you'll get a pop-up menu. Select Stop and the server will instantly change from the green triangle to a red square, indicating that the server is stopped.

The only problem would be that the server isn't stopped yet. Remember that the EM is actually a set of COM objects working for you. When you stop or start the server from these objects, what it really does is issue a command for the service to stop and marks the service visually as stopped but it doesn't wait around for confirmation. In SQL Server 7, you could actually try to start the server before it was finished stopping. In that case, the server would give you an error that it couldn't do that yet. SQL Server 2000 handles this better by simply disabling the Start and Connect menu options until SQL Server is fully stopped.

The SQL Server Service Manager Utility

The second method of starting and stopping SQL Server is by using the SQL Server Service Manager utility. To find that go to Start ≻ Program Files ≻ Microsoft SQL Server ≻ Service Manager. From here you have two drop-down boxes, a checkbox, and a couple of buttons. As you can see in Figure 3-7, the top drop-down lists servers and the bottom drop-down lists the various services associated with the server, including SQL Server, SQL Server Agent, and the Distributed Transaction Coordinator. By pressing the green arrow (start) or red square (stop) button, you can start and stop the service. The checkbox that is at the bottom is used to determine whether the service for that server automatically starts. If it isn't checked, then you'll need to start the service manually. As long as we're here, go ahead and drop down the Services box and select SQL Server Agent. If it isn't started, start the service and then check the box so it's started automatically.

Figure 3-7. Starting and stopping SQL Server from the Service Manager Utility

The Services Panel

The third way to start and stop SQL Server and any of its services is from the Services panel. Although the panel is hidden in different spots in Windows 2000 and NT, you can always do Start ≻ Run and enter Services.msc. That should bring up the Service panel. From here you should be able to scroll down and find MSSQLServer. That is the default server. Any other instances that you have created will be named MSSQL$*instancename*. As you can scc in Figure 3-8, several instances of SQL Server are running on this machine, including the one for this book: MSSQL$RELUCTANTDBA. Across the top of the window you will find the standard buttons to start and stop the service. Table 3-1 shows the naming conventions for all of the services.

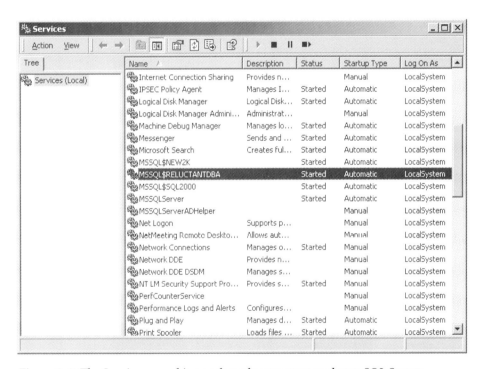

Figure 3-8. The Services panel is another place to start and stop SQL Server.

Table 3-1. Service Names and Instances Associated with the SQL Server's Default Installation

DESCRIPTION	SERVICE NAME
The server itself	MSSQL or MSSQL$*instancename*
SQL Server Agent	SQLServerAgent or SQLAgent$*instancename*
Distributed Transaction Coordinator	DistributedTransactionCoordinator. Runs per NT/2000 server and doesn't have separate services for each instance

The Command Line

The last way to start and stop SQL Server services that we need to cover is from the command line. Sometimes it's easier to do things from the command line, especially if you are trying to write a command file to process an update of some sort. The key is to know what the name of the service is (see Table 3-1). Once you know the name of the service you are trying to affect, you can use the NET STOP and NET START commands. If you wanted to stop the ReluctantDBA server, do something, and then start it again you could use the following in a Windows 2000 command file:

```
NET STOP SQLAgent$RELUCTANTDBA
NET STOP MSSQL$RELUCTANTDBA
REM Insert changes here
NET START MSSQL$RELUCTANTDBA
NET START SQLAgent$RELUCTANTDBA
```

It's important to note that this started and stopped the SQL Agent separately. Since Agent is actually dependent on SQL Server you could have just stopped SQL Server and that would have automatically stopped Agent. By that same token, starting Agent will start SQL Server if it isn't running. There are two reasons we didn't do this.

First, when you are stopping a service that has other services dependent on it, you'll get a prompt asking you if that's what you want to do. If you're at the command prompt trying to stop SQL Server for some reason, that's fine, but if you're trying to run a command file to do something, you probably don't want to have the user answering prompts.

The second reason has to do with programming. If you allow Agent to start SQL Server and there is an error, it makes it that much more difficult to write any error handling or to do any troubleshooting. Does the problem lie in SQL Server or Agent? (I'd rather know explicitly that the service started, but that's me.)

TIP   *One other way to start and stop SQL Server Services is to right-click on the SQL Server Services icon in your System Tray. From the menu that appears, select MSSQLServer Stop, MSSQLServer Pause, or MSSQLServer Start (grayed out when the service is running). This will apply to whichever instance of SQL Server is currently selected in the SQL Server Services program.*

What Is an Object?

OK, now you've got your server installed, registered in the EM and configured. What do you do with it? You manage it. The server is represented in the EM as a series of objects. Although we've said it before, we'll say it again; the EM is nothing more than a graphical user interface (GUI) for the Transact SQL commands to manage the database. You don't need to learn these commands, which is part of what makes SQL Server so easy to manage. Instead of writing out the commands to build a table or memorizing the syntax for creating and modifying a table, you can use the EM to point and click through most of those tasks.

This is not to imply that this is the most efficient *way of performing tasks. Everything that can be done through the EM can be done through Transact SQL as well. In many cases, the Transact SQL commands will be quicker. Not only that, there are certain things you cannot do through the EM. That doesn't diminish the ease of interaction with SQL Server that the EM provides.*

Every item displayed under the server is an object, a group of objects or a way to launch utilities to display their state. The easiest way to tell whether you're looking at an object or a group of objects is by whether you can drill down further through the tree. Figure 3-9 shows my newly registered server. Within that server I have drilled down to Databases, opened up the pubs database and listed all the groups of objects contained in that database.

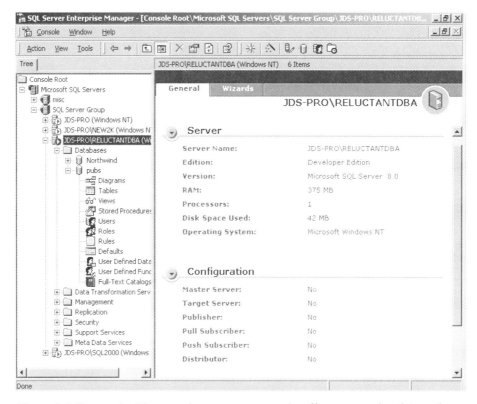

Figure 3-9. Enterprise Manager is an easy way to visually manage the objects that make up your SQL Server.

In the right-hand pane of the EM you can see a wealth of information about the server, including the server name, edition, version, RAM, number of processors, disk space used, and what operating system is being run. In addition, if you click on the Wizards tab you'll see a number of tasks that aid the management of the server. (Specific wizards are discussed throughout the book.)

Why Doesn't the EM Display All the Server's Information?

If the right side of your EM doesn't look like the one in the picture, then your MMC view has probably changed. For the server and the database level, there is a taskpad view that makes management easier by putting information and tasks at your fingertips.

To set the taskpad, make sure you are on either a SQL Server or a database in the tree and then select to View ➤ Taskpad. You will need to do this for each server and database. The taskpad views are actually Dynamic HTML pages. When you put your cursor over the yellow buttons with black triangles in them, you'll get menus for actions you can take. You can find these in the "80\Tools\HTML" directory if you want to take a look.

Now we're going to select a database and you can see that the taskpad view provides a host of useful information. You can see who owns the database, how big it is, how much disk space is allocated, and when it was last backed up.

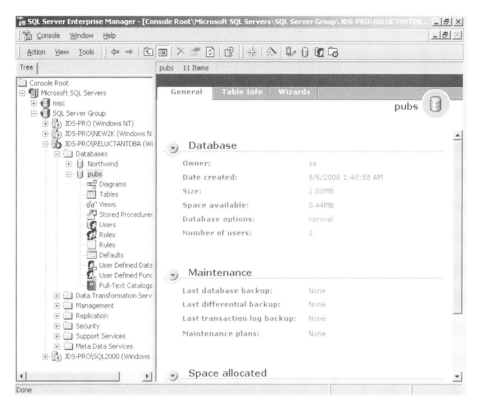

Figure 3-10. The database taskpad in the EM provides useful information about the database such as the size of the database and when it was last backed up.

 CAUTION *You may notice under Maintenance that this database has* never *been backed up. That's because the Pubs database is a sample database that comes with SQL Server 2000, and it can easily be re-created. A real database, on the other hand, should always have a recent backup!*

Across the top of the taskpad you'll notice there are three tabs: General, Table Info, and Wizards. Unfortunately, there's a bug in SQL Server 2000 that prevents the table tab from working completely correctly if you have more than twenty-two tables in your database. On the plus side, you can get around this by pressing the Go button without entering any data. For more information, check out

Knowledge Base article Q275024 (see "Resources" at the end of the chapter). Since the pubs database is small enough, though, all of the tables show up in this tab and you can see how many rows the table has, how much space it is taking up, and all of the indices associated with it.

How Do I Create a Database?

Creating a database is easy—we're going to do it *automagically* with a wizard! To do this, select your SQL Server in the tree of the EM and make sure the taskpad is in view. Next, click on the Wizards tab and select the Create a Database option (see Figure 3-11). This brings up a checklist showing the steps you need to take. Like many wizards, this has many informational and fill-in-the-blank (FITB) screens. We won't go through every single screen in the wizard, but there are some key screens to point out. You can create a database without using the wizard, but the wizard has an interesting and important twist at the end that you won't find in Transact SQL or the menus.

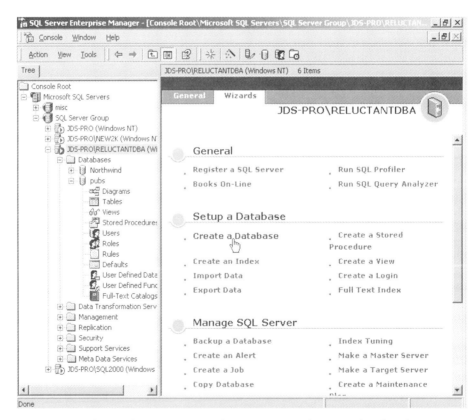

Figure 3-11. Choose the Create a Database option on the Wizards tab to begin creating a database.

You can also create a new database by right-clicking the Databases group under the server in the EM. This is the quickest way to create a database through the EM, but it doesn't provide a means to create maintenance plans.

Wizards, Menus, and Transact SQL, Oh My!

There are numerous ways to accomplish almost every task in SQL Server. The hardest way is to write the Transact SQL statement to accomplish the task; however, it's the most flexible way because you'll be able to perform any task—if you're willing to learn the syntax.[2]

The slowest way is to run a wizard and answer all of the prompts. This is also the most limiting way because the wizards are designed to help you perform the most common tasks and may not have all of the options you want to use. The best balance between functionality and ease of use is to use the menus. Having said that, the *best* way for you is whatever you feel most comfortable using.

Now it's time to FITB. You need to give the database a name and tell it where to create the files for the database. Database names can be up to 128 characters long. The first character must be a letter, underscore (_), at sign (@), or pound sign (#). Subsequent letters can be letters, numbers, underscores, at signs, pound signs, or spaces. The name cannot be a reserved word such as *database* or *table*. However, just because you can put a space in a database name doesn't mean you should. For this example, we're going to call this database RDBA1 and use the defaults for the location of the database files. There are two files, one for the data itself and one for the transaction log file.

SQL Server has always allowed for verbose naming; you should use it, but apply some discretion. Keep these rules in mind:

- The variety of users who will access the database could be quite diverse, so cryptic names will create more work for you when people start asking what the name of an object is.

- Names that are too long will drive troubleshooters nuts because much of their work is performed using Transact SQL and they will have to type in the names.

---

[2] Although this book is heavily oriented in using wizards and menus, I recommend you learn Transact SQL. There are some tasks that can only be done in TSQL, and there are others that are just quicker to write than going through menus or wizards. Further, TSQL commands will run faster because EM is just a front end to TSQL commands.

- Remember that the pound sign is used for temporary tables, and double pound signs (##) are used for Global Temporary tables.

 TIP *Avoid using spaces when naming objects in SQL Server. Although they are allowed, they can cause problems in any number of situations. When referencing them in Transact SQL, objects with spaces in their names must be bracketed between [and]. When referenced in client code, objects with space names require special handling. If you are using spaces for clarity, try using underscores (_) in the place of the spaces or use capitalization to ClarifyTheNameOfTheDatabase.*

Database Logs vs. Transaction Logs

Let's take a moment to look at the differences between physical files, virtual data, and transaction logs.

SQL Server stores the actual database in two (or more) separate files. The database file contains all of the data and objects related to the database. The server also handles all of the interactions between the user or program and the data. At the same time, it also maintains a log of all of the transactions that have occurred. This is a safety feature.

Every time data is inserted, updated (technically treated as a delete and then an insert) or deleted, two things happen. First, the actual change is made to the database through the use of a buffer. Second, just enough information about what was done is recorded in the database's transaction log file. That way, if your server should suffer some problem—say, a non-raided disk dies—and the database gets corrupted, you could restore the backup from the previous night (you are making backups, aren't you?). Then you can apply all of the transactions from the transaction log backups to bring the database up to the state it was in at the time of the last transaction log backup. Transactions will be covered throughout this book.

How Can I Define How Large My Database Should Be?

Now that the server knows where to put the files, it needs to know what you want to call them and how big you want them to grow. The good news is that SQL Server will help to grow your database, so you don't need to worry about outgrowing your database's physical files. Granted, you may outgrow your disks, but we'll cover how to take care of that in Chapter 16, "What Are System Monitor and Performance Monitor?" Generally, if you know the size of the data that you'll be loading into the database, you should make the initial database about 10MB larger that that. Unless there's a reason to change them, leave SQL Server's name of *dbname*_Data and *dbname*_Log alone.

The wizard's next screen requires a little bit of thought and planning before you fill in the blanks (see Figure 3-12). This is where you define the parameters for growing your database. You'll need to come back and revisit them every now and then to see if they are still appropriate. The first option is "Do not grow the database files." If you have an absolutely static database this may be a fine option. However, in most cases you will want to let the file grow rather than have it start generating errors because it has no room to store additional data once the physical file is full.

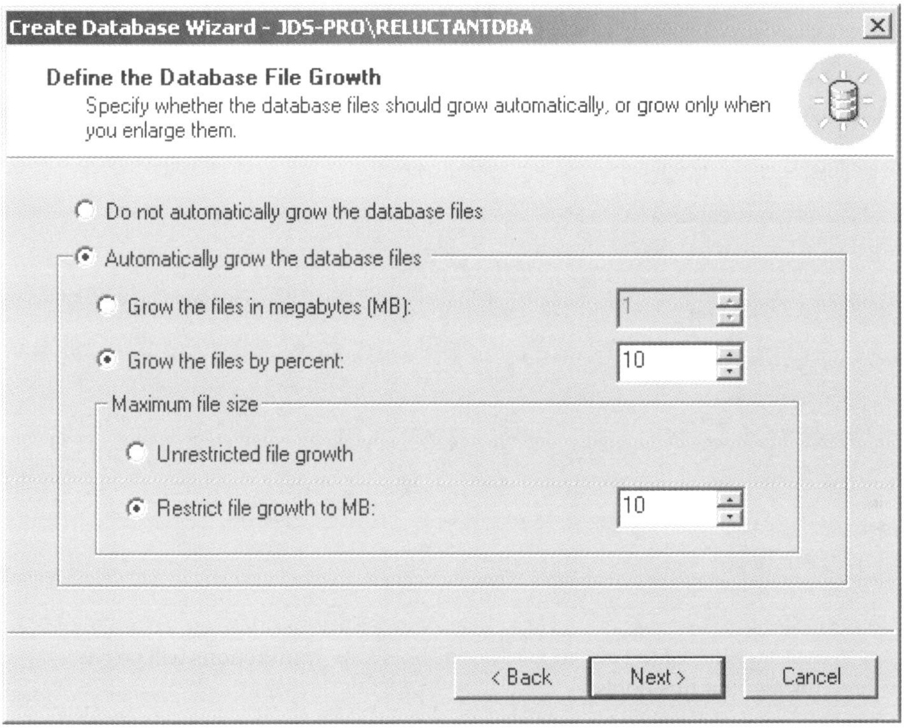

Figure 3-12. Determining how the database will grow requires some planning.

The next set of options requires the most thought for determining how your database will grow dynamically. That's because databases change over time. As they grow and reach the limits of the current physical file, that file needs to be made larger. If you started out with a 50MB database and set it to grow by 20 percent whenever it needs to, it will be growing the file by more than 50MB by the tenth increase. The rules of compound interest apply to databases as well as they do to money. That doesn't mean you shouldn't define growth as a percentage of the data, but it is important to remember how a database grows. How long will the database take before it uses the 50MB just allocated to it? As a general rule, when you're dealing with databases that could grow quickly, you should keep an eye on their growth and determine whether you need to set this to be a fixed increment or a percentage of the current database size.

> *Reluctant DBA* definition of a *runaway database*:
> Any database whose combined data and transaction log size exceeds disk capacity or vastly exceeds the amount of usable data in the database.

The next question is just as important: Do you really want a database to grow until it runs out of disk space? Although databases can take over the disks, they are generally one of two kinds: data warehouses or runaway databases. Runaway databases are created in a couple of different ways. One is by making lots of copies of tables that aren't really used. The important thing to remember is that, once a database has used up all available disk space, it's difficult to rein it in. For that reason, you should set some kind of limit on the database, high enough that it shouldn't be reached but low enough that it won't chew up all of the disk space available. Then, monitor the database size on a regular basis to ensure you won't run out of disk space or room in the physical database file.

Determining database size is a bit more complicated than this and the problems associated with incorrectly setting the parameters for database growth potentially far worse. Because most SQL Servers will have more than one database, you have to consider maximum sizes for each as well as the combined total. If you don't and one becomes runaway, all the space on the disk will be consumed and halt the database in question and invariably halt any and all other databases sharing the same drive space. This means you lose all databases on that disk. As you can see, setting realistic limits on data and log growth is important.

CAUTION *MSDE and Developer Edition database files can't grow larger than 2GB—but their log files can.*

Now that you've set the parameters for growing the database file, you need to do the same for the transaction log. Now, many runaway databases can be linked back to transaction log problems. In fact, we'll be talking about managing the transaction log in Chapter 4 under "How Do I Prevent Large Transaction Log Files?"

TIP   *The Log file can (and often should be) saved to a separate hard disk. This helps performance by having transactions processed by another disk drive.*

You have completed the Create Database wizard. You've got the Finish button and are all ready to go on to your next task, but the wizard has other plans for you because it is going to ask you if you want to create a maintenance plan.

What If My Database Is Larger Than My Disk Drive's Capacity?

Buy a bigger disk drive? That's not the answer, but it's always an option. Although the wizard lets you create multiple database and transaction log files, they all must be in the same location. This is a limitation of the wizard. SQL Server will let you create multiple database files for your database on different disks. In large data warehouses this is done not only because of the size but also for performance reasons. See "How Do I Modify the Database Size?" later in this chapter for more information on what to do when your database starts outgrowing your disk and how to handle adding additional database or transaction log files.

How Do I Create a Maintenance Plan (and Why Do I Need One)?

One way to create a maintenance plan is by selecting the Database Maintenance Plan wizard from the Wizards tab of the taskpad. But the EM thinks it's important enough to have a maintenance plan that it offers to let you build one as soon as you've finished building the database.

So why does SQL Server 2000 do this? After all, doesn't SQL Server 2000 automatically update index statistics, eliminating maintenance plans?[3]

---

[3]   Index statistics are covered in Chapter 7, "The Power of Indexing," but they are basically the data that SQL Server uses when determining which index to use when filtering data.

Well, yes, SQL Server 2000 does do a much better job of keeping statistics up-to-date, but a maintenance plan is so much more than just that. The first screen of the Database Maintenance Plan Wizard mentions the four tasks that it will help you accomplish:

- Run Database Integrity Checks. It's a simple fact of life that data will, on occasion, lose integrity. This is less likely to happen in SQL Server 2000 than it was in prior versions because the interface has been simplified, but it is still possible that disks can lose sectors. This will help reduce or eliminate these issues.

- Update Database Statistics. Statistics are what SQL Server uses to help streamline data access. An index that has a unique key will perform a quicker match than one with thousands of matches. By keeping track of these statistics, SQL Server is able to handle queries more quickly by knowing which index is most likely to provide a good match. And, although SQL Server 2000 does a much better job of this, there may be times you'll want to have it doing more or less sampling of the data.

- Perform Database Backups on a Scheduled Basis. If you are not doing this, please start. The data (and job) you save may be your own.

- Ship Transaction Logs to Another Server. Used for keeping multiple servers synchronized. Some companies like to keep their testing and development environments in synch with their production environment, and this is one of the easiest ways to accomplish this. See the "Resources" section at the end of the chapter for more information.

Once you've pressed Next on the wizard, you'll be shown a list of databases on the Server and asked which ones you want to back up. As you can see in Figure 3-13, the RDBA database is automatically selected.

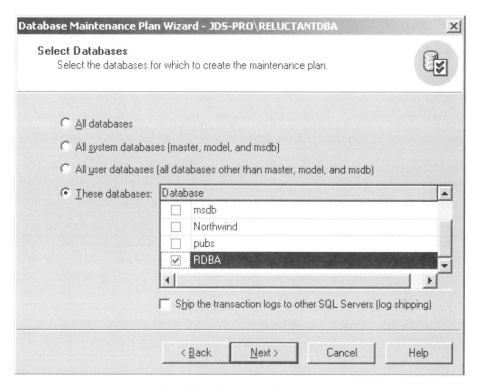

Figure 3-13. Determining which databases need to be part of the maintenance plans

Which Databases Should Have a Maintenance Plan?

That's a very good question and has an equally good answer: it depends. You probably shouldn't, for instance, put the **Northwind** or **pubs** databases under a maintenance plan. They are designed as sample databases and are rarely used for anything else, so there is no value to maintaining them. On the other hand, each and every production and critical system database should be part of a maintenance plan.

What Is a System Database?

There are four system databases: **master**, **msdb**, **model**, and **tempdb**. Of those four, **master** *definitely* should have a maintenance plan. The master database is just that. It contains information related to SQL Server and all of the databases maintained by the server, which includes, but is not limited to, User accounts, Passwords, and Permissions (access to databases). If it gets corrupted and you don't have a backup, you could be in for a tedious time rebuilding your SQL Server, not to mention that you might even lose your own databases!

The **model** database, on the other hand, needs a good backup only when you make changes to it. The **model** database is the one used as a template whenever you create a new database. If you want to make sure that every database you create on a server has one or more specific tables or objects, create them first in the **model** database. Then, every time you create a new database, these tables or other objects will be created as well.

The **msdb** database is where all of your job information is stored (schedules, steps, history, and so on), so it should be included for backups.

The **tempdb**, however, is one of the most fascinating databases. Every time SQL Server is started, **tempdb** is created anew. This database is a scratch database. When SQL Server needs to create a temporary table to join two tables together, that temporary table is created in the **tempdb** database. It doesn't need a maintenance plan. In fact, **tempdb** doesn't even show up as a database for which you can create a plan.

Data Optimization

The next screen in the wizard is where you can set optimization options for the database (see Figure 3-14). This screen separates into three sections: Indices, Database Size, and Scheduling.

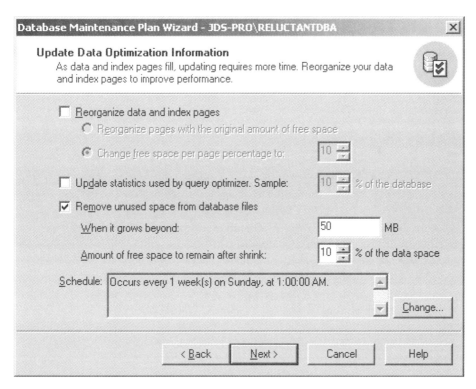

Figure 3-14. Setting the database optimization options

Indices

Indices will be covered in depth in Chapter 7, "The Power of Indexing," so we won't dwell on the index options in this chapter. The important thing to remember is that each of these options will automatically run an associated command:

- Reorganize Data and Index Pages. This will drop and rebuild all existing indices. This is one of those times that Transact SQL commands come in handy. Although this is a perfectly functional way to handle reorganizing your indices to keep them fast, the DBCC DBREINDEX command will accomplish a similar goal more quickly.

- Reorganize Pages with the Original Amount of Free Space and Change Free Space per Page Percentage To. The subject of free space is covered in depth in "The Power of Indexing" chapter.

- Update Statistics Used by Query Optimizer. Sample x% of the Database. This option will rebuild the data SQL Server uses when it optimizes queries. Now SQL Server 2000 stores statistics on indices but you might want a larger or smaller sampling of your data. This will be covered in Chapter 7, "The Power of Indexing."

Database Size

You can also tell SQL Server to automatically shrink the database. Although this doesn't get run often, it does help in keeping the database size in check. You can determine when to run it and how much free space to leave.

Several things could cause your database to grow and not all of them are good. A runaway query could start loading and expanding a table with millions of rows of data accidentally. Once that space has been added to the physical database file, even though the data that created the need for the space has been deleted, the space hangs around waiting to be filled. By shrinking the database you free up resources that can be used by other databases.

Scheduling

Scheduling is actually handled by the SQL Server Agent, which runs as a separate service on your server. Like any service running on your server, it can be turned off. In fact, it is dependent on SQL Server, so the Agent gets stopped every time SQL Server is stopped and it will need to be manually restarted. Each part of the maintenance plan can be scheduled independently to determine when it will occur. Some pieces, like the Data Optimization, can be run once a week or even once a month where others (backups!) should be run more often. You can accept the default of once a week on Sunday at 1:00 A.M., but we'll walk through what the screens look like if you need to change the schedule. (The SQL Server Agent will be covered in more detail in Chapter 12, "How Can SQL Server Agent Make Life Easier?")

To get to the schedule dialog box, press the Change button in the lower-right corner of the Database Maintenance Wizard. This will bring up the dialog box featured in Figure 3-15. The top section determines which day or days the maintenance will run. Jobs can be scheduled to run Daily, Weekly, or Monthly. Depending on which radio button you select, the box on the right will change to reflect options. Daily, for instance, lets you pick the number of days between jobs running. You can pick any number from 1 to 366.

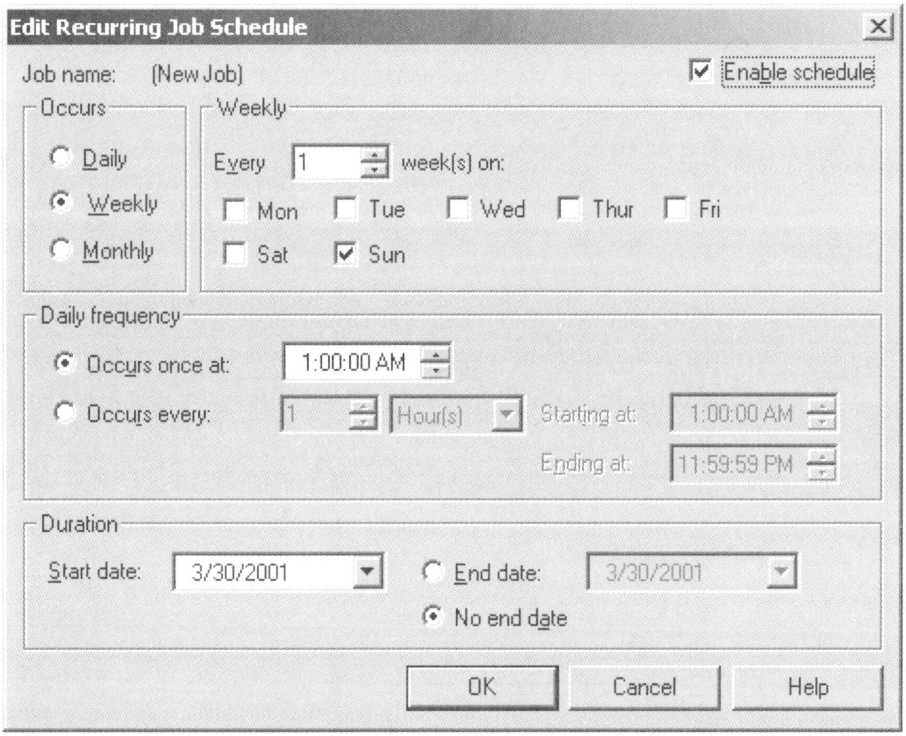

Figure 3-15. The maintenance plan has a variety of options for scheduling tasks to be run, all part of the SQL Server Agent.

Weekly seems to be the most frequently used schedule because it allows you to pick the days of the week. If a job needs to run on normal business days, you can select Weekly and then check Monday through Friday.

When you select Monthly scheduling you get two options. The first is to schedule the job to run on a certain day every x months. That means you could have a job scheduled to run on the 15th of every end of quarter month by setting it to Day 15 of every three months (you'd also need to set the start date, but we're getting there).

You can also set it to run on a particular day of the week, say the 1st, 2nd, 3rd, 4th, or last Sunday of the month. Again, you can schedule it to run every month, every 99 months, or any time frame in between.

The middle section is where you set the Daily Frequency of the task. You can set a task to run once at a specific time of day or as often as every minute.

Finally, there is the Duration. By default, new jobs start the day you set them and have no end date. If you go back to the job that should run on the 15th of every end of quarter that would be as simple as setting the start date to January 1, and it will work fine.

Now, to get back to the Maintenance Wizard, press either OK to accept your changes or Cancel to ignore them. Then click the Next button in the wizard to move onto the next task.

Database Integrity Check

Hey, isn't SQL Server supposed to be a bastion of programming, always ensuring that the data is good? Well, yes, but think of all the factors involved: the hardware or network could have issues, the application or application server could have a problem, and data could be corrupt and not caught by SQL Server. When you consider all the possibilities you find quickly that it's possible, though highly unlikely, that something could happen that may mess up the data or indices. Perhaps nothing noticeable happens, but it could affect performance. Always keep in mind that when a database is created, SQL Server attempts to grab as many contiguous blocks of space on the drive as it can. When data is stored and indices created, this information is placed on as many contiguous blocks as is possible. Most programmers are quite familiar with file fragmentation, but in SQL Server the problem can be exponential. First you have the "physical" space, then the "physical" data saved in that space, then you have the "virtual" references, like indices (which are in a tree structure), and very quickly you begin to realize the number of ways that performance can be degraded. For that reason you should run a weekly Database Integrity Check. The biggest decision to make here is whether you want the indices included in the check. By excluding the indexing function, you'll speed up the Database Integrity Check. Unless the database is massive, you can set the database integrity to check over the whole database.

SQL Server can also fix minor problems, if you let it. Minor problems aren't data errors, but rather errors with the physical file the database is stored in. SQL Server stores data in pages and, occasionally, a page can become "loose" or fragmented and SQL Server will fix these items for you.

You'll notice that there is an option to run these checks before every backup. Before SQL Server 7, running an integrity checks were almost a requirement. With SQL Server 2000, it is not required, at least not as something to be done every time you backup the database.

Database Backup Plan

Just in case you have missed my earlier comments, let me make this point:
BACK UP YOUR DATA CONSISTENTLY!
The simple truth is that SQL Server will back your data up for you without you needing to do much—but you still have to tell SQL Server to set up a maintenance plan to do so. If you don't set your maintenance plan to do anything else, have it back up your data. And always have the maintenance plan verify the

integrity of the backup when it has finished. That just tells SQL Server to take a quick look at the backup and make sure it can read the header files and read to the end of the file. There are more options to backing up your database than just selecting tape or disk and setting a schedule. You can also determine how many backups you keep and where they are stored.

There are actually two parts to the maintenance plan backup: one is for the database and the other is for the transaction log. Daily backups are recommended. When you move onto the next task in the wizard, backing up transaction logs, you can switch to something more frequent. For more information on backing up and restoring transaction logs, see Chapter 4, "How Do I Back Up and Restore My Data?"

> **CAUTION** *Backups are only as good as the restore you can get out of them. It's a good idea to test restoring your backups to another machine regularly. That way you'll know whether there is any problem with your backups. Trust me, it's far easier to do this in a controlled test environment where you can identify and fix any problems than it is to be under the gun to restore your company's data warehouse the day before accounting needs to use that data to present monthly financial information to your parent company. If you discover problems at that time, it could be an uncomfortable situation. This is an excellent opportunity to do testing of your own, like performance tweaking, testing schema changes, or experimenting in other ways that you couldn't do in production or other environments. You could also do some ad-hoc queries without affecting production. I'll cover backing up and restoring data in more depth in Chapter 4, "How Do I Back Up and Restore My Data?"*

The maintenance plan backups offer two more nice features. The easiest way to track file backups is to have the maintenance plan use the default backup directory ("\Program Files\Microsoft SQL Server\Backup") and then create a subdirectory for each database. That means that it would create a RDBA directory in the backup directory and store the backups there. Each backup that it creates will be automatically named with the database name and a timestamp. "RDBA_20010331030305.BAK" would be a backup made a little after 3:00 A.M. on March 31, 2001 of the RDBA database. In addition, you can have the plan determine how many days worth of backups to keep. As long as you have disk space, you could keep 14 days worth of database and transaction log backups on the disk. Every time the maintenance plan runs, it will remove any backups older than that.

CAUTION   *I know this sounds obvious, but I have to say it. If you are backing up your SQL Server to disk and then not backing up the backup files to either another machine or tape or some other media that is not a part of your server, then you still run the risk of losing all of your data if there is a disk drive problem.*

How Can I Know the Maintenance Plan Worked?

On the next page, the Maintenance Plan Wizard has an option that allows you to generate reports and keep a history of how the maintenance is going. The first option available is to have SQL Server Agent generate a report and store it in the "LOG" directory for SQL Server. The second option is to have it email an operator. (Email, operators, and all of that fun stuff are covered in Chapter 12, "How Can SQL Server Agent Make Life Easier?").

Unless it encounters an error, don't bother having it generate log files. Instead, set up an email account and have the server alert you proactively that there was a problem. The next (and almost final) page of the wizard is related to storing the history records. Keep the defaults here and go on.

The last page, before the wizard actually creates the maintenance plan, simply gives you a chance to name the plan and lists what the plan will do. Listing 3-1 shows the output from what we have just finished walking through.

Listing 3-1. A listing of the steps our maintenance plan will take

```
DATABASES
     master
     msdb
     RDBA
SERVERS
     (local)
OPTIMIZATIONS
     Occurs every 1 week(s) on Sunday, at 1:00:00 AM.
     Perform the following actions:
       Reorganize data and index pages, changing the free space to 10 percent of
the original space.
       Shrink database when it grows beyond 50 MB. Leave 10 percent of data space
as free space.
INTEGRITY CHECKS
     Occurs every 1 week(s) on Sunday, at 12:00:00 AM.
     Perform the following actions:
         Check database
```

```
COMPLETE BACKUP
    Occurs every 1 day(s), at 2:00:00 AM.
    Backup media: Disk
    Store backup files in the default SQL Server Backup directory.
    Delete backup files which are older than 2 Week(s).
    Verify the backup after completion.
    Create a subdirectory for each database, to store the backup files.
TRANSACTION LOG BACKUP
    Occurs every 1 day(s), every 2 hour(s) between 12:00:00 AM and 11:59:59 PM.
    Backup media: Disk
    Backup destination: D:\Program Files\Microsoft SQL
Server\MSSQL$RELUCTANTDBA\BACKUP
    Delete backup files which are older than 2 Week(s).
    Verify the backup after completion.
    Create a subdirectory for each database, to store the backup files.
```

Now, if we had built this database using the menus or Transact SQL commands, the maintenance plan would need to be added. It's important that every production database be part of a maintenance plan if only to get backed up consistently. Keep that in mind when you go to build your database through something other than the wizard.

How Do I Modify the Database Size?

OK. Our database is built and now we open it up in the EM and look at it through the taskpad to check out our handiwork and discover we've made one, tiny mistake. We were supposed to create the database and make it 10MB, but it's only 2MB! Not to worry, as long as you have disk space, you can easily increase the size of a database.

Right-click on the database and select Properties. If you are not connected to the server as the database owner (dbo), sa, or a member of the Administrators group, then Properties won't even appear on the menu. (For more explanation of the administrators group and dbo, see Chapter 11, "How Do I Secure My Data?") That's a good thing since the changes you make here can have some major impacts on your database. As you can see in Figure 3-16, the Properties of a database are sorted into several tabs to make it easier to find the settings you want to change. We'll look at the Data Files, Transaction Log, and Filegroups tabs.

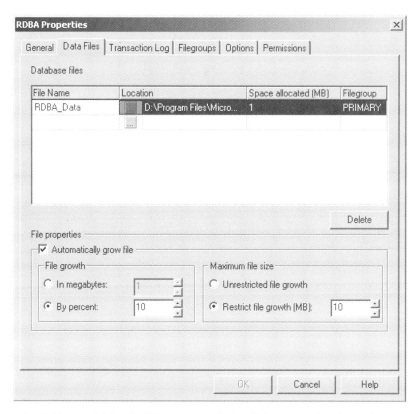

Figure 3-16. From within the EM, you can right-click on any database that you have sufficient permission for and make changes to the database's properties.

In Figure 3-16 the Data Files tab is open. Currently it has one file configured and that file is set to be 1MB large. When this database was created, it was set up so it could grow. If that's the case, you may be wondering why we want to increase its size now. The answer is relatively simple.

SQL Server will automatically increase the size of the files that make up a database. That usually happens when SQL Server is attempting to do something else. That means SQL Server has to temporarily halt the load of data while it increases the database size. To increase the file size to 10MB, it took approximately four seconds. Now that's not a large amount of time, but if you were preparing to load a couple hundred megabytes of data, it's just easier to set that file size ahead of time. So, put 10 in the file Space Allocated column and press OK.

This is also where you go to add new files and Filegroups to your database. There are a couple of reasons to do this, mostly related to performance issues. First, look at the "RDBA_Data" file. You can see that belongs to the Filegroup PRIMARY. There are two types of Filegroups: PRIMARY and user defined. Every database must have a PRIMARY Filegroup and that Filegroup must have one file in it. The PRIMARY Filegroup is where all of the system tables for a database are created and stored. In addition, one Filegroup must be the default. The default Filegroup is where any and all new objects in the database are created if a specific Filegroup isn't used.

Now that you've defined Filegroups, let's look at how SQL Server will use them to help us maintain our databases. Let's say we add a second database file to RDBA and it resides on another disk using a totally separate controller. If we put them both in the PRIMARY Filegroup, then SQL Server will automatically balance the data between the two disks. This provides a performance gain by allowing both disks to read data at the same time. Another possibility is to create a second Filegroup on a disk separate from your PRIMARY Filegroup to store indices on. Again, this helps by providing concurrent reads of the data.[4]

Adding a set of user-defined Filegroups is fairly simple. Go to the Filegroups tab and fill in the Name of the Filegroup. That's all you can do when you add a new Filegroup. Because there is no Apply button, you need to press the OK button and then come back in to the Property pages. When you come back in, your new user-defined Filegroup is available to be selected when you create a database file. However, you need to have a file in the Filegroup before you can do anything else, which means adding the file (or files) and pressing OK before you can come back and do anything else to the Filegroup. Once a file is associated with a Filegroup you can then set it to be the default Filegroup.

The Basics of Files and File Groups

Some basic rules apply to database files, transaction log files, and Filegroups.

- Every file can be used by one database and one database only.

- There must be at least one database file and one transaction log file when you create a database.

- You must have a PRIMARY Filegroup.

- Transaction Files do not belong to any Filegroup.

- Database files can belong to only one Filegroup.

- You cannot move database files between Filegroups. You would have to delete the database file (which you cannot do until you have removed all objects from it) and re-create it in the new Filegroup.

---

[4] If you are using Redundant Arrays of Independent Disks (RAID) technology, then you are already experiencing some of this benefit because concurrent reads from multiple disks is one of the benefits of RAID.

How Do I Drop a Database?

It is a sad but simple fact that sometimes you will need to get rid of a database. Perhaps it will have outlasted its usefulness, or maybe you just need to start your design over again from scratch. In any case, as long as you have dbo, sa, or administrator rights, you can get rid of the database easily.

> **WARNING**   *Dropping a database is an irrevocable act. The only way to get the database back once you've dropped it is to restore from your backups!*

One way to delete the database is to right-click on the database in the EM tree and select Delete. The EM will ask you if you really want to do this. If you've created a maintenance plan you'll also be asked if you want to remove the backup and restore history for the database. Ask yourself if you have a good backup of the database (unless you're *sure* you don't need one) and then hit the Yes button.

Another way to delete the database is to select the Database tab in the EM. This will fill the right pane of EM with all of your databases. Select the one you want to delete and then you can click on the red X in the toolbar at the top of the page.

> **NOTE**   *Both of these options are different from attaching and detaching the database, which is covered in Appendix A, "How Do I Load the Examples?" Attaching and detaching the database simply removes references to the database and transaction log files from the server and allows you to do other things with them, like put them on CD so someone else can load them onto their server.*

There is one more way to get rid of a database, but it's not recommended. However, someone could use this method to remove a database, so you should be able to recognize the symptoms that indicate someone has totally bypassed the system to get rid of a database. Begin by stopping SQL Server. Once it has stopped, go to the Data directory where you have created the database and transaction log files and then delete the file. If SQL Server is running, you'll get a sharing violation, but if it isn't, you can delete the underlying files of the database without a problem.

Now start SQL Server again and open up the Databases tab under the server. You will see one of your databases grayed out and marked Suspect. In this case it's suspect because the database file was deleted. It could, however, be marked suspect because the disk file is corrupted or the RAID array is having problems or . . . you get the picture.

The easiest way to correct this, assuming that the file is actually missing or corrupted is to delete the database and restore from your latest backup. Which just happens to be what I'm going to be talking about in the next chapter. If you don't have a backup then you'll be very busy rebuilding the database and the data that it had in it.

Last Words

In this chapter you were introduced to SQL Server's EM. It definitely qualifies as the Reluctant DBA's best tool for interacting with the database. Now you know how to interact with SQL Server, create databases, and create maintenance plans for the databases. As soon as you learn about backups in the next chapter, you'll be ready to start working with data.

Resources

- Learn how to ship transaction logs to another server:
  http://msdn.microsoft.com/library/psdk/sql/ht_servpem_8gtl.htm

- Get an introduction to the Microsoft Management Console:
  http://msdn.microsoft.com/library/psdk/mmc/mmcsg001_2z37.htm

- Read up on transaction log architecture:
  http://msdn.microsoft.com/library/psdk/sql/8_ar_da2_876t.htm

- Learn more about physical database files and Filegroups:
  http://msdn.microsoft.com/library/psdk/sql/8_ar_da2_9sab.htm

CHAPTER 4

How Do I Back Up
and Restore My Data?

*Yesterday an unnamed film crew plugged a gigawatt of lighting
equipment into one of our uninterruptible power supplies. Not
unexpectedly, it was interrupted, temporarily bringing down the user
database machine. At about the same time on the science database
machine one of the disks failed. Thanks to RAID, the hot swap disk
kicked in. Unfortunately the hot swap also failed, revealing a more
serious problem. It didn't automatically kick over to the second hot
swap. Today we rebooted the science database machine that brought
the second hot swap online. The RAID controller worked as advertised
and the science database kept operating with just a momentary
lapse and no data loss.*

—SETI@home, Technical Newsletter, November 2, 1999

NO MATTER HOW CAREFULLY you plan, the unexpected will happen. Somewhere,
sometime, you are going to need to recover from a problem. That's what hap-
pcncd to the SETI@home crew. They hadn't planned on bringing down the user
database machine the hard way, nor had they planned on having one of the disks
on their science database fail at the same time. Fortunately, they had everything
they needed to recover from that little problem and pick up where they left off.

Once again, if you are not consistently backing up your data, then you have
a disaster just waiting to happen. No matter how small the database, if you don't
have a backup you'll end up reinventing the wheel (rebuilding your database, in
other words), and every time you reinvent the wheel, you run the risk of invent-
ing one that won't roll.

In the last chapter you learned how to build a maintenance plan that would
automatically back up your database and transaction logs. In this chapter, we'll
discuss other ways to back up your data, where you should put your backups,
and how to restore your data and transaction logs.

Why Do I Need to Back Up My Data?

Well, for one, your job comes to mind. Of course there are many other reasons to back up data. It doesn't matter whether you are running a very large database (VLDB) or a small one, or whether your database is running on a basic computer with one disk drive or a mega-server with RAID 5 disks measuring terabytes in size. Backups should be a part of your life.

No matter how many preventative steps you take, you will someday need to restore your data. Recently I was working on a moderate data warehouse that had some really good equipment. All of the disks were RAID-5, the computer had dual-power supplies and a large uninterruptible power supply (UPS), and it was locked in a secure room. I was working on an update to the database to improve performance and made one, really small mistake. I accidentally deleted the WHERE condition on an UPDATE, which led to updating every single record in the database.

Why stop with updating every record, though? This change ultimately updated every single record multiple times (sometimes creative solutions have a way of biting back). By the time I was done, my data warehouse had been burned to the ground, and I was sifting the coals for clues. Did I grab my résumé and start calling recruiters? No. First, I was working on a duplicate copy of the database (to prevent destroying the real data warehouse from such an event as this) and second, because I had a backup of the database that I could restore and be up and running again.

This would have been a really good time for a hard shut down. Ask yourself, "Will I have to resort to a backup when this process is done?" If so, and the query hasn't yet completed (and it won't cancel), shut the power off. This may sound drastic, but SQL, as a general rule, will roll back the transaction upon restart and put the database back as it existed before the UPDATE, DELETE, *or* INSERT. *The recovery will take less time than performing a restore, and if the recovery fails, you already concluded before shutting down that you'd resort to restoring a backup anyway, so you haven't really "lost" anything in doing this.*

No matter how good the hardware and software, unexpected things happen, so you need to be ready to put your database back together from a backup if necessary.

So, How Do I Back Up a Database?

There are several ways to perform backups:

- SQL Server's SQL Agent can schedule backup jobs.

- Commercial backup products may have their own built-in schedulers.

- Backup Wizards in the Enterprise Manager (EM) can perform ad-hoc backups.

No matter which method you use to create or perform backups, be consistent! One method you can use is a SQL Server maintenance plan, which was covered in the last chapter. In this chapter you're going to learn how to do one-time back-ups from the EM and discuss some of the options for *where* to put your backed-up data. Here "where" means the physical location.

 CAUTION *Just because a database is part of a maintenance plan does* not *mean it is getting backed up. For the mainte-nance plan to run, the SQL Server Agent has to be configured correctly and be running, and the maintenance plan must have a scheduled job (which is likely if you use the wizard). Keep in mind that there are other factors that can prevent a job from running even when SQL Server Agent is running fine. Read Chapter 12, "How Can SQL Server Agent Make Life Easier?"*

The easiest way to cover all of the things that go into backing up a database is to use the wizard. Starting wizards from the taskpad was covered in the last chap-ter, so in this chapter we'll show you how to use the menus. From within the EM, select Tools Wizards. That will bring up the Select Wizard screen (see Figure 4-1). The Backup Wizard is not, as you might believe, under the Database section. Instead you'll find it under Management. That's because backing up your data-base is a global function of managing the database, just as job scheduling and logins are.

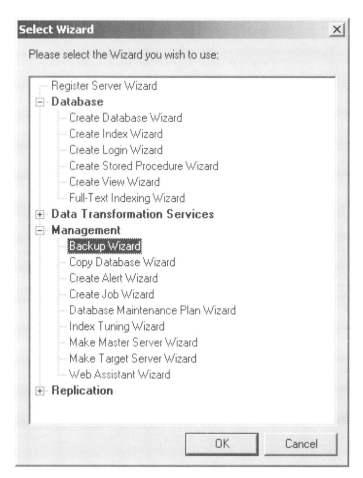

Figure 4-1. The Select Wizard screen shows you all of the wizards available in SQL Server 2000.

The Backup Wizard will step you through the four parts of a backup:

- Specifying the name of the database to be backed up and the type of backup to perform

- Specifying which devices to use in the backup

- Deciding whether to overwrite or append the backup data

- Verifying the backup

The first screen is the obligatory explanation of what the wizard is going to do. The second one isn't much more exciting—it lists all of the databases on the system.[1]

To follow the example from the last chapter, we'll choose the RDBA database and press Next. The next screen asks to name and describe the backup (see Figure 4-2). The backup name is *automagically* generated for you, but you can put whatever you want in the description. Make sure the description is something meaningful or intuitive—this will help you identify more easily what it is you are restoring, especially if you have multiple backups being made while you test some new functionality. The only down side is that the description, while written to the backup file, isn't displayed where it might make sense, but we'll cover that when we talk about restores in "How Do I Restore a Database from a Complete Backup?" For now, enter a description and press the Next button.

 The name you give a backup file may also follow a company standard. If no standard exists, now is a good time to create one and use it consistently. Since BAK is used as the default extension for backup files, it can be left out of the "logical" name. One of the most troubling issues with naming files is the use of spaces. Although it is great that we now have the ability to write long names and descriptions for files and such, there are still problems with shortcuts, queries, and other functionality in the operating system, applications, and even SQL Server that necessitate using underscores (_), capital letters, and no spaces. Although using capital letters to start each word within a name is certainly better than using spaces, underscores in general practice are more user friendly (for non-technical people).

---

[1] Even if you don't have the rights to back up a database, you can start the wizard and select a database to back up. Depending on the rights you *do* have, you can get to various points in the wizard before it generates an error. For more information, see Chapter 11, "How Do I Secure My Data?"

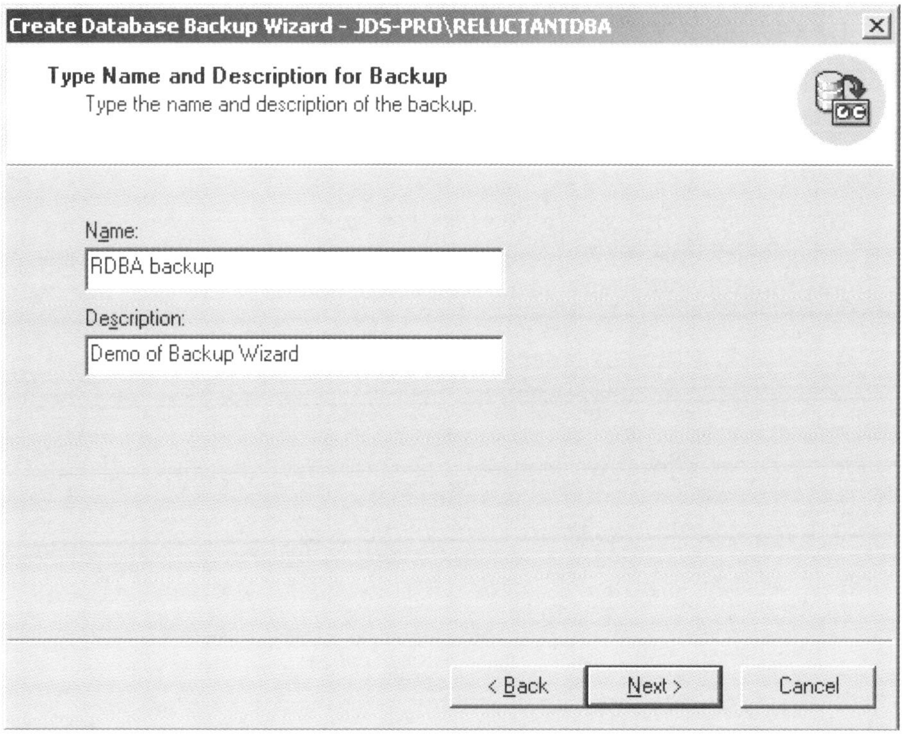

Figure 4-2. You can name and describe your backup to aid in restoring data.

What Do I Back Up?

The next screen lists three options for how and what to backup. We'll look at each in turn and then talk about how you could use each one as a part of your backup plan. For this walk-through, however, we're going to select a database backup.

> *Reluctant DBA* definition of a *database backup*:
> A backup is a *complete* copy of the database structure, all of the indices, constraints, and programming at a moment in time.

If your databases are small enough, you can run a complete database backup on them every day. Small is, by the way, a relative term. Some of these databases might be measured in terms of gigabytes, but they could still be backed up completely every night because the complete backup to disk could take only a couple of hours. This is the easiest backup to use because all it does is create a snapshot of the database in time. This backup is very much like a line drawn in the sand. When the backup starts, it is backing up the state of the database at that point in time. If the database is modified while the backup is going on, the backup won't capture what changes. That is left for differential database backups.

> *Reluctant DBA* definition of *differential database backup*:
> A snapshot of everything that has been changed since the last backup and up to the time the backup is executed. This requires multiple steps in restoring data to recover to a given point in time.

Differential backups are faster and smaller than full database backups, but this comes at a price. With a full backup, you can restore the backup and be done. Restoring a differential backup requires restoring the last full backup and then each differential backup *in sequence*. This makes restoring data using differential backups a lot more time consuming. However, if you have a large database that you can't get a complete backup of every day, you may want to do a weekly complete backup and a daily differential backup. This is covered in more detail in "How Do I Restore a Differential Backup?"

> *Reluctant DBA* definition of *transaction log backup*:
> A backup of all of the transactions that have occurred since the last full database backup or last transaction log backup, whichever is more recent, whether full, differential, or transaction log.

Unless you specifically tell the server to ignore it, everything that happens in the database is logged. This is especially handy when recovering data, which we'll cover in depth in "How Do I Restore a Transaction Log?" once we've finished talking about backups.

Where Do I Back My Data Up?

When it comes to backing up your data somewhere, the wizard offers you three choices: Tape, File, or Device (see Figure 4-3). Tapes are fairly obvious, but you can only use a tape if you have a tape drive installed. One potential down side to using tapes is they can be slow. Another is that the person responsible for putting the tape in the tape drive might not rewind it or might forget to put a new tape in, meaning you might overwrite last night's backup. With larger databases you may find it faster to back up the database to a disk file (this is the preferred method) and then back up the file to the tape using your normal backup software.

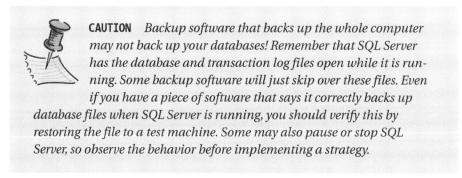

Figure 4-3. You have several options when it comes to determining where you will back up your data.

> **CAUTION**   *Backup software that backs up the whole computer may not back up your databases! Remember that SQL Server has the database and transaction log files open while it is running. Some backup software will just skip over these files. Even if you have a piece of software that says it correctly backs up database files when SQL Server is running, you should verify this by restoring the file to a test machine. Some may also pause or stop SQL Server, so observe the behavior before implementing a strategy.*

That leaves us with files and devices. So what's a backup device? Here's how Books On Line (BOL) explains it:

> *Disk backup devices are files on hard disks or other disk storage media and are the same as regular operating system files. Referring to a disk backup device is the same as referring to any other operating system file. Disk backup devices can be defined on a local disk of*

a server or on a remote disk on a shared network resource, and they can be as large or as small as needed. The maximum file size is equivalent to the free disk space available on the disk.

Actually, backup devices are structured files that contain header information related to the database, database files, transaction log files, and the description you provided when you backed up the database. Each backup file will be approximately the same size as the data it contains, which means that if you have 300MB of data to back up, you'll need 300MB of disk space free for the backup.

Although the backup file can reside on a network connection, there are two minor issues with that. The EM will not let you use the Universal Naming Convention (UNC) of "\\servername\path," though you can specify this in a Transact SQL (TSQL) script. The second thing is that there is a security issue that you'll need to work around. Remember that SQL Server runs as a service on NT/2000 machines and whatever user account the "service" is running under will need to be granted at a minimum read/write access to the network share.

For now we're going to accept the default that the wizard is offering. This creates a backup file in the "BACKUP" directory that exists wherever the server was installed, in this case in "D:\Program Files\Microsoft SQL Server\MSSQL$RELUCTANTDBA\BACKUP." In addition, the file will be named "*database*backup.BAK."

Where Should You Put Your Backup?

Although backing up your data is important, where you back it up to can be just as critical. If you set up nightly backups of your data to the same disk where the database is stored, and the disk drive crashes, you lose both your database *and* your backups. Keeping your backups on the same machine can lead to the same outcome.

Backing up your database to tape can help, as can backing up the database to disk and then copying the backup files to tape, *if* you use multiple tapes. It's important to remember to cycle through your tapes. I'll never forget one day when my department was being audited, and the auditor and I were visiting the remote offices where non-IT people were responsible for doing the backups. Although they had a step-by-step checklist to follow, we found that they weren't following it. Not only that, but they were using the same tape every night! Had we needed to restore data that had been deleted yesterday we would have been unable to do it.

Whether you use tapes, store your backup files on disk, or even write them to a CD-RW, make sure you can recover the data if need be. This is discussed in more detail in "How Do I Restore and Recover My Data?" later in this chapter.

Another reason to put backups on separate drives could be performance related. Although this may not be an issue starting out, it could become one as the database grows and as the demand for having the database accessible 24/7 grows. Having a separate channel improves things even more since data access and data backups aren't going across the same "pipe." These are just some of the subtle things that can be done to prevent performance pitfalls (but not necessarily to improve performance).

Should I Overwrite or Append My Backup File?

When we defined the maintenance plan in the last chapter, this wasn't an issue because the maintenance plan creates a new backup file every time it runs. That file has the database name, date, and time in the name of the file. When you do these one-time backups or when you are scripting them using TSQL, you have the option of overwriting the existing file or appending data to it. My *preference* is to overwrite the existing file. Let me explain why and then explain why you might want to append instead.

When making a backup using the wizard it is generally because you want a backup for a specific purpose. You might make backups like this when planning on testing an upgrade script and need to make sure you can restore the database to a specific state.[2]

If that is all you want to do, then you only need one copy of the backup.

The second reason I don't like using the append method has to do with obfuscation. Maintenance plan backup files are easy to understand. The filename says that it is for a specific database at a specific date and time. It is one file and it contains one copy of the database. When you append a backup to the end of an existing file it is harder to know what is in the file without going through SQL Server. If you always overwrite the existing file, then you know that it is a backup of the database and the file time stamp (though it *can* be modified) tells you when the backup was made. You can verify this information through SQL Server, but you get a good idea of what you're dealing with.

The final argument against appending backups to existing files is because it becomes an all-or-nothing type of file. If you have a backup file that contains multiple backups, and you don't need one of them any more, there is no way to delete just that backup. You would have to overwrite the whole device and wipe out *all* of the backups. And, if you're dealing with hundreds of megabytes of data that can lead to some large backup files.

---

[2] I handle normal maintenance backups through the maintenance plan.

Now that the reasons against using append have been explained, let's look at why you might want to use it. Using the append method guarantees that you won't overwrite an existing backup that you might want or need. Also, if you are performing a full backup once a week and partial backups the rest of the week, you can have all of your backups in the same file, making it easier to restore from.

If you choose to overwrite, you'll get a screen asking you if you want to initialize and label the media. This optional information is written to the header of the file or tape and can be used to prevent writing data to the wrong place. Once you are past that screen, or if you selected to append your data, you'll get the screen in Figure 4-4. This is the last set of options before the data gets backed up.

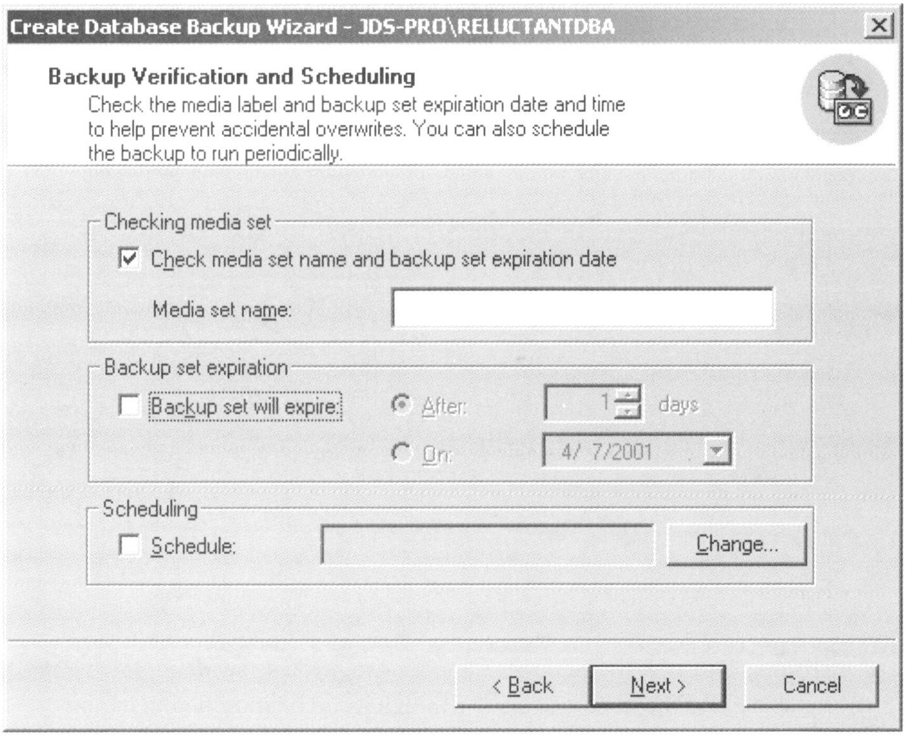

Figure 4-4. The final set of options in the Backup Database wizard

The first option is to check the Media Set Name. If you were overwriting data and had defined a Media Set Name then you can specify that name in this option. If the Media Set Name in the backup file or on the backup tape does not match the Media Set Name you are looking for then the backup is aborted with a message telling you that the media names are different. This checkbox does not, however, just verify the media name. It also checks to see whether the backup has expired and can be overwritten.

The second option box (which is disabled if you are doing an append) determines the expiration date of the backup. When making a backup you can specify how long the backup should stay around by checking this box and selecting either the number of days a backup should be kept or by specifying a date for the backup to expire. This is a handy way to prevent overwriting a backup you want to keep. For a backup that has data appended to it the first backup done determines the expiration date.

 CAUTION *This only works if you check the media set. If that first checkbox is not checked then you can overwrite the data whether it is expired or not.*

The final option is to schedule the job to be run. This is the same scheduling component that the maintenance plan uses because it is all part of the SQL Server Agent (see Chapter 12 for more information). However, here's a helpful shortcut. If you schedule the backup it will create a job that contains the TSQL commands to carry out the exact type of backup that you have just requested. If you are just learning TSQL, then you should take opportunities like this to create different backup plans and then go check out the TSQL commands that get created.

The wizard's final screen reviews what options you have selected. Then you can press Finish, and your database is backed up. Again, this is a good way to make one-time backups but use maintenance plans for consistent backups.

How Do I Back Up My Transaction Log?

While walking through the wizard you saw that you could perform three types of backups: Full, Differential, and Transaction Log. When you perform a full or differential backup you are backing up not only the data but the transaction log as well. Many times, however, it is helpful to back up your transaction log by itself. There are two main reasons for doing this. First, it will make your recovery a lot easier and second, it will help keep your database from growing out of control.

The transaction log is responsible for keeping track of what has happened in your database. Every time you do anything that modifies data, that modification gets recorded to the transaction log: inserting, deleting, or updating data, all of it is recorded in the transaction log. Well, almost all. Toward the end of the chapter in "What Is a Recovery Model?" we'll talk about how to turn the transaction log off for the entire database and how to turn it off for some things, but for now we're going to assume everything is being logged because that is the default setting.

On an active database, this can lead to a large transaction file (even larger than the database itself!). Even on a database that isn't very active, if left to its own devices, the transaction file will grow until one of three things happens:

- The transaction log runs out of disk space or hits the upper limit allowed when it was defined.

- The transaction log is truncated.

- The transaction log is backed up.

The problem with all three of these is that you still have a large transaction file to deal with, and it won't seem to shrink easily. The reason for this lies in the way the transaction log works. Imagine a row of couches lined up against a wall. Each couch represents a virtual transaction log within the physical transaction log file. People sit down in orderly fashion from left to right and, as one couch fills up, people start to use the next couch in line.

Now, before the people have finished filling up the couches, everyone who is sitting down gets up and leaves the room. That happens when you backup the transaction log. This does not mean that the next people who go to sit down will sit on the far left cushion. Instead they continue to fill the couches starting with the seat to the right of the last person to get up and continue filling the couches until they have no more couches. Then new people start to fill in at the beginning again.

This circular queue is similar to the way the transaction log works, with a couple of minor exceptions. If there are no more seats available, the server automatically provides a new couch (expands the transaction log) for people to sit on. The other exception is the part that causes so much trouble for people and that's related to how the transaction log is shrunk.

How Do I Shrink My Transaction Log?

Just as the server only adds couches to the right-hand side of the couch queue, it can only compress from right to left. If you suddenly add a large sectional that seats thirty and there is one person sitting in it with a thousand empty seats to the front, you can't remove any of the couches (shrink the log) until the last couch has been filled and is emptied. And, if the database is set to expand the log based on a percentage of physical log file size, you can get some pretty big couches added.

Once you have processed enough transactions that the last segment has been filled and only the couches on the far left have any one sitting down, then you can start removing couches. So, if you find yourself with a large transaction file, don't despair. Keep an eye on it and keep trying to shrink it, and it will shrink one day. In the "Resources" section you'll find a link to a great article on how to shrink the transaction log.

How Do I Prevent Large Transaction Log Files?

The wrong answer to this question is to turn transaction logging off. You can do that easily enough by setting a property in the database, but this can have dire consequences, and we'll cover those in just a bit.

The best way to prevent large transaction log files is to back up your transaction log. The more active your database, the more frequently you should back up the transaction logs. How often you should back up your log is something only you can determine by monitoring your database. Watch how your transaction log grows throughout a period of time and then schedule your backups accordingly. The more frequent the transaction log backups, the longer your recovery time will be because each log will need to be restored sequentially.

The final way to prevent large transaction log files is to truncate them. This effectively removes all transactions from the transaction log and invalidates your entire data recovery scheme, so we're not actually going to look at how you do that. You can find it in the BOL if you really want to know. Instead we're going to move on to restoring and recovering data, and we'll explain why turning logging off and truncating the transaction log are bad ideas.

 A fast-growing transaction log could be a sign of poor coding practice. If you see performance dropping off and a corresponding increase in transaction log size, you may have a problem with the way deletes or updates are performed. One instance is unqualified or poorly qualified UPDATEs *and* DELETEs, *where more records are touched than need be.*

How Do I Restore and Recover My Data?

You may be wondering about the question that frames this section, restore *and* recover? At first glance it appears to be something straight out of the *Handbook and Manual for the Society to Stamp Out and Abolish Repetition and Redundancy*, but these really are two different acts. To help illustrate this we're going to walk through a simplified set of transactions in a database and do a backup immediately after each transaction. Then we're going to restore the database step by step so you can see how everything fits together. Finally, we're going to discuss what would have happened if either transaction logging were turned off or the log was truncated.

Before we begin, though, understand that this example is simply to illustrate a point. We're not using TSQL code, and the transactions we're doing are somewhat oversimplified because we're not looking at transactions here, rather we are looking at the backup's restore and recovery procedure. For a more in-depth discussion of transactions, see Chapter 10, "Working with Data: Beyond the Basics."

The database in this example is a simple To Do list that can store a task and then record whether or not the task has been accomplished. At the beginning we have no tasks in the To Do list, and we have just restored the database from a backup that will be called "Backup0." Now, without further ado, let's begin. Table 4-1 shows the list of transactions and backups.

Table 4-1. Backing Up Data to Restore and Recover Data

STEP	TASK	BACKUP TYPE	BACKUP NAME
1	Add a task: Pick up laundry	Transactional	Transaction1
2	Add a task: Stop at bank	Transactional	Transaction2
3	Add a task: Get salad stuff	Differential	Differential1
4	Mark complete: Pick up laundry	Transactional	Transaction3
5	Mark complete: Get salad stuff	Transactional	Transaction4
6	Mark complete: Stop at bank	Complete	Backup1

OK, now that we have a list of transactions and backups, let's consider how we would restore and recover the database to some point in time. You can find the backup files with the extension of BAK in the "\Chapter04" directory of the accompanying CD.

How Do I Restore a Database from a Complete Backup?

This is the easiest restore to perform. There are no wizards for restoring and recovering, so you'll have to do it all by either TSQL commands or the menu options in the EM. To begin any restore, right-click on a database to bring up the pop-up menu and then select All Tasks Restore Database. Or you can choose Restore Database from the Tools menu. This brings up a window filled with options that relate to restoring your database (see Figure 4-5).

 CAUTION *Before you can restore a database, you need to make sure no one else is using it. We'll show you how to do this in Chapter 15, "Should I Bother to Learn SQL Profiler?"*

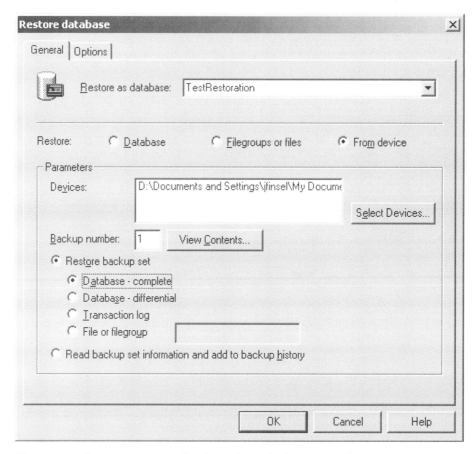

Figure 4-5. When you restore a database through the EM, you have a number of options to select.

Although you are presented with a list of databases on the server, we are going to restore to a new database. So, put TestRestoration in the database name. Next you need to define where the backup file is that you want to restore, so click on Select Device. This happens because SQL Server appears to be creating the device on the fly when you create a file, and it uses the terms *backup device* and *disk file* interchangeably within the EM.

This brings up a new dialog box that displays the list of disk files associated with the database. Because this is a new database, there won't be any devices listed. We're going to Add a device and then put in the path of the file we want to restore—in this case it would be the "Backup01.bak." Now, in the bottom part of the window, we need to tell the EM that this is a complete backup that we are restoring.

NOTE *You may remember when I made the backup I mentioned that you could provide a description of the backup but you couldn't get to it easily? If you select the View Contents button you can see the name you gave to the backup, but you can't see the description. The only way to get the description out of the file is to use TSQL commands. This is just one of those limitations of the EM.*

Once we've done that, we're ready to switch over to the Options tab, illustrated in Figure 4-6. This is where you need to set three important options. The first option is at the top where you can click Force Restore Over Existing Database. If the database you are trying to restore already exists, you'll need to check this box so that you can restore it *and* you'll need to make sure that nobody is using the database. This will be covered in Chapter 15, "Should I Bother to Learn SQL Profiler?"

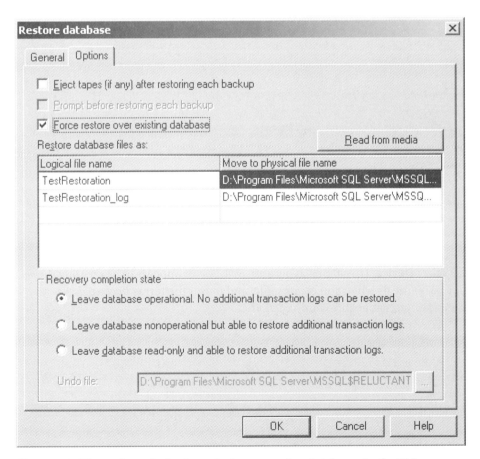

Figure 4-6. The option tab that's used when restoring databases in the EM

The second option that needs to be set is the middle where it lists the TestRestoration and TestRestoration_log. If you happen to have installed an instance of SQL Server in "D:\Program Files\Microsoft SQL Server" called RELUCTANTDBA, then you don't need to modify these. If you haven't done that (and you probably haven't), you need to put a valid directory for each of the files listed here.

> **CAUTION** *The Move to Physical File Name column has a file-name in it as well as the path. You need to replace only the "path" part of this string with a valid one, leaving the filename intact. If you change the filename, the restore will still work, you just have to remember the name you gave it if you wind up looking for the file or need to reference the file for some other reason. In a nutshell, try to keep the names the same.*

The final option that needs to be set is the bottom set of radio buttons. Since we're doing a complete restore of the database, keep the top radio button Leave Database Operational. No Additional Transaction Logs Can Be Restored. Press OK and the database will be created, mirroring how it was when we backed it up.

If you open that database in the EM and then click on tables, you should see a table listed called TaskList in the right-hand pane. Right-click on the table and select Open Table ➤ Return all rows. Now you should see three tasks, each with the Completed column showing 1. What if, however, something had happened *before* Backup1 was made? Let's look at three scenarios: restoring transaction logs, restoring a differential backup, and restoring transaction logs to a differential backup.

How Do I Restore a Transaction Log?

All restoration and recovery begins with the restore of a full backup, in this case Backup0. We're going to restore it by following the same steps we used in the previous section on restoring a full backup with one change. On the Options tab select the bottom radio button, Leave Database Read-Only and Able to Restore Additional Transaction Logs. (We're choosing this option, so you can see the changes in the database as we go through the steps.)

After you have restored the database you'll notice that it shows up in the EM somewhat differently. As you can see in Figure 4-7, the database is grayed out and says (Read-Only) after it. If you want, you can open the TaskList table and verify that it is empty. What we have just done is to *restore* the database in *recovery* mode. That means that you can take further action to bring the database to a certain point in time.

You may be wondering why we've left the database read-only. Assume for the moment that people need immediate access to the database—let's say it isn't time-sensitive information—but you don't want modifications taking place before you have a chance to restore the logs. If any updates take place before you restore the logs, the logs become invalidated and can no longer be restored.

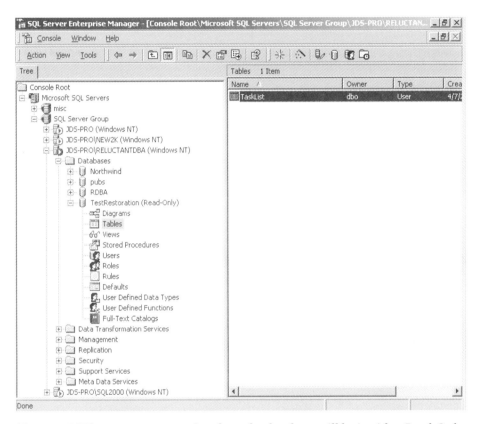

Figure 4-7. When you are recovering data, the database will be in either Read-Only mode or totally unavailable.

Now it's back to Tools ➤ Restore Database again. This time we'll restore Transaction1.bak. This time you need to select the Transaction log option (see Figure 4-8) and on the Option tab we'll again select Leave Database Read-Only and Able to Restore Additional Transaction Logs then press OK and restore that transaction log. Again, you can open the TaskList table and see that it has one row of data, Pick Up Laundry, and the complete column for that row is marked with a 0.

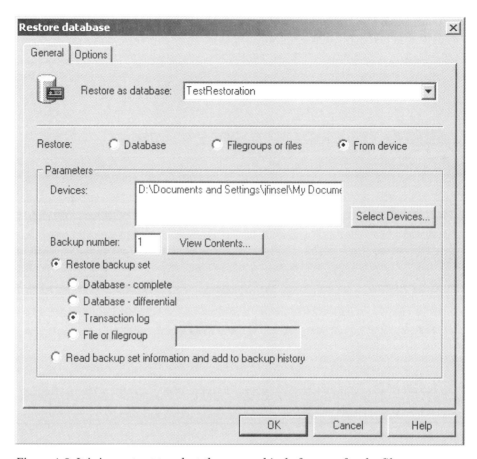

Figure 4-8. It is important to select the proper kind of restore for the file you are restoring.

Finally we are going to restore Transaction2.bak. This time, however, we're going to set the restore option to Leave Database Operational. No Additional Transaction Logs Can Be Restored. Once this transaction log has been applied, we are done with both the restore and recovery of data, and my database is in the same state it was before we took step 3 in Table 4-1.

Is It Possible to Restore Transaction Logs Out of Sequence?

The short answer is no. SQL Server tracks transactions with a log sequence number and any attempt to restore them out of sequence results in an error message like the one shown in Figure 4-9 when attempting to restore Transaction4.bak instead of Transaction2.bak. This means that if you are missing a transaction log backup then you will only be able to restore to the last sequential transaction log backup that you have.

Microsoft SQL-DMO (ODBC SQLState: 42000)

The log in this backup set begins at LSN 5000000005000001, which is too
late to apply to the database. An earlier log backup that includes LSN
5000000003000001 can be restored.
RESTORE LOG is terminating abnormally.

OK

Figure 4-9. Attempting to restore transaction logs out of sequence results in errors.

How Do I Restore a Differential Backup?

Differential backups include all changes since the last full or differential backup, but recovering data still requires starting with a full backup so we're going to restore Backup0.bak and leave the database Read-Only.

Once we've done that we can restore the differential backup, Differential1.bak. Because this includes all of the changes since the last database backup, we don't need to restore the transaction logs, although we can. Once the differential database is restored then the database is recovered to the state it was in after step 3. If we wanted to restore the database to where it was after step 4 we would just have to restore the transaction log backup Transaction3.bak.

Once you understand the concepts, restoring and recovering data becomes a follow-the-list method. Restore the last full backup, then sequentially restore any differential backups, and finally sequentially restore any transaction logs that exist. This brings your database back to a known state. It may not, however, have all of the data you want.

If the server lost power, the existing transaction log would automatically be applied when the server was started again. If, on the other hand, the disk itself were to go bad and you needed to restore your data from your backups, then you would lose whatever changes had occurred between the last transaction log backup and the time the disk drive went bad.

What Is a Recovery Model?

Now that you understand the basics of backing up, restoring, and recovering your data, it's time to look at the three different models of recovery: Full Recovery, Simple Recovery, and Bulk_Logged Recovery.

Full Recovery is the method of recovery that we have been talking about, and it is the default recovery model. Everything is logged, complete backups are made, and transaction log backups, differential backups, or a combination of them are made between complete backups. This recovery model has a great deal going for it since you know what your risk is. If you back up your transaction log hourly then your risk is that you'll lose, at worst, an hour's worth of data.

Simple Recovery is where the transaction log is either truncated on a regular basis or turned off. In either case, the only restore that can be made is from complete backups. That's because the act of truncating the transaction log prevents it from being backed up until a full backup is made to give it a starting point (and with the transaction log truncated you have no incremental data to back up).

Bulk_Logged Recovery is a little more complicated. When Bulk_Logged Recovery is set, certain operations aren't fully logged, they're more noted, almost footnoted. When operations like `BULK INSERT`, *bcp*, `CREATE INDEX`, `SELECT INTO`, `WRITETEXT`, and `UPDATETEXT` occur, the transaction log records the fact that the transaction occurred, but it doesn't log all of the details. This means that the transaction log files stay small and those operations run much more quickly since the SQL Engine is just writing the data to the database instead of to the database *and* the transaction log.

But, since TANSTAAFL[3] applies to everything in the galaxy, you still have to pay for this somewhere. In this case you pay for it in the transaction log backup. When the backup is made, it includes a copy of the bulk data so it can be restored correctly. That means that it doesn't affect how you restore and recover the database, but you might need to take the larger transaction log backups into account when you are planning how much disk space you need.

To change your recovery model, right-click on the database in the EM and select Properties. Go to the Options tab and select the model you want to use (see Figure 4-10).

---

[3]   There Ain't No Such Thing As A Free Lunch.

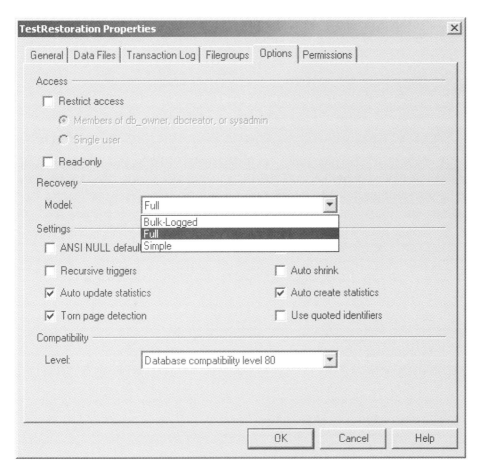

*Figure 4-10. You can set the recovery model for a database from the Database's
Property pages.*

Why Can't I Restore My Database?

You may try to restore a database only to find that you don't have enough disk
space. You may remember that a backup file would be only as large as the data
that needs to be backed up. That's different from what you need to restore
a database.

If you created a database that was 10GB in size but only contained 10MB of
data, the backup file would be 10MB in size. When you go to restore the database,
however, you will need 10GB of disk space for the database being restored. That's
one of the main reasons that the databases being included with this book are the
database files instead of backup files. If you can fit the database files on your disk
then you know you can attach and use the database.

Another thing that could be preventing you from restoring a database is that the database could be the wrong version. Although you can easily restore a SQL 7 database to SQL Server 2000, going the other way won't work.

Last Words

Now that we've covered the basics of database backups, restores, and recovery, we're finally ready to design and create database tables. However, you should take some time to document how you plan to back up and test your backups. After all, a backup will do you no good if you can't restore the data.

Resources

- Although the Knowledge Base Article Q119443, "Dump SQL DB to a Novell File Server," was written for SQL Server 4.2 and Novell, the basics of setting up the shared account and modifying the account that SQL Service runs under are still applicable:
  `http://support.microsoft.com/support/kb/articles/Q119/4/43.asp`

- Shrinking the Transaction Log by Andrew Zanevsky, *SQL Server Professional*, February 2000:
  `http://www.pinnaclepublishing.com/SQ/sqmag.nsf/Index /F36C151BD80FAD8F852568D0007799BE?opendocument`

- For a more in-depth discussion of how backups and Recovery Models actually work: Chapter 5 of *Inside Microsoft SQL Server 2000* by Kalen Delaney (Microsoft Press)

- Planning for disaster recovery:
  `http://msdn.microsoft.com/library/psdk/sql/ad_bkprst_7kvb.htm`

CHAPTER 5

How Do I Define and Structure a Database?

A rock pile ceases to be a rock pile the moment a single man contemplates it, bearing within him the image of a cathedral.
—Antoine de Saint-Exupery

IN THE FIRST CHAPTER you learned that the concept of databases has been around for a long time, and you learned that *database* is defined as any system that lets you organize and retrieve data. Although that definition is definitely true, there are differences between the way data is organized in a physical system and the way it is organized in an electronic system. The theory behind how to take a physical organizational system and make it an electronic one is the theory of databases—and what a theory it is!

This chapter will cover database theory as it applies to practical, everyday problems. When we talk about normalization,[1] for instance, we're not going to go into all six normal forms. We're going to cover the first three, because those are the ones you'll be using on a daily basis. In this book, tuples will be referred to as *rows* because that's how SQL Server presents them. We'll deal with entities in terms of Entity Relation Diagrams (ERD), but entities (tables are one example of an entity) will be referred to as *objects* because many programmers think in terms of objects rather than entities. If you feel more comfortable substituting the word *entity* for *object* or *tuple* for *row*, feel free.

Introduction to Problem Solving

Defining and creating a database is like writing a program. The first step is to identify what needs to be in the database. The goal of this section is not to define the layout of the database; we'll get to that in the sections "Can I Use Enterprise Manager to Design My Database?" and "What is Normalization?" In this section, we'll define what data needs to be in the database and get some rough ideas about how it all fits together. This would also be a good time to review business logic, because "physical" steps may not be duplicated precisely in the electronic

---

[1]   Normalization is the process of efficiently building a database.

form being built. You also don't want to miss critical points in the processing methodology of the business.

We'll start by identifying the concepts for which you should be looking. Then you'll read a section of text from "Anne," the head of information technology for an imaginary veterinary organization for which the sample database is being built. After that we'll point out the important items covered in her conversation. Finally, we'll walk through building and normalizing the tables based on that information. Keep in mind the process of gathering requirements is not a one-pass deal. You may have to go back to the customer multiple times as the project proceeds. Do yourself a favor and don't promise results in the first iteration.

How Do I Translate an Existing System into Database Layouts?

When you want to translate an existing system into a database, you need to think about four key concepts: objects, properties, relationships, and jobs. These four concepts are what you should look for as you take your notes when you meet with your client. In addition, there are two special properties for table objects: primary keys and foreign keys. As you read through Anne's comments in this chapter, you might want to use different color highlighters or some other form of notation to identify these six concepts.

- **Object:** An object (or entity) is a person, place, or thing that will translate into a table row. Take this book you are reading. It could easily represent a row in a table of books. Tables store zero to *n* rows—each describing a specific object in the set of known objects.

- **Property:** A property is some aspect of an object. Properties are represented in the table/object as a column or field. The properties of a book would include: title, author(s), subject, page count, chapter count, publisher, and price. These properties are then entered into their respective columns (or fields) in the object (table). When you're taking notes, you could indent properties under an object to clearly delineate them.

- **Relationships:** This is not to be confused with "related," which was covered in Chapter 1 when you learned about the concept of relational databases. Relationships are not those that occur between properties in an object but *between* objects. For instance, a book has a publisher and an author. Both the publisher and author are objects separate from the book, and they have some kind of a relationship to the book. When taking notes, you could use your margins to note the relationships between objects.

- **Jobs:** A job is an operation that takes place on an object either directly or via stored procedures, which is the preferred method as explained in Chapter 9, "Working with Data: Basic Stored Procedures." The result of that job may be the insertion or update of one or more rows into one or more objects. For instance, the publisher publishes books. In the course of the act of publishing, the publisher sells books, changing properties in an inventory object (update in-stock, adjust order quantities) and a royalty object (royalties accrued and paid). Through jobs, tables are manipulated and data is added, updated, deleted, archived, or moved to reporting servers (via Data Transformation Services or other process).

- **Primary Key:** A primary key is a special property or group of properties of an object that uniquely identify it from like objects. This book's ISBN number, for instance, is unique to this specific book and could function as a primary key.

- **Foreign Key:** The foreign key is the property or properties that links two related objects together. The property that identifies the publisher of this book must be an existing publisher. The foreign key will link to the related object's primary key.

It's important to understand that you will need to translate these key concepts twice. When you are gathering requirements, you'll need to translate physical objects into virtual objects and properties. At some point you're going to need to go back to the people who gave you your requirements and verify that what you're designing is what they need. If you start talking tables, columns, and keys, they will probably get confused and won't be able to help you do your job correctly the first time. You need to learn how to translate tables into objects as easily as you translate objects into tables. The good news is, once you learn translation one way, the other is easy to do. The hard part is making it a habit.

 You will be establishing not only the logical design of the database, but the naming conventions *as well. It is important to use names that not only serve their purpose dutifully, but do it in a way that decision makers will be able to quickly and intuitively identify the objects they need to use to complete their given tasks. Ask yourself: Do you really want to have to educate people on the names used for objects? Databases do exist that have numbers for object names and objects that have "lookup" information for the original objects: to look up the table's "real" name and purpose. This practice is commonly referred to as* cryptic *naming. Save yourself and your potential users some grief: KISS (Keep It Super Simple).*

If you have ever done any object-oriented programming, you may find that these concepts are remarkably like those in object-oriented programming. In fact, you can apply that same type of design logic—defining objects, their properties, and their methods—to creating databases.

What Kind of Data Can I Have in a Table?

The time has come to speak about data types. SQL Server has quite a few different types of data you can put into a table. Roughly speaking, they fall into four groups: characters (letters, numbers, and symbols), numbers (positive/negative, whole, and decimal), binary, and special data types. Let's look at characters first.

Characters

There are six different kinds of character types: CHAR, VARCHAR, TEXT, NCHAR, NVARCHAR, and TEXT. To simplify your task, let's first discuss what Unicode means, because the three character types that begin with *N* are simply Unicode variations of the other three.

The American Standard Code for Information Interchange (ASCII) is a 7-bit character set that represents the letters and symbols found on a standard U.S. keyboard. As you can imagine, that leaves some countries missing some data. Some countries can't fit all of their data into a 7-bit data set. Unicode (National Character sets) addresses that by using a 16-bit (sometimes referred to as *double byte*) encoding that allows for 2^{16} or 65,536 characters. The end result is that a string with 100 characters takes up 200 bytes. What does this mean to database administrators and programmers?

Well, the most obvious effect is that Unicode columns take up twice as much space as non-Unicode columns. That means you'll need twice as much disk space for storage and twice as much network bandwidth for passing data back and forth. It may also mean slightly more work in your stored procedures and Transact SQL (TSQL) code because you have to make sure that any strings you define are Unicode. Finally, the maximum column length is 4,000 characters instead of 8,000. So, what do you gain by using Unicode?

Well, how about the world, for starters? When using non-Unicode strings, each character takes up one byte, and what the bit pattern in that byte stands for depends entirely on the code page for that server. If the data you save in your database isn't Unicode and it gets restored on a database that was set up with a different code page, then the data that appears—although it is absolutely correct—will be interpreted incorrectly by the SQL Engine when it is displayed. As a general rule, all of your databases should be designed to embrace Unicode.

Now that we've covered Unicode, let's look at the differences between NCHAR and NVARCHAR. The main difference between the two is a trimming of data.

A 10-character NCHAR column that stores the word *database* will be stored as "database ". That's because SQL Server will pad the column with spaces because the length of an NCHAR specifies how long the string will be all of the time.

NVARCHAR, on the other hand, treats the column length as a maximum length and stores the actual length of the data. If the word *database* were stored in a 10-character NVARCHAR column, then it would only be 8 characters long and is stored as 8 characters (plus a couple of bytes overhead to store the length of the data). Both NCHAR and NVARCHAR have a maximum column size of 4,000 characters (8,000 characters for CHAR and VARCHAR).

So, which should you use, the variable or fixed-length? It depends. If you are going to store fixed-length data in a table, then you should use a fixed-length NCHAR. This has the advantage of not forcing SQL Server to determine how long the data is that it needs to return to you. A good example of this could be a part number that is always the same length. For almost every other case, a variable length string is preferred.

There are some cases when the combination of the extra byte or two to store the length of the data and the small amount of time it takes to get the variable length string can have an impact on performance. If you are storing short strings (5–10 characters), you may find a performance gain by using fixed-length instead of variable-length columns. The down side to this is that the fixed-length columns will be padding the data when it gets returned, and you may need to deal with that programmatically.

TEXT and NTEXT fields are different from the other character data types for two reasons. First, they can hold much more (up to 2GB for TEXT and half that for NTEXT), and second, they aren't physically stored with the rest of the row's data; however, it is possible to set the table up so that these data types can be stored in the row *if the size of the data in the column is small enough*. Let's take a look at how SQL Server handles NTEXT data types.

When you define either a TEXT or NTEXT column, SQL Server actually creates a column containing a pointer in the row. This pointer is used to tell SQL Server where to find special physical pages that contain the actual data. When this row of information is requested, SQL Server will take that pointer, get the page (or pages) that contain the NTEXT data, write it out to a temporary file, and then return it to whatever requested the information. This requires additional reads from the database and can impact performance.

It is possible, when you define a TEXT or NTEXT column, to specify that the data be saved in the row if it's small enough. You accomplish this by setting the Text in Row option on the table. When you enable Text in Row, what you are really doing is setting a threshold limit that says, if the TEXT field is less than a certain length (you can specify from 24 to 7,000 bytes, remember that Unicode will be half that many characters), then store it with the rest of the data for that row. If the data exceeds the length you specify, then it will be stored on a separate data page just as though the Text in Row option were not specified. Now that you have learned about this option, you should know you can't turn it on from within the Enterprise Manager (EM); you'll have to use the system stored procedure sp_tableoption in TSQL.

Storing Large Amounts of Data

When contemplating storing Large Objects (LOB), be they TEXT, NTEXT, BINARY, VARBINARY, or IMAGE data types, you should ask yourself two questions: Should you really do this, and why are you doing this? Just because it's possible to store 2GB pictures in a database doesn't necessarily mean it's advisable to do so, and that's not just because Microsoft Data Engine (MSDE) is limited to 2GB databases.

When you are dealing with a LOB, it is usually an item like an image or text document that could just as easily reside on a disk file. There are many reasons to consider storing such data separate from the database:

- Data stored in a disk file is easier to get to than data stored as a column in a table.

- SQL Server stores the data in 8K chunks, performing one input-output operation for each 8K of the file and writing it to disk. The time it takes to accomplish this is time it can't take to respond to other queries.

- LOBs are passed through the data cache, flushing whatever is there, meaning that "real" data and procedures are flushed from memory and have to be re-fetched instead of being handy to use immediately.

- When SQL Server delivers up a large field, it has to store the whole thing to disk anyway when it assembles it so why not save a step.

However, this doesn't mean you should *never* do this, just that you should think through the implications of creating large columns of data using the data types TEXT, NTEXT, or IMAGE.

Numbers

When it comes to storing numbers, SQL Server has a whole slew of options for you. Numbers can range from TINYINT (0 through 255) all the way up to MONEY (922,337,203,685,477.5807 monetary units) and all steps in between. Numbers are divided into INTEGER, DECIMAL, MONEY, and REAL data types.

What Is an Integer?

Integers are signed or unsigned whole numbers, with nothing to the right of the decimal place. In SQL Server integers come in four sizes: tiny, small, normal, and big. Table 5-1 lists the differences between them both in terms of the numbers they encompass and the amount of space they take up in the database.

Table 5-1. Integers

INTEGER TYPE	SIZE	NUMERIC RANGE
TINYINT	1 byte	0–255
SMALLINT	2 bytes	-2^{15} (–32,768) through $2^{15}-1$ (32,767)
INT	4 bytes	-2^{31} (–2,147,483,648) through $2^{31}-1$ (2,147,483,647)
BIGINT	8 bytes	-2^{63} (–9,223,372,036,854,775,808) through $2^{63}-1$ (9,223,372,036,854,775,807)

The BIGINT data type is new with SQL Server 2000. One of the many tasks a BIGINT has is to provide identity keys and to be able to handle counting rows in datasets with more than nine quintillion rows.

Will a BIT Save Me Space?

There is one more item to lump in under integers: BIT. A BIT can be either 0 or 1, and many people use this as a Boolean expression because it "takes up less room." A BIT can be only a 1 or a 0 and works well for a Boolean. In theory, a BIT takes up only 1 bit instead of 1 byte. In actuality, a single BIT field in a table takes up 1 byte. Up to 8 BIT fields will take up 1 byte as well, so you might want to use BIT fields if you are storing multiple flags. However, this has its drawbacks as well because BIT fields cannot be included in an index or a group by condition.

If you are faced with including a single BIT field you could use a TINYINT instead. They both take up the same amount of space and you can include them when you summarize data. The down side to this is that there are programs (Microsoft Excel, for instance) that interpret the BIT as a true/false value instead of interpreting it as a flag. On the other hand, a TINYINT works wonders when someone wants to change the database to include three options where there used to be only true and false.

If you are creating a table with multiple BIT fields and you are going to never use the BIT fields when summarizing data and they will always represent a binary flag, then it would be appropriate to use BIT fields. However, remember that any stored procedure you use will still push 1 byte for each BIT (as either a 1 or 0) over the wire to you. You'll need to use 1 byte each time you reference the data, so you only save space in the storage of the data, not its transmission.

DECIMAL, NUMERIC, Precision, and Scale, Oh My!

After integers come DECIMAL and NUMERIC data types. Since NUMERIC and DECIMAL are interchangeable, we're going to use the term DECIMAL to simplify things. A DECIMAL data type is any number between -10^{38} through and $10^{38}-1$ with a fixed precision and scale. Precision refers to the maximum number of digits that can be stored in the number on either side of the decimal place. Scale, on the other hand, refers to the number of digits to the right of the decimal. Table 5-2 has several examples of varying precision and scale. In one respect, the DECIMAL data type is like the NVARCHAR: the larger the precision, the more space the column will take up in the database. A precision of 1–9 will take up 5 bytes, 10–19 will take 9 bytes, 20–28 will take 13 bytes, and a precision of 29-38 will take up 17 bytes.

Table 5-2. Decimal Precision and Scale Samples

PRECISION	SCALE	MAXIMUM NUMBER
5	3	99.999
18	6	999,999,999,999.999999
5	5	0.99999

Can You Exchange Currency?

SQL Server supports a MONEY and SMALLMONEY data type. These values are actually BIGINT and INT data types with four decimal places built into the formatting. But what does it mean to have a MONEY data type? It means your programs can know a number represents money and display it correctly with the computer's settings.

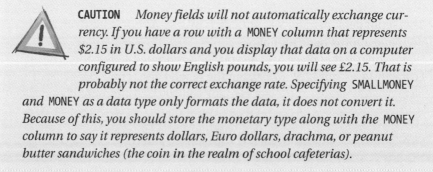

CAUTION *Money fields will not automatically exchange currency. If you have a row with a MONEY column that represents $2.15 in U.S. dollars and you display that data on a computer configured to show English pounds, you will see £2.15. That is probably not the correct exchange rate. Specifying SMALLMONEY and MONEY as a data type only formats the data, it does not convert it. Because of this, you should store the monetary type along with the MONEY column to say it represents dollars, Euro dollars, drachma, or peanut butter sandwiches (the coin in the realm of school cafeterias).*

What Are Approximate Numbers?

All of the numeric data types we've been talking about have been *exact numbers*. That means that they all occupy a specific point on a number line and, when you add two of them together, you get another specific point on the number line. That's because they have the same precision. Exact numbers are used in counting.

Approximate numbers, on the other hand, are used for measurement. The difference lies in how one actually does the math. Where you might take 2.5 and 3.04 and add them together to get 5.54, scientific math rounds the numbers to the same number of significant digits and gets 5.5 (3.04 gets rounded down to 3.0 to match the single decimal precision of 2.5).[2]

When you find yourself dealing with significant numbers of decimal places, it's best to turn to FLOAT and REAL data types. FLOAT and REAL give you plenty of zeros to play with but with an important caution. Not all numbers can be represented as accurately as exact numbers can be, thus the term *approximate number*. Though it can deal with small or large numbers, an approximate number in SQL Server only has a precision of up to 15 places. As a very simple example we're going to convert a BIGINT to a FLOAT and back again (see Listing 5-1).

Listing 5-1. Approximate numbers aren't good for counting because in certain situations they are only *close* to the number you want.

```
DECLARE @F1 float(24)
DECLARE @B1 bigint
SET @B1 = 1234567890
PRINT @b1
SET @F1 = CAST(@B1 as float(24))
SET @B1 = CAST(@F1 as bigint)
PRINT @b1
```

This script demonstrates what happens when converting between exact numbers and approximate numbers.

When you run that piece of code you get two printed statements. The first one correctly gives you 1234567890, but the second gives you 1234567936. That's a really minor difference of 46 (representing 0.000003726-percent difference) and acceptable for FLOAT and REAL data types. You shouldn't, however, use FLOAT or REAL numbers when you need an exact count.

---

[2] This reminds me of one of my favorite math quotes: 2 + 2 never equals 5, not even for large values of 2.

What Are Date Data Types?

Every database needs to track date information at some time or another. SQL Server has two date types designed to handle this task: DATETIME and SMALLDATETIME. The difference between the two can be found both in how much time they span and how small a unit of time they can track.

The SMALLDATETIME will store a date and time anywhere from 1/1/1900 through 6/6/2079 and can keep track of the value to the minute. At 8 bytes, the DATETIME data type is twice as large but covers more than twice the time period. The DATETIME data type can store a date anywhere from 1/1/1753 through 12/31/9999 down to three-hundredths of a second.

While DATETIME covers a large period of time, it doesn't necessarily cover all of the time periods you might want. If, for instance, you wanted to store information about antiques that date to before 1/1/1753, you would not be able to store them using the built-in date data types. You actually have a couple of options to handle this. First, you could use a character-based date and store the data as 6/15/1215. Or, if you'd rather, you could store the date as a number and use your own programming skills to interpret the date.

Don't forget: When dealing with SMALLDATETIME and DATETIME the data is *stored* as a four-digit year but that date will be *translated* into a four-digit year when passed as a two-digit year. This translation is based on the properties of the server (for more details, see Chapter 3, "How Do I Visually Manage Objects?"). Therefore, always specify all four digits!

What Are Binary Data Types?

A binary data type is just that—something that stores data as a non-translated binary string. Binary data types are used to store images, documents, executables, zip files . . . the list goes on. As long as you understand the overhead of having to pull the binary out of the database to a file and pass it along to whatever application is calling for the data, feel free to use them. There are advantages to storing binary data in the database. It's more difficult for someone to modify, for instance.

When converting values to BINARY *using the* CONVERT *function, the translation is based on the source data type. For example, if you pass the values 1234 and "1234" to* CONVERT, *you will get two different results. The first is treated as a number (in this case* INT), *but the latter is treated as* TEXT. *The first would be thought of as 1,234. The latter, being* TEXT, *is evaluated a position at a time from left to right. Choose your data types wisely, especially when defining variables. Know how they interact or your application will produce unpredictable results.*

Table 5-3 lists the three types of binary data types. We'll take this moment to point out that if you are going to store 2GB of binary data in a database, then that would be the only thing you could have in an MSDE database, because databases in MSDE are limited to 2GB. There are many reasons not to store large amounts of binary data in the database. Please see the sidebar "Whither to Store Large Amounts of Data?" earlier in this chapter for more information.

Table 5-3. Binary Data Types

DATA TYPE	SIZE	DESCRIPTION
BINARY	Up to 8,000 bytes	This is a fixed-length binary column.
VARBINARY	Up to 8,000 bytes	This is a variable-length binary column.
IMAGE	Up to 2^31-1 bytes (2GB)	This is a really big column.

What Is a Special Data Type?

There are more data types that don't really fit nicely anywhere else, and SQL Server defines them as "special data." One of these special data types, the BIT, was covered earlier along with integers. The next is the UNIQUEIDENTIFIER. The UNIQUEIDENTIFIER is a Globally Unique IDentifier (GUID), a 16-byte hexadecimal number randomly generated based on a number of variables, including the address of the network card. GUIDs are supposed to be unique across time and space. We will be discussing this further in "How Do I Define a Primary Key?"

Then there is the User-Defined Data Type (UDDT). Creating a UDDT allows you to define your data in a clearer fashion. For instance, you could define a PhoneNumber data type as NVARCHAR with a length of 20. Once this is done, then you can refer to the PhoneNumber data type whenever you are going to create a phone number field. Although this can be handy for making your database easier to use, there are some drawbacks. For instance, you cannot define a default value for a UDDT or perform any checking of the data.

Finally we come to the most confusing data type of all, the TIMESTAMP. In SQL Server 2000, the TIMESTAMP data type is a number that is automatically incremented and guaranteed unique within a database. You can't set the value of a TIMESTAMP column; you can only query it to see if it has changed. The TIMESTAMP is used to determine whether the row of data has changed because it is updated every time the row is updated. But Microsoft does not following the SQL-92 standards when it comes to this data type.

According to the standard, the TIMESTAMP data type is like SQL Server's DATETIME data type. And, with a name like TIMESTAMP you might easily believe that this is a column that marks the date and time that something occurred to the row rather than an incremental counter for changes being made to the row. You would be mistaken, at least currently. Books On Line (BOL) says this about TIMESTAMP:

> . . . timestamp is a data type that exposes automatically generated binary numbers, which are guaranteed to be unique within a database. timestamp is used typically as a mechanism for version-stamping table rows. The storage size is 8 bytes.
>
> The Transact-SQL timestamp data type is not the same as the time-stamp data type defined in the SQL-92 standard. The SQL-92 timestamp data type is equivalent to the Transact-SQL datetime data type.
>
> A future release of Microsoft® SQL Server™ may modify the behavior of the Transact-SQL timestamp data type to align it with the behavior defined in the standard. At that time, the current timestamp data type will be replaced with a **rowversion** data type.
>
> Microsoft® SQL Server™ 2000 introduces a rowversion synonym for the timestamp data type. Use rowversion instead of timestamp wher-ever possible in DDL statements. rowversion is subject to the behaviors of data type synonyms.

In other words, right now, it really has nothing to do with DATETIME, but it could be modified to be a true DATETIME data type in future versions so you should use ROWVERSION instead. And if you are going to use ROWVERSION, you'll have to do it outside of the EM because that's not one of the data types provided in the Table Design facility.

What Type of Data Are SQL Variants?

New to SQL Server 2000 is the SQL_VARIANT data type. If you have programmed in Visual Basic, then you know that a variant can hold any other type of variable type and the SQL_VARIANT is a close relation. In fact, BOL has the following to say:

> The sql_variant data type operates similarly to the variant data type in Microsoft® Visual Basic®.

Truth be told, however, it doesn't work exactly like the variant data type. With the religious wars that have been waged in the past over Visual Basic's variant, many will choose sides over the proper use of the SQL_VARIANT data type (or whether to use it at all).

Basically, this data type can take any data type except TEXT, NTEXT, IMAGE, TIMESTAMP, and SQL_VARIANT. Of course, this flexibility also makes it quite confusing. All of the documentation, not that there is much of it, states that you should specifically cast the data type you want to store in the SQL_VARIANT to avoid having SQL Server do it for you, especially because the data type that SQL Server chooses might not be the one you want to use. There are some pointers to more information in the "Resources" section at the end of this chapter. We'll also talk more about using SQL_VARIANTs in Chapter 9, "Working with Data: Basic Stored Procedures." For now, avoid creating a database table with any columns that are SQL_VARIANT data types.

Mind you, SQL_VARIANTs are neither good nor bad. This data type is a tool that needs to be understood before it can be used well, and it is a tool that can be used poorly easily, leading to many potential problems.

What Is the TABLE Data Type?

The TABLE data type is new to SQL Server 2000, and it is exactly what it sounds like: a data type that contains a table with columns and rows. You can't create a column in a table with this data type, but we'll be discussing it in Chapter 9, "Working with Data: Basic Stored Procedures."

What Is NULL?

NULL means unknown. This is different from 0 or "", which are frequently confused with NULL. A good example of this would be a genealogical database that stores information about someone's life. It could have a date field for birth and one for death. If you were entering information for someone who hasn't died, then you would not enter anything for the date of death, which would leave the respective column NULL (assuming it doesn't have a defined default value). Nothing is more frustrating than searching for NULL values in a database only to discover that unknown values were entered as BLANK or SPACE. Don't add to the confusion by doing this.

How Can I Determine Which Data Type Is Best?

Determining the data type for a column is important. Choosing the correct data type will give you an efficient database, one that will perform well. Granted, the database is one part of the whole system and if the network is not robust enough or the server isn't properly configured, you can run into other performance issues. But we're focusing on the database right now. We'll discuss some of these other issues in Chapters 15 and 16, "Should I Bother to Learn SQL Profiler?" and "What Are System Monitor and Performance Monitor?" respectively.

Not only does poor design mean a slow database, it also means more work for you. After all, because no one will use a slow database, you'll have to redesign and "upgrade" the underlying data structure. Changing the structure of a table that has 100 rows is a minor inconvenience. Doing the same thing to a table that has several million rows of mission-critical data is a nightmare. Even though SQL Server 2000 makes it easier to do accomplish such a change than having to write the code by hand, it is still a significant chore that is best avoided.

The first thing to consider when choosing a data type is size. The smaller you can make a row of data, the more efficiently your database will retrieve information. Take a phone number, for instance. That could be stored as a 10-character (for domestic phone numbers) column or an 8-byte BIGINT.

The second thing to consider is how that column will be used. Continuing with the phone number example, the phone number is a number but is often treated like a string of digits. After all, which is easier to read: 5135551212 or (513) 555-1212? If the phone number will frequently be formatted and parsed, then store it as a CHAR. The two bytes it costs in database size are offset by the savings in processing by not having to constantly convert the column from number to string and back again.

Keep the size of the data types and how each piece of information will be used in mind as you read the following introduction from Anne.

Introducing the Berkeley Area Vets

"About ten years ago, three of the local veterinarians got together and started to talk about the various expenses they had and decided to join together to see if they could save some money by buying items in bulk. This worked so well that several more veterinary practices joined over the years. As the Berkeley Area Vets (BAV) grew, they started looking at other ways they could cut costs. To that end, they wanted to put in place a central accounting system that handles all of the billing and collections, thus freeing up office staff to take care of the animals. After all, that is why most of them entered into veterinary practices.

"After looking at all of the systems in use by the various offices, we have decided to go beyond just accounting and do a better job of tracking our patients' histories as well. Not only that, but we have two emergency room hospitals included in our group. People who need to take a pet to one of the emergency rooms require a follow-up to their regular vet and more than 80 percent of the time, that vet is a member of the BAV. It would be nice if the emergency room staff could see the information that the regular vet had on the pet and also if the data they collect could be made available to the regular vet without having to send the chart home with the owner to take to the vet.

"We've already decided on a fairly open, third-party accounting system, so what we're looking for is a system that will store pet data and interface with that system.

"Each veterinary office has one or more veterinarians who spend their day in the office or sometimes out on house calls. Our vets run the gamut from those who deal mostly with house pets to a couple of large-animal vets who deal with horses and such. During a normal day, owners bring their pets in for scheduled appointments. The veterinary assistants take vital sign information such as weight, pulse, temperature, and the reason for the visit and mark all of that in a chart.

"The vet then conducts a more thorough exam and make notes in the chart about what is wrong, what actions to take, and gives specific instructions about care. When the visit isn't an emergency, it's good to have the animal see the same vet so that the vet can develop knowledge of the animal that goes beyond what is written in the chart.

"As each of these steps is taken, any billable task is checked off on a list of common billable items. When the vet is done, this is generally entered into the vet's billing system using standardized codes that are then translated into a bill for the owner.

"Each veterinarian generally works in only one office, though we do have a few who work at both a normal office and one of the emergency hospitals. Some veterinarians also need to be on call, especially our large-animal vets.

"Although this doesn't cover everything, it should be enough to get you started. Both I and my staff will be happy to answer any questions you may have."

Before you turn the page, how many objects did you find in that brief introduction from Anne? Were you able to identify any properties or relationships to go along with the objects? Could you see any of the jobs that the objects do? Let's see how you did.

Defining the Objects

Here are the objects that could be defined from reading Anne's comments:

- Veterinary Office

- Veterinarian

- Owner

- Pet

- Chart

- Appointment

- Billable Task

If you didn't get all of those objects, don't worry about it. Go back and look at Anne's comments again and see if you can find the ones you missed. Did you find any properties that go along with those objects? For instance, what type of information is stored in the chart? Did you see any relationships between the objects? How does a pet relate to a vet? Based on that relationship, how would a vet relate to an owner? In the next section we'll dig into those relationships more, but for now make note of these relationships so that you can build on them as you read.

How Do I Find Hidden Properties?

Let's take a look at the properties Anne has defined for these objects, starting with the Veterinary Office.

According to Anne, each Veterinary Office has veterinarians assigned to it and each office is either an Emergency Care facility or it isn't. Logically, however, we know there are more properties for each office than these. Each office also has to have a physical location (address), a phone number, fax, working hours, and so on. If you were to ask Anne, she'd agree wholeheartedly that those are all necessary pieces of information. So why didn't she think to supply them?

It comes down to a human trait of knowing something so well that you believe it to be common knowledge (the ability to read minds would come in really handy at this point). Another way of looking at it is those things are usually *not* documented but are common and necessary practices. It's this type of information that causes trouble in every project and usually comes out after the fact. A prime example would be a scheduling program that overbooks a facility because it tried to schedule seven simultaneous appointments when there are only five rooms. It would be common knowledge to the person who does the scheduling that there's a limit.

In hindsight, hidden properties always appear obvious but whenever we do something repeatedly, we tend to take certain aspects of that activity for granted because they become automatic. For this reason, it helps to keep asking questions. Although the sample database won't have the structure to handle scheduling, you can probably see at least some of the objects that would be required in terms of knowing how many simultaneous appointments can be handled at each office and how long each different type of appointment might take.

One way of gathering this common knowledge, especially when you are dealing with paper-based information, is to take a good hard look at the paper. If there is a section on the paper for some specific detail, then it is most likely a property of something. Take several copies of the paper and methodically cross out everything you have defined. Write down whatever is left and ask questions to identify it as a property and define to which object it belongs. Make sure you work with filled-out paperwork. Remember, a paper database isn't as stringent as the electronic version. You may encounter a missing property or relationship that boiled down to someone saying: "Oh, there isn't a place for that. We always mark that in the right margin."

Another helpful technique in identifying objects, their properties, and relationships is to write them down in non-technical language. Table 5-4 shows this in action. It lists each object, what properties it has, and how it relates to other objects but has attempted to put it in terms that non-technical people would understand.

*Table 5-4. Objects, Properties, and Relationships in the **RDBA05** Database*

OBJECT	PROPERTIES	RELATIONSHIPS
Veterinary Offices	Name, Address, Phone, Hours, Emergency Care	Vet Offices have Vets assigned. Vet Offices have Patients. Vet Offices handle certain types of pets.
Vets	Name, Address, Specialty, Pager	Vets have specific patients.
Pets	Name, OwnerName, Address, PrimaryVet	Pets belong to specific offices. Pets have specific vets.

In addition to making it easier for non-technical people to understand and provide input, it makes it easier for you to cross-reference your relationships. In looking over Table 5-4, you can probably see that Vets needs to belong to a specific office. Omissions like that will stick out in this format. Another advantage to doing your design work this way is it will make it far easier to normalize your data when you've already defined most of your objects, properties, and relationships.

How Do I Define a Primary Key?

Primary keys are important properties. Sometimes an object will have a property that sticks out as an obvious primary key, like the ISBN of a book. In other cases you may find a unique property after you've looked at all of the properties of an object. Sometimes it's possible to use multiple properties for a key; this is referred to as a *Composite key*. If there are no unique properties, you can always assign an arbitrary primary key in the form of an identity column that will automatically generate a unique number.

What Doesn't Make a Good Primary Key?

Any column that could change or be duplicated should never be used as a primary key. For instance, names make lousy primary keys. In college, I had two friends who shared the name Lisa White. To make matters worse, they were roommates. They shared an impish delight in confusing whoever might be calling for one or the other if that person didn't know them well enough to recognize which one answered the phone. We kept them straight by identifying them with their middle initials as Lisa M. and Lisa D. The school kept them straight because they had different student ID numbers.

Though that situation would cause enough confusion to recommend against using a name as a primary key, today they are married and have different names, and one rule of a primary key is it shouldn't change.

Unfortunately, none of the objects that have been defined have a naturally occurring primary key, so each of them will have to have a primary key property added to them.[3] SQL Server 2000 has two choices for primary keys. One is an integer-based identity column using either INT or BIGINT for the data type. The other (introduced in SQL Server 7) is a 36-character column that stores a GUID in the UNIQUEIDENTIFIER data type. You should take several things into account when considering what type of data to use for your identity field. An INT or even a BIGINT takes up less space than the 36 bytes of a GUID, and SQL Server provides an easy way to return the value of a newly inserted identity key.

When you know you are going to be passing similar data between multiple machines, you can use a RowGUID. A RowGUID is a UNIQUEIDENTIFIER used like an identity column. If you had a database being used between three different locations and they were trying to replicate data across the servers, then a RowGUID would serve much better than an integer. A row created on server A would not

---

[3] This is another one of those religious issues among database administrators. Some will tell you that you should *never* use a naturally occurring primary key because "constants aren't and variables won't." I'm avoiding the issue in the book but I prefer to add an identity column or RowGUID even if a natural key exists because I prefer the simplicity of dealing with integers that have a simple, consistent format.

overwrite data on servers B or C because the record is uniquely stamped with a RowGUID. Not only that, but the RowGUID won't repeat. The integer identity will restart with the same seed every time that the table is created.

> *Reluctant DBA* definition of an *identity column*:
> An identity column is one in which SQL Server automatically generates a value (beginning with 1 by default) for an inserted row and which is incremented with each subsequently inserted row. You can define the starting number (*identity seed*) and the increment value for each subsequent number. This identity seed gets reused every time the table is either truncated or re-created. Please note that SQL Server does not reuse numbers that have been deleted. Instead you simply have gaps in your numbers, as it should be.

Check over your list of objects and properties. Take time to make notes about what type of data each property should be. Do you think you have a good idea of what will be needed in the database? Good, because that's where we're heading next.

Can I Use Enterprise Manager to Design My Database?

SQL Server has a good design tool built into it and we're going to take full advantage of that as we demonstrate how to build and normalize the database. If you have a Modeling Tool, it doesn't hurt to familiarize yourself with SQL Server's built-in tool. Although not as robust, it certainly does the job for which it was intended. In this example, we are going to use the Diagramming tool to build our tables first, based on the objects identified, and then we will work on normalizing the data, defining normalization as we go. After we're through with the Diagramming tool, you'll learn how to work with tables in the EM.

To begin with, create a database called **RDBA05**.

NOTE   *See the section "How Do I Create a Database?" in Chapter 3 for more information.*

Once the database is created, it's time to create the database diagram. Figure 5-1 shows you how to create a new diagram. Because this is a new database, you'll get a message saying there are no tables to add. The Diagramming tool is actually an ERD tool. That is, it visually displays the entities (objects) and their relationships and lets you change them or define new ones.

> **NOTE** *When you are working with an existing database and create a new diagram, the New Diagram Wizard starts, providing you with an easy way to add existing tables. The wizard also starts on a new database if you have not set your SQL Server Registration to hide system objects. If you are following along and the wizard pops up instead of the message saying there are no tables, go ahead and select Cancel to start with a blank diagram.*

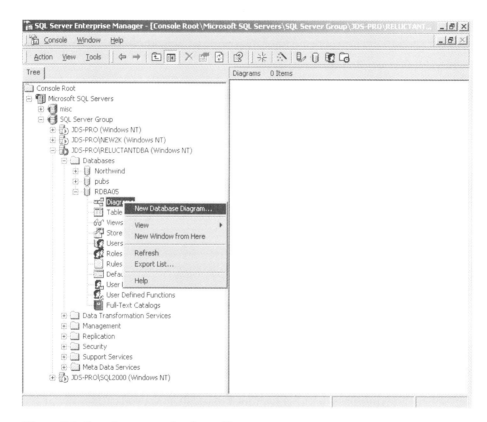

Figure 5-1. Creating a new database diagram

The Diagramming Tool's Toolbar

Before we get too far into using the Diagramming tool, we should look at the toolbar shown in Figure 5-2. The first button is Save, which will save the diagram but, more importantly, it will save any changes you have made in the diagram to the underlying tables and relationships. The next is the Properties button. which gives you easy access to many of the topics we're going to cover later in the "What Properties for a Table Are Exposed in the Diagramming Tool?" section.

Figure 5-2. Diagramming tool toolbar

The third button prints your diagram. Before you print your diagram, how-ever, you need to take two steps to ensure your database will look good on the printout. First, right-click in the white area of the diagram and you'll get a menu. Select Page Setup . . . and you can specify the printer that you want to use and whether you want the printouts to be landscape or portrait. Once you defined your printer you can right-click in the white area again and select View Page Breaks. This adds blue borders to your diagram that indicate where the page will break, handy when your diagram is more than one page long.

TIP *If this is the first time you're using the Diagramming tool, make sure the objects are long enough and wide enough to dis-play all the properties clearly (if possible). The Relationship lines can be manipulated, which means you can move them around to reduce or eliminate overlapping, thus reducing con-fusion for others that may reference your diagram.*

The fourth button allows you to save a script of the changes you have made. This is handy for upgrading databases. You can make the changes and save them to a script that you can use for upgrading the database. The script can also be used for automating updates to other environments or remote systems. The next set of buttons represent the standard Cut and Paste buttons.

The two buttons after the Cut and Paste buttons are both for adding tables to the diagram. The first one, marked with a light in the upper-right corner, is for creating a new table. The second one, with the plus symbol (+), is for adding an existing table to the diagram.

The magnifying glass defines how much of the diagram you can see at one time by increasing or decreasing the diagram size. The text list next to it changes your view of a selected table. You can view it as name only, columns as well as table name, keys, or a custom view. The little gold key is used to set the primary key for the column or columns selected within a table.

The button that's labeled "a|b" lets you put a text annotation on the diagram, handy for explaining why you did something or for making notes about some-thing that you still need to do. The button with three blue squares rearranges the tables on you—oops, *for* you—based on an internal algorithm. It'd be nice if you could disable this button. It is frustrating when you take the time to arrange the tables so they make sense, are lined up in a logical order based on relationships, and correctly placed to print only to then hit that button accidentally and have your work rearranged. Try to become habitual about saving so you can easily recover from such an error.

The last three buttons are for managing Relationships, Index/Keys, and Constraints. The Index/Keys button is a shortcut to the dialog box used for defining indices for a table, and indexing is covered in Chapter 7, "The Power of Indexing." We'll cover relationships in the upcoming section "How Do I Relate Tables Together in the Diagramming Tool?" We'll cover constraints toward the end of this chapter in the section "What Table Properties Are Exposed in the Diagramming Tool?"

How Do I Create a Table in the Diagramming Tool?

Creating a table in the Diagramming tool is as easy as clicking on the New Table button and giving it a name; we'll call this one "VeterinaryOffices." This creates a new table, all ready to be defined (see Figure 5-3). For the moment we are just going to put the column names in and default them to character fields with a length of 10. The asterisk (*) next to the table name signifies it hasn't been saved yet. Now that we've got placeholders for the properties that belong to a veterinarian's office, we can start examining them to determine what data type they should be, whether they need better names, and if they need to be split up.

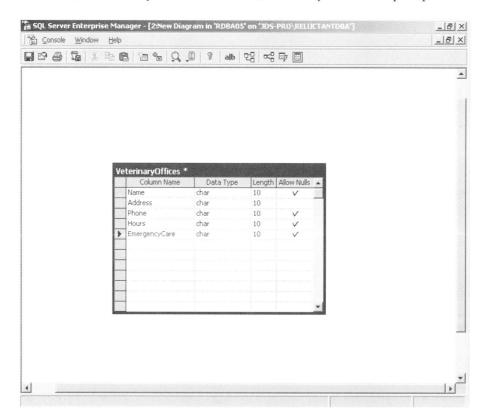

Figure 5-3. This is the first pass at designing the VeterinaryOffices table.

Naming Objects within SQL Server

If you have been in programming more than a month or two, you have seen some of the religious wars that go on. Visual Basic 6 versus VB.NET is a good example. There are people who have a "take no prisoners" approach to their beliefs about programming languages.

There are also people like that when it comes to naming objects in SQL Server. Some will tell you that each table should be named in the singular ("Veterinarian") because each row represents one of that type of object. Others will tell you that you should use the plural ("Veterinarians") because a table is a collection. Still others will tell you that you should prefix every single table with a "tbl," every view with a "vw," and so on in order to define what each object is. Let me give you the definitive rules to follow in naming objects within a SQL Server database:

- If you have a defined naming guide within your company, use that.

- If you do not have a defined naming guide within your company, create one and stick with it.

Let's be honest. Naming conventions are good things. They make it easier for a team to work together and for everyone to see what role an object plays by how it is named. They do not, however, affect how your database operates. For this book we are using the collections approach ("Veterinarians").

Each row represents one of an object, and a table (or view) represents a collection. With the "tbl" naming convention, things can change and you should try to minimize programming modifications. Let's say that a table has to be modified and split into two tables. It's quite possible that a view can be created to present the same set of data that the table used, but if you're prefixing all of the objects then you'll need to modify all of the code that referred to "tbl" to now refer to "vw" instead. If, on the other hand, you can create a view with the same name the table *used* to have (you'd have to rename the table when I split it in two) then you can minimize programming changes.

Check out the "WhitePapers\Naming" directory on this book's CD, which includes some naming convention documents that certain developers have agreed to share. You can use or adapt one for your company if you don't have one.

Take a good look at the table in Figure 5-3. The first field is called Name, but that's not very descriptive. If you take a look at the other objects identified, there are several Name fields: one for veterinarians, owners, even pets. So we're going to rename that field to OfficeName and set it to be a NVARCHAR with a length of 64. That's not really an arbitrary length; this will be explained in a moment.

The next field is more of a problem. Address isn't really one piece of information. There's a street address, city, state, and zip code, all of which make up an address. In some situations you have two address lines, for instance, 123 Main St. on the first line and APT 321 on the second. Instead of storing all of this data in one field, we are going to split Address into separate fields. In fact, we're going to split it as shown in Table 5-5, using the field length standards as set forth by the United States Postal Service (USPS).

Table 5-5. Data Structure for VeterinaryOffices

FIELD NAME	DESCRIPTION	DATA TYPE	LENGTH	NULLABLE?
OfficeID	Identity column	INT	8	No
OfficeName	Name of the office	NVARCHAR	64	No
OfficeAddress1	First Line Street Address	NVARCHAR	64	No
OfficeAddress2	Second Line Street Address	NVARCHAR	64	Yes
OfficeCity	Mailing City	NVARCHAR	30	No
OfficeState	Mailing State	NCHAR	2	No
OfficePostalCode	Mailing 5 Digit Zip	NCHAR	5	No
OfficePostal4	+4 Digits of Zip Code	NCHAR	4	Yes
OfficeHours	Hours of Operation	NVARCHAR	256	No
OfficePhone	Phone Number	NUMERIC	10	No
OfficeFax	Fax Number	NUMERIC	10	No
EmergencyCare	Flag determining whether Emergency care is provided at this office	BIT	1	No

Actually, the post office can go further and break down an address line into a street number, street name, and street type. There are two good reasons not to do that in this database. First, addresses are rather more complex than most people know. The USPS has defined twenty-seven different items of information that can appear on a mailing label. And that data may or may not contain a street address. What if the address is a post-office box? No, simplicity is a good rule to follow in keeping the street address as a distinct unit. The second reason is that the address line will always be used as one singular object. That means there is no need to split up and rebuild the data every time it is accessed.

We have refined the data structure, but it still lacks a critical piece, the primary key. The primary key is the column or columns that will uniquely define each row. Because there are no guaranteed unique columns in VeterinaryOffices, we are going to create one. We're going to highlight the OfficeName column by clicking in the gray box to the left of the field name and then right-clicking to get a menu (see Figure 5-4). Now we'll add a field called OfficeID and set it to an INT data type and non-NULL (not only shouldn't it be nullable, it can't if it's going to be an identity).

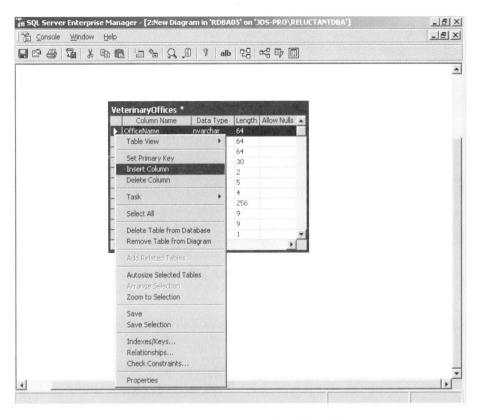

Figure 5-4. Inserting a field into a table can be done from the pop-up menu.

Now, however, we need to tell SQL Server that this will be an identity column. Before we can make this column an identity column, we need to set up SQL Server to correctly display more options for each column in the table. In previous versions, the standard view of a table in the Diagramming tool had more information than it does now. The information is still there, it's just not in the standard view, so we must create a customized view of the table. To do this, first, right-click on the table and bring up the menu. Select Table View ➤ Custom. Next, go right back to that menu but choose Modify Custom. Now you'll see a window like the one in Figure 5-5. From here you can select what data for the table structure shows up in the Custom view. An easy way to do this is to click on the >> to add all of the column information and then remove Condensed Type, Not for Replication, Formula, and Collation columns. Once you've done that you have all of the information at you fingertips to modify a table however you want.

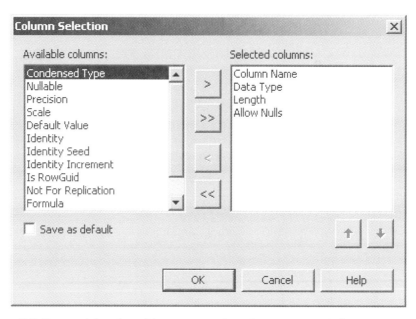

Figure 5-5. Customizing the table structure view gives you more information.

Now that we've added some extra columns to the view of field information we can finish defining the table. First click in the identity column for OfficeID. Now SQL Server will automatically increment the value in that column for every new row that gets added. You can also define the identity seed and identity increment. Those determine what the first value will be and how large an increment will be used between values.

Now, why would you want to use anything other than 1 for your seed and increment values? Well, there are a couple of reasons. Because an identity column *should* be just an arbitrary number to uniquely reference a row of data, you really shouldn't need to worry about what the seed and increment are. However, often you will find identity columns as customer numbers, invoice numbers, and so on. If that's the case, no one wants to display invoice number 1. It always *looks* better to have a higher number invoice.

For that reason identity seeds are often created with a date base, for instance 20010415 for a seed value on a table created on 4/15/2001. Sometimes people will want to specify an increment other than 1 just so they have some breathing room if they need to insert rows of data between existing data. For this table, however, we're going to leave the seed and increment at 1.

Only once have I considered modifying the increment value to provide room for inserting new data into existing data. I'm glad I didn't and would highly recommend against it. Everything in SQL is entered in some physical order (dictated by a clustered index or non-clustered index). If it is permitted to arbitrarily insert values "midstream," the true historical activity of a table is lost. Under many systems I've worked on, this would be a serious security breach and not condoned.

The last step to take in setting up this table is to set the identity column to be a primary key. This is really simple. All you need do is click on the gray box to the left of the column name to select the field and then click on the gold key in the toolbar. This puts a little key next to the column name (see Figure 5-6). If you have multiple columns to set, you can select them all at once and click on the gold key. As long as they are all set to Not Null *and* there are no duplicate values for these columns in the table already, your key will be created. Now, before we go any further we're going to save the diagram. This will not only save the diagram, but it will create the table in the database as well.

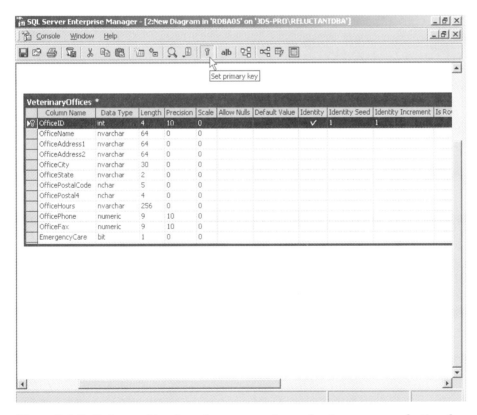

Figure 5-6. Defining an identity column as a primary key is as easy as selecting the columns and pressing the golden key on the toolbar. Primary key columns have a small key next to the columns that make up the key.

How Do I Relate Tables Together in the Diagramming Tool?

When we relate two tables together, it is because they have some common field. The table that will store data about veterinarians, Veterinarians, is related to the VeterinaryOffices table because it contains a foreign key.

> *Reluctant DBA* definition of *foreign key*:
> A foreign key is a column in one table (foreign/child) that references a unique row in another table (primary/parent). The data types of the columns being related between the two tables must match, and the value must exist in the referred table. Because that value was not generated in the current table, it is called *foreign*.

The easiest way to illustrate a foreign key is to create one. To that end, we're going to create another table, this one to hold veterinarian information. Table 5-6 shows the basic table structure.

Table 5-6. Data Structure for Veterinarians

COLUMN NAME	DATA TYPE	LEN.	DEC.	NULL	DEFAULT
VeterinarianID	INT identity	10	0	NO	—
VeterinarianSpecialty	NVARCHAR	50	0	NO	—
VeterinarianLastName	NVARCHAR	30	—	NO	—
VeterinarianFirstName	NVARCHAR	25	—	NO	—
VeterinarianPhoneNumber	NUMERIC	10	0	YES	—
VeterinarianPager	NUMERIC	10	0	YES	—
VeterinarianEmailAddress	NVARCHAR	100	—	YES	—
VeterinarianPrimaryHospital	INT	10	0	NO	—

NOTE *When naming primary keys and foreign keys, it's best to use a name that can be unique across the database. By using OfficeID instead of ID, for instance, you will know that wherever you encounter that column name, it refers to VeterinaryOffices. This is especially handy when producing a data dictionary.*

Once we've defined the second table we can create the foreign key. It's as simple as deciding which table is going to contain the reference and which is going to be referenced. In this case, Veterinarians is going to have a field that refers to a row in VeterinaryOffices. Defining the foreign key is as easy as selecting the OfficeID column in Veterinarians and dragging it to the VeterinaryOffices table, just as you would drag and drop anything in Windows. Once you've done that, you'll get a dialog box allowing you to further define the foreign key (see Figure 5-7).

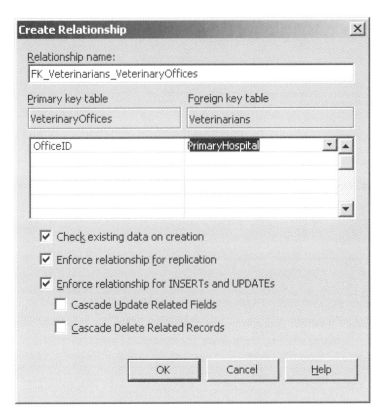

Figure 5-7. Defining a foreign key can be done through these handy dialog boxes that appear once you've dragged the foreign key column to the table that contains the primary key.

Let's go over the data found in the Create Relationship dialog box. The first thing is the name of the foreign key relationship. SQL Server does a good job of naming the relationship exactly what it is, a foreign key between the tables Veterinarians and VeterinaryOffices. The next thing it does is to define which is the primary key table and which is the foreign key table. The primary key table is the one that has the field as its primary key, and the foreign key is the table referring to the primary key table. Creating foreign keys is actually a way of ensuring Declarative Referential Integrity (DRI).

> *Reluctant DBA* definition of *Declarative Referential Integrity*:
> Declarative Referential Integrity is a fancy term that means "verifying that the data being used as a foreign key exists in the primary key table."

 In the old days we wrote triggers to enforce Referential Integrity (RI), which is known as procedural integrity. *With DRI you've literally "declared" what values are acceptable. This is sort of like declaring variables in Visual Basic. When SQL Server checks RI it's doing it at a system level as opposed to running a script like a trigger or stored procedure.*

The primary key table will always list all of the fields that make up its primary key. SQL Server will attempt to match up the columns based on name and type, which is another good reason to name columns consistently. Next come five checkboxes that require some further explanation.

Why Wouldn't I Want to Check Existing Data on Creation of a Foreign Key?

This sounds like one of those trick questions, but it is an important consideration. If you are working with an existing database that wasn't properly built with foreign keys, then you might have some . . . uh, inconsistent data.[4] Therefore, you can tell SQL Server that you don't want to test all of the existing data to ensure that all of the values in the one table have corresponding values in the primary key of the other table. Many DBAs will not allow data like this to exist. When they are creating foreign keys on a database that has inconsistent data, they will frequently pull all of the data that would violate the foreign key constraint out of the database to prevent problems with the data later.

Actually, if you are trying to create a foreign key between two tables with a lot of rows, you *might* want to check this to keep from tying up the database while all of those rows are cross checked, but this isn't recommended. It's a bad idea not to check the data when you create foreign keys. It just leads to headaches down the road if there are any inconsistencies, because users will find them when their programs start encountering errors.

---

[4] If you put garbage in a computer, nothing comes out but garbage (GIGO: Garbage In, Garbage Out). But this garbage, having passed through an expensive machine, is somehow ennobled and none dare criticize it.

CAUTION *Never exit the Diagramming tool without saving your work first, especially if you are creating relationships. If there is a relational error in your diagram, you may regret not saving first. When you create foreign key relationships in the Diagramming Tool, they don't exist nor are they checked to see if they could exist until they are saved. At that time SQL Server will attempt to create the relationship and report on any problems. If it finds that it cannot, then it will tell you there is a data error trying to create the key. When you exit, you are prompted to save if you have made any changes, however, you don't get an option to cancel the exit and come back into the Diagramming tool to fix any errors that might be encountered. Instead, it will ask you if you want to save the changes to a script. At that point you can either save it to a script so you can try to fix the inconsistencies later using Query Analyzer or you can tell it not to save the work you've been doing. Therefore, always save before exiting the Diagramming tool.*

Why Wouldn't I Want to Enforce Foreign Key Relationships for Replication?

This is a little more complex, and we're not really dealing with replication in this book. Still, it is reminiscent of the age-old question: Which came first, the chicken or the egg?

If you are replicating data, then you are passing the data between two servers. If you have table A that has a foreign key relationship to table B and a row gets replicated for table B before the corresponding row is replicated for table A, then you get a foreign key error. The server where the data was created *should* maintain the foreign key relationship, and the data *should* be replicated with the primary key table first, so this should be a non-issue. But if you are having replication errors, you can modify this option.

If you were using Merge Replication (a subject beyond the scope of this book), then SQL Server would take care of handling these issues for you. If you are planning on creating this type of replication scenario and handling it without the use of Merge Replication, every time you re-create the wheel you run the risk of creating a wheel that doesn't roll (or at least one that doesn't roll smoothly).

Why Wouldn't I Want to Always Enforce a Foreign Key Relationship?

It may sound crazy to create a foreign key relationship that SQL Server won't actually enforce, but some people feel they need to do this. Having a foreign key *does* create a miniscule amount of overhead because SQL Server has to verify the existence of data whenever inserting or updating rows. The truth is that SQL Server has been built so this requires minimal overhead, far less than if a separate program was handling this enforcement. Further, performance on DRI hasn't been an issue since 6.5 when DRI was introduced.

Even so, sometimes you inherit historical data that needs to be in a foreign key relationship but that relationship can't be created. This happens most often when working on normalizing an existing database that wasn't properly designed. When that happens, you should still define a foreign key in the Diagramming Tool and uncheck all of the boxes so there is no enforcement of the relationship. That way you at least have a visual representation of how the data *should* relate so you can start work on cleaning it up until you *can* enforce DRI.

I've always negotiated to remove "orphan" data with the goal of re-inserting it as parents are identified or created.

Cascading Foreign Keys

The last two checkboxes cannot be checked unless you enforce the foreign key relationship for inserts and updates. That's because the cascading updates and deletes rely on the existence of the foreign key relationship.

As explained earlier, primary keys *shouldn't* change. Sometimes a naturally occurring primary key might need to be modified. On other occasions, a primary key might need to be deleted. Unfortunately, if that primary key is being used as foreign key, you cannot just modify or delete it, especially if that row is being used as another table's foreign key. In those instances you need to follow certain steps. To modify an existing primary key you would need to:

1. Insert a row with the new primary key value.

2. Update all foreign keys referencing the old primary key value to reflect the new value.

3. Delete the row with the old primary key value.

To delete a primary key value, you would need to:

1. Delete all rows referencing the foreign key to be deleted, recursively if a deleted row has a primary key being used as a foreign key.

2. Delete the row with the old primary key value.

You can have SQL Server handle all of these tasks for you, however, if you select the Cascade Update Related Records and Cascade Delete Related Records. This is not without cost, though. If you have half a dozen tables that are all inter-related by foreign keys and you delete a row from the top-most table, you could end up deleting rows from all six tables, complete with all of the overhead and locks involved in such an undertaking.

We want to create one more table now, this one to hold pet information. Table 5-7 defines the fields that will be in Pets. In addition, Pets will have Veterinarian ID and OfficeID as a foreign key relationship to Veterinarians. Figure 5-8 shows the final diagram.

Table 5-7. Data Structure for Pets

COLUMN NAME	DATA TYPE	LEN.	DEC.	NULL	DEFAULT
PetId	INT identity	10	0	NO	—
PetName	NVARCHAR	50	0	NO	—
OwnerName	NVARCHAR	30	—	NO	—
PetPhone	NUMERIC	10	—	NO	—
OfficeID	INT	10	0	NO	—
VeterinarianID	INT	10	0	NO	—

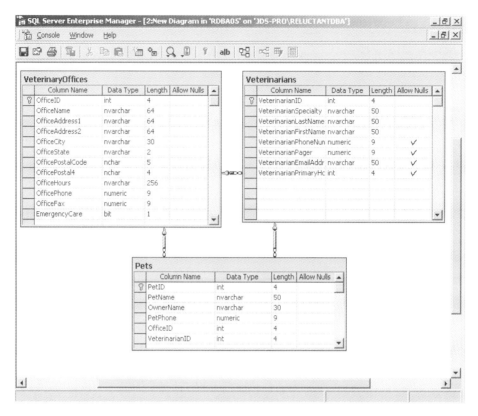

Figure 5-8. The first pass at building tables and defining relationships.

What Is Normalization?

Now that we have created tables and you can see how they are related, it's time to talk about *normalization*. In its broadest format, normalization is a blueprint for how a database *should* be built. However, databases can be "over-normalized," so as we discuss the benefits of normalization, we'll also talk about when to pull back and why.

When E.F. Codd first defined relational databases in 1969, he defined three normal forms that data take on. There are currently six normal forms, but we're only going to cover the first, second, and third normal forms.

Let's take another look at Veterinarians. There is one field that isn't quite correct, the VeterinarianSpecialty field. That field is designed to hold information about the vet's specialty. For instance, perhaps they are a small-animal veterinarian or one who specializes in horses or reptiles or some combination of the three. What if a vet had more than one specialty?

Let's begin by adding two more columns to the table, VeterinarianSpecialty1 and VeterinarianSpecialty2, both NVARCHAR 50 and both allowing nulls. This, however, introduces new two new problems. First it limits the number of specialties for each vet. Second, it makes querying the database more complex.

In the first pass of Veterinarians it would have been easy to find a small-animal vet by filtering the data selection with `VeterinarianSpecialty = 'small animal'`. With the additional veterinarian type fields it now becomes necessary to enclose that in a parenthetical WHERE clause so you end up with a convoluted SQL statement like this:

```
SELECT LastName, FirstName from Veterinarians WHERE (VeterinarianSpecialty =
'small animal' OR VeterinarianSpecialty1 = 'small animal' OR
VeterinarianSpecialty2 = 'small animal')
```

Having multiple fields with duplicate functionality leads to truly unmanageable SQL statements. Remedying this also leads directly to the first normal form of a database.

What Does First Normal Form Mean?

Anytime you find yourself creating fields with numbers (Field1, Field2, and so on) or fields that contain the same information (multiple address fields, for instance), you should take a hard look to determine whether those fields should be placed into an additional table and related back to the original one. In this case we are going to create a new table called VeterinarianSpecialties. VeterinarianSpecialties will have two columns, VeterinarianID and VeterinarianSpecialty. In addition, it will have a foreign key relation to Veterinarians (see Figure 5-9). The VeterinarianSpecialty in the VeterinarianSpecialties table will take the place of the VeterinarianSpecialty column in Veterinarians, so we will remove that column altogether.

> Reluctant DBA definition of *first normal form*:
> First Normal Form is a database where all repeating properties are separated into a table as rows and linked back to the original table using foreign keys.

Figure 5-9. By separating out the VeterinarianSpecialty into a separate table, we remove the limit on how many different specialties a vet can have.

This is much better. First, it expands the number of types that a veterinarian can have to infinity (or at least as much disk space as the server has). Second, it makes the SQL easier to write when you want to search for a veterinarian with a particular specialization. The convoluted checking of multiple fields is simplified to a subquery:

```
SELECT LastName, FirstName from Veterinarians WHERE VeterinarianID IN
(SELECT VeterinarianID FROM VeterinarianSpecialties
WHERE VeterinarianSpecialty = 'Small animal')
```

When *Not* to Normalize

If you look carefully at the tables defined so far in this chapter, you will find at least one thing that defies the first normal form. In VeterinaryOffices there are two fields for the street address. Could those two address lines be normalized into a separate file linked back to VeterinaryOffices just as with the VeterinarianSpecialty field? Of course they could, but unlike the VeterinarianSpecialty, the addresses are not repeating data. The second address line is commonly used for Apartment #, Suite #, or even a Care Of notation.

You might also note there are several tables that use postal addresses. In some cases it might make sense to create a separate address table and then create relationships, much as was done with the VeterinarianSpecialties. Is it necessary, though? To date, all of the owners have used only one address at a time, so Anne assures us the multiple addresses aren't necessary. Even if they were necessary, you might still build one of the addresses into the Owners table so that the most frequently used address is available without having to use multiple tables. That's the type of situation to address on a case-by-case basis.

Now that VeterinarianSpecialties exists, it is possible to see some new potential problems. First, we don't have a primary key defined for it. If we use

VeterinarianID, then we are limited to one per vet, which we don't want to do. So, the only option is to make both columns the primary key. But there are other problems with this table. Most of the vets, according to Anne, are small-animal vets. That could easily lead to data that looks like the data in Table 5-8.

Table 5-8. Data from VeterinarianSpecialties

VETERINARIANID	VETERINARIANSPECIALTY
1	Small Animal Vet
1	Herpetologist
2	Small Aminal Vet

Do you see any problems with the data shown in Table 5-8? The word *animal* is misspelled for VeterinarianID 2. Problems like this are taken care of by advancing to the next level of normalization.

What Does Second Normal Form Mean?

In first normal form, you remove repeating fields and place them in separate tables. Second normal form does the same thing with repetitive data within a table.

> *Reluctant DBA* definition of *second normal form*:
> Second normal form is a database where all repeating data values are put into one separate table and linked back to the original table using foreign keys.

Examining VeterinarianSpecialties will show why it should be further normalized: Potential misspellings can be better defined as inconsistent data. Separating the actual description into a separate table ensures that the VeterinarianSpecialties will always be spelled exactly the same way, not to mention the beauty of having to make the change in only one place! The first step in doing this is to redefine the VeterinarianSpecialties table. Instead of a VeterinarianID, give it a VeterinarianSpecialtyID and make that an identity column and primary key. Next create a table that is really nothing more two columns that will relate the data from Veterinarians with the data in VeterinarianSpecialties. We'll call this table VeterinarianVeterinarianSpecialties, and it will contain two columns, VeterinarianID and VeterinarianSpecialtyID. You can see how this all fits together in Figure 5-10. This type of table is called a *junction table*, also referred to as a *cross reference* or *xref table*. Some people may actually use *xref* in the name of the table, which is nice, but you must be consistent in your naming conventions.

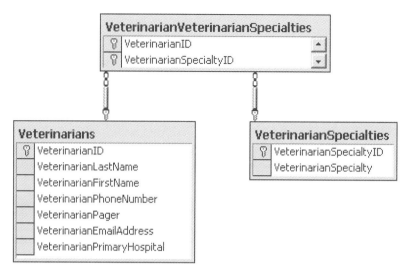

Figure 5-10. Using a junction table

> *Reluctant DBA* definition of a *junction table*:
> A junction is a table where every column is a part of the primary key that is designed to relate two tables together in a many-to-many relationship.

What Does Third Normal Form Mean?

The purpose of a relational database is to have data in each table related by some unique feature. Every column of data in a table should be related to the primary key of that table. If there is a column that doesn't, then that column is probably in the wrong table or belongs in a totally new table. Anytime you find data that could be duplicated, you should probably pull it into a separate table.

> *Reluctant DBA* definition of *third normal form*:
> Third normal form is a database where all fields in a table are directly related to the primary key of that table.

Take a look at the data structure for Pets (see Table 5-7). Do you see any columns that do not relate directly to the pet? OwnerName and PetPhone are both properties of the owner, not of the pet. That means we need to take these columns from Pets and put them into Owners. Table 5-9 shows that structure.

Table 5-9. Data Structure for Owners

COLUMN NAME	DATA TYPE	LEN.	DEC.	NULL	DEFAULT
OwnerID	INT identity	10	0	NO	—
OwnerLastName	NVARCHAR	30	—	NO	—
OwnerFirstName	NVARCHAR	25	—	NO	—
OwnerAddress1	NVARCHAR	64	—	NO	—
OwnerAddress2	NVARCHAR	64	—	NO	—
OwnerCity	NVARCHAR	30	—	NO	—
OwnerState	NCHAR	2	—	NO	—
OwnerZipCode	NVARCHAR	10	—	NO	—
OwnerPhoneNumber	NUMERIC	10	0	NO	—
OwnerEmailAddress	NVARCHAR	100	—	YES	—

OwnerID, an INT and identity column, serves as the primary key for the table. You can replace the OwnerName and PetPhone fields in Pets with an OwnerID column and then create the foreign key relationship between the two tables. Now all of the columns in Pets pertain only to that pet, and the columns in Owners relate only to the OwnerID. Any information for the owner of a specific pet can be referenced through the OwnerID field in Pets.

More on Relating Tables

Throughout this chapter we've been defining how tables relate to one another. Our diagram now has six tables, all interrelated (see Figure 5-11). These relationships are referred to by the number of rows in each of the two tables being related. Take the relationship of VeterinaryOffices to Veterinarians. Because the OfficeID is a required field (not nullable) in the Veterinarians table, then each vet must have a valid OfficeID. There can be multiple veterinarians for each office, however. We call this a one-to-many relationship because every one row in the VeterinaryOffices table can have none, one, or multiple rows in the Veterinarians table.

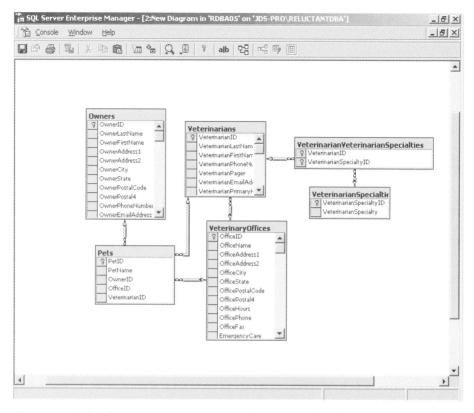

Figure 5-11. This figure shows how the six tables defined so far all relate to each other.

Although using a junction table like VeterinarianVeterinarianSpecialties actually creates two one-to-many relationships (one for each table it is related to), the junction table is generally not mentioned. Instead, the Veterinarians table and the VeterinarianSpecialties table are referred to as having a many-to-many relationship.

There is one more type of relationship that we need to address, but Anne will bring that up because, although there are still a couple of tables to be defined related to tracking appointments and billing, Anne has some comments about the structure of our database so far:

"I like what you've done so far, but there are a couple of things that I think we need to address. I see that you are tracking a veterinarian's primary hospital, but several of the veterinarians actually work at both a regular office and at an emergency room as well, and we'd like to keep that information in the database.

"Speaking of emergency room offices, I see that you define offices as being either an emergency room or not. That's not quite true. We actually define our offices as non-emergency, weekend-emergency, or 24-hour emergency. The difference between weekend-emergency and 24-hour emergency is that the weekend-emergency offices are open for a few hours on the weekend to treat emergency cases only, not regularly scheduled visits.

"Finally, we have some of our veterinarians mentoring newer veterinarians. Although that doesn't impact appointments and such, it would be handy if that mentoring information were stored in the database so we could easily retrieve who is mentoring whom for some of our reports."

This is one reason that regular reviews are good. Catching these changes now is a lot easier than trying to make these changes after the project has been implemented. Anne has asked for three changes to be made. First, there needs to be a junction table between Veterinarians and VeterinaryOffices. Second, the BIT field for EmergencyCare in VeterinaryOffices needs to be modified to handle more than true/false states. Finally, the Veterinarians table needs to store management information.

Adding a junction table would be handled just as it was for the VeterinarianSpecialties, so we're not going to review that. Changing EmergencyCare in VeterinaryOffices to a TINYINT is equally easy even though it also involves adding a table to store what the EmergencyCareID means and creating the correct relationships. What we want to focus on is adding the mentor information to Veterinarians.

How Can a Table Relate to Itself?

For each of the relational examples covered so far, there have been two tables on each side of the relationship. What Anne has asked us to do, however, is to link Veterinarians to itself so the relationship involves only one table. The first step is to add a column to Veterinarians, in this case MentorID. This will be an INT data type because it is going to link back to VeterinarianID and that is an INT. Unlike VeterinarianID, however, MentorID will allow NULL as a valid value.

Earlier in the chapter you learned that NULL is the absence of any value. That is perfect for a situation like this one where a vet may not have a mentor. Putting the vet's own VeterinarianID in the MentorID would imply that the vet was self-mentoring, which is incorrect. Because that's not the case, we allow NULLs for vets who have no mentors.

Once we've added the MentorID column, we can click in the gray box to the left of the column name to select the column. Here comes the tricky part: Drag the mouse out of the table and up to the top. SQL Server will bring up the Create Relationship dialog box with the same table listed for the primary and foreign key tables, but the primary key will be VeterinarianID and the foreign key will be MentorID. There is one thing to note about a self-referencing table. The bottom two checkboxes of the Create Relationship dialog box are not available. You can't cascade updates or deletes within this type of relationship.

How Are NULLs Handled by DRI?

Because all the other relationships we've defined have been on columns that haven't allowed NULL, now is a good time to answer this question. Talking about DRI means talking about building a foreign key relation. And all foreign key relations must have a primary key column defined in the primary key table. And, by definition, a primary key cannot contain a NULL, so that's never an issue on that side.

On the foreign key table, however, it's different when using a column that allows NULLs. Because a NULL means there is no data available, then there is no need to verify that the data exists in the primary key table. And that's not a problem. In our MentorID relationship, it is valid that a veterinarian will not have a mentor and so, by leaving the foreign key column (MentorID) NULL, SQL Server won't try to match it up with the VeterinarianID.

This is how SQL Server is designed to act. It is, however, a behavior that can have unintended consequences. When you are joining two tables together based on the foreign key relationship, you will have to specify that you want to see those records that don't match. We'll cover this in more detail in Chapter 6, "What Is a View?"

What Table Properties Are Exposed in the Diagramming Tool?

If you remember way back to the beginning of this chapter, one toolbar button displays the properties of a table. It's the second from the left and looks like a hand holding an index card, that's the Table Properties button. If you select VeterinaryOffices and press that button now, you'll see a dialog box like the one shown in Figure 5-12. Almost everything in this chapter can also be done from within this dialog box.

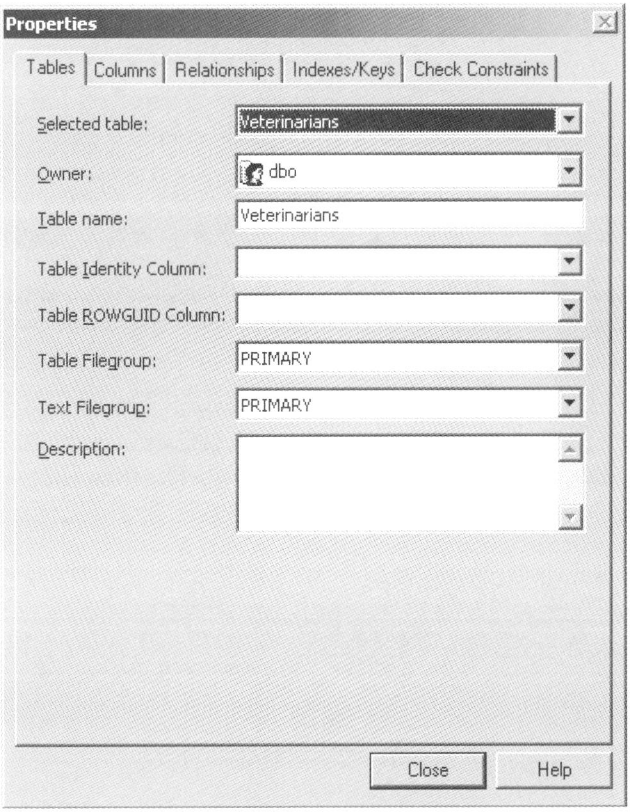

Figure 5-12. The Property dialog box for VeterinaryOffices

The first tab is related to the table as an object. Here you can select a differ-ent table, rename the table, or set a couple of key properties such as which column is the identity column and which is the ROWGUID column. Although we won't cover the differences between Primary and Secondary file groups, those can be set from this tab as well. The final section on this tab lets you fill in a description of the table and stores it as an extended property of the table so it is available in other situations.

How Is the Columns Tab Different from Filling in the Values in the Diagramming Tool?

You've learned how to modify the columns in a table from the custom view of the Diagramming tool, now you'll learn how you can modify the definition of a col-umn through the table's properties. Next, you'll learn how to use the EM more directly to create and modify tables. Which is the best way to do it?

It all depends on which way you feel most comfortable doing it. All of these ways are equally valid, and the only real differences lies in the interface.[5]

> **NOTE** *My preference is to do my initial table building through the Diagramming Tool using the custom view, but I have used the other ways as well. It all depends on what tool I'm using when I discover I need to make the change. Doing the changes through the Table Property dialog box does allow you to focus on one column at a time, much the way that the EM does.*

The drop-down box (see Figure 5-13) lets you select the name of the column you want to edit or you can type it in. You cannot, however, add new columns through the Table Properties dialog box. Also, be careful what you type because the Enter key will close the dialog box.

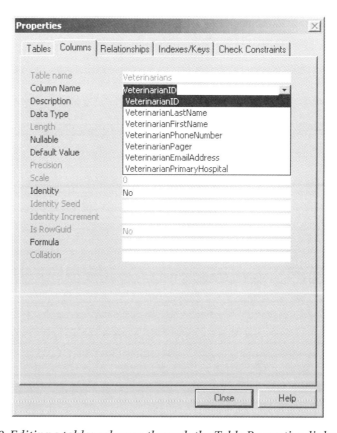

Figure 5-13. Editing a tables columns through the Table Properties dialog box

---

[5]   Not only that, but you can build tables through the SQL Language itself. The different front ends are all just different ways of building TSQL code.

Why Build a Relationship through a Dialog Box?

If you're a visual person who finds it easiest to drag and drop your relationships through an ERD tool like the Diagramming tool, then you'll probably prefer to do it that way. Some people, however, work better without diagrams, and this handy tab is one way to build relationships non-visually.

As you can see in Figure 5-14, this tool gives you all of the parts you need to build a foreign key relationship without dragging and dropping. You can select a table from the drop-downs (and when you tab out of the drop-down it will automatically change the name of the foreign key to reflect the new tables). This dialog box is similar to the one shown in Figure 5-7.

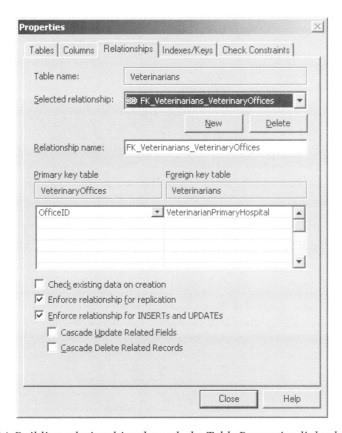

Figure 5-14. Building relationships through the Table Properties dialog box

What Is a Constraint?

You may remember that foreign keys help maintain DRI; in other words, they prevent a value from being entered as the foreign key in a table when no such value exists in the parent table as a primary key. That is a constraint. Primary keys must be unique within a table. That is also a constraint. Whether a column is allowed to have NULL data or not is another constraint. Table 5-10 shows all of the types of constraints.

> *Reluctant DBA* definition of *constraint*:
> A constraint is a rule used to enforce data integrity on a SQL Server database.

Table 5-10. Constraint Types

TYPE	DEFINITION
PRIMARY KEY constraints	Column(s) must be unique.
FOREIGN KEY constraints	Column(s) must exist as a primary key in another table.
UNIQUE constraints	Data must be unique within table.
CHECK constraints	Used to enforce domain integrity
DEFAULT definitions	If no data is supplied use this default value.
Nullability	Must contain data or not

We've covered each of these constraints except the CHECK and DEFAULT constraints, so let's finish this section with the CHECK constraint and then cover setting a DEFAULT value for a column in the last section of this chapter.

> *Reluctant DBA* definition of a *check constraint*:
> A check constraint works like a foreign key restraint except that the allowed values aren't contained in another table but defined within a Boolean statement.

Let's take a look at the Owners table. It could be a requirement that all last names of owners must begin with a letter from A to Z. To handle a rule like this you could create a CHECK constraint that read:

```
UPPER(Left(OwnerLastName,1)) IN ('ABCDEFGHIJKLMNOPQRSTUVWXYZ')
```

This code will check to make sure that the uppercase value of the left-most character of the OwnerLastName column is in the set of data from A to Z. Figure 5-15 shows how easily that is accomplished.

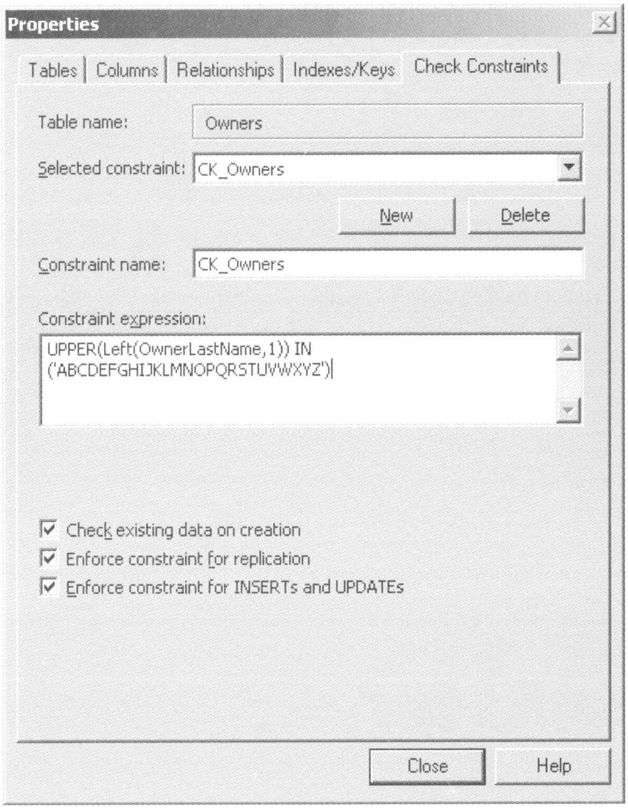

Figure 5-15. Creating a CHECK *constraint*

Now, if you try to enter a row in the Owners table that violates this rule (say, a last name that begins with 9), you'll get an error like the one shown in Figure 5-16. This error will be passed back to whatever program was trying to insert the data.

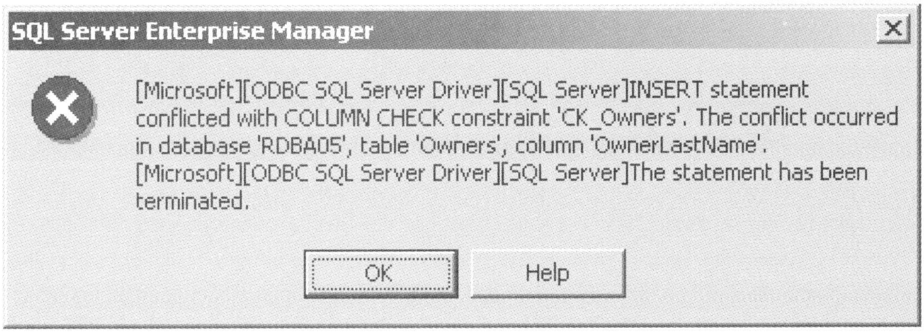

Figure 5-16. A CHECK *constraint violation*

How Do I Work with Tables without Using the Diagramming Tool?

Another way to work with tables is directly from the EM. If you've been following along on your computer through the chapter, save your diagram and then close the Diagramming tool. Now that you've got the EM's tree showing again, click on the Tables collection and you should see the tables you've created in the right-hand pane (see Figure 5-17). Once you have Tables open, you can see some basic information related to each table, the name of the table, the creator/owner of the table, what type of table it is, and when it was created. If you have hidden the system objects (see Chapter 3, "How Do I Visually Manage Objects?"), then you should only see User tables. (We'll talk about the creator/owner properties of the tables in Chapter 11, "How Do I Secure My Data?")

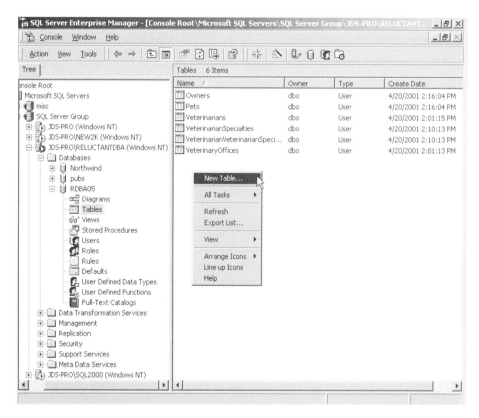

Figure 5-17. You can create and change tables from the Tables collection of the EM.

If you right-click in the right-hand pane, you'll get a pop-up menu. From here you can do numerous table related tasks, but for now select New Table. This brings up a new screen as you can see in Figure 5-18.[6]

If you've used older versions of SQL Server, this screen looks different than it did in the past. The older versions of SQL Server had an interface much like the customized view in the Diagramming tool. The new screen is similar to Microsoft Access. The top section of the screen contains a grid that holds the columns that make up the table. Within the grid you can set the name of the column, the Data Type, Length, and whether or not it allows NULL values.

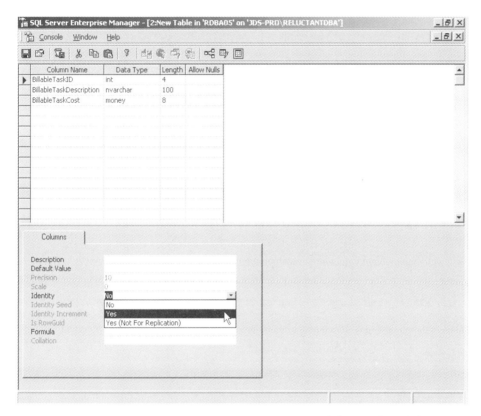

Figure 5-18. From the Enterprise Manager, you can add, delete, and modify the columns of a table.

The bottom section lets you make further adjustments to the column depending on the data type. As you can see in Figure 5-18, we're working with the column BillableTaskID. That column is an INT data type that we're going to make an identity column for this table. In the bottom section, you can see that some of

---

[6]   You can also get this screen for an existing table by right-clicking on a table and selecting Design Table from the pop-up menu.

the options are grayed out. Precision and Scale, for example, are not relevant to INT data types, so those are disabled. The Identity Seed and Identity Increment are also disabled because we haven't actually set the column to be an identity column yet. Once we do, those two parts will be enabled and we can specify the values for each.

Once we've done that, we can also set the primary key by clicking on the Key in the toolbar. By the way, does that toolbar look familiar? It should, it's a subset of the toolbar that's available in the Diagramming tool. It's missing a couple of buttons specific to the Diagramming tool (printing, annotating the diagram, adding tables) but the Key button still marks the selected columns as part of the primary key, and the hand holding the card is still the Properties button. In fact, if you press the Properties button, you'll get the same dialog box that shows up in the Diagramming tool with one exception. It doesn't have the tab for Columns because you are already working with the columns of the table.

Another similarity that is shared with the Diagramming tool is that your changes don't happen in real-time. The table isn't created or modified until you save the changes by clicking on the Save button or closing the window. For the same reasons outlined for the Diagramming tool, always save your changes before exiting, just in case there is an error in relationships. When you save the table for the first time or when you exit before saving (but you really shouldn't), you will be asked to provide the table's name. Then, once you've closed the Design Table tool, you should see your new table in the Tables collection.

To finish designing the sample database, we need to add four more tables in addition to the BillableTasks used in Figure 5-18. We're going to define these tables in Table 5-11 and then outline their data structures in Table 5-12. We won't go through the steps involved in creating each one, but we will look at the end results in Figure 5-19.

Table 5-11. The Remaining Tables in the Sample Database

TABLE NAME	DESCRIPTION
Appointments	This table is used for setting up appointments.
BillableTasks	This is a lookup table that contains all of the billable items and associated cost.
BillableEntries	This table contains a historical record of what billable tasks occurred at an appointment.
Charts	This table contains chart entries that the veterinarian makes during the appointment.

Table 5-12. Data Structure for the Remaining Tables

TABLE NAME	FIELD NAME	DESCRIPTION	DATA TYPE	LENGTH	NULLABLE?	FOREIGN KEY RELATION
Appointments	AppointmentID	Identity column/primary key	INT	4	No	—
—	PetID	Link to Pets	INT	4	No	Pets
—	OfficeID	Link to Office	INT	4	No	Offices
—	VeterinarianID	Link to Veterinarians	INT	4	No	Veterinarians
—	AppointmentDate	Date and time of appointment	DATETIME	8	No	—
BillableTasks	BillableTaskID	Identity column/primary key	INT	4	No	—
—	BillableTaskDescription	This will appear on the bill.	NVARCHAR	100	No	—
—	BillableTaskCost	This charge will appear on the bill.	MONEY	8	No	—
BillableEntries	BillableEntryID	Identity column/primary key	INT	4	No	—
—	AppointmentID	Link to Appointments	INT	4	No	Appointments
—	BillableTaskDescription	This will appear on the bill.	NVARCHAR	100	No	—
—	BillableTaskCost	This charge will appear on the bill.	MONEY	8	No	—
Charts	ChartEntryID	Identity column/primary key	INT	4	No	—
—	PetID	Link to Pets	INT	4	No	Pets
—	AppointmentID	Link to Appointments	INT	4	No	Appointments
—	ChartEntry	Text of the entry in the chart	NVARCHAR	2048	No	—

You may have noticed there is something odd about the BillableEntries and the BillableTasks tables. They have two columns with the exact same name, but there is no link between them. In fact, BillableTasks is not linked to any other table. This breaks the rules of normalization, but we're breaking that rule for a good reason. The BillableEntries table is a historical table that will store entries from the BillableTasks table, but those entries should never change. If the BillableEntries table contained a link to the BillableTasks table, then you could end up with the following scenario:

An owner brings his pet in for a routine checkup that costs $20 according to the BillableTasks table. A link to the Routine Checkup entry in BillableTasks is stored in BillableEntries. This gets passed to the accounting system, and the customer is charged $20. A month goes by and the cost of that checkup is modified in the BillableTasks table to be $25. Another month goes by and accounting wants to audit this database against their accounting system. When they go to review the data in the database for this appointment, it will show up as $25 when the owner was only charged $20! To prevent this kind of error, BillableTasks acts as current lookup table, and BillableEntries acts as a historical reference.

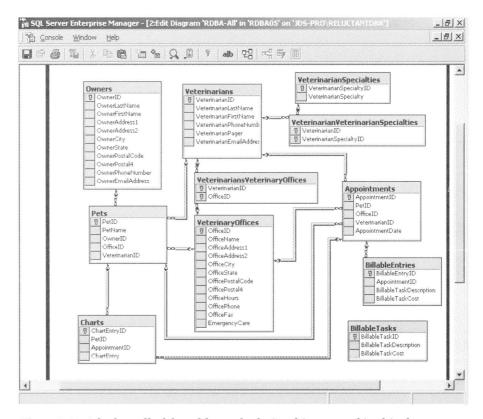

Figure 5-19. A look at all of the tables and relationships created in this chapter

Last Words

We've covered a lot of ground in this chapter, from deciphering requirements into a database specification to creating a database. Now that we've covered how to split the data apart into normalized tables, we're going to cover how to put them back together using Views in the next chapter.

Resources

- For an article on displaying TIMESTAMPS programmatically, read Knowledge Base Article Q170380:
  `http://support.microsoft.com/support/kb/articles/Q170/3/80.asp`

- Learn how to simplify SQL variants in this article by Josef Finsel, *Visual Basic Programmer's Journal*, March 2001:
  `http://www.devx.com/premier/mgznarch/vbpj/2001/03mar01/sq0103/sq0103.asp`

- Learn more about Globally Unique Identifiers:
  `http://www.opengroup.org/onlinepubs/9629399/apdxa.htm`

- For an article on precision and accuracy in floating-point calculations, look at Knowledge Base Article Q125056:
  `http://support.microsoft.com/support/kb/articles/Q125/0/56.asp`

CHAPTER 6

What Is a View?

'What tremendously easy riddles you ask!' Humpty Dumpty growled out. 'Of course I don't think so! Why, if ever I did fall off—which there's no chance of—but if I did—' Here he pursed up his lips, and looked so solemn and grand that Alice could hardly help laughing. 'If I did fall,' he went on, 'the King has promised me—ah, you may turn pale, if you like! You didn't think I was going to say that, did you? The King has promised me—with his very own mouth . . . to . . . to . . . .'
—Lewis Carroll, *Through the Looking Glass*

THE LAST CHAPTER DESCRIBED some of the benefits of normalizing your database structure, but it seems that such normalization can make it trickier to access the data. After all, now that the data is split apart, how do you put it back together? Fortunately, you won't need all the king's horses and all the king's men—you can use a view.

NOTE *Throughout this chapter we'll be using the sample database called **RDBA06** (see Appendix A for how to install this database on your computer).*

Reluctant DBA definition of a *view*:

A view is a virtual table that doesn't really exist. In more technical terms, a view is a stored Transact SQL (TSQL) statement that has a name. When that name is used, SQL Server replaces the name with the predefined TSQL statement.

You can use a view almost anywhere you would use a table. It's important to remember, however, that a view is *not* a table. Instead, views function very much like C++ substitution macros. They are Transact SQL (TSQL) statements that provide a convenient shorthand name. Whenever this statement is referred to by the name of the view, SQL Server substitutes that predefined TSQL statement within the body of your original TSQL statement. Although this may seem to be a fine distinction to be making, you'll see the effect this distinction can have on performance.

The TSQL used in creating a view is the SELECT command. We're going to be creating the views through the Enterprise Manager (EM) using the View Designer and, as you create the views, you will see the TSQL statement being built. This makes the View Designer a handy shortcut to building SELECT statements. We'll also use it in Chapter 8, "Introduction to Query Analyzer."

How Do I Create a View?

Let's begin by creating a simple view. Open up the **RDBA06** database, right-click on the Views collection, and select New View from the pop-up menu. This will open the View Designer (see Figure 6-1). The Designer is split into four sections and each section can be hidden or displayed.

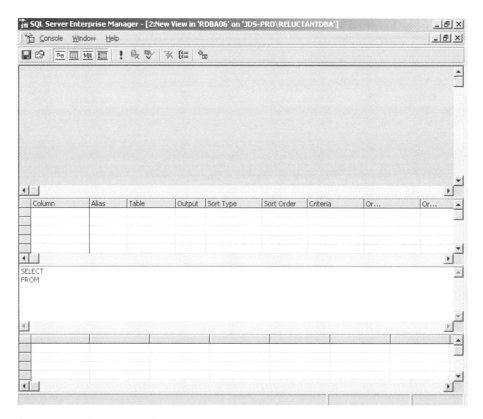

Figure 6-1. The View Designer provided in EM makes creating views simple.

The gray section at the top is the Diagram pane, where a graphic representation of any tables that you want to use shows up. The Grid pane in the second section displays information related to the columns you want to include in the view. The third section, the SQL pane, is where the TSQL code that makes up the view appears. Finally, the bottom grid, the Results pane, contains the results of the view. A change made in any of the top three grids results in the other two grids being modified to reflect the change. If any of the top three grids are modified while data is displayed in the Results pane, that data will be grayed out to indicate it is no longer consistent with the other panes.

 CAUTION *Most* SELECT *options can be parsed and displayed without a problem. There are some* SELECT *options, such as* UNION, *that are perfectly valid in a view but can't be diagrammed. In this case, the View Designer will warn you that it can't parse the statement and leave it at that.*

Across the top of the View Designer is a toolbar (see Figure 6-2).

Figure 6-2. The View Designer toolbar

Each button has a specific function:

- The Save button saves your view. Just as in the Diagramming tool, the changes aren't made to the view until you actually save it.

- The Properties button, next to the Save button, is where you set the properties of the selected object.

- The next four buttons let you hide or show the four panes. They affect the Diagram pane, Grid pane, SQL pane, and Results pane, respectively.

- The Run button has the red exclamation point and attempts to execute the TSQL and fill the Results pane.

- The Cancel Execution and Clear Results button to the right of that, disabled in Figure 6-1, cancels a running query and clears the Results pane.

- The Verify SQL button, displaying "SQL" with a checkmark, verifies the code in the SQL pane is syntactically correct. It does not, however, verify the code will actually run. If you type in the SQL pane and misspell a column name, this button tells you everything is syntactically correct, but you will get an error when you press the run button.

- The disabled funnel button (Remove Filter) removes any filter that has been applied.

- The next to the last button is the Use Group By button, and it creates subtotaled views.

- The Add Tables button adds tables to the view, which is exactly what we're going to do next.

When you click the Add Tables button, you get a dialog box that lists the three types of objects you can use in a view: tables, other views, and functions. Because we have built neither views nor functions yet, we are going to concentrate on creating views that use tables. Double-click on Owners to add the Owners table to this view. The Diagram pane will display the Owners table and all of its columns, and the SQL pane will add dbo.Owners after the word FROM. To create a phone list of all of the owners, select OwnerLastName, OwnerFirstName, and OwnerPhoneNumber from the columns listed. If you click on the red exclamation point in the toolbar, then the Results pane displays the results (see Figure 6-3).

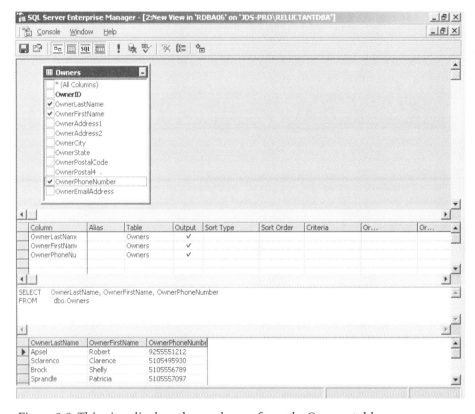

Figure 6-3. This view displays three columns from the Owners table.

If you look at the Diagram pane in Figure 6-3 you will see one column listed that isn't really a part of the Owners table. That would be the first one listed: ** (All columns)*. Selecting this option instead of individual columns will place one row in the Grid pane for all columns, represented by the asterisk (*). Although this may *appear* to select all of the columns, it is different from actually doing so.

Is It Really Wrong to Use SELECT *?

Using SELECT * is not necessarily wrong as much as it usually isn't right. That's because there is a difference between SELECT * and SELECT followed by all of the column names, particularly when you are using a view. You see, even though the view may use SELECT *, it only knows about the columns that existed at the time the view was created. If you add a new column to the table, you will need to re-create the view to add that column to the view.

Conversely, if you remove a column from a table, any view defined as SELECT * against that table will fail because the view has more columns defined than the table has. There's a simple SQL Script called "ViewsWithSelectStar.sql" in the "\Chapter06" directory on the CD that will show you this as well as one other consequence of using SELECT * in a view.

If you have a table with three columns and create a view that uses SELECT *, then drop a column and add a totally new column, you'll get the old column headings for the new columns!

With that in mind, it is always best to select each column individually in a view. We'll cover one place to use SELECT * in Chapter 9, "Working with Data: Basic Stored Procedures."

---

*One other issue involved with SELECT * is performance. The fewer columns selected the better because less parsing is involved and less data needs to travel along the wire to the client. Limiting your select to the columns needed helps performance.*

Well, we've got a list but it doesn't really do us much good. After all, there is no rhyme or reason to how the data is being displayed. Actually, that's not true: it's being displayed in OwnerID order because that's the primary key, but that doesn't make the data very useful to us. So we're going to sort the data by Owner-LastName, OwnerFirstName. To do that, we're going to use the Grid pane.

The Grid pane is where individual options for each column of data can be set. Each column of the grid lets you set some part of the column that is appearing in the view. The first one, labeled Column, contains a drop-down list that has all of the columns for all of the tables in the view. Selecting a new column will check the box for that column in the Diagram pane and add the column to the TSQL statement in the SQL pane. The next column, Alias, lets you specify another name for the column. This is handy when you have the same column showing up more than once because you aren't allowed to duplicate column names in a view. We'll look at this when we create a view of Mentors in the "Do NULL Values Affect Joins?" section. The third column is for selecting the table the column comes from and is set by default when you either check the box for a column in the Diagram pane or select from the first column.

The next two columns allow you to define your sort order. Each column can be sorted ascending, descending, or not sorted at all. Because this view represents a phone list for Owners, we're going to sort it by OwnerLastName, OwnerFirstName. When you do that, you can see that several things happen (see Figure 6-4):

- The Owners table in the Diagram pane now shows the columns in the sort order.

- The Sort Order column in the Grid pane now has numbers to indicate the order that the columns are to be sorted.

- The SQL pane shows two changes: TOP 100 PERCENT is added after SELECT and before the column names and an ORDER BY clause has been added listing the columns to sort.

- The Results pane shows that the grid has been disabled. This indicates that the data in the grid is no longer consistent with the view as it is currently defined.

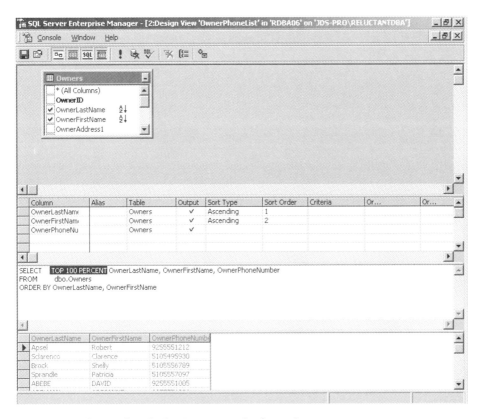

Figure 6-4. The results of selecting sort order for a view

 I recommend against sorting in a view unless you're absolutely certain the view won't be sorted again, such as if someone writing a report decides to change the sort order to descending or joins the view to another view or table and sorts the results of that. Re-sorting a sorted view adds a lot of overhead to SQL and may have a serious impact on performance. Use sort wisely and sparingly in views.

Remember that a view is a virtual table that doesn't really exist. Instead, SQL Server inserts that predefined TSQL code in the place of the view. Because it appears to function just as a table does, you can sort the results of a view. If you were to save this view right now and call it OwnerPhoneList, you could start Query Analyzer and use the following TSQL to get a data back:

```
SELECT OwnerFirstName, OwnerLastName, OwnerPhoneNumber
FROM OwnerPhoneList ORDER BY OwnerPhoneNumber
```

When this code is run, however, SQL Server is going to sort the table Owners by OwnerLastName, OwnerFirstName because that is how the view is defined and then *re-sort* the resulting row set by OwnerPhoneNumber.

NOTE   *In previous versions of SQL Server you were not allowed to add the* ORDER BY *clause to a view; however, if you are running an instance of SQL Server 7 on a machine that has SQL Server 2000 installed, you'll find that you can add sort functionality to a view. Even in SQL Server 2000 you aren't allowed to use the* ORDER BY *unless you specify a* TOP *qualifier to limit what is being returned. In this view the* TOP *qualifier doesn't do much good because you're specifying the* TOP 100 PERCENT, *but it will become more important when we talk about summarizing data in a view in the "How Do I Summarize Data?" section.*

Why Wouldn't I Just Want to Join Tables Using TSQL Commands?

At this point you may be wondering what the value of a view is because it seems like it would be more work to create the view and reference it in your code than it would be to use the TSQL statements to access tables directly. Well, there are a couple of reasons to use a view.

The first reason is to control the available data, both for ease of use and security. Although none of the tables in this database contain data that would be considered confidential, some databases need to consider this. By creating a view that includes certain columns and excludes others, it is possible to limit what an individual can see (we'll discuss this in more depth in Chapter 11, "How Do I Secure My Data?"). The view we just created limits the columns that it returns to OwnerFirstName, OwnerLastName, and OwnerPhoneNumber.

The second thing you can control with views is what rows are presented. If you use the Criteria column of the Grid pane to create a WHERE clause, you can filter out what gets displayed in the view. For instance, if you put the word "Apsel" in the Criteria column for OwnerLastName and then execute the view, then you would only get one row back (see Figure 6-5). Through this method you could create a separate view of all of the veterinarians in each Veterinary Office by filtering on the OfficeID. (Though you could do this, a better way would be to create a stored procedure that would return the data based on a parameter. We'll do this in Chapter 9, "Working With Data: Basic Stored Procedures."

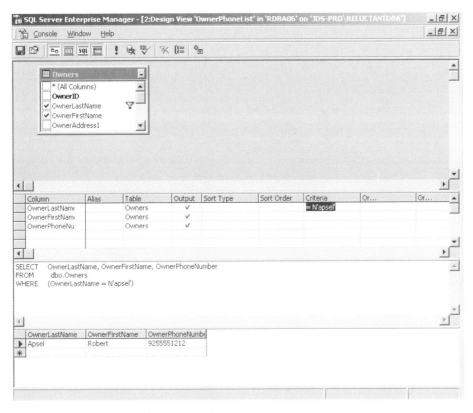

Figure 6-5. The result of filtering a view

In addition to limiting the number of columns, views are easy ways to join your normalized tables for programmers to use.

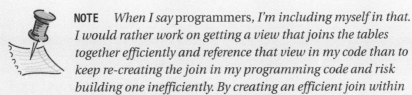

NOTE   *When I say* programmers, *I'm including myself in that. I would rather work on getting a view that joins the tables together efficiently and reference that view in my code than to keep re-creating the join in my programming code and risk building one inefficiently. By creating an efficient join within a view, all programmers can take advantage of it.*

Not only that, but if programmers are using views and you need to make a change to the underlying view, then you can modify it once, leading to fewer programming changes that need to be made. Also, a change to a view is often easier to back out than a change to a table. Now it's time to put views to some practical use by rejoining data split apart when the database was normalized. First, however, we're going to save the view we've been working on and call it OwnerPhoneList.

How Do I Join Two (or More) Tables?

When data from two or more tables is put together to form one coherent view, we say that we are *joining* the data together. *Join* is a term that has some specific connotations associated with it and there are several different types of joins, each with a different purpose. Let's start with the simplest of them, however, the Inner Join.

What's an Inner Join?

> *Reluctant DBA* definition of an *Inner Join*:
> An Inner Join matches two tables based on one or more column both tables have in common, usually a foreign key relationship. Both tables must have matching rows in order to display data. It's best to have the smallest result set as the first table listed in the view.

To demonstrate how this works, we're going to create a new view and we're going to select the VeterinaryOffices table and from that table we're only going to select the OfficeID and OfficeName columns. When we execute that view, we'll get the results listed in Table 6-1. As you can see, there are five offices and each one has a separate OfficeID.

Table 6-1. OfficeIDs and OfficeNames in the VeterinaryOffices Table

OFFICEID	OFFICENAME
1	Emergency Pet Care of Orinda
2	Standard Pet Care of Walnut Creek
3	Emergency Pet Care
4	Standard Pet Care
5	Xavier's Pet—Animal Ready Care

Now, we're going to add the VeterinariansVeterinaryOffices table. Start by right-clicking in an empty part of the Diagram pane, selecting Add Table, and then choosing the table you want. This adds that table to the Diagram pane and, because there is a foreign key relationship between the two, there is a link joining them together (see Figure 6-6). In addition, you can see that the SQL pane now has an additional section that says Inner Join. We'll come back to this syntax in just a moment. When you execute the view now, however, you'll get back four records and one of them is repeated! That's because VeterinariansVeterinaryOffices contains entries for only three OfficeIDs and one of them is in there twice. The Inner

Join tells SQL Server not to show the OfficeIDs that are in VeterinaryOffices unless they are also in VeterinariansVeterinaryOffices *and* to show them *every* time they match.

That's fine if we want to see only offices that have veterinarians employed. What if we need to see all of the office, whether there are veterinarians associated with the office or not? Then we use an Outer Join.

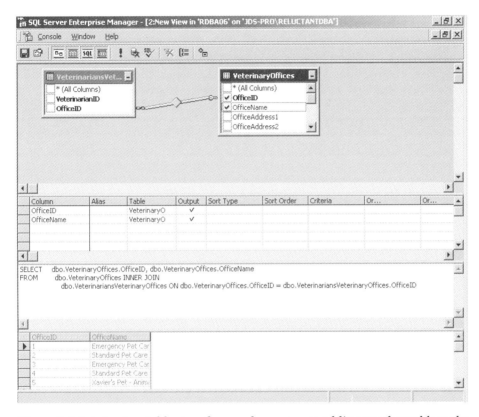

Figure 6-6. Joining two tables together can be as easy as adding another table to the view, provided there is a foreign key relationship between them.

What's an Outer Join?

> *Reluctant DBA* definition of an *Outer Join*:
> An Outer Join displays *all* records from one table and the matching records from the other. If there is not a matching row in the joined table, NULL is displayed for that table's selected columns.

Perhaps the easiest way to explain an Outer Join is to demonstrate. Using the view that we have displayed, we're going to do two things. First, click on VeterinarianID in the table VeterinariansVeterinaryOffices so it will be displayed in the view. Next, click on the line that joins the two tables and then click on the Properties button in the toolbar (see Figure 6-7). As you can see, this brings up a dialog box that gives you the choice of selecting all of the rows from one table or the other (or both). We're going to choose Select All Rows from VeterinaryOffices. This will change the diamond so that it has half of a square on the side toward that table indicating that all rows from that table will be selected. More importantly, it will change the SQL pane to say:

```
SELECT     dbo.VeterinaryOffices.OfficeID, dbo.VeterinaryOffices.OfficeName,
dbo.VeterinariansVeterinaryOffices.VeterinarianID
FROM        dbo.VeterinaryOffices LEFT OUTER JOIN
                    dbo.VeterinariansVeterinaryOffices ON
dbo.VeterinaryOffices.OfficeID = dbo.VeterinariansVeterinaryOffices.OfficeID
```

Running this code will generate the data you see in Table 6-2.

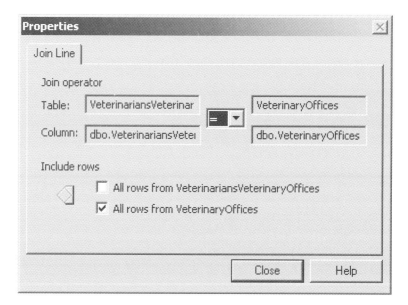

Figure 6-7. Specifying an Outer Join can be accomplished through the property menu of the relationship that joins the two tables.

Table 6-2. The results of a Left Outer Join means that NULL *is used for data that has no match.*

OFFICEID	OFFICENAME	VETERINARIANID
1	Emergency Pet Care of Orinda	NULL
2	Standard Pet Care of Walnut Creek	NULL
3	Emergency Pet Care	1
3	Emergency Pet Care	3
4	Standard Pet Care	2
5	Xavier's Pet—Animal Ready Care	3

Why Is It Called a Left Outer Join?

How can it be a Left Outer Join when the table is on the right side in the Diagram pane? The terms *Left Outer Join* and *Right Outer Join* refer to the order of the tables in the TSQL command. Since VeterinaryOffices is to the left of VeterinariansVeterinaryOffices in reading the TSQL from left to right, which is how TSQL is interpreted. The Left Outer Join specifies that all rows from that table be used.

If you reversed the table order in TSQL and changed *left* to *right* you would still get the same results.

We've got one more step to take to make this a usable view. If you remember from the last chapter, VeterinariansVeterinaryOffices is a junction table designed to relate two tables in a many-to-many relationship. What we need to do is to add the Veterinarians table to the view. Again, we right-click in the Diagram pane and choose Add Table. Because there is a foreign key relationship defined between this table and VeterinariansVeterinaryOffices, it is automatically joined. Right-clicking on the join between the two is a shortcut to the join properties, and you can select from the pop-up menu that you want to have All Rows from Veterinarians. Figure 6-8 shows the result of executing the view.

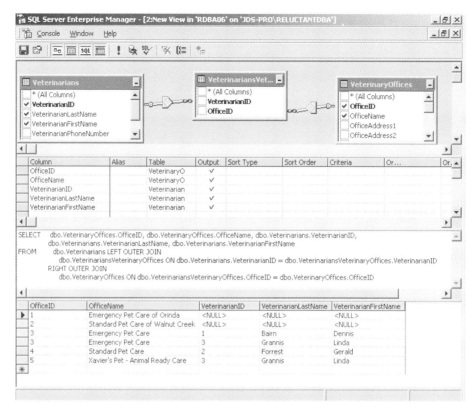

Figure 6-8. Joining three tables together to rejoin data that has a many-to-many relationship.

Do NULL Values Affect Joins?

Most of the tables that have been defined for the sample database contain for-eign key relationships *and* have a constraint on the foreign key column requiring data to be entered. There is one, however, that doesn't. The table Veterinarians has a reference to itself to provide information on Mentoring and that is a handy tool for demonstrating how NULL affects a join.

We're going to create a new view and add the table Veterinarians. Then, once that is in the Diagram pane, we'll add a new table and select Veterinarians again. As you can see in Figure 6-9, the View Designer will add a copy the Veterinarians table to the Diagram pane and rename it to Veterinarians_1. This is also taken care of in the TSQL. If you look closely you'll see that the text after Inner Join is dbo.Veterinarians Veterinarians_1. The View Manager automatically assigns an alias for the table Veterinarians so that it can be referenced correctly.

Reluctant DBA definition of *alias*:

An alias is another name given to an object. Aliases can be used for clarity when two objects of the same name are used in a TSQL statement (such as referencing two copies of the same table). Aliasing is often used for compatibility, to make table or column names "friendlier" or to minimize typing, such as using initials for tables with long names. The latter is probably one of the more common uses.

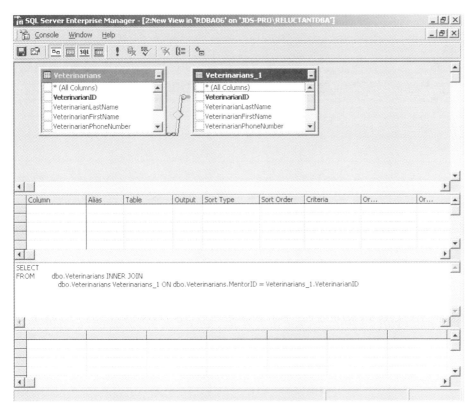

Figure 6-9. When duplicating tables in a view it is necessary to rename one of them. This is taken care of automatically in the View Designer.

Now, let's add the columns of data that need to appear in this view. We want to display the vet's name and the mentor's name. To accomplish this we are going to select the VeterinarianLastName and VeterinarianFirstName from both tables (see Figure 6-10). Because each column must be uniquely identified, View Designer sets the Alias column in the Grid pane to read Expr1 and Expr2 and renames the columns in the SQL pane. These are easy enough to fix. You just update the Grid pane by typing over Expr1 with "MentorLastName" and Expr2 with "MentorFirstName."

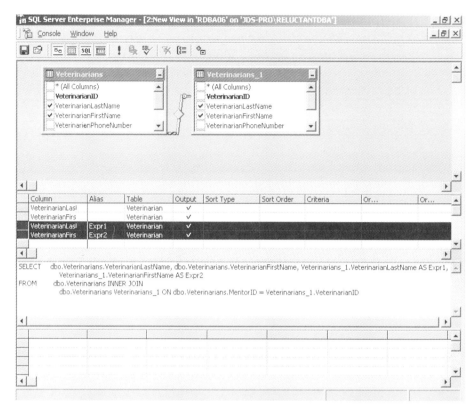

Figure 6-10. If the View Designer encounters duplicate names, it will automatically add a non-descriptive alias for the columns.

There's one last thing that needs to be done to make this view usable. "Veterinarians_1" isn't a very descriptive label. The label "Mentors" would more accurately reflect the role the second reference of Veterinarians is playing. Now, there are two ways to do this change. The hard way is to go into the SQL pane and replace all of the Veterinarians_1 with Mentors. Unfortunately, the SQL pane doesn't have a Ctrl-H (Replace All) function, but there is a simpler way to do this. Click on the Veterinarians_1 table in the Diagram pane and then select the Properties button from the toolbar. You'll get a dialog box that has only one thing you can change, the table's alias. Type in "Mentors" and press the Enter key. Voila, the name is applied throughout the SQL pane. Your code should read:

```
SELECT    dbo.Veterinarians.VeterinarianLastName,
dbo.Veterinarians.VeterinarianFirstName, Mentors.VeterinarianLastName AS
MentorLastName, Mentors.VeterinarianFirstName AS MentorFirstName
FROM  dbo.Veterinarians INNER JOIN dbo.Veterinarians Mentors ON
dbo.Veterinarians.MentorID = Mentors.VeterinarianID
```

If you execute this view, you'll get three records back. That's because three vets have mentors assigned. The vets that do not appear have a MentorID of NULL. Since NULL means no value assigned, they can't be matched up in this JOIN.

How Do I Get All of the Data?

OK, some day you're going to need to see *all* of the data, not just the ones that match on one or the other tables. Go back to the properties of the link between the two tables and check both Select All Rows from Veterinarians and Select All Rows from Mentors. Now you're going to be selecting all data from one side of the join along with all the matching records from the table on the other (outer) side of the join. Table 6-3 lists the values in the table for VeterinarianID and MentorID. Can you guess what the results of selecting all records from both tables will be?

Table 6-3. VeterinarianID and MentorID Columns from Veterinarians Table

VETERINARIANID	MENTORID
1	NULL
2	2
3	2
4	NULL
5	1

Remember, we're creating this Full Outer Join based on the MentorID joined to the VeterinarianID, so the resulting data will have all of the matching combinations of these values. If you guessed twenty-five rows (five by five), then you're on the right track. But that would be a Cross Join, a subject we're not going to cover in depth but will touch upon toward the end of this chapter in "What on Earth Does *= Mean?" Instead, the Full Outer Join will return eight rows, as shown in Table 6-4.

If we did an Outer Join that selected all rows from the Mentors alias then we would get six rows, those that have been italicized in the table. That's because the three rows that have NULL for the first two columns represent veterinarians who are not mentoring anyone and the other three rows represent the mentoring relationships that exist. If we had used an Outer Join that selected all rows from Veterinarians then we would have gotten five rows, one for each veterinarian. The Full Outer Join performs both Outer Joins and then removes duplicate rows, leaving us with these eight rows.

Table 6-4. Results of the Full Outer Join of VeterinarianIDs and MentorIDs

VETERINARIANID	MENTORID	VETERINARIANID2	MENTORID2
NULL	*NULL*	*3*	*2*
NULL	*NULL*	*4*	*NULL*
NULL	*NULL*	*5*	*1*
1	NULL	NULL	NULL
2	*1*	*1*	*NULL*
3	2	2	1
4	NULL	NULL	NULL
5	1	1	NULL

How Do I Join More Joined Tables to Already Joined Tables?

That sounds like a mouthful, but when a database has been normalized it often requires that you join multiple tables together in a daisy-chain fashion. Let's say you wanted a list of all of the veterinary offices with the specialties that the vets at that office have. The path from VeterinaryOffices to VeterinarianSpecialties will take five tables (see Figure 6-11).

Although this seems complex, it really is straightforward, especially since there are foreign key relationships defined between all of the tables. If you were trying to do this view by hand, it is quite possible you could end up with one that would have the wrong join. It's even possible that you could end up with a lot of unnecessary data. On a small set of data like what's included in these tables that wouldn't be much of a problem; but on a larger data set you could end up with a monstrous set of data that was absolutely useless—or worse it could "hamstring" the server for an indefinite period.

The key to getting a complex join like this correct is to be methodical. Add and join the tables one at a time, verifying the data looks the way you want it to, especially if you are going to be mixing Inner and Outer Joins. In this view there are three inner joins linking VeterinarianSpecialties to VeterinarianVeterinarianSpecialties and VeterinarianVeterinarianSpecialties to Veterinarians and Veterinarians to VeterinariansVeterinaryOffices. The fourth join is an outer join, joining VeterinariansVeterinaryOffices to VeterinaryOffices, selecting all offices whether they have any veterinarians or not. By starting with VeterinarianSpecialties and VeterinarianVeterinarianSpecialties it is easy to add the tables one at a time and ensure the view is built correctly. If the tables already have foreign key relationships defined, your job will be much easier.

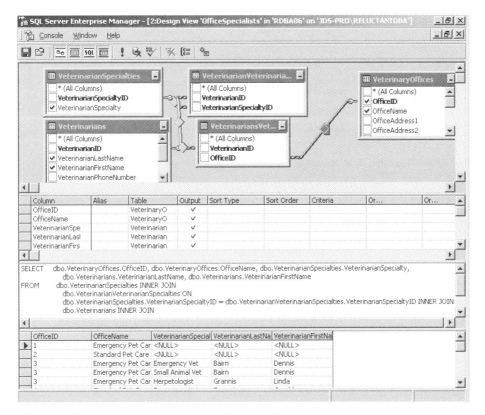

Figure 6-11. It's a lot easier to join multiple tables together through the View Designer.

How Do I Summarize Data?

Raw data isn't very useful for some things. At some point in time, someone is going to want to summarize the data in the database. Fortunately that's easy to accomplish, and the View Designer has the functionality to create these types of views.

We're going to create an extremely simple summary view that counts the number of pets that each owner has in the database. We're going to create a new view and add owners and pets to it. Then we're going to check the OwnerLast-Name, OwnerFirstName in the Owners table and PetID in the Pets table. At this point the view is no different from any of the other views we've created in this chapter. Now, however, we're going to press the Group By button in the toolbar (the next to the last one on the left). That adds a new column to the Grid pane, Group By. As you can see in Figure 6-12, this column contains a drop-down box populated with choices we can use for how to define this column. Every column in a Summary view must be either a part of the grouping or a summary function. Table 6-5 lists the most commonly used Summary options you have for a column. Some of the options are only available for specific data types. After all, how can you add up a column of names? We're going to select COUNT for PetName, so we can see how many pets each Owner has.

Table 6-5. Common Summary Functions

NAME	DESCRIPTION	LIMITATIONS
AVG	Averages a column of numbers.	Not applicable to character data types.
COUNT	Returns a count of the rows.	When no column is specified, returns a count of *all* rows, even those with NULL values. If a column is specified that contains NULLs then the number will exclude NULL values and give you a message explaining that it has ignored data that contained NULL.
COUNT_BIG	Same as count but uses the BIGINT data type.	—
MAX	Returns the largest value found.	Excludes NULL values. When used on character data types returns highest string as though sorted alphabetically, for Dates the most recent.
MIN	Returns the smallest value found.	Excludes NULL values. When used on character data types returns lowest string as though sorted alphabetically, for Dates returns earliest date.
SUM	Adds up all values found.	Excludes NULL values and not applicable to character data types.
STDEV	Returns the standard deviation found in the column.	Excludes NULL values and not applicable to character data types.
STDEVP	Returns the standard deviation for the population found in the column.	Excludes NULL values and not applicable to character data types.
VAR	Returns the statistical variations found in the column.	Excludes NULL values and not applicable to character data types.
VARP	Returns the statistical variations for the population found in the column.	Excludes NULL values and not applicable to character data types.

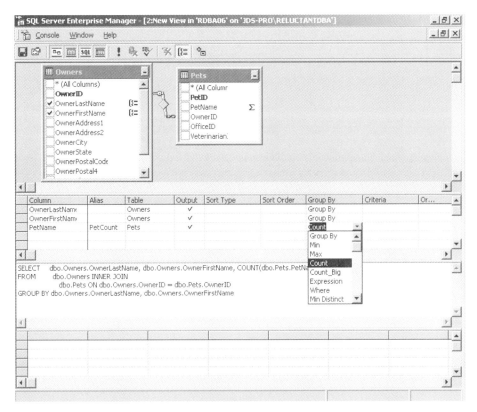

Figure 6-12. Creating a Summary view is as simple as selecting the summary function from the Group By drop-down list.

Before we execute this view, there are a couple of other things that need to be done. Summary views are *grouped* by the columns specified but are not *sorted* that way unless specified. We're going to sort the results by OwnerLastName, OwnerFirstName. Then we're going to execute this view and wait. And wait. And wait some more. Once the data comes back it's fairly obvious why we had to wait: the first person in the list has 768 pets!

Is there something wrong with this view? Nope. The Pets table has been loaded with a lot of duplicate data specifically for Chapter 7, "The Power of Indexing." By the time we've finished the next chapter, this view will be lightning fast. But an index isn't the only thing that impacts performance. Let's take a quick look at the how table order can have an impact.

The Owners table has 2,359 rows, and Pets has 1,527,296. When we built this view, we selected Owners first because it was first alphabetically and, in this case, it works well because it is the smallest table. In Query Analyzer, executing this view returns all of the data in five seconds.

If the only thing we changed was the order of the tables, then there is a dramatic impact on the query. The following code takes fifteen seconds to return the same data! That's a dramatic difference. So always join the smaller tables to the larger tables.

```
SELECT    TOP 100 PERCENT dbo.Owners.OwnerLastName, dbo.Owners.OwnerFirstName,
COUNT(dbo.Pets.PetName) AS PetCount
FROM          dbo.Pets INNER JOIN
                    dbo.Owners ON dbo.Pets.OwnerID = dbo.Owners.OwnerID
GROUP BY dbo.Owners.OwnerLastName, dbo.Owners.OwnerFirstName
ORDER BY dbo.Owners.OwnerLastName, dbo.Owners.OwnerFirstName
```

When the TOP keyword isn't present, the SELECT statement will return all rows that match the various criteria in the WHERE and join clauses. But what if you don't want *all* of the data?

You can use TOP and BOTTOM to limit how much data gets returned. Unfortunately, they need to process through the whole data set before they can limit the data. Below you have two TSQL statements. The only difference between the two is that the first wants 100 percent of the data and the second wants only the first 100 rows. When SQL Server processes the first one, it joins the tables, sorts the result, and returns everything. When the second one is processed, however, SQL Server does everything the same until the last step. Then it deals out 100 rows from the top of the sorted results and returns only them. So, although TOP and BOTTOM limit your data, they don't necessarily limit the amount of work that needs to be done.

```
SELECT    TOP 100 PERCENT dbo.Owners.OwnerLastName, dbo.Owners.OwnerFirstName,
          COUNT(dbo.Pets.PetName) AS PetCount
FROM      dbo.Pets INNER JOIN dbo.Owners ON dbo.Pets.OwnerID =
dbo.Owners.OwnerID
GROUP BY dbo.Owners.OwnerLastName, dbo.Owners.OwnerFirstName
ORDER BY PetCount
SELECT    TOP 100  dbo.Owners.OwnerLastName, dbo.Owners.OwnerFirstName,
          COUNT(dbo.Pets.PetName) AS PetCount
FROM      dbo.Pets INNER JOIN dbo.Owners ON dbo.Pets.OwnerID =
dbo.Owners.OwnerID
GROUP BY dbo.Owners.OwnerLastName, dbo.Owners.OwnerFirstName
ORDER BY PetCount
```

Now, if you were to modify these two TSQL statements to ORDER BY Owner-LastName, OwnerFirstName instead of PetCount, you *would* see a quicker result. That's because SQL Server will sort the Owners table and join the top 100 rows from that to the Pets table. Because the initial result set is smaller, the join is more efficient.

> *Reluctant DBA* definition of TOP and BOTTOM:
> TOP and BOTTOM are keywords used in SELECT to limit the amount of data that will be returned. They may or may not impact the amount of processing that needs to be done to return data.

What on Earth Does *= Mean?

Back in the old days, joins were written somewhat differently. Instead of using the word JOIN, the join was performed in the WHERE clause. For instance, the view that showed Mentors would be written like this:

```
SELECT     dbo.Veterinarians.VeterinarianLastName,
dbo.Veterinarians.VeterinarianFirstName, Mentors.VeterinarianLastName AS
MentorLastName,  Mentors.VeterinarianFirstName AS MentorFirstName,
dbo.Veterinarians.MentorID, dbo.Veterinarians.VeterinarianID
FROM         dbo.Veterinarians, dbo.Veterinarians Mentors
WHERE dbo.Veterinarians.MentorID = Mentors.VeterinarianID
```

The join is actually defined with WHERE MentorID = VeterinarianID. Because the equals sign was used, this is an Inner Join.

If you wanted to create an Outer Join, you would use an asterisk (*) to indicate which table would give you all of the rows. To get a Left Outer Join you would use the following code:

```
SELECT     dbo.Veterinarians.VeterinarianLastName,
dbo.Veterinarians.VeterinarianFirstName, Mentors.VeterinarianLastName AS
MentorLastName,  Mentors.VeterinarianFirstName AS MentorFirstName,
dbo.Veterinarians.MentorID, dbo.Veterinarians.VeterinarianID
FROM         dbo.Veterinarians, dbo.Veterinarians Mentors
WHERE dbo.Veterinarians.MentorID *= Mentors.VeterinarianID
```

This would list all of the Veterinarians whether they had a mentor or not.

CAUTION *You should* not *use this format for making join. It is confusing and easy to make mistakes! I'm including it solely because you might encounter something written this way and will need to understand it. I highly recommend modifying it to use the Inner Join and Outer Join syntax. Another good reason to avoid this kind of syntax is because of an expensive error you can create. If the* WHERE *clause isn't specified, you will get a Cartesian table, a one-for-one match of every row in one table with every row in the other table. Such a join of Owners and Pets would create a data set with 3,602,891,264 rows!*

 TIP *Microsoft has been threatening to stop supporting this method of making joins since 6.5, but it still hasn't. Fortunately, it is easy to modify any TSQL you encounter in this format. Just start the View Manager and then cut and paste the old-style code into the SQL pane. The View Manager* automagically *reformats it into ANSI-92 format!*

Last Words

In this chapter you've been introduced to views, or virtual tables referenced exactly like a table. Views are handy for restricting access to rows or columns within a table and for providing an easy way to reference data split into multiple tables as though it were in one. You've also learned how the View Designer in the EM is a handy way to create joins and why you should specify the smallest table first in your joins.

In the next chapter we're going to look at how indexing will speed up data access. We'll also discuss how indexing affects views and how an indexed view can affect performance.

Resources

- "No Result Set From Tables Joined with Outer Then Inner Join" (Knowledge Base Article ID Q108893):
  `http://support.microsoft.com/support/kb/articles/Q108/8/93.asp`

- "Handy Utility Refreshes Views" by Ken Spencer, *SQL Server Magazine*, December 1999:
  `http://www.sqlmag.com/Articles/Index.cfm?ArticleID=7816`

CHAPTER 7

The Power of Indexing

Knowing you have the book you want does you no good if you can't find where you have put it. —Anonymous

LIBRARIES ARE A GOOD EXAMPLE of a database because they are designed to make the search and retrieval of books easier and more efficient, as mentioned in Chapter 1, "Where Did Databases Come From?" In this chapter we are going to use libraries to illustrate how indexing works. My own personal library is a modest affair of a couple hundred books crammed onto shelves in no particular order. I know, approximately, where any book I might need is located. If I don't know where a book is, it doesn't take too long to scan all of the titles to find it.

Compare that to the Library of Congress. According to its Web site, the Library of Congress preserves a collection of more than 121 *million* items. If these books weren't organized in some fashion, then you could spend a lifetime searching for a book you might never find! Obviously, some standardized means of finding a book is necessary.

 NOTE   *This chapter relies heavily on the **RDBA07** database. You'll find instructions for installing that database in Appendix A, "How Do I Load the Examples?" This chapter also makes use of the Query Analyzer (QA). If you haven't used that tool before, don't worry; it's covered in depth in Chapter 8, "Introduction to Query Analyzer."*

How Does Indexing My Data Speed Up Access?

Reluctant DBA definition of an *index*:
An index is a sorted subset of the fields that make up a table and includes a pointer to where each row that makes up the rest of the row of data is located.

Let's take a brief look at how non-fiction data in a library is stored. Each book is grouped into a broad category such as Science or Biography. All of the science books are stored in one area of the library and all of the biographies are in another area. Each category is further broken down into sub-categories, such as Chemistry and Physics sub-categories for the science books. These sub-categories each have their own sub-categories. This continues down into several more sub-categories until there are no more sub-categories needed.

Alas, Poor Card Catalogs, I Knew Them Well, Horatio. . .

Card catalogs aren't really going away, but they have changed dramatically in the last decade. Every library used to have a collection of small drawers storing a collection of 3×5 cards, hence the name *card catalog*. Many libraries still have a small set of these drawers, but its functionality is limited because the data has been put into a large database. People looking for a particular book can now use computer terminals to access the data. But even with online access to the data, the card catalog is still used like an index to the various physical books in the library.

In addition to being physically stored on a shelf somewhere in the library, the location of a book is also recorded in the card catalog, along with several other pieces of information, including the author and the title of the book, both handy pieces of information to look up books. Once you have the reference number of a book, you could use it to find the book within the library. Let's say you wanted to find a copy of *Business @ the Speed of Thought* by Bill Gates. Looking in the catalog, you would find the reference number—let's say it's 658.4038.

To find this book, you would first check a map that would show where the 600 series of books (the Technology category) are located. Within that section of the library, there are several bookcases. Along the ends of each set of shelves there would be a listing of the range of books contained on each bookcase. One bookcase should have a set of books that would contain the book with the reference number 658.4038. Once you've narrowed your search down to that bookcase, you can check the left-most book on each shelf to see if it is less than or equal to 658.4038. Once you find the shelf you can then start scanning to the right to find the exact book for which you're looking.

Indexing in SQL Server works much the same way. An index is a collection of pointers to the location of the physical row of data for which you're searching. Each row of physical data can be compared to a book. Taking the comparison further, each row is stored on a *page* of disk space. If the table contains fixed-length columns (all books are the same size), then the number of rows (books on a shelf) that will fit on each page is predefined. If you are using variable-length columns (different-sized books), then the amount of data (the number of books) that can fit on each page will vary depending on the size of all of the data elements of each row.

To carry the analogy one more step, each page is part of an *extent*—a group of eight pages. An extent is similar to a bookcase containing eight shelves of books. When people speak about extents, they generally are referring to *uniform extents* and *mixed extents*. Uniform extents are those where all eight pages are for data related to the same object, much like an entire bookcase in the library might contain chemistry books. Mixed extents contain pages for different objects, much like a bookcase that has the top four shelves filled with chemistry books and the bottom four with physics books.

To complicate matters just a little more, indices are stored in the exact same manner as the physical data rows, in pages and extents, with the same limitations on how much data fits on a page.

Now that we've defined some of the basics of an index, let's see how to use them.

How Does an Index Help?

We created an aggregate view that was somewhat slow toward the end of Chapter 6, "What Is a View?" You'll find that view, called OwnerPetCount, in **RDBA07**. If you start up the QA and enter SELECT * FROM OwnerPetCount, it takes 16 seconds to get all of the data back. That's because SQL Server scans the entire Pets table, sorts it by OwnerID, and then creates a summary table containing the OwnerID and the number of rows. That table is then joined with Owners and the results returned. To put this in terms similar to the library example, it's like looking at all 1.5 million books in the Pets section, counting up the books by author. That's a *lot* of work.

Let's take the first step toward improving this process. Go into the EM, open the **RDBA07** database and the tables collection, and then right-click on the Pets table. From the pop-up menu, select All Tasks Manage Indexes (Figure 7-1). This brings up Select New.[1]

---

[1]   Whenever SQL Server actually uses the term *indexes* in a menu, I will use that term. Everywhere else, I'll use the term *indices* to indicate the plural of *index*. Call me old-school, but that's how I learned it, and it's a hard habit to break.

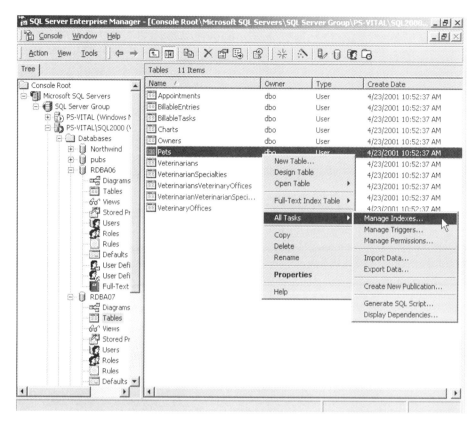

Figure 7-1. You can create indices from a pop-up menu in the Enteprise Manager (EM).

This brings up a dialog box with a number of options (see Figure 7-2). Creating an index is as easy as giving it a name, selecting the column or columns to index, and pressing OK. For this example we're going to call the index "ixPetsOwnerID" and select the OwnerID column. Then we'll press OK, and the database will create the index. This will take a couple of minutes because the index covers a lot of records. Before we get into the options available in setting up an index, let's see if the index helps.

Did That Index Really Help?

You have to be careful when testing indices because indexing isn't the *only* way SQL Server has to speed up data access. Another way SQL Server will improve performance is to cache data. This means that you could see an improvement in performance just because SQL Server already had the data cached in memory. To prevent this from happening when you are trying to test index performance, you can issue a command from the QA to clear the cache. DBCC FREEPROCCACHE will clear the cache and let you judge the effectiveness of a new index.

However, you don't want to run this on a production server. DBCC FREEPROCCACHE clears the cache of *everything*, meaning that stored procedures will be recompiled and execution plans re-created, which will slow down the processing on the server.

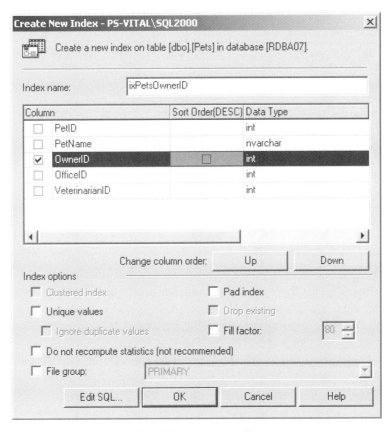

Figure 7-2. There are many options for creating indices.

Go back to the QA and re-run the `SELECT * FROM OwnerPetCount` and watch as it finishes in three seconds, less than one-fourth of the time! That's because SQL Server no longer needs to sort the Pets table by OwnerID; it can use the existing index. That's how easy it is to create an index, but the key to performance improvements is creating the *right* index.

How Do Indices Work?

As a Reluctant DBA, you are probably willing to let SQL Server handle many tasks for you. Indexing, however, is one area where you need to understand how SQL Server is using indices to create effective ones.

That's because proper indexing can help make your SQL Server hum along like a finely tuned sports car while improper indexing can hurt performance drastically. SQL Server uses a B-tree format for indexing. You can find resources at the end of this chapter should you desire to dive into the more technical aspects of a B-tree, but let's look at a general introduction now.

B-trees are so called either because they are "balanced" or because R. Bayer introduced them in 1972, no one is quite sure which. The theory behind B-trees involves a lot of heavy mathematics, but the concept is fairly simple.

B-trees are made up of nodes. Each node contains either pointers to other nodes or it contains pointers to actual data. Each node also has a physical limit to how much data it can contain. When an attempt is made to add more data to a node than it can hold, the node is split in two and the data added to either the old node (which gets roughly half the data) or the new node (which gets remainder). Unlike binary trees, which can grow to be quite deep, the B-tree is wide and shallow.

The B-tree has one node specified as the entry point (referred to as the *root node*). Under that node is a level of nodes that contain pointers to other nodes. These nodes may have a similar level of nodes under them. At the bottom of the B-tree, however, are nodes that contain only data links. These are called *leaves*. Although this is a generalized concept, clustered indices and non-clustered indices implement this differently, but we'll cover this in more detail as we go.

Having a general idea of how the B-tree works is important because every time you insert, delete, or update a row, SQL Server needs to maintain the B-tree structure. Usually it walks the nodes to find the leaf it needs to update, but in some cases SQL Server may find that the leaf it needs to update has no room left to store a new entry. In that case, it takes the leaf and splits it into two new leaves, each one containing half of the data. This necessitates updating the nodes that point to these leaves or, possibly, splitting that node in two as well. A poorly indexed database can spend almost as much time updating the indices on a table as it does updating the table itself. Now that you have an idea of why incorrect indexing can lead to problems, let's look at how to build good indices, starting with determining an index's size.

Does Size Matter?

The smaller the index data size is, the more rows can fit on a single leaf. The more rows on a leaf, the quicker SQL Server can access the data because it spends more time accessing data and less time getting the next leaf. You might easily assume that indexing a single INT column of 4 bytes means you could fit 2,000 of them on each leaf.[2]

The only problem with tis assumption is that SQL Server stores the value plus a value called the RowID (and internal counter used by SQL Server). The RowID is 8 bytes in length, which means wee need to add 8 to the size of the column, giving us a total of 12 bytes. Now we can take the total size and divide it into the 8000 bytes we started with, and if you have roughly 600+ rows that can be inserted. Remember, SQL Server can't split the 23 bytes, so if there were 9 bytes left on a page, the next entry would have to go onto a new page. This changes if the table being indexed has a clustered index.

What Is a Clustered Index?

> *Reluctant DBA* definition of *clustered index*:
> A clustered index physically sorts the table according to the index. The leaves of a clustered index, instead of containing pointers to the physical location of the data in the table, *are* the physical location of the table. Including all of the data for that row in the index eliminates the need to walk through both the index and the table.

Because a clustered index physically sorts the table, you can only have one clustered index for each table. Clustered indices are usually created for primary keys. In fact, if a clustered index doesn't exist on a table at the time the primary key is defined, the primary key is clustered by default.

Clustered indices have some benefits that aren't obvious at first glance. It makes sense that they would be more efficient than a non-clustered index because SQL Server doesn't need to read the table to get the data it wants, so does it make sense for other indices to point to the clustered index value instead of the RowID? Let's find out.

Let's take a look at what SQL Server would need to do if it used the RowID as the pointer in a non-clustered index on a table that has a clustered index defined. Every time that data is added to the table, the clustered index could change.

Let's take a look at what would happen to a non-clustered index on a table that has a clustered index associated with it if SQL Server used the RowID in the non-clustered index instead of the clustered index value. When a row is added to a table that has clustered index, it is possible that the new record would require

---

[2]   Each leaf, like all other objects in SQL Server 2000, is stored on a physical page having a size of 8192 bytes. The first 8000 bytes is used for data. The remaining 192 bytes are used for housekeeping.

a reordering of the table. When the table gets reordered, the RowIDs change, requiring that all of the indices get updated to reflect the new RowIDs. As you might imagine, that would lead to a lot of excess disk reads and writes. By using the clustered index value *instead* of the RowID, reordering the physical file doesn't require any changes to the non-clustered indices on a table. This results in faster processing on the table.

It *can* also result in smaller indices. Take Pets for instance. Because it has a primary key defined, it has a clustered index defined on PetId, an INT. An index for OwnerID on this table would only need to store 8 bytes (4 bytes for the OwnerID and 4 bytes for the PetId) instead of 12 bytes (4 bytes for the OwnerID and 8 bytes for the RowID). And the more data you can fit onto an index leaf, the faster the data will be returned.

What if the Clustered Index Size Is Larger Than 8 Bytes?

Neither primary keys nor clustered indices are limited to using INT or BIGINT datatypes. Invariably you will find yourself using values that take up more than 8 bytes for your clustered indices. That *does* mean that non-clustered indices on that table will be larger than they would be without the clustered index. However, that is not a bad thing. The purpose behind a clustered index is to speed up access to the data. Even when the clustered index value is larger than 8 bytes, access to the data based on that key is faster than access without the clustered index and you still get all the benefits of reduced management on your non-clustered indices.

How Much Space Does a Clustered Index Take Up?

This is a legitimate question. In addition to the data, a clustered index adds nodes that contain index row, which in turn point to the leaves that contain the data, where a table without a clustered index would have, in effect, only leaves. If you had a table that already had data in it and you wanted to add a clustered index, you would find the end result would be a table about 20 percent larger than the original ($1.2 \times [data\ size]$). Thus a one-megabyte table would take up about 1.2 megabytes.

By the way, you need to have 1.2 megabytes available in your database to add the primary key. Because SQL Server needs to physically rearrange the table, it effectively creates a new table with the primary key, moves the old data into the new table, and then drops the old table.

Another thing to take into account when creating a clustered index on an existing table is the time it will take to create. Not only will the table be rebuilt into the clustered index, but also all of the indices that exist on that table will be rebuilt to point to the clustered index value instead of the physical location. Thus, when creating new indices on a table, it makes sense to create the clustered index first.

When re-building clustered indices, keep in mind that the table's size can have a significant impact on performance, so changes should take place "off peak" so as not to impact users. In addition to this, any non-clustered indices that exist will be re-built as well. Changing clustered indexes may also impact RowIDs, which of course impacts non-clustered indices.

What Is Fragmentation?

> *Reluctant DBA* definition of *fragmentation*:
> A table is fragmented when it has empty holes in the pages and extents that it takes up.

Fragmentation occurs as a result of page splits and deletion of rows of data. This could happen if a large number of rows are deleted. Because primary keys are not supposed to be reused, new data is added to the physical end of the table, leaving a hole that slows down accessing the data. To resolve fragmentation, you can rebuild the clustered index. For more information on this, see "How Do I Create a Maintenance Plan (and Why Do I Need One)?" in Chapter 3, "How Do I Visually Manage Objects?" This type of hole is not to be confused with the holes you might leave on purpose when you create an index, those are called *fill factor* of an index.

What Is a Fill Factor?

> *Reluctant DBA* definition of *fill factor*:
> The fill factor determines how much free space is created within the leaves of an index when it is created.

The fill factor is used to specify how "full" each leaf of the B-tree should be when the index is created. Let's say we had an index that could hold 100 rows of data on each leaf. When SQL Server needs to add another row to a full leaf, that leaf will be split into two leaves with approximately 50 rows in each one, and the new row added to whichever leaf is most appropriate. The splitting of the leaf (and possibly the nodes pointing to the leaf) takes more time than just adding a new data row.

This is where the fill factor comes in. The fill factor dictates how full the index page will be as a percentage. In other words, a fill factor of 50 means that the page would be filled to 50-percent capacity, thus leaving room for additional rows of data. Let's go back to the index that holds 100 rows per leaf. If the table had 1,000 records and we created an index, it makes sense to assume the index would have 10 leaves. The problem with building an index this way is that the first new row we add will cause a split in a leaf in the index, leaving us with 9 leaves that are full, 1 leaf of 50 rows, and 1 leaf of 51 rows. Even worse, it's possible that the first 10 inserts could hit in such a way as to split every one of the original leaves. Not only is this inefficient in terms of maintaining the index, but it doubled the number of leaves by increasing the number of records by only 1 percent! This, of course, leads to fragmentation. Can you say, "Give me more hard drives, please!"

If, instead of filling the pages completely, SQL Server left some room on each leaf for growth, then adding 10 rows shouldn't create 10 splits. This can easily be accomplished by specifying a fill factor of 90. That means that each leaf would be filled only 90-percent full, leaving room for growth.

 NOTE *Fill factors are used only when the index is created. The whole purpose behind the fill factor is to make the database more efficient. If it were forced to maintain the fill factor, then leaves would get split more often (at 90-percent full instead of 100 percent), resulting in more nodes to be processed to find the data. Because reads in a database typically outnumber the number of writes, anything that can be done to speed up reads is a good thing, and filling as many leaves as possible to 100 percent is the most efficient way to use an index.*

What Happens If We Don't Specify a Fill Factor?

If you don't specify the fill factor, then SQL Server uses the default. Although you can change SQL Servers default setting, it's not recommended because you can always change the fill factor when you create an index. So what does Microsoft think the best value for the fill factor is?

Zero. Yes, the fill factor can be any value between 1 and 100, but Microsoft says the default fill factor is 0. That's because a fill factor of 0 is just like a fill factor of 100—well, almost. Don't believe me? See what Microsoft has to say:

The default for fill factor is 0; legal values range from 0 through 100. A fill factor value of 0 does not mean that pages are 0 percent full. It is treated similarly to a fill factor value of 100 in that SQL Server creates clustered indexes with full data pages and non-clustered indexes with full leaf pages. It is different from 100 in that SQL Server leaves some space within the upper level of the index tree.

—SQL Server Books On Line, Fill Factor Option

In other words, SQL Server's default fill factor of 0 fills the leaves completely and leaves room in the nodes so that a node split isn't necessary when an insert takes place.

In general, you can leave the fill factor set to the default of 0. There aren't many situations where you'll have to change the fill factor. An exception would be if you have a large table that you know is going to be read-only, you can specify a fill factor of 100. That way you know that you will have the most efficient index built because there will be no empty space and, because the data is read-only, you don't need to worry about node or leaf splits.

When creating tables that are expected to grow rapidly early on, it's wise to create some cushion in the form of a smaller fill factor. Later as the table stabilizes, the clustered index can be re-built using 0 or something close to 100, and so on. This can really take some load off a server early on.

What Is Selectivity?

Reluctant DBA definition of *selectivity*:
Selectivity is the amount of uniqueness in an index. The more unique hits per the total number of rows, the more effective the index and the higher the selectivity is.

Let's take a look at the Pets table, which has 1,527,296 rows and 3,817 unique names. That means that, on average, each unique name averages roughly 0.25 percent of the rows in the table. That makes this a good candidate for an index. OwnerID has 2,539 unique values, meaning that each unique value averages 0.17 percent of the table. In other words, PetName has higher selectivity than OwnerID, though both columns appear to have enough unique values to make a good index. The primary key, because it must be unique, will provide the highest selectivity on any table.

Why is this important? The whole purpose of an index is to speed up finding specific data. When SQL Server is looking to find data *and* it has an index that helps limit what it has to look for, it performs remarkably well. If the selectivity isn't high enough, SQL Server might not use the index at all, determining that the costs of walking through the index and then coming back to get data out of the table is higher than the cost of performing a table scan. We'll cover one of the ways to see whether SQL Server is using the indices you've created in "How Do I Create an Index?"

How Does SQL Server Determine Selectivity for a Column?

SQL Server determines selectivity by keeping a set of statistics on the column or columns of an index once that index has been created. When you create an index, SQL Server stores information about the selectivity. Then, when a certain percentage of rows have been inserted/updated/deleted, SQL Server updates this selectivity statistic by using a statistical sample of the data in the table. This functionality is Auto Update Statistics and wasn't available in earlier versions.

However, it is also possible to create statistics on non-indexed columns and see the results to determine whether an index should be created. This is done through the use of two SQL commands: CREATE STATISTICS and DBCC SHOW_STATISTICS.[3] CREATE STATISTICS, as the name implies, creates a statistical sample based on parameters. This is the syntax for CREATE STATISTICS:

```
CREATE STATISTICS statistics_name
ON { table | view } ( column [ ,...n ] )
[ WITH
[ [ FULLSCAN
| SAMPLE number { PERCENT | ROWS } ] [ , ] ]
[ NORECOMPUTE ]
    ]
```

This is what the options mean:

- statistics_name: A set of statistics is an object, like any other, so it must have a unique name. You could name all of your statistics with an "sts" prefix, for example.

- Table or view name: This is the name of the table or view you want to create the statistics on.

- Column(s): Using multiple columns not only gives you the overall selectivity but shows you how columns get increasingly selective as they are added together. You can have up to sixteen columns, just like a real index.

- FULLSCAN/SAMPLE: There are two ways to create statistics. They can be created on a full scan of the table or they can be created on a statistical sampling. Any table less than 8MB will have a full scan done regardless.

---

[3] The QA provides a tool for managing statistics, and you can use that for creating statistics (from within the QA, select Tools ➤ Manage Statistics). You cannot, however, view those statistics from the tool, so I'm going to take you through the SQL code necessary to create and view statistics.

- SAMPLE PERCENT/ROWS: If you decide to sample the data rather than perform a full-blown table-scan, then you can specify whether you want to sample 1 to 100 PERCENT or any number of ROWS.

- NORECOMPUTE: Don't use this! This option exists for backward compatibility. It will not keep the statistics up-to-date, and out-of-date statistics can lead to poor performance. In fact, you shouldn't use this option even on a read-only table for two reasons. First, if you allow SQL Server to RECOMPUTE statistics, it won't happen until the data in the table actually changes. Second, read-only tables rarely are.

DBCC Show_Statistics, on the other hand, takes only a table or view name and the name of the statistics object. Let's take a look at using these commands and what they tell us. The ShowStatistics.SQL script in the "\Chapter07" directory on the CD has the following commands in it:

```
CREATE STATISTICS stsOwnerID ON Pets (OwnerID) WITH fullscan
GO
dbcc show_statistics (Pets, stsOwnerID)
go
drop statistics Pets.stsOwnerID
go
```

What this set of TSQL commands will do is to create a histogram of statistics for the column OwnerID in Pets and then display the statistics. At the end of the code, we are dropping the statistics because statistics, although not an index, still have the overhead of maintenance. If they aren't being used, why keep them around? After running these commands we get three tables of results, shown in Tables 7-1, 7-2, and 7-3.

What Is a Histogram?

Histograms are not the things in pollen that cause you to sneeze. A *histogram* is a mathematical way to represent how data is distributed. The histogram that SQL Server creates for index effectiveness takes the data spread across various leaves of the B-tree and determines how much unique data there is, how quickly could the data be reached, and whether the data is too skewed by not containing enough unique rows.

It does this by splitting the data into bins with an upper and lower boundary, then separates the data elements into those parts, and displays information related to how the data was separated.

Table 7-1. Results of Statistics Gathering

UPDATED	ROWS	ROWS SAMPLED	STEPS	DENSITY	AVERAGE KEY LENGTH
Apr 29 2001 5:14PM	1527296	1527296	173	4.3160061E-4	8.0

This first table has some general information related to the statistics. Updated tells you when the statistics were gathered. Rows indicates the total number of rows in the table. Rows Sampled is the number of rows actually used for gathering statistics. Because we requested a full scan, Rows and Rows Sampled are the same. The Steps column indicates the number of distribution steps. Density indicates the selectivity of the first index column, with lower densities being preferred. Average Key Length is just that, the average length of the key. You'll notice that it's 8 bytes even though OwnerID is a 4-byte INT datatype. That's because Pets has a 4-byte PetId for the primary key and that primary key is stored in a clustered index, so SQL Server would store both the OwnerID and PetId in the index to be able to find the data. This table of statistics is maintained only on the first column in a multi-column index.

> *Reluctant DBA* definition of *distribution steps*:
> Distribution steps indicate the number of bins that the data has been split into for the histogram.

Table 7-2. Selectivity Results of Statistics Gathering

ALL DENSITY	AVERAGE LENGTH	COLUMNS
4.2390744E-4	4.0	OwnerID
6.5475194E-7	8.0	OwnerID, PetID

This second set of data is related to how valuable this index would be for use in a query and shows how the selectivity changes as you get further into the columns that make up the key. All Density reflects the selectivity for this column and is displayed using Scientific Notation. The lower this number is, the better the selectivity. You'll notice that the second row shows a smaller number (0.00000065475194) than the first row (0.00042390744), meaning the combination of columns is more selective than the first column. The second column shows the average length of the key, 4 bytes for OwnerID and 8 bytes for OwnerID and PetID. The last column tells you which columns were included in generating these numbers.

Table 7-3. First Eight Rows (of 173) Representing the Histogram

RANGE_HI_KEY	RANGE_ROWS	EQ_ROWS	DISTINCT_RANGE_ROWS	AVG_RANGE_ROWS
1	0.0	767.0	0	0.0
21	11007.0	1024.0	19	579.36841
33	6912.0	1024.0	10	627.36365
46	6400.0	1024.0	12	533.33331
59	5632.0	1024.0	11	469.33334
78	10240.0	256.0	17	567.88892
90	5632.0	1024.0	11	512.0
109	12800.0	256.0	18	711.11107

Table 7-3 represents the actual histogram. It will have n-rows of data where *n* is the number in the Steps column from the first set of data, 173 rows in this case. Range_Hi_Key shows the upper bound for the histogram step. Range_Rows shows the number of rows from the sample that fall within this step/bin that aren't equal to the upper bound of the bin. EQ_Rows indicate the number of rows that equal the upper bound of the bin. Distinct_Range_Rows are the number of distinct values in the bin, and Avg_Range_Rows are the average number of duplicate values in a bin.

Let's take a quick look at one bin to get a better idea of what the values in Table 7-3 represent. VerifyHistogram.sql in the "\Chapter07" directory of the CD has the following code that mimics one of the bins of the histogram with a lower boundary of 91 and upper boundary of 109:

```
- Verify Bin Information for OwnerID in Pets
- Lower Boundary of Bin = 91
- Upper Boundary of Bin = 100
- Verify Range_Rows
- This excludes OwnerID 109
SELECT COUNT(*) AS Range_Rows FROM Pets WHERE OwnerID BETWEEN 91 AND 107
- Verify EQ_Rows
- This includes only OwnerID 109
SELECT COUNT(*) AS EQ_Rows FROM Pets WHERE OwnerID = 109
- Verify Distinct_Range_Rows
- This excludes OwnerID 109
SELECT COUNT(DISTINCT OwnerID) AS Distinct_Range_Rows FROM Pets
WHERE OwnerID BETWEEN 91 AND 107
```

This returns a Range_Row of 12800, an EQ_Rows of 256, and a Distinct_Range_Row of 18, just like the statistics did. Avg_Range_Rows is figured by taking the Range_Rows/Distinct_Range_Rows. In this case, 12800/18 is equal to 711.11.

All of this information shows that OwnerID would be a reasonable column on which to index. It has a fairly low density. In general, any value that isn't small enough to show up in a scientific notation is probably not a good candidate for an index.

Why Do I Have More Tables Than the Three You Listed, and What Is This _WA_Sys_OwnerID_?

If you ran the ShowStatistics.SQL in grid mode, you may have noticed you got more recordsets returned. If you ran it in text mode, you might have noticed that above the fourth set of data was something like Statistics for collection '_WA_Sys_OwnerID_6B24EA82'. Anytime you see an index that starts out with _WA_Sys_, then you are seeing a reference to the statistics histogram. SQL Server creates these statistics for every index that you have created and uses the data in the statistic to determine whether an index should be used for a query.

NOTE *When Auto Update Statistics is on (the default for a database in SQL Server 2000), then you will find statistic histograms that you didn't create.*

Can I Use More Than One Column in My Index?

You can use up to sixteen columns for an index, but the total length of the key cannot exceed 900 bytes. When considering a multi-column index, however, there are other things that need to be taken into account.

The 900-Byte Limitation of SQL Server Indices

The 900-byte limitation that SQL Server has for the size of an index entry is a big "gotcha," but not because of its size. You can create an index with columns whose *potential* length is greater than 900 bytes, which means you cannot insert a row whose index key is greater than 900 bytes. It is possible, for example, to create a composite index on three columns that are all VARCHAR data types of 500 bytes each. As long as the length of the data inserted into the columns is less than 900 bytes, there isn't a problem. The moment you try to insert data that exceeds that limit, SQL Server complains. In the "\Chapter07" directory on the CD you will find a SQL script named TestIndexSize.sql. This simple script creates a table with two columns, each VARCHAR(500), and then creates an index on them.

When the index is created, a warning is generated, but the index *is* created. Next the script attempts to do three inserts: The first inserts 500 spaces into the first column and a NULL into the second. The next insert puts 450 spaces into the first column and 450 into the second—again no problem. The third one, however, attempts to put 450 spaces into the first column and 451 into the second, resulting in a key of 901 bytes. At this point, SQL Server generates an error. Finally, just to be a good citizen, the script deletes the table it created.

To Microsoft's credit, you cannot create an index that could have more than 900 bytes through the EM. It treats the warning as an error and won't let you do it. The fact remains, however, that you shouldn't create an index that *could* be larger than 900 bytes. If you are certain the data will never exceed 900 bytes, then change the length of the columns!

We're going to walk through how SQL Server uses a multi-column index by looking at one query statement executed four different times. The first time will be with no index, then with a single column index, then with a composite index, and finally with the composite index not being used. In each case the basic SQL statement won't change:

```
SELECT OwnerID, OwnerLastName, OwnerFirstName  FROM Owners
WHERE OwnerLastName = 'marion' AND OwnerFirstName = 'eula'
```

The first time this is run, SQL Server performs a table-scan of all of the rows, returning the matching ones.

Before we run it again, we're going to create an index based on OwnerLast-Name. With the index in place, SQL Server uses the index to find all of the rows where `OwnerLastName='Marion'`. Then it takes that much smaller subset of data and scans it to find the rows where `OwnerFirstName = 'Eula'`. Finally we're going to create an index using both OwnerLastName and OwnerFirstName. When we run the query this time, SQL Server needs only use the composite index. In fact, since we're not asking for any data outside of the index, SQL Server doesn't even need to access the table to give us the data for which we're looking. This is called a *covered query*.

> *Reluctant DBA* definition of a *covered query*:
> A covered query is one in which every single column referenced in the query is contained within an index and no reads of the physical data file need to be made to return data.

Indices, however, are only good if they are used. In this example we have an index based on OwnerLastName, OwnerFirstName, and SQL Server uses that index because the `WHERE` clause is in that order. If we were to reverse the `WHERE` clause so we were looking for `OwnerFirstName = 'Eula'` *and* `OwnerLastName = 'Marion'`, the SQL Server could do a full table-scan, even though all of the data is sitting in an index.

 NOTE *Ordering columns in your* `WHERE` *clause is one of those gray areas of tuning. In previous versions, ordering the columns in your* `WHERE` *clause differently than they are ordered in your* `INDEX` *would cause a full table-scan. In SQL Server 2000 this tends to happen less frequently, though it is still possible. That's good news for developers because it means we get an added bonus in our performance tuning, but it can still reach out and get you. Thus, it's always best to put your* `WHERE` *columns in the same* `INDEX` *order.*

Does Selectivity Affect Composite Indices?

When building a composite index, SQL Server only looks at the selectivity of the first column of the index to determine whether it should use that index. That means you should put the column with the most unique entries (highest selectivity) first.

How Do I Create an Index?

Now that we've covered all of the basics of indexing, let's look at how you create *usable* indices. If you have skipped to this section because you're desperate to create an index to improve your database's performance, it's highly recommended that you at least skim over the previous section. Just creating an index won't do you any good unless SQL Server actually uses it.

We're going to create an index on Owners and, at the same time, show you how to tell if the index is really doing you any good and modify it to make it better. For this exercise you'll need to open the QA and enter the following SQL command:

```
SELECT OwnerID, OwnerLastName, OwnerFirstName  FROM Owners
WHERE OwnerLastName = 'marion' AND OwnerFirstName = 'eula'
```

Let me show you one of the reasons that the QA has earned the title Analyzer (and why often we build indices through the QA instead of the EM). Press Ctrl-L or from the Query menu, select Display Estimated Execution Plan. This is going to open up a new tab in the bottom pane (see Figure 7-3).

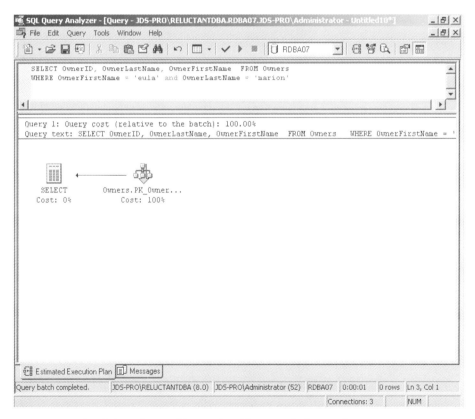

Figure 7-3. The QA's Estimated Execution Plan can help you fine-tune your indexing.

Figure 7-3 shows SQL Server's estimate of what it is going to take to run the query in the Query pane, including what objects are involved in the query. Because Owners has a clustered index associated with it and a clustered index physically orders the data in index format, SQL Server shows the clustered index object rather than the table object. And the estimated plan tells us that 100 percent of the processing is going to take place in a scan of that clustered index.

When we put the mouse over the Select icon, a new box will pop up (see Figure 7-4). Although we are not going to go into these numbers in detail, the important number to track is the Estimated subtree cost. This field indicates the amount of input/output that went into getting the data. The smaller this number is, the more efficient the query.

SELECT
Retrieves rows from the database. Allows
selection of one or many rows or columns from
one or many tables.

Physical operation:	SELECT
Logical operation:	SELECT
Estimated row count:	1
Estimated subtree cost:	0.0691

Figure 7-4 Determining the cost of the query is easy when you look at detailed parts of the execution plan.

Now, we're going to see if we can get a number smaller than 0.0691. To do that, we're going to create an index, something we can do right in the QA. Open the Tools menu and select Manage Indexes. This brings up a window we can use for managing indices. In the Tables/views drop-down list,[4] select Owners.

This option automatically displays the primary key index that exists and we can press the New button to create a new index. We're going to give the index a descriptive name (ixOwnersByOwnerLastName) and then select the OwnerLastName column (see Figure 7-5). Before going any further, let's discuss the few remaining options related to indices, because they show up in this window.

---

[4] This only applies to indexed views under SQL 2000 Enterprise Edition, and I'll be talking about indexing views at the end of this chapter.

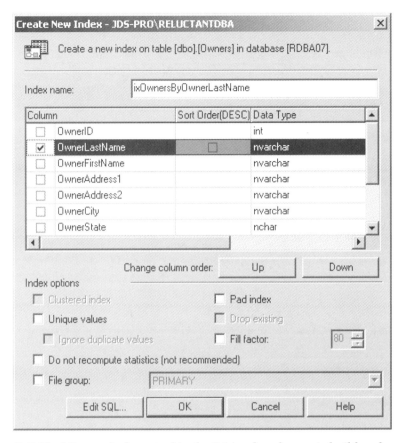

Figure 7-5. The Manage Indexes tool in the QA is a handy way to build and maintain your indices.

What Is a UNIQUE Index?

A unique index is exactly what it sounds like, an index where every entry is unique. If you're thinking that sounds a lot like a primary key, you're right. Primary keys are unique indices that enforce that uniqueness as a constraint, not allowing any duplicate entries to be added to the table. The most confusing part of creating a unique index has to do with the checkbox Ignore Duplicate Values.

If that box isn't checked and you try to create an index on a table where the columns being indexed are not unique, you'll get an error. Then again, if it *is* checked and you try to create the index, you'll get an error. This checkbox has one purpose and that is to deal with bulk operations.[5]

---

[5] I'll discuss bulk operations in detail in Chapter 14, "What Are the Data Transformation Services (DTS)?"

Let's say you have a table populated with data that has a unique index. Now you issue a bulk insert command for 500 rows and, within those 500 rows there are two duplicate keys. If the Ignore Duplicate Key isn't checked, all 500 rows will be rolled back as an invalid transaction. If it is checked, then only the two rows that would be duplicates are rolled back. Of course, then you have to find out which two rows were affected. Rolling them all back is easier, so we leave the box unchecked.

What Does Pad Index Mean?

Pad Index goes hand in hand with fill factor. Let's say you are creating an index and you want that index to set the fill factor to 90 percent, meaning that each leaf of the B-tree is only filled 90 percent. The nodes that lead to the leaves will still be filled 100 percent, leading to the need to create new nodes on leaf splits.

If you check the Pad Index checkbox, then the same concept behind fill factor is applied to the nodes. The SQL Server default for the fill factor (0) automatically creates some empty nodes. Again, this option is best left alone unless you have a table with very little data that you know is going to be growing rapidly.

Was the Index Effective?

OK, we've created the index, clicking the OK button and then the Close button. Now let's see if it did any good. The number to beat is .0691, so we're going to go back to the QA and press Ctrl-L again to refresh the Estimated Execution Plan.

The Estimated Execution Plan has changed quite a bit (see Figure 7-6), but the question remains: Is it more efficient? When we hover the mouse over the SELECT to see the numbers, we get a subtree cost of .0126, almost one-sixth of the execution time. Now, let's take a look at the execution plan and see what it tells us.

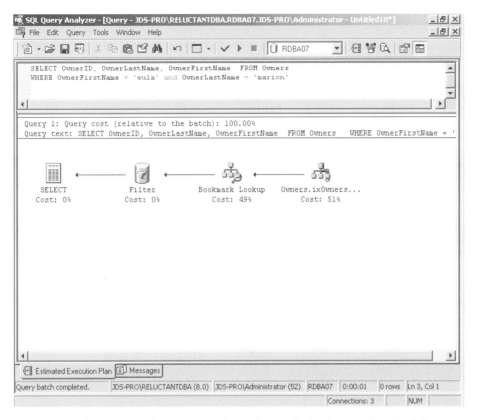

Figure 7-6. The Estimated Execution Plan using an index is more involved than one that doesn't use an index, but it is more efficient.

The first thing that jumps out about this execution plan is that it does more than the first one. Figure 7-3 showed that SQL Server had to scan the table Owners and return the data. When there is an index, however, there are additional steps.

First, SQL Server looks up the data in the index (which takes 51 percent of the time). Next, it takes the pointers from the index and uses them to look up the data in the clustered index (49 percent of the time) and then it filters the data. It has to filter the data because the number of rows that were returned from the index might be more than was asked for since the index doesn't contain all of the columns used in the WHERE clause. Even with the extra steps, there is a significant time savings, but is it possible to speed it up any more?

Of course it is. We're going back to the Tools menu and Managing Indexes again. Once we've selected Owners we're going to double-click on ixOwnersByLastName to open up the index and then we're going to check the box next to OwnerFirstName. Once we've clicked OK to create the index and OK to exit the Manage Index tool, we've got a composite index.

The Estimated Execution Plan in Figure 7-7 looks like the same one that was in 7-3 with two exceptions. Instead of scanning PK__Owners the Estimated Execution Plan is using the ixOwnersByLastName index and the subtree cost here is estimated at 0.00640! That's half of what the single column index was and almost one-tenth of the non-indexed version. That's because all of the data necessary was in the index, removing the need to go back to the table. If we add a column that's not in the index, then the speed goes back to .0126 because SQL Server now has to access the table.

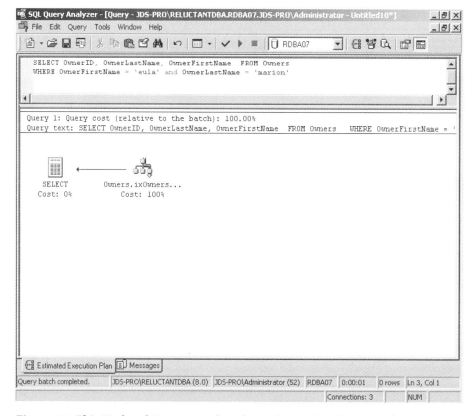

Figure 7-7. This Updated Execution plan shows the results of a covered query.

What Is the Index Tuning Wizard?

The QA can do more than tell you how an existing index will affect a SQL statement; it can even make recommendations for new indices. For example, if we go into the QA and enter the following code and execute the query, it takes several seconds to get the data back:

```
SELECT PetID, PetName FROM Pets WHERE PetName = 'Francheska'
```

Although several seconds may not seem like much, if many people are hitting the database, several seconds per person can really add up. Not only that, but a quick check of the execution plan shows that the query is doing a table-scan. We should be able to get that list back much more quickly. So we ask SQL Server what it thinks we should do about it by pressing Ctrl-I and starting the Index Tuning Wizard.

The Index Tuning Wizard starts with a nice splash screen that details some of its functionality. Press the Next button and you'll come to the first Option Screen. You shouldn't need to change any data on this screen. It should have your current database already selected from the drop-down box and Keep All Existing Indexes should be checked. All you need to do is press the Next button.

The second option page is covered in more detail in Chapter 16, "What Are System Monitor and Performance Monitor?" You can collect information on what SQL Server is doing and process it through at a later date and let SQL Server recommend changes in terms of indices and such, but for now you just need to make sure that the Query Analyzer radio button is selected and press the Next button.

The next page lists all of the tables in the database and the number of rows they contain. Click on Pets to select it and then press the Next button. The Index Tuning Wizard analyzes the database and comes up with a suggestion for creating an index that would help the query run more efficiently (see Figure 7-8). In this case, not surprisingly, it recommends creating an index on PetName and suggests that this will represent a 99-percent savings. We're not going to go into the analysis information here because it will be covered in depth in Chapter 16, "What Are System Monitor and Performance Monitor?" Instead, we're going to press the Next button.

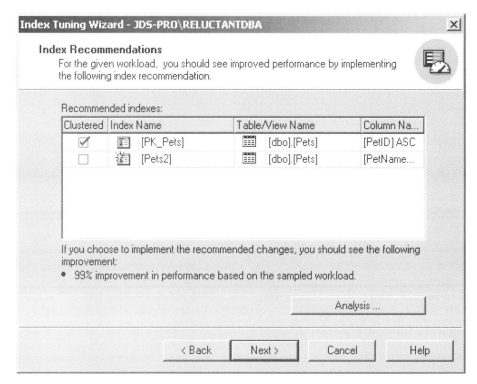

Figure 7-8. The Index Tuning Wizard recommends, not surprisingly, that an index be built on PetName.

The next page offers us the opportunity to create the index now, schedule it for later, or save it as a script. We're going to go ahead and create it now, but we have one more page before we actually create the index. That page contains a warning that we should back up the database before committing this change. That's important because if we hadn't selected Keep All Existing Indexes, then we would find all of our indices gone!

With the new index created, we can execute the SELECT and the data is returned instantaneously! Properly applied indices are great for speeding up data access.

Why Index a View if Views Aren't Real?

We've discussed the good things that can come of indexing (and the bad that can come of over-indexing), so it's time to discuss how an index can exist on a view. If you remember, last chapter we defined views as macro-like pieces of TSQL code that are substituted for the view name when the TSQL is executed. Indexing macros sounds puzzling, no?

The short answer is that SQL Server Enterprise Edition allows you to create an index on a view. In fact, SQL Server even allows you to create a clustered index on a view, changing the view from a virtual table to one that is more (or less) permanent. In other words, if we created a clustered index on the view MentorList, then every time someone accessed MentorList, they would actually be reading from a physical table instead of having SQL Server join Veterinarians to itself. Before you rush off to start creating clustered indices on all of your views, let me give you the down sides because TANSTAAFL rules even in terms of indexed views.

First, creating an indexed view adds complexity to the maintenance of tables. Every time that one of the tables is modified, the indexed view, just like any indices on the table, must be modified. The exeception ia that the indexed view could have several tables that are updating it unlike an index taht only has one table.

Second, you can't index a view without using TSQL code. Not that this is a bad thing—it's highly recommended you learn TSQL, but that's not the focus of this book. In fact, if you right-click on a view in the EM and select All Tasks, the Manage Indexes function is disabled.

Finally, there are a number of restrictions on using indexed view. Options need to be set before the index is created and then those same options must be in place before the indexed view can be accessed. Don't despair, however. The references in this chapter's "Resources" section will aid you in learning more about indexed views.

Last Words

In this chapter we've covered not only how to create indices but how to create useful ones as well. We've also touched briefly on the QA tool. So, the time has come to dig into more of what that tool offers in Chapter 8, "Introduction to Query Analyzer," and get your feet wetter when it comes to TSQL code.

Resources

- Improving performance with SQL Server 2000 indexed views:
  `http://www.microsoft.com/technet/sql/indexvw.asp`

- "Introducing Indexed Views" by Kalen Delaney, *SQL Server Magazine*, May 2000: `http://www.sqlmag.com/Articles/Index.cfm?ArticleID=8410`

- "B-Trees: Balanced Tree Structures" by Peter Neubauer:
  `http://www.public.asu.edu/&tilde;peterjn/btree/`

- The Library of Congress Web site: `http://www.loc.gov`

CHAPTER 8

Introduction to Query Analyzer

Get the habit of analysis—analysis will in time enable synthesis to become your habit of mind.　　　　　　　　　　—Frank Lloyd Wright

IN THE PREVIOUS CHAPTER, the Query Analyzer (QA) was introduced as a tool useful for analyzing data and creating indices. Now, you may be asking yourself why you need a tool like the Query Analyzer. After all, you can create and manipulate your database in the Enterprise Manager (EM), and tools like the View Designer create joins for you to use. Aren't we taking a step backward when talking about what—on the face of it—is a non-graphical tool? Well, we shall see. This chapter will provide a brief introduction to the QA. Then we'll look at some Transact SQL commands that every Reluctant Database Administrator should know, and finally we'll go into a few of the QA's new features.

 NOTE *The examples in this chapter use the* **RDBA07** *database from Chapter 7, "The Power of Indexing." You'll find instructions for installing that database in Appendix A, "How Do I Load the Examples?"*

Why Do I Need the Query Analyzer?

Whatever language you program in, be it Visual Basic (VB), Visual C++ or C#, that language will communicate with the database through SQL statements and view data returned in terms of either rowsets or output values. In fact, all of the visual interface elements of the EM are simply shells hiding the Transact SQL (TSQL) statements and formatting their results.

The QA is a great tool made even better in SQL 2000. About the only thing it lacks is Intellisense—with that addition, it would be perfect. Its official name, according to the Books On Line (BOL), is SQL Query Analyzer, but everyone calls it either the *Query Analyzer* or the *QA* for short. The QA is the TSQL tool to use when you want to get into the nuts and bolts of SQL.

Of course, it's also handy to see if your SQL statements work the way you expect they should. You can cut and paste the command from your VB app into the Edit pane and see what you're really getting back rather than relying on what VB says you're getting. Once you know your TSQL statement works, the QA has tools that help analyze how efficient the TSQL code is.

How Do I Start the Query Analyzer?

You can start the Query Analyzer in two ways. The first is from the EM's menus: Tools ➢ Query Analyzer. The second is from the Start menu: Start ➢ Program Files ➢ Microsoft SQL Server ➢ Query Analyzer. Either way will start the QA; the biggest difference is that starting the QA from the EM automatically logs you into the server you were working with in the EM and in the selected database (assuming one is selected) when you started.

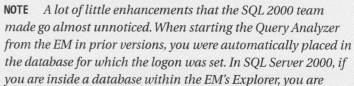

NOTE *A lot of little enhancements that the SQL 2000 team made go almost unnoticed. When starting the Query Analyzer from the EM in prior versions, you were automatically placed in the database for which the logon was set. In SQL Server 2000, if you are inside a database within the EM's Explorer, you are automatically set to that database without having to worry about changing your database before getting to work. Another nice touch in SQL 2000 is that it defaults to showing results in the grid format.*

If you have started the QA from the Start menu or you didn't have a server selected within the EM when you started it, you first have to log on to a server through the Connect to SQL Server dialog box (see Figure 8-1). This requires telling QA which server you want to connect to and whether you want to use Windows NT Authentication (a trusted connection) or specify a user ID and password. If you start the QA from the EM with just the server selected, you are placed into the default database for the account logged into the machine, or the default database for the SQL Account logged in with. If a database is selected when the QA is started from EM, that is the database you will be in, except when you don't have permissions to access that database, in which case you will be placed in the default.

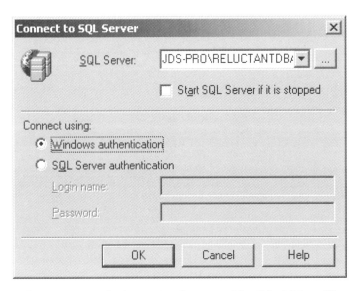

Figure 8-1. When you start the Query Analyzer outside of the EM you'll need to enter the SQL Server name and the account (Windows authentication or SQL Server authentication) with which to connect.

NOTE   *When you are connecting to the main server on your local machine, you have three different ways to specify it in the Connect to SQL Server dialog box. You can specify it by name, as it is in Figure 8-1, or you can use (local), or you can use a period.*

Once you have connected you'll find yourself with a dialog box called the Editor pane. Note that the database listed in the drop-down list on the Toolbar is your default (or that of the account used to log into SQL Server). This is where you can type SQL Statements to be processed. Figure 8-2 shows what the QA looks like with data. Although we won't touch on everything that you can do in the QA in this chapter, we'll cover all of the basics. First, let's go over the most important parts of the QA.

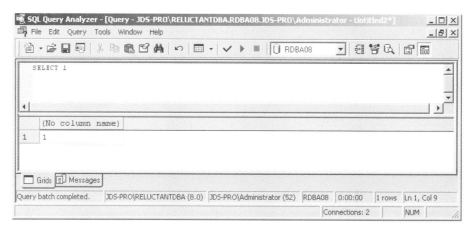

Figure 8-2. Sample Query Analyzer screen

We'll start by going over the QA toolbar. The first three buttons are pretty standard. The New Query button (a sheet of paper) creates a new query in the same database, the Load SQL Script button (an open folder) opens a stored query, and the Save Query/Result button (a disk) saves the query. The fourth button, the Insert Template button, is for inserting a template, something we'll cover in more detail toward the end of the chapter in the section "What Is a Template?"

You're probably familiar with the next set of buttons, which provide the standard edit and paste functionality. The Execute mode button (to the right of the edit and paste buttons) contains a drop-down list that allows you to change whether you see the results in a grid format, as shown in Figure 8-2, or see them as text. Grids are easier to use when you need to review information because you can easily adjust the column width by dragging the column's side. But there may be times when you want to use the text display instead.

NOTE *In prior versions, the default for the results pane was the text display. In SQL Server 2000 the default is the grid pane.*

The next set of buttons consists of a blue checkmark, a green triangle, and a disabled red square. If you've used Access much, you can probably guess at what they are:

- The blue checkmark, the Parse Query button, parses your SQL statement to see if it's correct. It doesn't execute the statement, it just checks it to see if it is syntactically correct and lets you know where any errors might be. This does not mean that the SQL statement will actually *work*, mind you, just that it is formed correctly.

- The green triangle, the Execute Query button, executes your
  SQL statements.

- The disabled red square, the Cancel Query Execution button, is not a trib-
  ute to the triumph of democracy over Soviet Communism. Rather, it is the
  button for stopping a query while it is running.

When you run a query, the Execute Query button is disabled and the Cancel
Query Execution button is enabled.

The drop-down box to the right of the Cancel Query Execution button shows
you which database you are currently in and what databases are available. To
change databases, just select the one you want. Unlike the old versions of the QA,
the current version gets a list of databases every time the drop-down box gets
focus. A nice new feature is found in the last entry of the list. In the old versions,
this was labeled "<Refresh>" and would get you an updated list of the databases.
In the 2000 version it is labeled "<Details. . .>" and it provides the list of current
databases along with some new information (see Figure 8-3). At a glance you can
see all of the databases, which level of SQL Server the database is for, and what
the current status of the database is. All of these databases are SQL Server 2000
databases (as shown by the Compliance Level 80, SQL Server 7 shows as Compliance Level 70) and are ready to be used.

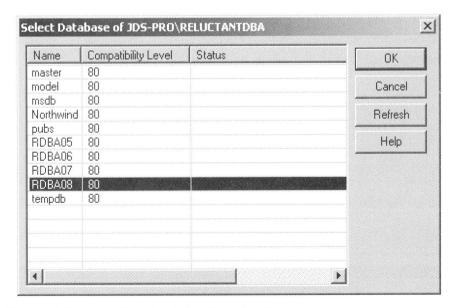

Figure 8-3. Database Details window from the QA

We've already covered the Editor pane, so we're going to skip to the two tabs along the bottom of Figure 8-2, the Grids and Messages tabs. As you can see, the Grids tab is the default tab, and it shows the results of the SQL statement. Another nice enhancement of the current version is the fact that if you execute a statement that returns multiple rowsets (grids), they now show up in sequential order in the Grids tab. In prior versions they would show up as separate tabs, forcing you to switch between tabs to see the results.

The Messages tab is where SQL Server delivers messages to you about what has happened. In most cases you want to see messages like "The command(s) completed successfully" or "25 row(s) affected." Messages like these tell you if everything is working fine or if there is a problem executing the query. If you should select the text display for your output, you'll find these informative messages interspersed with your results. One reason people use text results instead of grids is to put such messages within the context of where they are being returned.

That covers the basics of SQL QA. Table 8-1 shows you common keyboard shortcuts that you can use with the QA. Now it's time to dig into SQL and put the QA through its paces.

Table 8-1. Handy Key Combinations for the QA

KEY COMBINATION	ACTION
Ctrl+N	Creates a new query in the same database.
Ctrl+S	Saves the current query.
Ctrl+Shift+F	Saves the results to file.
Ctrl+Shift+Ins	Inserts a template.
Ctrl+D	Shows the results in a grid.
Ctrl+T	Shows the results as text.
Ctrl+E or F5	Executes a query.
Alt+Break	Stops a query.
Ctrl+F5	Parses a query.
Ctrl+O	Opens a new database connection.

What Is Transact SQL?

Reluctant DBA definition of *Transact SQL*:

SQL Server's Transact Structured Query Language (TSQL) can be used for everything you do in SQL Server, including creating new tables, putting data into them, getting data out of them, and changing the properties of the database itself. Its syntax is kind of like the English language, only not.

One of the goals of TSQL is that the syntax is supposed to be easy to learn. TSQL has a definite structure; in many cases it has a verb-noun type of structure. Take the following TSQL command, for instance:

```
SELECT OwnerLastName FROM Owners
```

This returns all of the data in the OwnerLastName column from the Owners table. We'll start our review of TSQL with the SELECT statement because it is the most easily understood and most often used. Then we'll cover the INSERT, UPDATE, and DELETE commands.

NOTE   *Teaching TSQL in depth is not a goal of this book. Many books do a good job of that, and a couple of them are listed in the "Resources" section at the end of this chapter. The goal of this section is to introduce the basics of four commands that you will often use with the SQL Server:* SELECT, INSERT, UPDATE, *and* DELETE. *Although SQL Server's graphical interface tools will let you perform many tasks without knowing any TSQL, it really is in your best interests to learn it because there are some things you just can't do without it.*

What Am I Selecting?

SELECT is a useful SQL command used for pulling data out of one or more tables. In its simplest form, the SELECT statement looks like this:

```
SELECT ColName FROM tablename
```

This SQL SELECT will return all rows for a specified column from a table. In some cases you'll want to return *all* table columns, and you can accomplish this by using an asterisk (*) instead of listing all of the column names. However, this is not a good idea. For lots of reasons discussed in the books on ActiveX Data Objects (ADO) programming listed in the "Resources" section of this chapter, using SELECT * is problematic at best. It says, "OK, let me have all the columns currently defined for this table. I don't care what's been added since I wrote this program four months ago, my code can handle it."

In older versions of SQL Server, TSQL statements were frequently written this way because no one really wanted to type in every single column name. With the new version, however, it isn't necessary. In a few pages we'll look at the Object Browser, which makes listing any (or all) columns in a table as easy as using SELECT *.

Let's try a SELECT query by selecting all of the data owners from the **RDBA07** database. Start the QA and point to the **RDBA07** database and enter this TSQL command:

```
SELECT OwnerID, OwnerLastName, OwnerFirstName, OwnerAddress1, OwnerAddress2,
OwnerCity, OwnerState, OwnerPostalCode, OwnerPostal4, OwnerPhoneNumber,
OwnerEmailAddress FROM Owners
```

Before executing the command, check the drop-down box to make sure you are in the **RDBA07** database. If you are not, then you might get an error that says "Invalid object name 'Owners.'" If you are in the correct database and you spelled everything correctly, you should get something similar to Figure 8-4. It's all of the rows and columns of the Owner table.

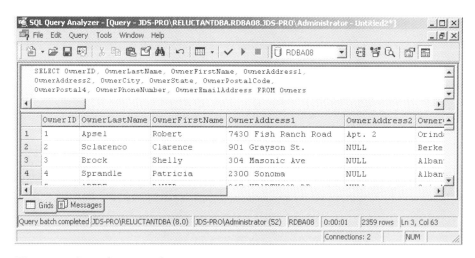

Figure 8-4. Sample output from a SELECT *statement*

White Spaces, Line Breaks, Comments, and TSQL

TSQL is a forgiving language when it comes to formatting your data. It will ignore white spaces and carriage returns. It also won't fuss if white space and carriage returns are missing. If you want to use two spaces between each word or indent continued lines, TSQL won't care. For instance, this line:

```
SELECT OwnerFirstName FROM Owners
```

is the same as

```
SELECT OwnerFirstName
          FROM Owners
```

When you comment your code, you have two choices. The first is two dashes (--). This will comment all code until the next line break. Your second alternative is to use /* */. When /* is encountered, everything until the matching */ is considered to be a comment. This is covered in more detail in Chapter 9, "Working with Data: Basic Stored Procedures."

Using SELECT is the first step in getting data out of a table, but there's more to getting the *correct* data out. Getting the correct data out means retrieving only the data that's needed in terms of both columns and rows. If you need to understand why you should limit the rows being returned, just consider this. If you need one row of data and you are returning one thousand, then you are forcing the server to use resources for your query that it could be using elsewhere. In addition, you are pushing more data through the network pipes than you need, tying up even more resources.

One good reason to define the columns being returned is that the programmers (including yourself) will probably thank you for it. Many VB programmers know that the fastest way to access columns in a recordset is to reference them by number. This eliminates the need for the database component to map the string field name to the column number at runtime (late binding). All of this is fine and dandy, even if you use SELECT * as long as the table never changes structure. What happens, however, if you add a new column in the middle of the old ones? Suddenly, every column from that one on will be out of sync. If the columns are defined in the SELECT statement, it becomes an easy task to put that new column at the end of the column list and not break working code.

NOTE *Reluctant DBAs have the potential to make the best DBAs in a programming environment as long as they can wear two hats at the same time. Our experience with programming helps us understand how the programmer will use the data, often giving us insight that a traditional DBA might lack. It's important to always have both hats on, making sure that the DBA and programmer always balance one another in terms of helping each other work more efficiently.*

So the general rule is, even if you need all of the columns from a table, spell them out individually in your SELECT statement.

How Do I Rename a Column?

There are times when you will need to temporarily name or rename a column in the rowset that your SQL statements return. If you look back at Figure 8-1, you'll notice that the rowset contains one row and one column, and the column name is "(No column name)." Most people would agree that, as column names go, that is less than useful. So, let's change that SQL statement to (re)name the column. This is as easy as adding the keyword AS and providing a name to use as an alias. Once a column has been given an alias, it can be referenced by that alias.

You'll want to provide a column alias whenever you SELECT an expression such as an aggregate. We'll rename the column to SampleColName using the SQL code SELECT 1 as SampleColName. As you can see in Figure 8-5, the column now shows up with a useful name.

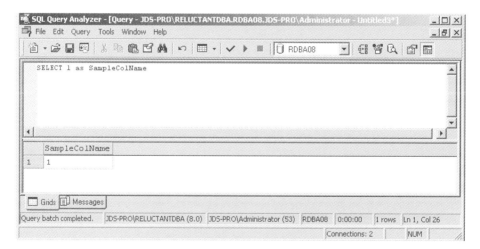

Figure 8-5. Sample SELECT *with the column renamed*

How Do I Sort the Data?

Unless there's a clustered index, there is no real rhyme or reason to the order of the data SQL Server will return. Simply rearranging the order of the filter you're applying to a table can result in reordering the data unless you specifically ask SQL Server to sort it before returning it to your application.

Ordering data is as easy as using the ORDER BY keywords followed by column names (or aliases). By default, ORDER BY will sort in ascending order, but you can use the keywords ASC (ascending order) and DESC (descending order) to modify how it sorts.

To sort the Owners by OwnerCity ascending and OwnerPhoneNumber descending you would use:

```
SELECT OwnerID, OwnerLastName, OwnerFirstName, OwnerCity, OwnerPhoneNumber FROM
Owners ORDER BY OwnerCity ASC, OwnerPhoneNumber DESC
```

When this is run in the **RDBA07** you'll see that the city for the first two rows is Albany and the phone numbers are sorted in descending order. When a table doesn't have a clustered index on it, it will be returned in whatever order it was physically entered. If there is a clustered index, then the data is physically sorted by that index so it will be returned in that order.

Using the ORDER BY clause can radically change the way SQL Server performs the query and constructs the rowset. Unless you are using a fully covered query, SQL Server has to fetch all of the rows into **TempDB** and sort them *before* returning any of them to your application. Once in **TempDB,** SQL Server applies the ORDER BY and sorts the data as it returns it to your application. This takes time and more server-side resources, not to mention having to revert to table-scans in some cases to run the query. You can, in many cases, sort (or re-sort) the data using ADO's Recordset Sort property once the rows arrive. If you will consistently be using a particular sort order, you can use QA's Index Tuning Wizard to build the most efficient index for the TSQL statement, just as we did in the last chapter.

How Do I Filter the Data?

There are two methods of filtering data. The first is by choosing the columns of data to return, and the second method is by using the WHERE clause. The WHERE clause allows you to specify the criteria to be used in selecting rows to be returned or updated. In its simplest form, the WHERE clause looks for matches on one column:

```
SELECT OwnerId, OwnerLastName, OwnerFirstName, OwnerCity FROM Owners WHERE
OwnerCity = 'Orinda'
```

As you can see in Figure 8-6, the data shows only data where the city name is Orinda.

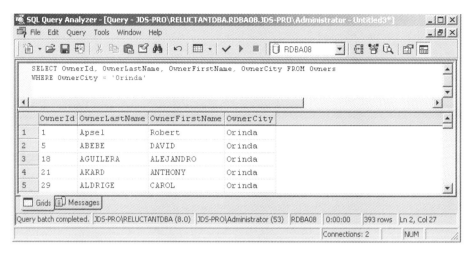

Figure 8-6. Using the `WHERE` *clause filters the data that gets returned.*

As you can see, this SQL statement returns only the records that match what was asked for. How do we know that it selected the right data? We can easily check. Highlight the first portion of the SQL, excluding the `WHERE` part and then execute the query. You can see in Figure 8-7, Orinda isn't the only OwnerCity that shows up when the `WHERE` filter is removed, so the `WHERE` clause is correct.

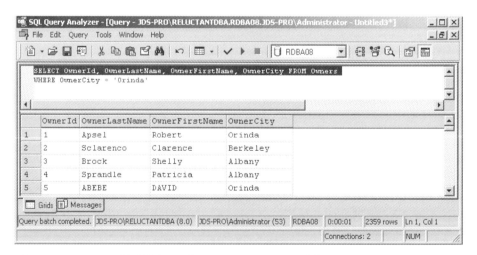

Figure 8-7. You can highlight and run just a portion of the TSQL that's in the SQL pane as long as it is a complete TSQL statement.

TIP *When you are working in the QA, you can highlight a portion of the TSQL statement, press the Execute Query button and only that portion will get executed. This is a handy way to check part of a SQL statement without having to comment out or delete parts of it.*

There are a number of different symbols and words that you can use with WHERE. These are called *operators* and include intuitive ones like =, <, > and <> along with some others that are less intuitive. First we'll look at Boolean symbols. These will return true, false, or unknown. You can use a Boolean symbol against every data type except text, ntext, or image columns. Table 8-4 lists the Boolean operators you can use in WHERE clauses.

Table 8-4. Boolean Operators for Use in WHERE Clauses

OPERATOR	MEANING	SAMPLE
=	Equals	1 = 1
>	Greater than	2 > 1
<	Less than	1 < 2
<>	Not equal to	1 <> 2
>=	Greater than or equal to	2 >= 1
<=	Less than or equal to	1 <= 2

CAUTION *Boolean means* TRUE *or* FALSE. *In SQL Server, however, it is also possible to have* UNKNOWN. UNKNOWN *is not a member of the Boolean set, and many programmers who are not used to considering* UNKNOWN *get tripped up because they forget about it. If you have 100 records in a table and find out that forty-five of them have a value in a column of less than two, do not assume that the other fifty-five are greater than two. If the column you are evaluating allows* NULL *values, it is possible that some number of the records contain the value* NULL.

Figure 8-8 shows a perfect example of an UNKNOWN. If you look at how the Owners table was designed you'll see that the OwnerAddress2 column allows NULL. Figure 8-8 shows two SQL statements, both of them filtered on the Address2 column. The first one finds all of the records where Address2 is "Apt. 2" and the second one looks like it should find the rest of the rows. You can see the two separate grids in the Results pane, but the second one isn't showing any data. Why?

It doesn't show any results because all of other rows in the table have NULLs in the Address2 column and resolve to an UNKNOWN. To find *all* of rows that aren't equal to "Apt. 2" you have to use IS NULL.

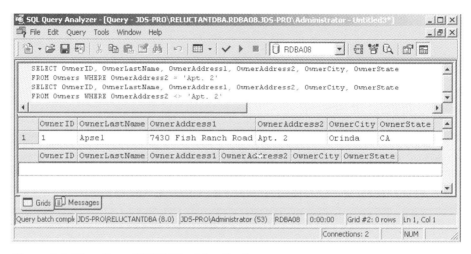

Figure 8-8. The effect of UNKNOWN *with a Boolean operator*

When dealing with columns that may or may not be NULL, it's always wise to consider IS NULL or IS NOT NULL. IS NULL does exactly what you think it should. It evaluates a column to determine whether the column has a value. Figure 8-9 shows the results of using IS NULL in addition to the <>. It also uses the OR operator, which is a logical operator.

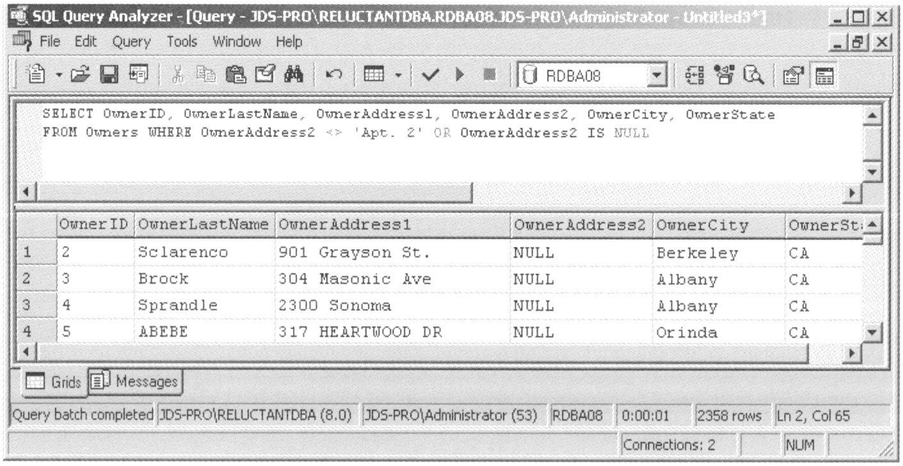

Figure 8-9. Using IS NULL *in a* WHERE *filter to get all of the data*

What Are Logical Operators?

A logical operator resolves to a Boolean value. In SQL that means it can return TRUE or FALSE. There are ten logical operators (see Table 8-5) and most of them are fairly intuitive, but I'm going to run through all of them with samples to make sure that you understand how and when to use them.

Table 8-5. Logical Operators

OPERATOR	DESCRIPTION
AND	Takes two expressions and returns TRUE only if *both* of them are true.
OR	Takes two expressions and returns TRUE if *either* of them are true.
NOT	Reverses the value of the expression, making TRUE FALSE and vice versa.
BETWEEN	Will find all of the values between two values, including the two values used.
IN	Will check to see if the expression exists in a set of data provided.
LIKE	Used for pattern matching within text. See the CHARINDEX string function too.
ALL	Checks a set of expressions to see if they all are TRUE.
ANY	Checks a set of expressions to see if any of them are TRUE.
SOME	Checks a set of expressions to see if some of them are TRUE.
EXISTS	Checks to see if a value exists in a subquery.

Before we dive into examples, let's take a quick refresher course in precedence from algebra. Precedence is nothing more than the order in which the WHERE clause is evaluated. Take the earlier query that was looking for rows where Address2 wasn't equal to "Apt. 2." That query returned 2,358 rows according to the status bar at the bottom of the QA. But what if we wanted to restrict our selection to cities that did not include "Berkeley"? We could use the following SQL to accomplish that:

```
SELECT OwnerID, OwnerLastName, OwnerAddress1, OwnerAddress2, OwnerCity,
OwnerState FROM Owners WHERE OwnerAddress2 <> 'Apt. 2' OR OwnerAddress2 IS NULL
AND OwnerCity <> 'Berkeley' ORDER BY OwnerCity
```

If you run this, you'll get 1,972 rows back and Berkeley doesn't appear to be in the listing. But is it correct? Try this:

```
UPDATE Owners SET OwnerAddress2 = '' WHERE OwnerID = 2
SELECT OwnerID, OwnerLastName, OwnerAddress1, OwnerAddress2, OwnerCity,
OwnerState FROM Owners WHERE OwnerAddress2 <> 'Apt. 2' OR OwnerAddress2 IS NULL
AND OwnerCity <> 'Berkeley' ORDER BY OwnerCity
```

The third row contains a Berkeley resident. Why didn't the WHERE clause filter out Berkeley? Because of the precedence involved. When SQL Server parses that SELECT statement it doesn't necessarily read from left to right. Instead, it groups the WHERE based on the precedence of the operators. AND has a higher precedence than OR, so SQL Server groups the WHERE clause and interprets it as follows: First, collect all rows where OwnerAddress2 IS NULL and OwnerCity <> Berkeley, then collect all rows where OwnerAddress2 isn't "Apt. 2." Given that information, SQL did just what we asked it to.

Why did the WHERE filter work the first time? Because there was no data that met the requirements until we modified OwnerAddress2 for OwnerID 2. This set up a case where OwnerAddress2 was not NULL but not equal to "Apt. 2" either.

If you really want to, you can memorize the precedence orders within SQL, but it is much easier to just use parentheses around the groups that you want to keep together because parentheses are at the top of the precedence group. Not only is this easier to get correct when writing your code, it's also much easier to understand the precedence in several weeks when you have to look at the TSQL code again. By forcing SQL Server to put the Address2 selections together within the parentheses you'll end up with the correct data:

```
SELECT OwnerID, OwnerLastName, OwnerAddress1, OwnerAddress2, OwnerCity,
OwnerState FROM Owners WHERE (OwnerAddress2 <> 'Apt. 2' OR OwnerAddress2 IS
NULL)  AND OwnerCity <> 'Berkeley' ORDER BY OwnerCity
```

AND/OR/NOT

AND and OR are logical operators that both take two expressions and evaluate them in terms of each other. NOT takes one expressions and reverses the evaluation. Table 8-6 demonstrates how each of the expressions reacts in cases of TRUE, FALSE, or UNKNOWN. There is a SQL Script on the CD in "\Chapter08" called AndOrNot.sql that will reproduce the table so you can see for yourself how it works.

Table 8-6. AND/OR/NOT *Evaluations*

EXPRESSION	VALUE
TRUE AND TRUE	TRUE
TRUE AND FALSE	FALSE
TRUE AND UNKNOWN	FALSE
FALSE AND UNKNOWN	FALSE
TRUE OR TRUE	TRUE
TRUE OR FALSE	TRUE
TRUE OR UNKNOWN	TRUE
FALSE OR UNKNOWN	TRUE
NOT TRUE	FALSE
NOT FALSE	TRUE
NOT UNKNOWN	FALSE

Although SQL was loosely patterned after English syntax, an English sentence doesn't always do what you want it to do. In spoken language, even if you don't say precisely what you mean, the listener often can figure out what you meant. For example, suppose you gave the following instructions to a co-worker looking through the address file: "Find everyone who lives in Orinda and Berkeley." Your colleague would not translate your instructions literally as:

```
SELECT OwnerID, OwnerLastName, OwnerAddress1, OwnerAddress2, OwnerCity,
OwnerState
FROM Owners WHERE OwnerCity = 'Berkeley' AND OwnerCity = 'Orinda'
```

Such a statement would never return data because the OwnerCity column cannot simultaneously be Orinda and Berkeley. A human being would figure out that you really wanted the records from *both* cities, requiring OR:

```
SELECT OwnerID, OwnerLastName, OwnerAddress1, OwnerAddress2, OwnerCity,
OwnerState
FROM Owners WHERE OwnerCity = 'Berkeley' OR OwnerCity = 'Orinda'
```

Of course, putting a large number of ORs into a SQL statement can make it confusing. If you wanted to choose all rows for ten different cities you would need ten different OR statements. Then, assuming that you might have addresses from differing states, you would need to put those ORs between parentheses and add an AND statement after all of the ORs to filter based on OwnerState. If only there were a better way.

How Do I Filter Results Based on a Set of Data?

Filtering on a set of data is as easy as pie when you use IN. The IN operator allows you to specify a data set and checks for every row where a specific column's value matches the data set you specify. The basic syntax of the IN operator is:

```
Colname IN (var1, var2, var3-varN)
```

If you wanted to get all of the rows that have Orinda or Berkeley for the city, you simply say:

```
SELECT OwnerID, OwnerLastName, OwnerAddress1, OwnerAddress2, OwnerCity,
OwnerState FROM Owners WHERE OwnerCity IN ('ORINDA', 'Berkeley')
```

If you need to restrict your rowset to a specific state you simply add
AND OwnerState = 'CA' and you're finished.

How Do I Filter Data Based on Another Table?

Although IN uses a data set, you don't have to type in the data set to use it. You can use a separate query to give you the data. This is known as a *subquery*. Subqueries enable you to pull data from one table based on the data in another table.

> *Reluctant DBA* definition of a *subquery*:
> A subquery is a part of a SQL statement that could stand on its own as a query but is included as a filter in another query.

Subqueries are useful when you have lookup tables. They enable you to filter the data in your primary table based on the data in a secondary table. Because this database has been through the normalization process, there are a couple of good examples we can use for building subqueries. For instance, every row in the Pets table contains an OwnerID pointing to that pet's owner. If we wanted a list of all of the pets that live in Albany we could get this data using a subquery:

```
SELECT PetID, PetName FROM Pets WHERE OwnerID IN (SELECT OwnerID FROM OWNERS
WHERE OwnerCity = 'Albany')
```

This TSQL statement first gets a list of OwnerIDs that meet the criteria requested in the subquery. Then, using that list of OwnerIDs, it filters the requested columns from Pets. The important thing to remember about subqueries is that they can only return one column of data at a time.

Is That the Only Way to Filter Based on Another Table?

No. It is more efficient to use a join instead. This code produces the exact same results as the one using the IN but is slightly more efficient:

```
SELECT PetID, PetName FROM Owners INNER JOIN Pets on Pets.OwnerID =
Owners.OwnerID WHERE OwnerCity = 'Albany'
```

> **NOTE** *The natural tendency of programmers seems to be to use subqueries. I include myself in this statement because I still think through solving a problem by creating a set of data from one table that I can use to filter the data in another table. The problem with subqueries is that they are not as efficient as joins. I frequently create a subquery first because it's the easiest way to get the correct information, and then I work on joining the tables to match the data in the subquery.*

How Do I Get All of the Data between Two Values?

You probably prefer to keep your data requests as simple as possible. Of course, any time you want a rowset that contains an upper and lower limit of records you can do that by hand using something similar to:

```
SELECT colnames FROM tablename WHERE columnname >= lowlimit AND columnname <=
highlimit
```

There really isn't a problem with this, but Transact SQL has a BETWEEN operator that takes two values and uses the AND operator. The value of using the BETWEEN operator is two-fold. First, it makes the statement easier to read. Second, it eliminates the possibility that you might forget the equal symbol and have > instead of >=. Here's a sample SQL command using BETWEEN:

```
SELECT VeterinarianID, VeterinarianLastName, VeterinarianFirstName,
VeterinarianPhoneNumber,  VeterinarianPager, VeterinarianEmailAddress, MentorID
FROM Veterinarians WHERE VeterinarianID BETWEEN 2 AND 4
```

How Do I Find Data That Matches a Pattern?

SQL Server has several ways to find pattern matches. The most common is the LIKE operator. The LIKE operator searches for matches in a specific column using wildcard and other operators. It can be used on numeric, character, and even datetime data types. Not only that, but you can search for groups of letters as well. Table 8-7 shows you the wildcards; we'll look at each in turn.

Table 8-7. Wildcard Expressions for the LIKE *Operator*

WILDCARD	DESCRIPTION
%	Matches a string of characters of any length. g%s would match *gas, gears* or *gs*. For those migrating from Access, this replaces the wildcard character (*).
_	Matches any single character. g_s would match *gas* but not *gears* or *gs*.
[ ]	Matches a range of characters. Using [d-g]ear would match *dear, fear* and *gear*. It would also match *eear,* but that's not a word.
[^]	Matches all *except* a range of characters. Using [^b-d]ear would exclude *bear* and *dear* while matching *fear* and *gear*.

The most important thing to remember about using LIKE is that you have to match your data exactly. Searching for '%ears' will find *gears* but not *gears* with a space after it, because the extra space on the end causes the match to fail.

> **TIP** *Most of the time I am searching for a string in the middle of a column so I will always put a % on either end, so instead of searching for '%ears' I would search for '%ears%'; that way I'd get both matches. However there are performance implications when using the wildcard character at the beginning of the string. In most cases, this syntax triggers use of a table-scan instead of an index scan (if the searched column is keyed).*

First we'll use the wildcard character (%) to pull all of the pet owners from our database that have last names that begin with *s*. The SQL is simple enough:

```
SELECT OwnerID, OwnerLastName, OwnerFirstName, OwnerPhoneNumber FROM Owners
WHERE OwnerLastName LIKE 'S%'
```

Executing that returns a number of rows, all starting with *s*. If we had put another % in front of the *s* (%S%) we would have gotten Robert Apsel and Art Abramson and many others whose names contain the letter *s*, still including those that begin with *s* as well. For our second LIKE example, we put a NOT in front of the S% and got the rest of the rows. We get the same results as we do with our last example using the caret wildcard (^), but it is far easier to read this one.

 NOTE NULL *columns work about as well with* LIKE *as they do with the equal sign (=). If you have a* NULL *column in your table, remember to use* OR colname IS NULL *in your query as well. If you were to run* SELECT * FROM Owners where Address2 NOT LIKE 'A%' *you won't get any of the rows where the* Address2 *is* NULL.

The underscore (_) represents one character. 'S__a%' tells SQL Server to look for one *s*, two letters of any kind, one *a* and then anything else it finds. If you were to substitute 'S_r%' you would get back Patricia Sprandle and EM Sardanetta.

Another way to search for a specific string in a column is to use the PATINDEX and CHARINDEX functions. CHARINDEX is faster than the '%x%' technique, easier to understand, and returns the position in the column (string) containing the searched-for argument. The down side is that it works only with the beginning of the string and doesn't allow wildcards. PATINDEX works with a pattern match for the whole string, but it often causes table-scans.

Some Final Words on SELECT

The SELECT statement is the most used command in my TSQL experience. It is often misused with either SELECT * or using WHERE filters that have no index relevance. I strongly encourage you, once you think you know how to use it, to get a copy of *Advanced Transact SQL for SQL Server 2000* by Ben-Gan and Moreau. The book is chock full of ideas that will help you better understand how to write more efficient TSQL code.

Until you get to that point, remember that the View Designer will help you build a lot of your SELECT statements, especially when joining tables together.

How Do I INSERT Data?

The INSERT command is designed to add one row of data to a table. The basic format is:

```
INSERT INTO tablename colname1, colname2 VALUES(value1, value2)
```

You supply the name of the table that the data is being inserted into, a list of the columns, and the list of values *in the same order* as the columns.

To List Columns or Not to List, *That* Is the Question

Listing column names is optional, but it's recommended that you do so, especially since the QA's Object browser (covered later in this chapter) makes it so easy to do. If you don't include the column names, then you need to list a value for every column in the VALUES section of the INSERT statement.

Not a problem, you say? Imagine if you will, that you have coded an INSERT statement into a VB program without specifying column names. Then, because nothing stays static, you add a column to the table. You even think far enough ahead that you give the column a default value and add it to the end of the columns. When your program attempts to insert the data, SQL Server determines that the number of values passed doesn't equal the number of columns in the table and generates an error.

If, on the other hand, you had specified the column names, then SQL Server would have processed your INSERT and used the default for the columns that aren't specified.

INSERT is a fairly straightforward command affecting one row on one table at a time.[1] It is possible to use the INSERT command on a view, but there are limitations involved with that, not the least of which is that once a view reaches a certain level of complexity you can no longer INSERT data into it. It's very possible to have a view that you are performing INSERTs on and then you add one column and suddenly it no longer works. Now you'll have to modify all of your code to use the tables instead. One other note—it is a common practice to create views in a security context (limiting what columns users can see from a table). If someone attempts to insert data through a view that doesn't have all of the columns, and one of the missing columns is a required column that doesn't accept NULL and doesn't have a default, then your INSERT would fail.

How Do I UPDATE Data?

The UPDATE command is similar to the INSERT command. The UPDATE command looks something like this:

```
UPDATE tablename SET colname1=value1, colname2=value2 WHERE condition
```

---

[1] Actually, you can do bulk inserts and updates using another table for the source, but I'll cover that in more detail in the next chapter.

Why is the WHERE condition in that example in boldface? It's boldfaced because you don't want to UPDATE a set of data and perform the update on every row in the table! And sometimes it isn't easy to get your data back when you make a mistake like that. Even if you've got a good backup and have transaction log backups, unless you have a transaction log backup from just prior to executing the UPDATE, you'll probably mess up some data.

> **TIP** *When building an* UPDATE *or* DELETE *statement, always build a* SELECT *statement first. That way you can verify that your* WHERE *clause is getting just the rows that you want to update or delete. Then you can modify the first part of the code to perform the* UPDATE *or* DELETE.

How Do I DELETE Rows?

There are two ways to delete rows. The first and preferred way is to use the DELETE command. As you can see from the next example, it simply takes a table name and a WHERE condition. The WHERE condition is important because issuing DELETE FROM tablename will delete *all* rows.

```
DELETE FROM tablename WHERE condition
```

If the row you are trying to delete has any other rows dependent on it in a foreign key relationship, you will be unable to delete it until those rows are deleted. Using the DELETE command is good because it is a logged command. If you have a table that doesn't have any other table dependent upon it, you *could* use TRUNCATE TABLE, but this is a bad command to use.

TRUNCATE TABLE is an unlogged command, and it will invalidate your backup scheme unless you perform a full backup right away. TRUNCATE has one other peculiarity that is different from DELETE—when TRUNCATE is used on a table with an IDENTITY column, the column is reset back to 1. In other words, the first new row inserted (not inserted with BULK INSERT, or SELECT INTO, or BULK COPY (bcp)) will have the IDENTITY value of 1. If you insert into the table with one of the three methods just mentioned, the counter automatically picks up from the largest value, so if the largest value in the column were 2,345, then the next row inserted would contain 2,346.

Is That All There Is to TSQL?

No, not by a long shot. You really need to learn TSQL, so you should read through some of the references in this chapter's "Resource" section. These four commands (SELECT, INSERT, UPDATE, DELETE) are simply a small part of what exists in the TSQL language. In fact, what this chapter has covered about these four commands is a small fraction of what you can do with them. Throughout the rest of this book, however, you'll find these commands referenced and, as necessary, expanded upon them. In Chapter 9, "Working with Data: Basic Stored Procedures," for instance, you'll learn how to use UPDATE and INSERT for multiple records based on a SELECT statement. But for now, we'll get back to the QA.

How Do I Get TSQL Help in the Query Analyzer?

The QA has two help keys. The first, F1, is the key that calls up Help for the QA. The second, Shift-F1, calls up Help for whatever TSQL command you have highlighted. For instance, if you type the word "SELECT" into the QA's SQL pane, highlight it, and press Shift-F1, BOL appears, pointing to the SELECT statement in TSQL (see Figure 8-10). This is referred to as *context-sensitive* Help. This kind of Help is especially helpful when you want to use a "system" stored procedure in your code but can't recall the correct syntax. Shift-F1 gets you to the answer quickly.[2]

However, this is only the beginning of the assistance that you can get, and it was available in SQL Server 7. New for 2000, however, is the Object Browser.

---

[2]   I told you that SELECT is more complex than what I've covered.

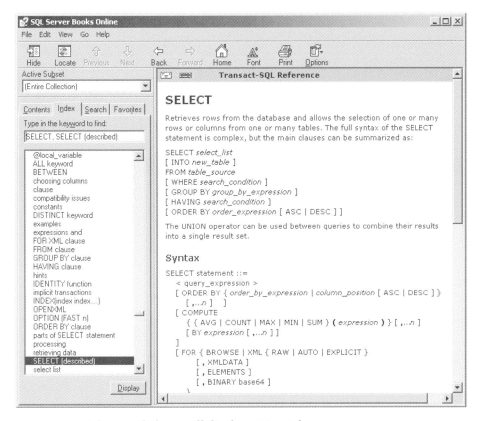

Figure 8-10. Selecting Shift-F1 will display TSQL Help.

What Is the Object Browser?

The QA Object Browser is one of the really nice enhancements that make upgrading to SQL Server 2000 worth it. When exploring views, you learned you should never use SELECT * over individual column names. One of the ways to specify individual column names in SQL Server 7 was to go into the QA and issue:

```
SELECT * FROM tablename WHERE 1=0
```

Using WHERE 1=0 guarantees that no rows will be returned, just the column names to the Results window. Then highlight all of the column names and paste them into a new query window. Use Ctrl-H to replace all double spaces with single spaces until there are no double spaces left, then replace each space with a space and comma. Now you have a list of column names that you can use. Tedious, no? In SQL Server 2000's QA, it's as simple as dragging and dropping.

The first thing to do is to open the Object Browser by selecting F8 and then drill down to the object that you want to use. If you're going to list all of the possible veterinarian specialties, you would drill down through **RDBA07**, User Tables, dbo.VeterinarianSpecialties, and Columns. Once you have the columns folder open, you can click on it to select it, and then drag it over to the SQL pane. Once you do that, all of the column names appear in the SQL pane (see Figure 8-11).

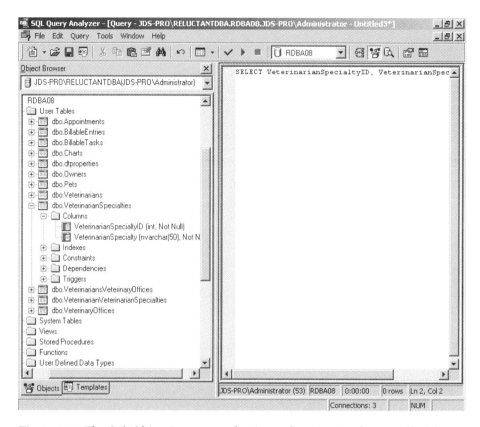

Figure 8-11. The QA's Object Browser makes it much easier to reference all of the columns in a table by name.

NOTE *When you drag and drop, the objects are displayed wherever the cursor was last, so if you accidentally place the cursor in the middle of a name, the objects you've selected will be placed in the middle of the name.*

Now that you've got the column names, you can type "FROM" and then drag the table name over, particularly handy with either long table names or a lot of columns. You'll notice that when you bring the table name over, it also supplies the "table owner" name prefixed to the table name, typically `dbo..tablename.`

> **NOTE** *If you try to drag the Columns folder before you open it, you'll get a message that says "No Script Generated." That's because the Object Browser doesn't actually query SQL Server for information until it needs to display it in the browser.*

If this were all that the Object Browser could do, it would be a fine addition, but there's much more to it. If you right-click on the VeterinarianSpecialties table (which displays a menu), you'll see a smorgasbord of choices available for this object. From here you can have the Object Browser open a new query window and insert a `SELECT`, `INSERT`, `UPDATE`, or `DELETE` statement that will have all of the columns defined (see Figure 8-12). It may not be perfect, but it sure is a much better starting point than having to cut and paste the column names.

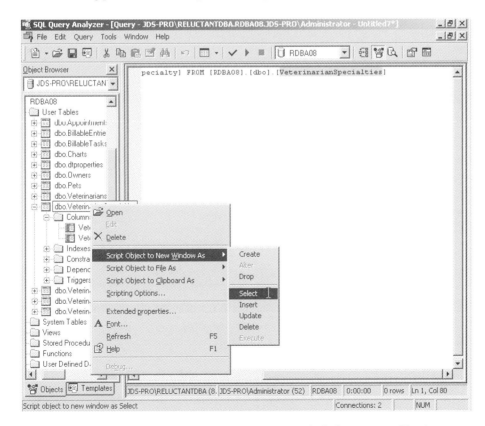

Figure 8-12. The QA's Object Browser offers point-and-click creation of basic `SELECT`, `INSERT`, `UPDATE`, *and* `DELETE` *TSQL code.*

CAUTION *When right-clicking on a view or table, do not select Open from the QA or the EM. You can lock up your table and cause all kinds of problems. Granted, the mere act of opening the table and browsing through it doesn't cause problems, but if you change any data, even by accident, you will lock that row. To verify this, I opened a table in the **NorthWind** database through the QA and modified one row. Then, with that QA window still open, I switched to another QA window and tried to use TSQL to* UPDATE *the row I had modified. That* UPDATE *was still waiting four hours later when I closed the editable grid. Once the grid closed, the* UPDATE *took place.*

Not only can you have Object Browser generate TSQL commands for you, you can choose where it creates the code. You can have it placed in a new QA window, save it to a file or copy it to the clipboard.

Can the Object Browser Help Me with Other TSQL Commands?

Having the Object Browser has made it much easier to build TSQL commands, both by providing a drag-and-drop data dictionary and by generating TSQL code, but there is one other really handy feature in the Object Browser.

After you've been using TSQL awhile, you'll discover that someone is going to want time-related information. For instance, you may want to know how much time has elapsed between two dates. You may need this if you're running a test to see whether one way of doing something is more efficient than another. SQL Server has several date functions and one, DATEDIFF, is handy for just such an occasion. But you probably won't use it often enough to have committed it to memory, so with SQL 7 you could type DATEDIFF into the QA, highlight it, and hit Shift-F1 to look up what parameters it had.

In the QA's Object Browser, however, all you need to do is to scroll to the bottom of the Object Browser to find the Common Objects section. As you can see from Figure 8-13, one of those handy items is a Date and Time Functions folder. When you open it, you can find DATEDIFF and right-click on it to script it to a new QA window. Then you just fill in the blanks and you're ready to go—well, almost ready to go. Sometimes you still need to hit BOL to find out what the datepart is for others you don't use that often, such as quarter (qq) or week (ww), for example.

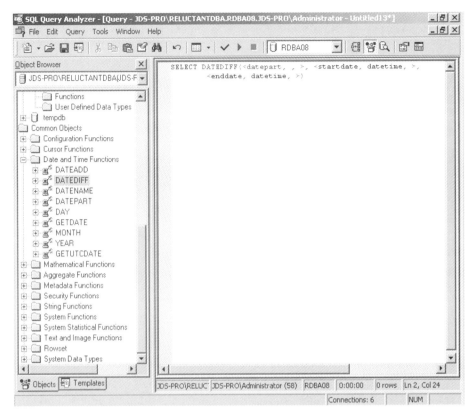

Figure 8-13. The QA's Object Browser offers a handy reference to TSQL functions.

Once you've got the DATEDIFF function listed in the SQL pane, then you've got another tool you can use to finish filling in the parameters. Looking at the code listed next, it almost seems as though the Object Browser was trying to tell you not only what each parameter was named but also what type of data it required. Well, it is doing that. Not only that, but you can easily fill in the parameters of this query by pressing Ctrl-Shift-M:

```
SELECT DATEDIFF(<datepart, , >, <startdate, datetime, >,  <enddate, datetime, >)
```

Ctrl-Shift-M brings up the Replace Template Parameters window. As you can see in Figure 8-14, this window lists the parameter name, the type of data it requires (if there is one), and gives you a place to fill in the values you want to use. When you press Replace Values, it changes all of the parameters for the ones you specify. Based on Figure 8-14, I should be able to replace the values and execute the query and get –7, right?

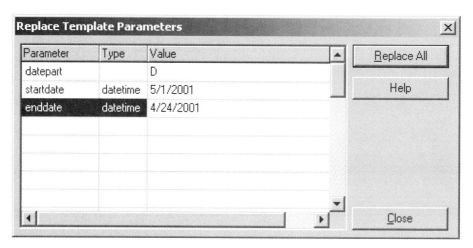

Figure 8-14. When the Object Browser creates a script with parameters, you can use the Replace Template Parameters window (Ctrl-Shift-M) to easily edit and replace them.

Wrong. I don't get –7, instead you get 0. Is there something wrong? Yes, but with these inputs, not with SQL Server. Even though the Replace Template Parameters window tells me that I need to use a DATETIME data type, I typed in 5/1/2001. Looks like a date, doesn't it? But SQL Server needs to have '5/1/2001'; the quotes define the date as a single entity instead of a mathematical equation. When you add quotes around both dates, you'll get –7, which is the correct result.

 CAUTION *The Replace Template Parameters window only lists data type as a convenience. It doesn't attempt to enforce that what you entered is of that data type.*

What Is a Template?

So, if the QA has a Replace Template Parameters window, does that mean it supports templates? Yup. In fact, if you look down at the bottom of Figures 8-11, 8-12, or 8-13 you'll find a second tab marked Templates. But what's a template?

A template is something that serves as a pattern. If you've used a wizard to generate stub code, then the stub code is a template for your program. It's got enough there to guide you in finishing the job. The QA templates serve the same function. They have just enough code and explanation to serve as a guide to accomplishing some task using Transact SQL. Templates are different from the script object menus because they tend to be more complex objects such as joins and cursors.

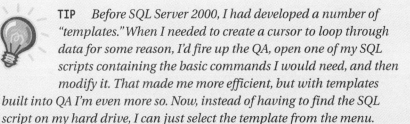

TIP   *Before SQL Server 2000, I had developed a number of "templates." When I needed to create a cursor to loop through data for some reason, I'd fire up the QA, open one of my SQL scripts containing the basic commands I would need, and then modify it. That made me more efficient, but with templates built into QA I'm even more so. Now, instead of having to find the SQL script on my hard drive, I can just select the template from the menu.*

How Do I Use a Template?

Using a template is as easy as double-clicking on one to open it. Open the Create Table folder and double-click on Create Table Basic Template. This will open up the template into a new QA window. Now that you've got the template open, you can save it and then modify it. Figure 8-15 shows the template for creating a temporary table.

CAUTION   *When you use a template, the first thing you should do is to save the file with a different name! If you don't, you can overwrite the template. One way to avoid overwriting your templates is to mark all of your template files as read only. That way you cannot overwrite them accidentally.*

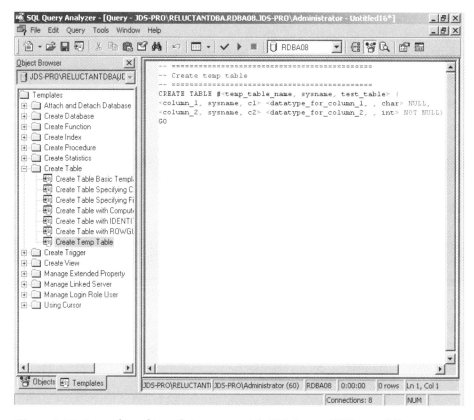

Figure 8-15. A number of templates come with SQL Server 2000, providing blueprints of TSQL code for common tasks such as creating tables.

Once the template is open, you'll notice a number of funny looking commands between < and >. Those are template parameters. Let's open a template and take another look at the parameters. Open the Create Table folder and then the Create Temp Table template. Now we're going to update the parameters using Ctrl-Shift-M, just as we did with the DATEDIFF function.

NOTE *I could have gone to Edit Replace Template Parameters, but I'm a shortcut kind of guy. Speaking of which, you'll notice that many of the menus displayed when you right-click include the shortcut keys as well. Happy shortcuts!*

If you've been following along at your computer, you may have noticed something different about what happened when you opened the Replace Template Parameters window this time. That's because the parameters all have default values assigned. Once again, you can make any changes and click Replace All, and the TSQL is ready to be used.

 CAUTION *Don't hit the Enter key. Hitting Enter will execute the Replace All. In addition, the Tab key takes you from the Grid to the buttons. Use the Up and Down arrow key to move between the rows to input your values.*

Can I Create My Own Query Analyzer Templates?

Of course, even with the more than 50 templates provided with SQL Server 2000, it won't have everything for everyone.

Making a QA template file is as simple as 1-2-3:

1. Open a new query window and write your Transact SQL statements.

2. For each part of the template you want to replace, use a parameter definition (see below).

3. Save the query with an extension of TQL for a template.

The trickiest part of building a template is putting the parameter definitions in place. Parameter definitions are simple. The first parameter in the definition is the parameter name, the second is the data type, and the third is the default value. Let's create a template. It's not a useful one since SELECT statements can be built from the Script Object To menu, but it will demonstrate how to build a template as well as a surprise benefit of templates:

```
-- Comments can be <comment,varchar,'anything you want'>
SELECT <SELECTLIST, , > FROM <tablename, , Veterinarians> WHERE <FilterClause,,>
```

Four parameters are defined for this template. One is the SELECTLIST where you can put in the columns that you want. Second is the tablename, and third is the WHERE clause. If you were to do an Edit ➢ Replace Template Parameters and press the Replace All button without changing anything, you'd get something that could almost be run.

```
-- Comments can be 'anything you want'
SELECT  FROM Veterinarians WHERE
```

Templates allow you to put parameters within the comments. That means that if you would like to have a standardized header for each stored procedure or view or whatever, you could incorporate them into a template with parameter definitions in the comments section. Then, as long as you build everything from the templates, you can just fill in the data without having to worry about how it looks.

Where Are My Templates Stored?

When you install SQL Server, the templates are stored in a shared directory, generally "Program Files\Microsoft SQL Server\80\Tools\Templates\SQL Query Analyzer." Each directory under this shows up as a folder in the Templates Tab, so you can easily create project specific folders and store your templates there.

Last Words

In this chapter you've been introduced to the Query Analyzer and some basic TSQL commands. In the next chapter you'll learn how to unleash the power of these commands through the use of stored procedures and user-defined functions. Along the way we'll also talk about why using stored procedures can make your programs more robust and how to build stored procedures (and tables and views) that will work well with other programs, even if the database needs to be changed.

Resources

There's no two ways around the simple fact that you have to learn Transact SQL. As much as you can do through the EM, there is more that you can do when you can write and modify the TSQL on your own. To that end, here are some great resources:

- Not necessarily the best resource for learning TSQL, but the original reference for all of the TSQL commands: SQL Server Books On Line.

- OK, this book is one that I recommend you have on your bookshelf but these guys do a pretty good job of explaining the details of TSQL: *Microsoft SQL Server 2000 Administrator's Companion* by Garcia, Reding, Whalen, and DeLuca (Microsoft Press).

- Once you've got the basics of TSQL down, get this book and work through it. One advantage of this book is that it starts with TSQL statements that look a lot like the ones I'm used to writing and demonstrates how to change them so they are much more efficient: *Advanced Transact SQL for SQL Server 2000* by Ben-Gan and Moreau (Apress).

- Bill does a good job of covering SQL related information while showing you how to program the client side of things: *ADO Examples and Best Practices* by William R. Vaughn (Apress).

- Another one of those books recommended for your bookshelf: *SQL For Smarties: Advanced SQL Programming, 2nd Edition* by Joe Celko (Morgan Kaufman).

CHAPTER 9

Working with Data: Basic Stored Procedures

A stored procedure is a group of SQL statements compiled into a single execution plan.
—SQL Server 2000 Books On Line, SQL Stored Procedures Overview

THIS CHAPTER AND CHAPTER 10, "Working with Data: Beyond the Basics," cover working with data. If you have turned to this chapter first because you need to start using stored procedures to improve performance, then you should at least skim through the preceding chapters. Performance improvements through programming within a database are only as good as the foundation they are built upon. No matter how well-crafted a stored procedure is, if you haven't built the underlying database efficiently to begin with, then your stored procedures won't give you the performance you seek.

Bear in mind that two chapters of a book are not enough to handle all of the nuances of programming a database. Although we're going to cover how to write stored procedures, user-defined functions, and triggers as well as some important and related concepts, this is just the beginning of what you need to know to program well in SQL Server. The "Resources" section at the end of this chapter will point you to additional resources.

In addition to learning the fundamentals, you should approach database programming with the goal of not breaking existing code. For example, if you were programming a COM object, you would define the methods and properties of the object and, once you had defined them, you would freeze them. If you needed to add parameters to a method, you would add them as optional parameters at the end of the parameter list. That way, any program that was using the object wouldn't necessarily break when the updated object was installed. The same philosophy should apply to database programming as well.

NOTE *This chapter relies heavily on the **RDBA09** database. You'll find instructions for installing that in Appendix A, "How Do I Load the Examples?" In addition, a number of SQL files in the "\Chapter09" directory on the CD contain the code for creating the various stored procedures and functions in this chapter. When the source code is available, the filename is listed in the caption of the code listing.*

What Is a Stored Procedure?

> *Reluctant DBA* definition of *stored procedure*:
> A stored procedure is a set of Transact SQL (TSQL) statements that function like a Visual Basic (VB) sub or an object's method. TSQL stored procedures allow for flow control, parameters, and output functionality.

In many ways, a stored procedure is like a Visual Basic (VB) sub or function. It can have parameters, and it can return data. The basic format for creating a stored procedure is:

```
CREATE PROCEDURE ProcedureName AS (TSQL CODE)
```

Let's start off by creating a stored procedure that returns a rowset. The TSQL code in Listing 9-1 can be found in the "\Chapter09" directory on the CD. It's in the file called ListOffices1.sql. All this procedure is going to do is return a rowset of data in the VeterinaryOffices table.[1]

There are two ways to create a stored procedure:

- Through the Query Analyzer (QA) by using the CREATE PROCEDURE command

- Through the Enterprise Manager (EM) by right-clicking on the stored procedures collection in the database where the procedure needs to be and selecting New Stored Procedure

Because a stored procedure is a collection of TSQL commands, you'll find that the editor for stored procedures is very plain. It has a large white area for entering the TSQL commands and six buttons along the bottom (see Figure 9-1).

---

[1]   For the traditionalists among you, you can find a HelloWorld.SQL in the "\Chapter09" directory on the CD.

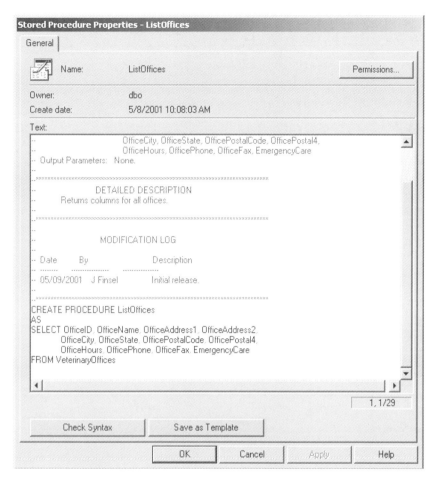

```
--                        OfficeCity, OfficeState, OfficePostalCode, OfficePostal4,
--                        OfficeHours, OfficePhone, OfficeFax, EmergencyCare
-- Output Parameters:  None.

-- ***********************************************************************
--
--                  DETAILED DESCRIPTION
--           Returns columns for all offices.
--
-- ***********************************************************************
--
--                  MODIFICATION LOG
--
-- Date       By            Description
-- --------   ------------  --------------
-- 05/09/2001   J Finsel       Initial release.
--
-- ***********************************************************************
CREATE PROCEDURE ListOffices
AS
SELECT OfficeID, OfficeName, OfficeAddress1, OfficeAddress2,
        OfficeCity, OfficeState, OfficePostalCode, OfficePostal4,
        OfficeHours, OfficePhone, OfficeFax, EmergencyCare
FROM VeterinaryOffices
```

Figure 9-1. The stored procedure edit window in the EM is sparse but functional.

The Check Syntax button does just that; it verifies there are no syntactic errors in your code and that all of the columns actually exist in any tables that are being referenced. The Save As Template button saves the procedure as a template.[2] The OK button saves the stored procedure and closes the edit window. The Cancel button closes the edit window without saving (though it prompts you if you have made any changes so you won't lose them). The Apply button saves any changes you have made but leaves the edit window open so you can make further changes. Finally, the Help button takes you to a description of the edit window. And no, Shift-F1 doesn't give you syntax help like it does in the QA, though it would be a nice enhancement. Type in the code below and then press the OK button. Assuming that you didn't mistype anything, then you should be returned to the EM and there should be a stored procedure listed named ListOffices.

---

[2]   Templates are covered in more detail in Chapter 8 in the section "What Is a Template?"

Listing 9-1. Creating a stored procedure to return a rowset of all offices. (ListOffices1.sql)

```
CREATE PROCEDURE ListOffices
AS
SELECT OfficeID, OfficeName, OfficeAddress1, OfficeAddress2, OfficeCity,
OfficeState, OfficePostalCode, OfficePostal4, OfficeHours, OfficePhone,
OfficeFax, EmergencyCare
FROM VeterinaryOffices
```

Listing 9-1 shows a fairly straightforward, though boring, stored procedure. It executes a single SELECT statement, exactly as if you had just put the SELECT statement into the QA. At least it should. To test it, start the QA, make sure you're in the correct database and then execute the following statement: EXEC ListOffices. If everything ran correctly, you should see a list of veterinary offices like the ones shown in Figure 9-2. Of course, you could have gotten the same information by issuing the SELECT statement directly in the QA window, raising the question of why should you use stored procedures.

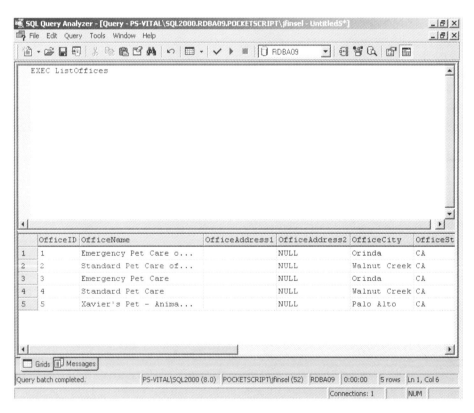

Figure 9-2. Executing ListOffices returns a rowset containing information for veterinary offices.

Commenting on Comments

The ListOffices1.sql file has a lot of text above the actual stored procedure in the form of a standard comment header that I use on all of my stored procedures, triggers, user-defined functions, and so forth. You'll find these header comments in the samples on the CD, but I am excluding them from the examples listed in the book. That's because the standard header I use has 20 lines in it. This header may look a little strange when a stored procedure is viewed in the EM because it uses a different font than the QA. That different font means the Modification Log columns don't appear to line up correctly when viewing an existing stored procedure in the EM.

Let me take a moment to go over the parts of the header, a template of which can be found in the StdHeaderComments.sql file in the "\Chapter09" directory on your CD and displayed in Listing 9-2. As you can see, all of the parts that need to be modified are set up as parameters that can be replaced using the QA's Parameter Replacement function. Having a header that explains what is going on and what changes have been made makes maintenance of any programming much easier, but using comments to create headers is only the tip of the iceberg for comment usage. I'll go over other areas and types of comments as I reach appropriate places to insert comments in the stored procedures.

Listing 9-2. A standardized header for procedures and functions (StdHeaderComment.sql)

```
--*************************************************************************
--    Stored Procedure : <NAME,,>.
--    Brief Description: <DESC,,>.
--    Parameters       :  Nonc.
--    Rowset Data      :  None.
--    Output Parameters:  None.
--*************************************************************************
--    DETAILED DESCRIPTION
--*************************************************************************
--    MODIFICATION LOG
--    Date          By                  Description
--    ____      _____-          _____
--    <InstallDate,mm/dd/yyyy,>    <Programmer,,>           Initial release.
-*************************************************************************
```

Why Use Stored Procedures?

We could probably spend a goodly amount of time detailing the benefits of stored procedures; in fact, we'll spend the next two chapters discussing not only how to build stored procedures and user-defined functions but *why* you should use them. For now, however, you should consider three simple points. The first two will be expanded upon as you go through this chapter. The third will be covered in more detail in Chapter 11, "How Do I Secure My Data?"

- Performance: We'll talk about the performance gains that you get because of the compiled execution plan in the next section, "What Is a 'Compiled Execution Plan'?" You also get performance gains because a stored procedure can take advantage of TSQL's branching logic to perform several steps in one call.

- Maintainability: When changes to the database are necessary, modifications can usually be made to the stored procedures to take these changes into account without requiring changes to the programs accessing the data. This is especially handy in n-tier applications.

- Security: We'll cover security in more depth in Chapter 11. For the moment, just remember that stored procedures are an integral part of providing manageable security.

What Is a "Compiled Execution Plan"?

Many programmers, when they start using SQL Server, read that SQL Server creates compiled stored procedures and misunderstand completely what the Books On Line (BOL) is trying to say. To understand how compiled execution plans work, let's take a look at how SQL Server treats a TSQL request for data.

If you were to isolate the SELECT statement from the ListOffices stored procedure and place it into the QA, you could press Ctrl-L and have SQL Server generate an execution plan. When SQL Server creates this execution plan, it takes the data and filters that you are requesting and analyzes them to determine the most efficient way to return the data. Once the most efficient manner of executing your request has been developed, SQL Server executes the TSQL.

Now, creating the execution plan takes some amount of time depending on the complexity of what is being requested. For very simple SELECT statements it could be a couple of milliseconds. More complex joins will take SQL Server longer to find the most efficient execution plan. This may be a matter of milliseconds, but it still adds up.[3] Once the execution plan has been created for an ad-hoc query like this, however, the plan may or may not be stored in cache. If it isn't stored in cache and an identical TSQL request comes along, the whole process of creating the execution plan takes place again. The execution plan for a stored procedure, however, is created the first time the procedure is executed and the plan is stored in cache. Then, whenever SQL Server executes the stored procedure, it checks to see if the plan is in cache. If it is, it uses the cached plan and executes that much more quickly.

What Are Parameters?

> *Reluctant DBA* definition of *parameters*:
> Parameters are named buckets that hold data that is passed between
> a program and a stored procedure or function.

OK, you now know why you should use stored procedures and we've created a stored procedure that returns a list of all of the Veterinary Offices. What if we wanted to get information for a single office? To accomplish this, we need to be able to tell the stored procedure how to filter the data we want. That means using parameters and expanding our stored procedure.

The first thing to consider when building a query that will filter a rowset is which column should be the filter. For this example we're going to use the table's primary key, OfficeID. Including parameters is fairly simple. All we need to do is add the parameter name and data type between the procedure name and the AS keyword. Parameters (and variables) are prefixed with the at symbol (@). System variables (coming up in a few pages) are prefixed with two at symbols (@@).

---

[3]   I encountered a situation where a process running under SQL Server was running in 500 milliseconds or half a second. Although that may seem a short time, it was being run so often that it was taking up almost eight hours a day of processing! Saving milliseconds can mean the difference between a system that can handle a few users or a lot.

Now, instead of adding a new stored procedure, we're going to modify the one we just created. In the EM we can double-click on the stored procedure and open the edit window. We're going to modify the stored procedure to have one parameter, shown in boldface. It is called @OfficeID and is defined as an INT data type. In the last line this parameter is used as a part of the WHERE condition.

Listing 9-3. Modifying ListOffices to filter based on the OfficeID specified as a parameter
```
CREATE PROCEDURE ListOffices @OfficeID int
AS
SELECT OfficeID, OfficeName, OfficeAddress1, OfficeAddress2, OfficeCity,
OfficeState, OfficePostalCode, OfficePostal4, OfficeHours, OfficePhone,
OfficeFax, EmergencyCare
FROM VeterinaryOffices WHERE OfficeID = @OfficeID
```

If you go back into the QA and put a 2 after the EXEC ListOffices, the data for Standard Pet Care of Walnut Creek (OfficeID 2) is returned. There's only one minor problem with this particular stored procedure—it's not backward compatible. If you try to execute ListOffices without a parameter, then you will get the following message:

Listing 9-4. Error messages occur when stored procedures that now have parameters are called by programs that were written to call the procedure with none.
```
Server: Msg 201, Level 16, State 3, Procedure ListOffices, Line 0
Procedure ListOffices expects parameter @OfficeID, which was not supplied.
```

That's not good. When programs change in ways that work differently, many people get upset, from programmers to users. Right now, we're really just defining and testing the stored procedure, but what if we had been modifying one that was in production? One goal of this chapter is to teach you how to build backward compatibility into stored procedures to limit the amount of code changes that need to be made on other tiers of n-tier programs. The first step in that direction is using default values to create optional parameters and then incorporating "logic" to deal with the parameters.

CREATE PROCEDURE or ALTER One?

Although the EM always displays CREATE PROCEDURE in the edit window, it doesn't really create a new procedure every time you edit the procedure. The only time you really *need* to use CREATE PROCEDURE is when the stored procedure is brand new. This does a couple of things, but most importantly it creates an object in the database with a unique ID number. This ID is used to determine what other objects are dependent upon the procedure, what security is related to the object, and a few other such tasks.

In TSQL you have two choices when it comes to changing a stored procedure (or table or index or . . . well, you get the general idea). The first is to use the DROP command (DROP PROCEDURE ListOffices for instance) followed by the CREATE command. The problem with this approach is that even if you re-create the exact same stored procedure, SQL Server will create a totally new object with a new ID and any security or references may be no good.

ALTER PROCEDURE was introduced in SQL Server 7 to resolve this issue. Using ALTER modifies the stored procedure without changing the ID, meaning that all of the other relationships associated with the ID are kept. When you click either the Apply or OK button in the edit window, the EM changes the CREATE PROCEDURE to an ALTER PROCEDURE and then executes the command. It's a subtle difference but one that you need to be aware of.

Despite all that, the code listings for this chapter all drop the object if it exists and create a new one. That's because I do not know whether you are running the code in order and I try not to assume. It would be possible to build a SQL script that would ALTER or CREATE as necessary, but it would be unnecessarily confusing for these samples.

What Are Optional Parameters?

> *Reluctant DBA* definition of *optional parameters*:
> Optional parameters are parameters for a stored procedure that contain a default value. Specifying a default value for the parameter means that the parameter doesn't need to be provided when calling the procedure.

As with many other programming languages, TSQL lets you predefine a default value for your parameters by using the equal sign (=) and the value after the data type definition. For instance, if you wanted to set a default value of 2 for the OfficeID, you could use CREATE PROCEDURE ListOffices @OfficeID int = 2. Now that you know how to provide a default value, you need to determine which value should be used for the default.

For this stored procedure, the answer is fairly easy. If we accept that the stored procedure's interface should never "break" when you modify it, then whenever there is no value provided, the stored procedure should return all rows as it did before we modified it. Fortunately, SQL Server has just the thing for specifying an unknown value, NULL. However, it isn't as easy as setting the default value for the @OfficeID to NULL. If that were the only step you took then the WHERE condition would never return any rows because the OfficeID column is a primary key and cannot be NULL. To modify this stored procedure to return all rows or a specific row it is necessary to do a little flow control programming.

This is a simple matter of adding an IF statement that checks to see if a value was provided. If there is no value then the stored procedure returns all rows; otherwise, it uses a WHERE condition. The resulting code looks like Listing 9-5.

Listing 9-5. ListOffices modified to have a default value for the parameter and to act like it did before the parameter was added if the parameter is not added (ListOffices2.sql)

```
CREATE PROCEDURE ListOffices @OfficeID int =NULL
AS
IF @OfficeID IS NULL -- Return all of the data
  SELECT OfficeID, OfficeName, OfficeAddress1, OfficeAddress2,  OfficeCity,
   OfficeState, OfficePostalCode, OfficePostal4, OfficeHours, OfficePhone,
   OfficeFax, EmergencyCare
  FROM VeterinaryOffices
ELSE -- @OfficeID is not null so return data for the requested OfficeID
  SELECT OfficeID, OfficeName, OfficeAddress1, OfficeAddress2,  OfficeCity,
    OfficeState, OfficePostalCode, OfficePostal4, OfficeHours, OfficePhone,
    OfficeFax, EmergencyCare
  FROM VeterinaryOffices WHERE OfficeID = @OfficeID
```

Now we have a stored procedure that can return either a rowset with one row or multiple rows, all depending on whether a parameter is passed.

To execute this stored procedure, go into the QA and execute the commands in Listing 9-6.

Listing 9-6. Displaying the differences between calling ListOffices with a parameter and without

```
EXEC ListOffices
EXEC ListOffices 2
```

This lists all of the Veterinary Offices in one rowset and just those for Standard Pet Care of Walnut Creek in the second. This a fairly straightforward piece of work.

Flow Control in TSQL

This book isn't designed to teach TSQL because there are some good books to handle that task already. And I am writing this book under the assumption that you already know how to program. With that in mind, I'm not going to attempt to teach you how to use an IF ELSE statement, but I am going to give you a quick rundown on the flow control statements used in TSQL. If you want more in-depth discussions of these, check the "Resources" section at the end of the chapter for some TSQL programming resources.

- **BEGIN** and **END** These two words bracket a piece of code and mark it as a complete section, much the way curly braces do in C++. These can be nested and it's recommended that you indent these just as you do any other control structure.

- **IF...ELSE** The biggest problem with the IF ELSE constructs is that they don't let you use THEN. The structure is "IF *condition* do this ELSE do that." If you are going to be performing more than one TSQL command you will need to use BEGIN and END. You'll see this demonstrated in this chapter.

- **WHILE ... CONTINUE ... BREAK** WHILE loops in TSQL have a BEGIN and an END. You'll see this demonstrated in the next chapter when I discuss Cursors. In the midst of the WHILE loop you can use CONTINUE and BREAK to go back to the beginning of the loop or exit out of the loop.

- **CASE ... WHEN ... THEN ... ELSE** This is used for conditional branching where you have multiple conditions. This is handy especially in UDFs.

- **Commenting Control Structures** Commenting your control structures is important. Although the IF part of an IF ELSE statement might be easy enough to understand, you should always comment your ELSE statement. This is particularly true when you start nesting IF statements so you know which ELSE applies to what. Whenever you are coding a part of a control statement you should add a brief comment to explain what you are doing.

Do I Have to Return a Rowset from My Stored Procedure?

Nope. In fact, there are many times when you won't want to return a rowset at all. Why, you ask? Because there is overhead associated with creating and returning a rowset, and not just on the server side. If you are updating or deleting a row of data, for instance, you may not need a rowset.

The short version of what happens is this: SQL Server collects all the information it needs for the rowset. Then it assembles the metadata that describes each column of data being returned and finally it assembles the data and returns all of this in one big package (unless you're using asynchronous recordsets and then it returns it in a bunch of smaller packages). Then, on the client side, the client needs to read the metadata and discover that the first column is called OfficeID and is an integer, and the second column is a string that can be so long and . . . you get the idea.

Rowsets vs. Output Parameters?

As far SQL Server is concerned, there is no difference between rowsets and output parameters. In one test I ran I created one stored procedure that returned a single-record rowset with two columns containing the values 1 and 2. Then I created a second stored procedure that returned the same data as output parameters. When I compared the two in a V B 6 program I found that it took 3 seconds to execute the output parameter stored procedure 10,000 times and *10* seconds to execute the one that returned the row set. According to SQL Server profiler, each stored procedure took the same amount of time to process, so all of the excess overhead was contained in the process of creating and returning the recordset.

This procedure is fine if you're returning a list of offices but when you only need the data for one office, it seems to be a little more work than the server or client needs to perform. To simplify life we can create a stored procedure that returns data via output parameters.

> *Reluctant DBA* definition of *output parameters*:
> Output parameters are parameters that can return data, much like using the ByRef keyword in VB. If the value is changed within the context of the stored procedure, the new value can be used by the client.

Creating an output parameter is easy—just add OUTPUT after the data type. The OUTPUT keyword tells SQL Server that these are two-way parameters; output parameters can have data passed into them and can be used to pass data back out. For the GetOffice stored procedure, we can define a parameter for each of the columns. All of the parameters except @OfficeID are output parameters.

Listing 9-7. Using output parameters is more efficient than returning one rowset of data. (GetOffice1.sql)

```
CREATE PROCEDURE GetOffice @OfficeID int, @OfficeName nvarchar (64) OUTPUT,
    @OfficeAddress1 nvarchar (64) OUTPUT,@OfficeAddress2 nvarchar (64) OUTPUT,
    @OfficeCity nvarchar (30) OUTPUT, @OfficeState nvarchar (2) OUTPUT,
    @OfficePostalCode nchar (5) OUTPUT, @OfficePostal4 nchar (4) OUTPUT,
    @OfficeHours nvarchar (256) OUTPUT, @OfficePhone numeric(10, 0) OUTPUT,
    @OfficeFax numeric(10, 0) OUTPUT, @EmergencyCare tinyint  OUTPUT
AS
  SELECT @OfficeName = OfficeName, @OfficeAddress1 = OfficeAddress1,
         @OfficeAddress2 = OfficeAddress2,  @OfficeCity = OfficeCity,
         @OfficeState = OfficeState,  @OfficePostalCode = OfficePostalCode,
         @OfficePostal4 = OfficePostal4, @OfficeHours = OfficeHours,
         @OfficePhone = OfficePhone, @OfficeFax = OfficeFax,
         @EmergencyCare = EmergencyCare
  FROM VeterinaryOffices WHERE OfficeID = @OfficeID
```

The hardest part about putting output parameters in a stored procedure is using them on the client side. The ListOffices stored procedure only required using EXEC ListOffices 2 to return a rowset. To use the GetOffice stored procedure, there are a number of steps that need to be taken. You need to declare a variable for each of the parameters, execute the stored procedure using OUTPUT after each output variable, and finally you need to print out the variables.[4]

To make it easier to understand how to use output parameters in TSQL, we're going to discuss each section of code separately: defining variables, executing, and then printing the results of the stored procedure.

What Is a Variable?

> *Reluctant DBA* definition of *variables*:
> Variables are named buckets that hold data that can be manipulated by name. They are named with the DECLARE keyword and require that the data type of the variable be specified.

If you think the definition of a variable sounds a lot like the definition of a parameter, you're correct. Parameters are just special variables. You create a variable by using DECLARE @variablename data type. Once you have declared a variable, you can reference it for as long as it remains in scope.

Variables remain in scope from the time they are created until the time the group of TSQL statements they are defined in is finished processing. TSQL state-

---

[4]   This is for executing the Stored Procedure in TSQL. If you want to use ADO you'll need to use a Command Object. Check out Bill Vaughn's *ADO Best Practices* book (see Appendix C, "Recommended for the Bookshelf") and make sure you download the Visual Basic add-in from his Web site that will write the VB code for you.

ments are grouped together by batch. A *batch* is either all of the TSQL statements to be run, or everything between the start of TSQL statements and a GO, or everything between GO statements. Scope also affects the variables within the stored procedure. Although you can name your variables any legal name, we're going to name each variable with the parameter name. SQL Server has separate buckets for the parameters and variables and keeps them separate even though they appear to have the same name. It is easier to track which variable is for which parameter that way. Listing 9-8 shows how to set up the variables that we'll use for displaying output parameters.

Listing 9-8. Setting up variables for the output parameters (included in GetOffice1.sql)

```
DECLARE @OfficeID int, @OfficeName nvarchar (64), @OfficeAddress1 nvarchar (64)
DECLARE @OfficeAddress2 nvarchar (64), @OfficeCity nvarchar (30)
DECLARE @OfficeState nvarchar (2), @OfficePostalCode nchar (5)
DECLARE @OfficePostal4 nchar (4), @OfficeHours nvarchar (256)
DECLARE @OfficePhone numeric(10, 0), @OfficeFax numeric(10, 0)
DECLARE @EmergencyCare tinyint
```

What Is GO?

GO is not a SQL keyword. Instead, it is a special command for the utility that is processing the TSQL. If you look at the SQL files for the stored procedures created so far in this chapter, you'll notice that they have the CREATE PROCEDURE command and all of the TSQL that goes into that, then the word GO, and then the code to execute the stored procedure.

When the QA processes these scripts, it takes all of the code above the GO and uses it to create the stored procedure. It then takes all of the code below the GO and processes it next.

Now that we've got variables defined, we need to fill them. Filling a variable in this instance requires placing the word OUTPUT after the variable in the parameter list. An OUTPUT stored procedure parameter doesn't require the OUTPUT keyword when you execute the procedure. If you don't specify the OUTPUT for a parameter on the client side, you simply don't get data back. If you specify OUTPUT for a parameter on the client side that isn't an OUTPUT parameter in the stored procedure, then you get an error back. Listing 9-9 shows the actual execution of the stored procedure using output parameters.

Listing 9-9. Using variables to store output parameters (included in GetOffice1.sql)

```
EXEC GetOffice 2, @OfficeName OUTPUT, @OfficeAddress1 OUTPUT,
     @OfficeAddress2 OUTPUT, @OfficeCity OUTPUT, @OfficeState OUTPUT,
     @OfficePostalCode OUTPUT, @OfficePostal4 OUTPUT, @OfficeHours OUTPUT,
     @OfficePhone OUTPUT, @OfficeFax OUTPUT, @EmergencyCare OUTPUT
```

OK, so we've defined variables and passed them to the stored procedure specifying OUTPUT. Now all we need to do is display them so we can see how they worked. The easiest way to do that is to use the PRINT command. PRINT, as you might guess, displays data to the client. PRINT expects to be handed one variable to display. This leads to a couple of interesting side effects when PRINT tries to translate multi-data types to a single data type.

For instance, NULL added to anything creates NULL and NULL isn't really anything so PRINT 'This is a test of ' + NULL results in a blank line because the whole string is translated to NULL.[5] Another problem that can occur with PRINT happens when you attempt to print numbers. PRINT 5+55 will correctly display 60. The only problem is, so will PRINT '5' + 55. Even though PRINT takes a string or anything that can be translated to a string, it will first try to translate to numbers if they are present. In fact, if you try to do PRINT 'Four is ' + 4 the error message you get back is a syntax error converting 'Four is ' to an int! Listing 9-10 demonstrates how to print out the results of populating the variables with data from the stored procedure.

Listing 9-10. Printing the results of the OUTPUT parameters (included in GetOffice1.sql)

```
PRINT 'OfficeName = ' + @OfficeName
PRINT 'OfficeAddress1 = ' + @OfficeAddress1
PRINT 'OfficeAddress2 = ' + ISNULL(@OfficeAddress2, 'NULL')
PRINT 'OfficeCity = ' + @OfficeCity
PRINT 'OfficeState = ' + @OfficeState
PRINT 'OfficePostalCode = ' + @OfficePostalCode
PRINT 'OfficePostal4 = ' + ISNULL(@OfficePostal4, 'NULL')
PRINT 'OfficeHours = ' + @OfficeHours
PRINT 'OfficePhone = ' + CONVERT(varchar(20),@OfficePhone)
PRINT 'OfficeFax = ' + CONVERT(varchar(20), @OfficeFax)
PRINT 'EmergencyCare = ' + CONVERT(Varchar(3),@EmergencyCare )
```

---

[5]   This is actually a configurable option. Check out BOL under CONCAT_NULL_YIELDS_NULL.

CAUTION *One side effect of* PRINT *is that it generates a phantom recordset back to ActiveX Data Object (ADO). For this reason, putting* PRINT *in a stored procedure is generally not a good idea.*

To get around these two limitations, we have used an ISNULL function to display the string NULL. If we hadn't done this, OfficeAddress2 would show up as a blank line. We also used CONVERT to change the non-character data to character based so that we wouldn't get any errors. Once this is run, the data is returned and displayed correctly.

Can an OUTPUT Parameter Also Be Used for Input?

Yes. Just because you are returning data doesn't mean you can't pass the data into the stored procedure as well. Let's modify GetOffice to take either the OfficeID *or* the OfficeName. That requires two changes. One to make OfficeID an output parameter, and the other is to provide branching logic to look based on whichever parameter is provided. This code can be found in GetOffice2.sql on your CD.

Listing 9-11. Writing a stored procedure to use parameters for both INPUT **and** OUTPUT **(GetOffice2.sql)**

```
CREATE PROCEDURE GetOffice @OfficeID int = NULL OUTPUT,
@OfficeName nvarchar (64) = NULL OUTPUT, @OfficeAddress1 nvarchar (64) OUTPUT,
@OfficeAddress2 nvarchar (64) OUTPUT, @OfficeCity nvarchar (30) OUTPUT,
@OfficeState nvarchar (2) OUTPUT, @OfficePostalCode nchar (5) OUTPUT,
@OfficePostal4 nchar (4) OUTPUT, @OfficeHours nvarchar (256) OUTPUT,
@OfficePhone numeric(10, 0) OUTPUT, @OfficeFax numeric(10, 0) OUTPUT,
@EmergencyCare tinyint  OUTPUT
AS
IF @OfficeID IS NOT NULL -- Filter the data by the OfficeID
   SELECT @OfficeName = OfficeName, @OfficeAddress1 = OfficeAddress1,
        @OfficeAddress2 = OfficeAddress2,  @OfficeCity = OfficeCity,
        @OfficeState = OfficeState,  @OfficePostalCode = OfficePostalCode,
        @OfficePostal4 = OfficePostal4, @OfficeHours = OfficeHours,
        @OfficePhone = OfficePhone, @OfficeFax = OfficeFax,
        @EmergencyCare = EmergencyCare
   FROM VeterinaryOffices WHERE OfficeID = @OfficeID
ELSE -- OfficeID was NULL so filter by OfficeName
   SELECT @OfficeID = OfficeID, @OfficeAddress1 = OfficeAddress1,
        @OfficeAddress2 = OfficeAddress2,  @OfficeCity = OfficeCity,
```

```
        @OfficeState = OfficeState, @OfficePostalCode = OfficePostalCode,
        @OfficePostal4 = OfficePostal4, @OfficeHours = OfficeHours,
        @OfficePhone = OfficePhone, @OfficeFax = OfficeFax,
        @EmergencyCare = EmergencyCare
  FROM VeterinaryOffices WHERE OfficeName = @OfficeName
```

SET or SELECT, Which Is Correct?

So far, we've been using SELECT to set all of the variables, usually in the form SELECT @VariableName = value. That's because we have been setting multiple variables at the same time. At some point you'll see me doing SET @VariableName = value. The real difference between them is that SET works on one variable at a time and SELECT works on several.

What Is the Return Code?

The last type of parameter is the Return Code. This parameter doesn't *need* to be defined; it is built into every stored procedure. BOL calls it a *return code*, but VB treats it like a parameter.

The way it works is fairly simple. At the exit point of the stored procedure you put the keyword RETURN and follow it by an integer value. Any time the return code is not explicitly defined, it is returned as a 0. Take a look at the sample in Listing 9-12. It takes one parameter, an INT, and then compares to see if it is equal to 1 or not. If the parameter equals 1, then the procedure exits using RETURN and no parameter. If it is not equal to 1 then it prints a message and returns 1. Return codes are frequently used to flag that an error has happened. Many programmers set the return code to 1 to indicate a problem occurred.

Listing 9-12. Creating a stored procedure to demonstrate return codes (ReturnCodeSample.sql)

```
CREATE PROCEDURE TestReturnCode @iVerify int
AS
IF @iVerify = 1
    RETURN
ELSE  — Verify is not 1
    PRINT '@iVerify must = 1'
RETURN 1
GO
DECLARE @iTest int
EXEC @iTest = TestReturnCode 1
PRINT @iTest
EXEC @iTest = TestReturnCode 2
PRINT @iTest
```

After the stored procedure is created, we define a variable and then call the stored procedure to get the return code. To get the return code we simply put a variable and an equal sign between the word EXEC and the stored procedure name.

Updating Data through Stored Procedures

There are two broad categories of stored procedures: those that manipulate data and those that retrieve data. The procedures we've shown so far have all been those that return data, generally filtered data in some fashion. Now the time has come, however, to look at data manipulation through stored procedures.

A great deal has been written about how to build n-tier applications that separate data, business rules, and the user interface. Sometimes this separation leads programmers to believe that simply using SQL Server is "data" enough for the data portion, and they overlook the benefits of stored procedures, preferring to use SELECT, INSERT, UPDATE, and so forth from the whichever tier is connecting to the database. At the beginning of the chapter you read several reasons why stored procedures are preferable to executing TSQL directly, but this section is going to focus on two of those reasons:

- Stored procedures execute multiple statements in a single network call, eliminating the overhead of multiple calls between the client and SQL Server.

- It is easier to maintain one set of code in a stored procedure than to have to find every instance of that code throughout your programs when modifications are required.

To demonstrate these two points you're going to learn how to create stored procedures for manipulating data. Let's begin by taking a look at some of the tools SQL Server gives us for creating stored procedures.

Stored Procedure Wizardry

SQL Server has a wizard for helping with the creation of basic data manipulation stored procedures. Let me walk you through creating a set of procedures for inserting, updating, and deleting a row of data from Owners. To begin with, start the Create Stored Procedure Wizard. To do this, select Tools ➢ Wizards from the EM wizard. This brings up the Select Wizard tool. Under Database in the tree you'll find Create Stored Procedure Wizard (see Figure 9-3).

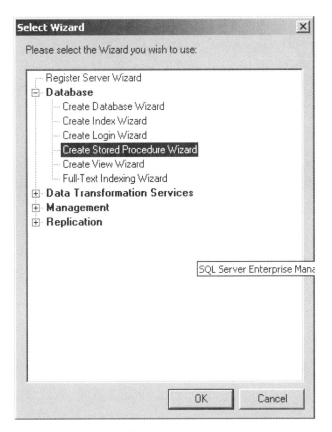

Figure 9-3. SQL Server has a wizard for creating stored procedures.

The wizard tells you that it is going to let you select a database, generate stored procedures to update, insert or delete data, and give you an opportunity to modify the stored procedure properties and the TSQL statements that make up the new stored procedures. Click Next and you'll be presented with a drop-down list of the databases on the server. Select **RDBA09** and then click Next. The next screen will list all of the tables in the database with checkboxes for Insert, Delete, and Update. For now, click on all three options for Owners and then select Next (see Figure 9-4).

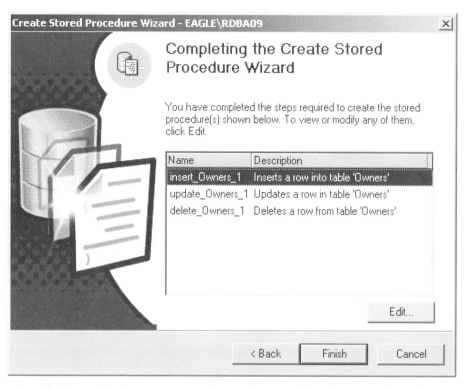

Figure 9-4. The wizard lets you create insert, delete, and update procedures for each table.

Now the wizard displays three stored procedures: insert_Owners_1, update_Owners_1, and delete_Owners_1. You can now make modifications before the procedure gets created. Before we do that, however, let's look at the output from the wizard for insert_Owners_1 in Listing 9-13. We've eliminated some of the white space so the output fits better on the page, but you can see the basics. The wizard creates a parameter for each of the columns in the table. You can modify the stored procedure by clicking on the Edit button before finishing the wizard.

Listing 9-13. insert_Owners_1 as created by the wizard

```
USE [RDBA09]
GO
CREATE PROCEDURE [insert_Owners_1]
  (@OwnerID_1 [int], @OwnerLastName_2 [nvarchar](30),
  @OwnerFirstName_3 [nvarchar](36), @OwnerAddress1_4 [nvarchar](64),
  @OwnerAddress2_5 [nvarchar](64), @OwnerCity_6 [nvarchar](30),
  @OwnerState_7 [nchar](2), @OwnerPostalCode_8 [nchar](5),
  @OwnerPostal4_9 [nchar](4), @OwnerPhoneNumber_10 [numeric],
  @OwnerEmailAddress_11 [nvarchar](50))
```

```
AS INSERT INTO [RDBA09].[dbo].[Owners]
  ( [OwnerID], [OwnerLastName], [OwnerFirstName], [OwnerAddress1],
  [OwnerAddress2], [OwnerCity], [OwnerState], [OwnerPostalCode],
  [OwnerPostal4], [OwnerPhoneNumber], [OwnerEmailAddress])
VALUES ( @OwnerID_1, @OwnerLastName_2, @OwnerFirstName_3,
  @OwnerAddress1_4, @OwnerAddress2_5, @OwnerCity_6,
  @OwnerState_7, @OwnerPostalCode_8, @OwnerPostal4_9,
  @OwnerPhoneNumber_10, @OwnerEmailAddress_11)
```

As you can see in Figure 9-5, the Edit button brings up a window that lists all of the columns for a table and lets you select or deselect the columns, rename the stored procedure, and even edit the TSQL of the stored procedure. As stored procedures go, it's not bad, but it's also not necessarily the best either. To begin with, insert_Owners_1 lets you pass in a value for OwnerID, an identity column. If you attempt to execute this stored procedure, you'll end up with an error because you're not allowed to insert explicit values for identity columns unless you take other steps!

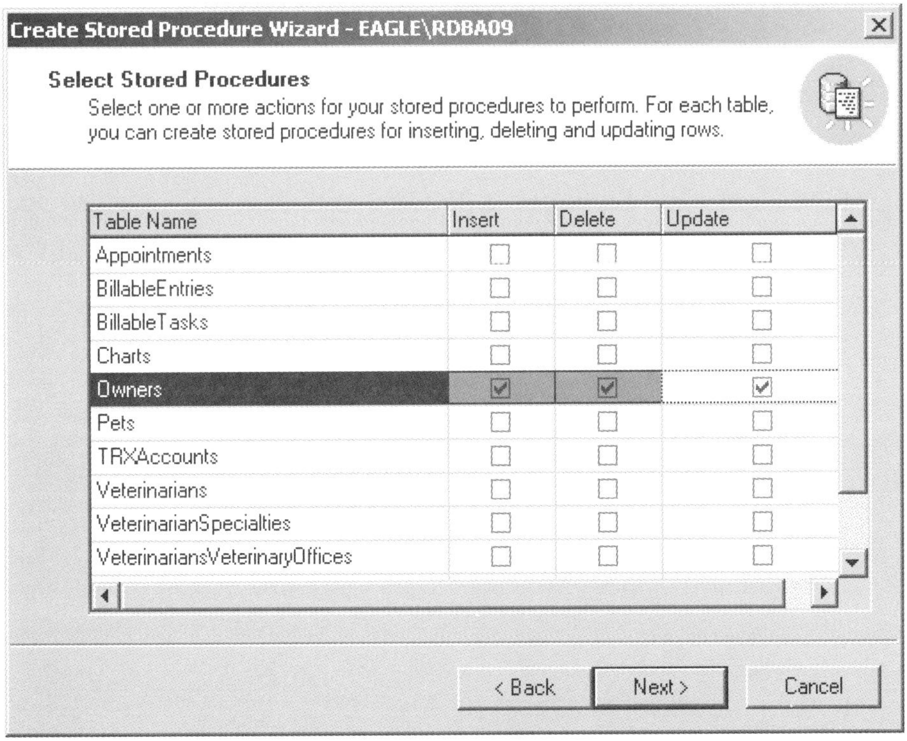

Figure 9-5. You can edit which columns are included in the stored procedure, rename it, and even modify the TSQL code from the edit window of the CreateStored Procedure Wizard.

The Create Stored Procedure Wizard also generates two procedures that do similar things: Insert and Update both modify data in a table. Wouldn't it be nice to put the two together so that you don't have to make changes in multiple procedures when you make changes to a table? How about an intelligent stored procedure that knows whether you're inserting or updating?

Intelligent Stored Procedures

An intelligent stored procedure is one that can react appropriately to the data given to it. The last chapter introduced EXISTS, and this chapter is going to use it to give our stored procedure some intelligence. Instead of having the client determine whether to insert or update data, the stored procedure will do it. The first thing the stored procedure does is determine whether the @OwnerID exists in the Owners table. If it doesn't exist there, then the data is inserted and the identity column is returned in an output parameter. If the data does exist, then the existing data is updated. To force an insert, a value like –1 is used for the OwnerID.

Listing 9-14. An intelligent stored procedure (usr_Owners_up.sql)

```
CREATE PROCEDURE usr_Owners_up
@OwnerID int OUTPUT, @OwnerLastName nvarchar(30),
@OwnerFirstName nvarchar(36), @OwnerAddress1 nvarchar(64),
@OwnerAddress2 nvarchar(64), @OwnerCity nvarchar(30),
@OwnerState nchar(2), @OwnerPostalCode nchar(5),
@OwnerPostal4 nchar(4), @OwnerPhoneNumber numeric(18,0),
@OwnerEmailAddress nvarchar(50)
AS
IF NOT EXISTS (SELECT * FROM Owners WHERE OwnerID = @OwnerID )
BEGIN
INSERT Owners (OwnerLastName,OwnerFirstName,OwnerAddress1,OwnerAddress2,
OwnerCity,OwnerState,OwnerPostalCode,OwnerPostal4,OwnerPhoneNumber,
OwnerEmailAddress)
VALUES(@OwnerLastName,@OwnerFirstName,@OwnerAddress1,@OwnerAddress2,@OwnerCity,
@OwnerState,@OwnerPostalCode,@OwnerPostal4,@OwnerPhoneNumber,
@OwnerEmailAddress)
SELECT @OwnerID = @@Identity
END
ELSE
UPDATE Owners
SET OwnerLastName= @OwnerLastName,OwnerFirstName= @OwnerFirstName,
OwnerAddress1= @OwnerAddress1,OwnerAddress2= @OwnerAddress2,
OwnerCity= @OwnerCity,OwnerState= @OwnerState,
OwnerPostalCode= @OwnerPostalCode,OwnerPostal4= @OwnerPostal4,
OwnerPhoneNumber= @OwnerPhoneNumber,OwnerEmailAddress= @OwnerEmailAddress
WHERE OwnerID = @OwnerID
```

One advantage to having a multi-use stored procedure like this is that it is easier to maintain one stored procedure than it is to maintain multiple procedures. If a change is made to the Owners table, say a column is added to store some demographic information, you only need to change one stored procedure, although you'll need to modify the Parameter list, the insert and update parts of the procedure.

A second advantage to this type of procedure is that it cuts down on network calls. You could accomplish the same thing from the client, check to see if the primary key exists, and then insert or update as appropriate, but that takes two calls to the server where this takes one.

A final advantage to this stored procedure over the wizard is that it returns a valuable piece of information, the value of the newly created identity column. For our purposes, it allows the client program to create the Owner and get the OwnerID back so that whatever pets need to be added can be added without having to make another call to the server to find out what that value was.[6]

Introducing User-Defined Functions

New in SQL Server 2000 are user-defined functions (UDFs). UDFs are functions similar to VB functions. They can take parameters just like a stored procedure but the similarity ends there. Two types of UDFs exist: those that return a simple value and those that return a table. A UDF that returns a single value can be used anywhere that a variable or constant can be. A UDF that returns a table can be used anywhere that a table can be. Let's start with a simple UDF that returns one value: the OwnerID associated with phone number.

UDFs take parameters, just like stored procedures do, but they can't be output parameters. In addition, UDFs require an explicit RETURN, and the code for the UDF must be bracketed between BEGIN and END. Just like a VB function, UDFs require a strongly typed return value, in this case an INT. This function takes a phone number, looks up the associated OwnerID, and returns the value of the OwnerID.

Listing 9-15. A UDF to return the OwnerID associated with a phone number (OwnerByPhone.sql)

```
CREATE FUNCTION dbo.OwnerByPhone (@PhoneNumber numeric(18,0)) RETURNS int
AS
BEGIN
DECLARE @OwnerID int
SELECT @OwnerID = OwnerID FROM Owners WHERE OwnerPhoneNumber = @PhoneNumber
RETURN @OwnerID
END
```

---

6. Now, I'm going to have to be honest and admit that another reason I like this multi-use stored procedure is that I wrote a utility to write them back when SQL Server 6.5 was around before the wizards came on the scene. In my humble opinion, my stored procedures are better than those the wizard creates.

Whenever you reference a UDF you need to qualify it with owner of the function. We'll cover this in much more depth in Chapter 11, "How Do I Secure My Data?" Suffice it to say that every object that gets created is associated with an owner of that object. In many cases that owner will be dbo (database owner), but it is possible to have objects owned by other logins. If you have appropriate permissions, you can use dbo when you create an object, just as we have in this UDF, and then it will be created with dbo as the owner. To get data from this UDF, we're going to put the following into the QA: PRINT RDBA09.dbo.OwnerByPhone(5105495930). When this runs, it returns the value 2.

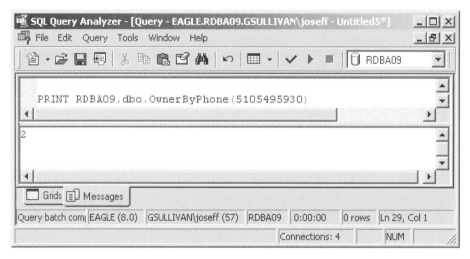

Figure 9-6. UDFs can return a single value.

Now that we have UDF that returns an OwnerID, wouldn't it be neat if we could use it in a stored procedure as a parameter? If you know the phone number of an owner but not the OwnerID, wouldn't it be great to make one call to the database using something like this:

```
EXEC GetOwner dbo.OwnerByPhone(5105495930)
```

Well, it would be great but it doesn't work. To understand why not, you'll have to turn to BOL, which states:

When a stored procedure is executed, input parameters can either have their value set to a constant or use the value of a variable. Output parameters and return codes must return their values into a variable. Parameters and return codes can exchange data values with either Transact-SQL variables or application variables.

In other words, the parameter must contain either a variable or a value, but it can't contain anything that requires further resolution, say a UDF or even a simple equation like 1+1. So you would need to get the value from the UDF and then turn around and use that value in the GetOwner stored procedure.

Non-Data Related Functions

Although many of the functions in this book are related to manipulating data, you don't need to use any data manipulation routines in a UDF. One example frequently used in programming manuals is creating a function that returns the minimum of two values. With that in mind, we're going to create an iMin function that takes two integers and returns the lower of the two.

First, let's look at the classic MIN function in Listing 9-16.

Listing 9-16. Classic psuedo-code for a MIN function

```
Function Min(x,y)
   if x < y
      return x
   else
      return y
```

This UDF may not work the way you think it would. The first problem with the classic pseudo-code is that a UDF can only have one return point. So instead you'll have to store the minimum value in a variable and return it after you have finished evaluating the values, as displayed in Listing 9-17.

Listing 9-17. First pass at iMin (iMin1.sql)

```
CREATE FUNCTION iMin(@x int, @y int) RETURNS  int
AS
BEGIN
DECLARE @MinValue int
IF @X < @Y
   SET @MinValue = @X
ELSE – @X > @Y
   SET @MinValue = @Y
RETURN  @MinValue
END
```

A much better way to handle this is to use the CASE...WHEN...THEN...ELSE structure.[7] There are two ways you can use the CASE structure. The first is just like

---

[7] I discovered this after reading Jason Rein's great introduction to UDFs, "Implement Easier Reuse," in the April 2001 edition of *Visual Basic Programmer's Journal.*

in VB: evaluating multiple WHEN statements against a single value, as shown in Listing 9-18. This is the simple great introduction to UDFs and requires that each WHEN be evaluated as equal to the same variable. In this case, with @Price set to 12, the ELSE statement will be used because 12 is not equal to 10 or 20.

Listing 9-18. CASE **statement evaluating a single variable (SimpleCaseSample.sql)**

```
DECLARE @Price int
SET @Price = 12
SELECT CASE @Price
    WHEN 10 THEN 'Cheap'
    WHEN 20 THEN 'Moderate'
    ELSE 'If you have to ask you can''t afford it'
    END
```

The second form of the CASE, the *searched* CASE, allows for each WHEN to have an expression to be evaluated. This is the CASE that can be used with iMin to make it a simpler function, as demonstrated in Listing 9-19. The one line says that WHEN @x is less than @y return @x else @y. We'll be revisiting this function in Chapter 10, "Working with Data: Beyond the Basics."

Listing 9-19. An improved iMin **using the searched** CASE **statement (iMin2.sql)**

```
CREATE FUNCTION iMin(@x int, @y int) RETURNS  int
AS
BEGIN
RETURN CASE WHEN @x < @y THEN @x ELSE @y END
END
```

How Do I Return Rowsets from a UDF?

Back in Chapter 5, you learned there was a data type that can't be used as a column, the TABLE data type. Now that we've gotten to the point of using UDFs, let's explore the TABLE data type. There are two ways that you can return rowsets from a UDF:

- Inline functions

- Multistatement table functions

Inline Functions

Inline functions are often referred to as *parameterized queries* because they are returning a rowset like a query but they can be filtered by their parameters.

> *Reluctant DBA* definition of *inline functions*:
> A UDF that returns a rowset that uses the function parameters to filter the data in the WHERE condition of the SELECT statement. Inline functions can be used in the FROM clause of a SELECT.

Let's say that you want to generate a mailing list for owners that are associated with a specific office. One option is to create a view that joins all of the relevant tables together, from Owners to Pets to VeterinaryOffices. Then, once the view is together you can use a WHERE condition to filter only the records you want. That leads to the TSQL that you see in Listing 9-20.

Listing 9-20. Joining tables together to get a mailing list

```
SELECT DISTINCT dbo.Owners.OwnerLastName, dbo.Owners.OwnerFirstName,
dbo.Owners.OwnerAddress1, dbo.Owners.OwnerAddress2, dbo.Owners.OwnerCity,
dbo.Owners.OwnerState, dbo.Owners.OwnerPostalCode, dbo.Owners.OwnerPostal4
FROM dbo.Owners INNER JOIN dbo.Pets ON dbo.Owners.OwnerID = dbo.Pets.OwnerID
INNER JOIN dbo.VeterinaryOffices ON dbo.Pets.OfficeID =
dbo.VeterinaryOffices.OfficeID
```

You could easily turn this cumbersome join into a view but then you'd need to add dbo.VeterinaryOffices.OfficeName to the list of available columns, which might just cause confusion. It would be possible to create a separate view for each office, filtering each view to only contain the Owners for that office but that would create a maintenance nightmare. Or you could create a UDF using Office-Name as the parameter that returns a filtered rowset. That's exactly what we're doing in Listing 9-21. Once you've finished creating the UDF, you can use it anywhere you would reference a table, for instance SELECT * FROM MailingListByName(N'Emergency Pet Care').

Listing 9-21. A UDF can return a rowset of data that is filtered by the parameter(s) (MailingListOffice.sql)

```
CREATE Function MailingListByOffice(@OfficeName nvarchar(64))
RETURNS TABLE
AS
RETURN(
SELECT DISTINCT dbo.Owners.OwnerLastName, dbo.Owners.OwnerFirstName,
dbo.Owners.OwnerAddress1, dbo.Owners.OwnerAddress2, dbo.Owners.OwnerCity,
dbo.Owners.OwnerState, dbo.Owners.OwnerPostalCode, dbo.Owners.OwnerPostal4
```

```
FROM dbo.Owners INNER JOIN dbo.Pets ON dbo.Owners.OwnerID =
dbo.Pets.OwnerID INNER JOIN dbo.VeterinaryOffices ON dbo.Pets.OfficeID =
dbo.VeterinaryOffices.OfficeID
WHERE dbo.VeterinaryOffices.OfficeName = @OfficeName)
```

UDF or Stored Procedure?

Now, you may be wondering why a UDF would be better than a stored procedure in this case. After all, both of them can return a rowset, both can use a parameter to filter the rowset. What's so special about a UDF?

Well, it's true that you can return a rowset of data from a stored procedure, but if you want to do anything with that on the SQL Server side, you'll need to jump through some hoops to use it. Let's say that we wanted to send a mailer to folks in one zip code from one office. If we had a stored procedure that returned the mailing list we would need to:

1. Create a temporary table to store the results of the stored procedure.

2. INSERT the results of the stored procedure into the temporary table.

3. SELECT using a WHERE condition to get the data needed.

4. DROP the temporary table.

This compares to using one line of TSQL code with a UDF. Listing 9-22 shows the difference between the two methods.

Listing 9-22 Filtering data from a UDF is much easier than filtering the results of a stored procedure (SprocVFunction.sql)

```
-- This is required for the Stored Procedure
CREATE TABLE #tmp (
    [OwnerLastName] [nvarchar] (30) ,
    [OwnerFirstName] [nvarchar] (36) ,
    [OwnerAddress1] [nvarchar] (64) ,
    [OwnerAddress2] [nvarchar] (64) ,
    [OwnerCity] [nvarchar] (30) ,
    [OwnerState] [nchar] (2) ,
    [OwnerPostalCode] [nchar] (5) ,
    [OwnerPostal4] [nchar] (4)
) ON [PRIMARY]
GO
INSERT INTO #tmp  EXEC MailingListByOfficeP 'Emergency Pet Care'
SELECT * FROM #tmp WHERE OwnerPostalCode = 94710
```

```
DROP TABLE #tmp

-- This is for the UDF
SELECT * FROM MailingListByOffice('Emergency Pet Care')
WHERE OwnerPostalCode = 94710
```

UDFs are better than stored procedures whenever the stored procedure is returning a single rowset that uses parameters to filter the data and returns only one rowset. But there are certain limitations to UDFs that can be summed up by saying that a UDF must not change the database. That means that a UDF cannot:

- Modify the database structure or database data in any way.

- Communicate with the outside world through email.

- `COMMIT` or `ROLLBACK` transactions.

- Use indeterminate functions.[8]

Outside of these minor limitations, UDFs create a powerful extension to your programming abilities in SQL Server.

Multistatement Table Functions

We've just finished demonstrating how the inline function works for returning a `TABLE` data type, but there is another way to do the same thing. The multistatement table function is similar to the inline function, but there is a fundamental difference between the two: the multistatement table function returns a fully declared table variable.

The best way to explain that is with a demonstration. We're going to build a new function called MailingListByOfficeML (ML for Multi Line in this case). As you can see from Listing 9-23 there are two differences in the way the UDF is built. In an inline function you merely define the `RETURNS` data type. In a multistatement table function you define the whole table. The second is that the `BEGIN` and `END` are required. The really big difference, however, lies in the way that SQL Server treats the two when caching execution plans.

---

[8] Indeterminate functions are those that change when called. For instance NewID and GetDate return different values every time they are called so you aren't allowed to use them in a UDF.

Listing 9-23. A multistatement table function returns a fully declared table variable (MailingLIstByOfficeML.sql)

```
CREATE Function MailingListByOfficeML(@OfficeName nvarchar(64))
RETURNS @MailingList TABLE ([OwnerLastName] [nvarchar] (30) ,
    [OwnerFirstName] [nvarchar] (36) ,
    [OwnerAddress1] [nvarchar] (64) ,
    [OwnerAddress2] [nvarchar] (64) ,
    [OwnerCity] [nvarchar] (30) ,
    [OwnerState] [nchar] (2) ,
    [OwnerPostalCode] [nchar] (5) ,
    [OwnerPostal4] [nchar] (4) )
AS
BEGIN
INSERT @MailingList
SELECT DISTINCT dbo.Owners.OwnerLastName, dbo.Owners.OwnerFirstName,
dbo.Owners.OwnerAddress1, dbo.Owners.OwnerAddress2, dbo.Owners.OwnerCity,
dbo.Owners.OwnerState, dbo.Owners.OwnerPostalCode, dbo.Owners.OwnerPostal4
FROM dbo.Owners INNER JOIN dbo.Pets ON dbo.Owners.OwnerID =
dbo.Pets.OwnerID INNER JOIN dbo.VeterinaryOffices ON dbo.Pets.OfficeID =
dbo.VeterinaryOffices.OfficeID
WHERE dbo.VeterinaryOffices.OfficeName = @OfficeName
RETURN
END
```

When SQL Server encounters an inline function, it treats it much like a view and substitutes the TSQL behind the function as part of the overall TSQL to be parsed and processed. With a multistatement table function, on the other hand, SQL Server treats it just like a table. Figure 9-7 shows the execution plans for using both MailingListByOffice and MailingListByOfficeML. As you can see, MailingListByOfficeML is much quicker. In fact, the estimated subtree costs for MailingListByOffice is .252 compared with .0376 for the MailingListByOfficeML, a much faster response.

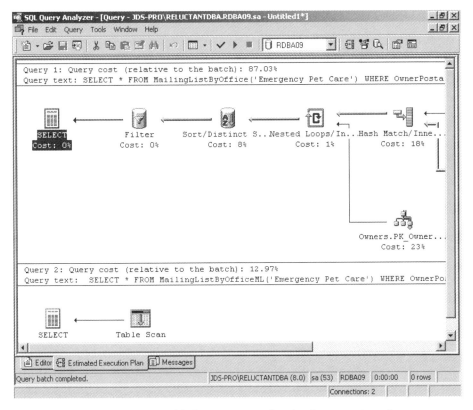

Figure 9-7. Multistatement table functions cost less in the execution plan.

Last Words

In this chapter you've been introduced to the basics of programming stored procedures and user-defined functions. We're also looked at the benefits of using them as opposed to ad-hoc queries of the database. In the next chapter we'll cover some of the more advanced topics related to this type of programming, including error handling, extended stored procedures, and system stored procedures/functions.

Resources

- Not necessarily the best resource for learning TSQL, but the original reference for all of the TSQL commands: SQL Server Books On Line.

- Once you've got the basics of TSQL down, get this book and work through it. One advantage of this book is that it starts with TSQL statements that look a lot like the ones I'm used to writing and demonstrates how to change them so they are much more efficient: *Advanced Transact SQL for SQL Server 2000* by Ben-Gan and Moreau (Apress).

- Another one of those books recommended for your bookshelf: *SQL For Smarties: Advanced SQL Programming, 2nd Edition* by Joe Celko (Morgan Kaufman).

CHAPTER 10

Working with Data: Beyond the Basics

As soon as we started programming, we found to our surprise that it wasn't as easy to get programs right as we had thought. Debugging had to be discovered. I can remember the exact instant when I realized that a large part of my life from then on was going to be spent in finding mistakes in my own programs. —Maurice Wilkes, 1949

IN THE LAST CHAPTER, we covered the basics of creating both stored procedures and user-defined functions (UDFs). In this chapter we're going to introduce Transact SQL (TSQL) error handling, transactions, triggers, system stored procedures, and extended stored procedures.

> **NOTE** *This chapter relies heavily on the **RDBA10** database. You'll find instructions for installing the database in Appendix A, "How Do I Load the Examples?" In addition, a number of SQL files in the "\Chapter10" directory on the CD contain the code for creating the various stored procedures and functions in this chapter. When the source code is available, the filename is listed in the caption of the code listing.*

How Do I Handle Errors?

If you've done any programming, you know that things can and will go wrong. The wrong data will be supplied or some file that should exist doesn't. Experienced programmers know they have to deal with errors when they occur. The problem is, error handling in TSQL isn't as straightforward as it is in some other programming languages—or at least the mechanisms for dealing with it are not as well developed.

Whenever someone starts talking about error handling in TSQL, they start talking about @@ERROR. @@ERROR is a system variable that stores an error code. This error code is reset with *every* TSQL statement. This means that if you don't save the error code, then you lose whatever value it contained. Confused? Let me give you an example in Listing 10-1. We'll cover RAISERROR in just a moment, but for now let me say it raises an error and sets @@ERROR to 50000. The first line raises the error, and the second line prints the error code of 50000. The third line prints an error code of 0 because it is reporting on any errors from the second line.

Listing 10-1. Error codes get reset with every TSQL statement.

```
RAISERROR ('This is an error',1,1) WITH SETERROR
PRINT @@Error
PRINT @@Error
```

Defining What Really Constitutes an Error

You can handle errors in many different ways. Some people don't handle them at all, preferring to let SQL Server and the client determine what the problem is. Just like in Visual Basic (VB) 6, the error will bubble up through the calling TSQL until either an error handler is found or the processing stops. Other people put error handling around all of their statements. But to truly understand how to implement error handling, we first need to answer the question: What is a trappable error?

Providing the wrong type of data to a parameter would be an error, but it is not a trappable one because SQL Server raises the error before it executes the stored procedure. Actually, SQL Server attempts to convert the data first. If the data can't be converted (say, 'A' to an INT data type), then SQL Server generates an error and does not go any farther. OK, we don't need to worry about error handling for parameter datatypes, so let's look inside a stored procedure.

Take the code in Listing 10-2. This is a bad coding example because it uses a parameter that is a different datatype than the column it will be referencing. You should never do this in your code, but this demonstrates how SQL Server handles this. Once this stored procedure is defined this way it is perfectly legal to execute ListOffices with a parameter of 2. SQL Server converts the numeric 2 into a VARCHAR "2" and then converts it back into a numeric 2—not the most efficient way to do something, but it works and returns a rowset for Standard Pet Care of Walnut Creek. But what happens when you call it with a parameter of 'A'?

Since the parameter datatype is VARCHAR, SQL Server doesn't fuss about accepting 'A' as the parameter. We know that OfficeID is an integer so SQL Server fails when it attempts to execute the SELECT and then it prints out the error code, right?

Listing 10-2. When this stored procedure is called using 'A' for the parameter you get an error, but not the one you might expect. (BadListOffices.sql)

```
CREATE PROCEDURE BadListOffices @OfficeID varchar(10) =NULL
AS
DECLARE @ErrorID int
IF @OfficeID IS NULL --Return all of the data
SELECT OfficeID, OfficeName, OfficeAddress1, OfficeAddress2,  OfficeCity,
OfficeState, OfficePostalCode, OfficePostal4, OfficeHours, OfficePhone,
OfficeFax, EmergencyCare
FROM VeterinaryOffices
ELSE -- @OfficeID is not null so return data for the requested OfficeID
BEGIN
SELECT OfficeID, OfficeName, OfficeAddress1, OfficeAddress2, OfficeCity,
OfficeState, OfficePostalCode, OfficePostal4, OfficeHours, OfficePhone,
OfficeFax, EmergencyCare
FROM VeterinaryOffices WHERE OfficeID = @OfficeID
SET @ErrorID = @@Error
SELECT @ErrorID as 'Error'
END
```

When you execute `BadListOffices 'A'` you discover that the error handling code doesn't get called. In fact, SQL Server complains about a *syntax* error! Why? To understand that, you need to understand how SQL Server treats variables. In a TSQL statement like this:

```
SELECT OfficeID, OfficeName FROM VeterinaryOffices WHERE OfficeID = @OfficeID
```

When SQL Server parses and then attempts to execute it, it replaces the variable with the variable's value. Even though @OfficeID is a VARCHAR data type, SQL Server knows that it can sometimes translate that data to an INT so syntactically it's allowed. Once the value of 'A' enters the picture, however, the parser complains. Instead of executing the SELECT followed by the error code, the stored procedure simply stops.[1] OK, so we can't trap syntax errors even though we can create them to sit like time bombs waiting to stop our program dead. And some errors we never see because SQL Server returns errors before executing our code. So why worry about errors at all?

---

[1]   It would be possible to use ISNUMERIC to see if the OfficeID is convertible to a number but if I was going to go through that much trouble I'd just as soon modify the parameter to be an INT to match the datatype of the column it references.

What Good Is Error Handling?

Now that you know where SQL Server *won't* let you trap errors, you'll learn where error handling will be useful. I'm going to create a stored procedure that will insert data into the VeterinariansVeterinaryOffices table. As you may remember, that table is a junction table containing two columns, VeterinarianID and OfficeID, both of which make up the primary key for the junction table. That means that the combination of the two columns must be unique. As you can see from the stored procedure in Listing 10-3, all the procedure does is to take two parameters and insert them into the table.

Listing 10-3. Stored procedure to insert data into before error handling is added

```
CREATE PROCEDURE usr_VeterinariansVeterinaryOffices_Ins
(@VeterinarianID [int],  @OfficeID [int])
AS INSERT INTO [VeterinariansVeterinaryOffices]  ( [VeterinarianID],  [OfficeID])
VALUES ( @VeterinarianID,  @OfficeID)
```

Once the stored procedure has been created, it can be run, and we're going to run it with the parameters 1 and 3. Because this OfficeID/VeterinarianID combination already exists, we're going to get an error message telling us that we cannot insert a duplicate key into a primary key. Finally, a trappable error. Let's add some error handling code to the stored procedure. In Listing 10-4 three lines have been added that do nothing but print out that there was an error. Now when we run the stored procedure with the parameters 1 and 3 we won't have any more problems, right? Well, unfortunately, that's not quite the case either. We get the same error as before, but this time we *also* get the error message that we programmed in. If the SQL Server error still gets sent back to the client, what's the purpose of putting error handling in the code?

Listing 10-4. Stored procedure with error handling code (usr_VeterinariansVeterinaryOffices_Ins.sql)

```
CREATE PROCEDURE usr_VeterinariansVeterinaryOffices_Ins
(@VeterinarianID [int],  @OfficeID [int])
AS
DECLARE @ErrorID int
INSERT INTO [RDBA09].[dbo].[VeterinariansVeterinaryOffices]
( [VeterinarianID],  [OfficeID])
VALUES ( @VeterinarianID,  @OfficeID)
set @ErrorID = @@Error
if @ErrorID <> 0
PRINT 'There was an error, number ' + convert(varchar(20), @ErrorID)
```

To understand the purpose behind putting error handling in TSQL code, we need to take a look at why we are trying to trap errors. In the example we're working with, the purpose behind calling the stored procedure is to insert a row into a junction table. When we attempt to do this using 1 and 3 for the parameters, we are attempting to insert a row of data that already exists. Even if the insert fails, the end result of having a row of data with the values 1 and 3 is met so there really isn't an error. If, however, we were to execute this stored procedure with the values 91 and 3, we would get a very different error.

Since the purpose of a junction table is to join two tables together, both the OfficeID that is being inserted needs to exist as a valid OfficeID in VeterinaryOffices and the VeterinarianID needs to exists in the Veterinarians table. Because 91 is an invalid VeterinarianID, the row can't be inserted. The end result, having a row with 91 and 3, doesn't happen and we have a real error, an error that affects transactions. Being able to control transactions is the real purpose behind error handling in TSQL.

What Are Transactions?

Transactions are at the heart of SQL Server. After all, the language is called *Transact* SQL for a good reason. Each command entered is considered to be part of a transaction. When dealing with SQL Server it is best to get yourself in the mindset of dealing with groups (sets) of records. Even if you are dealing with just one record, think of it as a very small group. But what is a transaction?

> *Reluctant DBA* definition of a *transaction*:
> A transaction is a group of commands that are either *all* completed successfully or none of them are.

Now, the sample database we've created for this book is not a complicated one, and there is no real need for transactional processing *per se*. Many databases that Reluctant DBAs create can get by without worrying about transactions, but the concept of transactions permeates the essence of SQL Server, so it is necessary to understand transactions, how SQL Server implements them explicitly and implicitly as well as the effect transactions can have on the database. To this end, we're going to use the most common transaction example given, the case of a bank transferring money between two accounts—say, checking and savings.

There is a table named TrxAccount in this database built especially for this demonstration. It is a simple table consisting of a column with the AccountID (say checking or saving) and a balance. In addition, a constraint on the table prevents the balance from dropping below 0.

Let's say each account has a balance of $100, for a total of $200, and we need to transfer $25 from savings to checking. Before we start we have a total of $200 in the two accounts, and when the transaction is done we should still have $200. Transferring money shouldn't be too hard; you just remove $25 from savings and put it into checking. When you're finished, savings has $75, and checking has $125. But it's not really that simple.

Suppose we've taken the money from savings but, before we put it into checking, the cleaning person unplugs the server to plug the vacuum cleaner into the UPS. In this case savings has $75, but checking only has $100. We've lost money and that upsets customers (but makes the bank happy). Alternately, what if we put the $25 into the checking account and *then* removed the money from the savings account? If the server should fail before we are finished, the checking account has $125, but the savings account still has $100. This is called *creative bookkeeping*, and the government tends to frown on it. Although the account owner might be happy, the bank is not.

The answer is to make sure that the two transactions—withdrawing the money and depositing it in another account—are handled as *one* combined transaction. Either all of the parts of the transaction complete successfully, or none of them do. If this account transfer is rewritten as a single transaction and the power goes out after the money has been withdrawn but before it is deposited, the multi-step transaction fails. When SQL Server starts up again, it goes through its transactions (in the transaction log) and says, "Hey, this didn't finish. I've got $25 that is floating around loose. Let's put everything back the way it was before I started messing with it." It's as simple as that. And no, you don't have to do anything special to make sure the server recovers—it's done automatically. However, it is also possible for you to control the status of a transaction and what happens to it.

Once a transaction begins, one of two things needs to happen.

- If the transaction finishes without running into any problems, then it needs to be committed.

- If the transaction encounters an error that prevents it from finishing, it needs to be rolled back and the entire transaction is erased, just as though it never happened.

Let me demonstrate how you would roll back a transaction using the bank example again.

> *Reluctant DBA* definition of *rollback*:
> Rolling back is not merely stopping a transaction, it is resetting the database to the state it was in *before* the transaction started. Rolling back a transaction doesn't exit a set of TSQL statements.

First, let's create a stored procedure to transfer the money. It's a simple stored procedure and outlined in Listing 10-5. It takes two accounts and transfers money from one account to another.

Listing 10-5. First attempt at a stored procedure to handle transferring money (Transaction1.sql)

```
CREATE PROCEDURE TransferAcctTrx @AccountIDFrom nvarchar(50),
        @AccountIDTo nvarchar(50), @Amount money
AS
UPDATE TrxAccounts set Balance = Balance - @Amount
            WHERE AccountID = @AccountIDFrom
UPDATE TrxAccounts set Balance = Balance + @Amount WHERE
            AccountID = @AccountIDTo
GO
```

It looks fairly straightforward, but it has a subtle error. Unless you explicitly define a transaction, SQL Server will autocommit each transaction individually. Take a look at the code in Listing 10-6. First it deletes any data in the table and then it inserts two records. Next it attempts to execute the stored procedure to transfer $50 from checking to savings. Although the first transaction fails because there is a constraint to keep the balance above 0, the second transaction *stands alone and is committed!* Figure 10-1 shows the results of using autocommit for two interdependent transactions.

Listing 10-6. This code demonstrates how the autocommit feature works. (included in Transaction1.sql)

```
DELETE FROM TrxAccounts
GO
INSERT INTO TrxAccounts VALUES(N'SAVINGS',100)
INSERT INTO TrxAccounts VALUES(N'CHECKING',25)
GO
SELECT AccountID, Balance FROM TrxAccounts
go
TransferAcctTrx 'CHECKING', 'SAVINGS', 50
go
SELECT AccountID, Balance FROM TrxAccounts
go
```

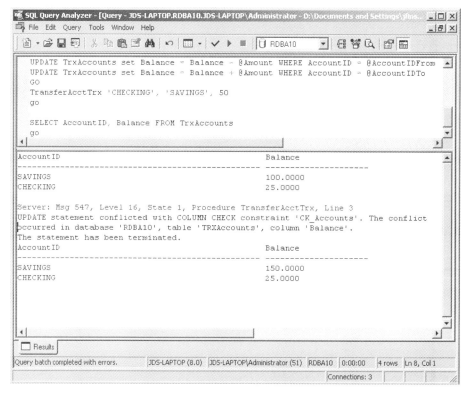

Figure 10-1. Even though one of the transactions failed, the other one was processed because autocommit treats each SQL statement as an individual transaction.

Figure 10-1 clearly shows that savings held $100 and checking held $25 before executing TransferAcctTrx. When the procedure is run, the attempt to remove $50 from an account that only has $25 causes the constraint to keep the transaction from processing but the second update command is its own transaction and goes ahead without a problem. The result is that the two accounts have $50 more than when they started. In order to fix this, we need to explicitly define the transaction.

How Do I Explicitly Define Transactions?

Explicitly defining transactions is not difficult. It simply requires using keywords to tell SQL Server when you are beginning a transaction and when you are either committing it or rolling it back:

- BEGIN TRANSACTION explicitly marks the beginning of an explicit transaction for a connection. For each individual transaction there can be only one BEGIN statement per SQL statement, but transactions can be nested.

- ROLLBACK TRANSACTION explicitly resets the database back to the state it was in when the transaction began. This means the transaction has *failed*. You can have many points within a transaction that rollback the transaction.

- COMMIT TRANSACTION explicitly finishes the transaction. It marks the transaction as having completed *successfully*. This should only be called when the entire transaction has completed successfully.

Each transaction needs a beginning and an end and as many points of failure as necessary. Let's fix the TransferAcctTrx procedure so that it works correctly. The first step is to add a BEGIN TRANSACTION statement before starting the UPDATE process. The next step is to add an error check after each update to see if we need to ROLLBACK the transaction. Finally, if everything works, we need to COMMIT the transaction. At this point in time you might be thinking that you can modify the procedure as in Listing 10-7, but this won't work the way you might think.

Listing 10-7. Incorrectly implementing transactions can lead to the same problems as not having transactions.

```
CREATE PROCEDURE TransferAcctTrx @AccountIDFrom nvarchar(50),
          @AccountIDTo nvarchar(50), @Amount money
AS
BEGIN TRANSACTION
UPDATE TrxAccounts set Balance = Balance - @Amount
    WHERE AccountID = @AccountIDFrom
IF @@Error <> 0
ROLLBACK TRANSACTION
UPDATE TrxAccounts set Balance = Balance + @Amount
    WHERE AccountID = @AccountIDTo
if @@Error <> 0
ROLLBACK TRANSACTION
ELSE
COMMIT TRANSACTION
```

Remember, ROLLBACK sets the database back to a known condition, but it doesn't exit out of the middle of TSQL statements. If the first UDPATE statement encounters a constraint error, the *transaction* will be rolled back but, since the stored procedure isn't stopped, the second UDPATE processes as an autocommitted transaction and the accounts are still out of synch. The key to successfully handling errors in transactions is to exit the procedure when you ROLLBACK a transaction. Listing 10-8 shows the complete and correct method of handling this transaction.

Listing 10-8. The corrected `TransferAcctTrx` **to properly exit the stored procedure after rolling back a transaction (Transaction2.sql)**

```
CREATE PROCEDURE TransferAcctTrx @AccountIDFrom nvarchar(50),
                @AccountIDTo nvarchar(50), @Amount money
AS
BEGIN TRANSACTION
UPDATE TrxAccounts set Balance = Balance - @Amount
        WHERE AccountID = @AccountIDFrom
IF @@Error <> 0
    BEGIN
ROLLBACK TRANSACTION
RETURN 1
END
UPDATE TrxAccounts set Balance = Balance + @Amount
        WHERE AccountID = @AccountIDTo
if @@Error <> 0
    BEGIN
ROLLBACK TRANSACTION
RETURN 1
END
COMMIT TRANSACTION
```

You may remember that the return codes are frequently used to indicate errors. Well, that's exactly what this code did. If the transaction needs to be rolled back we set the return code to 1 and exit the stored procedure. Now the client program needs to check to see what the return code is in order to know everything worked correctly.

Can a Transaction Have an Error That Doesn't Generate @@Error?

Of course, just because @@Error is equal to 0 doesn't mean there isn't an error; it just means there hasn't been an error SQL Server recognizes. For instance, executing `TransferAcctTrx` with an account that doesn't exist won't generate an error. The `UDPATE` statement executes even though it doesn't update any rows. This is perfectly legal within the TSQL syntax and represents a different type of error that needs to be addressed.

Fortunately, another system variable can tell us the number of rows affected by an INSERT, UPDATE, DELETE, or SELECT statement. @@RowCount contains the number of rows affected by the TSQL statement anytime the statement could affect a row. This requires a minor modification to the error handling, as shown in Listing 10-9. Even now, however, we're not quite finished. The code correctly handles rolling back the transaction, but it doesn't inform the client that the transaction had a problem. To do that, we need to raise our own error.

Listing 10-9. Checking for both errors and rows affected is the best way to determine whether to roll back the transaction. (included in Transaction3.sql)

```
IF @@Error <> 0 OR @@RowCount = 0
BEGIN
ROLLBACK TRANSACTION
RETURN 1
END
```

How Do I Tell the Client Something Is Wrong?

In Listing 10-1, we used RAISERROR. Now it's time to look at this command in more depth. As explained, RAISERROR raises an error back to the client program, but it can do more than that. The basic format consists of an error number or error message, the severity of the error, the state of the error, any arguments to be used in formatting the error message, and an option.

Listing 10-10. The basic format of RAISERROR

```
RAISERROR ( { msg_id | msg_str } { , severity , state } [ , argument [ ,...n ] ] )
[ WITH option [ ,...n ] ]
```

All errors can be either ad-hoc errors or defined errors. An ad-hoc error is one that you raise by passing RAISERROR a message string. All ad-hoc errors generate an error ID of 50000, just like the one in Listing 10-1 did. Defined errors can be either existing system errors or user-defined errors. Since the screens for defining an error separate out each option neatly, we're going to walk through defining a unique error to cover the individual parts of an error and then show how those parts work with an ad-hoc error.

Ad-Hoc or User-Defined Errors?

There are advantages and disadvantages to both using ad-hoc errors and using fully defined custom errors. One advantage with designing a custom error has is that you can define a unique error number and the client side can code to trap that error. Using ad-hoc errors means that the client code must trap for error 50000 and then attempt to take action based on the text of the error message.

The down side to using a custom error message is that these messages are *system*-wide messages. If your database wants to use error number 55000 and another database on the same server wants to use 55000, then you will have a conflict, and it could be that whoever gets installed last wins. Your code might still raise error number 55000, but the error message it displays could be wrong and make no sense to whomever is interpreting the error message. The worst case is that the error could be expecting an entirely different set of parameters for the message and your RAISERROR statement could generate a system error!

My preference is to use ad-hoc error messages that raise error number 50000 but make the first part of my error message a unique number that can be trapped in the client-side error code. That's my preference because most of my projects are on servers that have both in-house and commercial databases installed. If the database you are developing is strictly for in-house use, or you can completely control the SQL Server it will be installed on, then you won't encounter problems using unique error codes.

How Do I Find System Errors or Define My Own?

When you need to find the right error, especially if you want to raise a system error, you have two choices. You can search through Books On Line, or you can search through a list of all of the errors that are defined on the server. Although getting there isn't the easiest task, the Manage SQL Server Messages dialog box is a handy tool.

Start the Enterprise Manager (EM) and then open the server where you want to work with messages. Under the server, open the Management folder and then expand the SQL Server Agent collection. Right-click on Alerts and select New Alert (see Figure 10-2). Chapter 12 covers the SQL Server Agent and alerts.

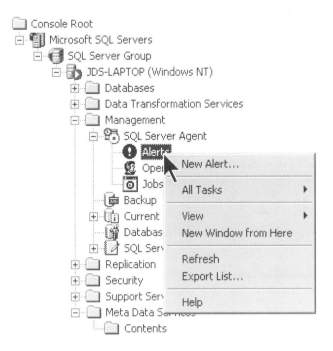

Figure 10-2. SQL Server Agent includes a means for monitoring alerts. This is the first step toward opening a window to search error messages.

Once you've opened the New Alert Properties window, you can select Error Number and then press the browse button (with the ellipses) to the right of the error number input. This will bring up a Manage SQL Server Messages window (see Figure 10-3). From this window you can filter the type of messages you want to look at by one or more of the following criteria:

- Message text

- A specific error number

- Message severity

- Only include logged messages

- Only include user-defined message

If you click on Find without filling anything in, you'll get a list of all of the messages defined on the server.

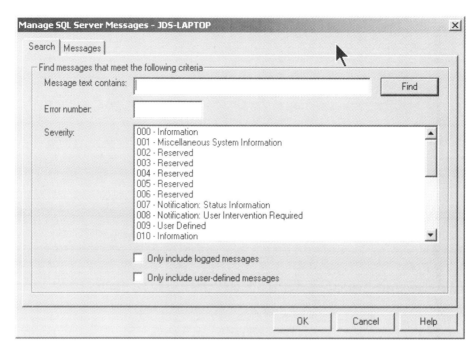

Figure 10-3. From this window you can set up a filter and then view all of the messages on the server that meet your criteria.

To get a list of all of the user-defined messages, click on the Only Include User-Defined Messages box labeled and then press the Find button. This will take you to the Messages tab, which should now display all of the user-defined messages. Now you can press the New button along the bottom of the screen to get the window displayed in Figure 10-4. This window lets you fill in the blanks to create a user-defined message. We'll use it to talk about the parts of a message, whether user-defined or system.

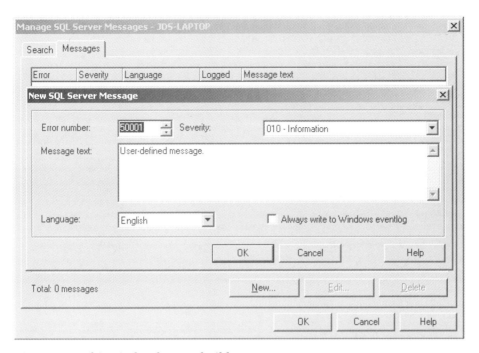

Figure 10-4. This window lets you build your own error messages.

User-defined errors must have a MessageID less than 0 or greater than 50000 because those MessageIDs are reserved for SQL Server. Since SQL Server is storing the error number as an integer and SQL Server Integers can be fairly large, -2^{63} (–9,223,372,036,854,775,807) through $2^{63}-1$ (9,223,372,036,854,775,807), you probably won't run out of error message numbers you can use. Because a message number could be in use by another application, raising all errors as ad-hoc but including a unique error number in the message text is a good idea.

The severity level of an error will do certain things, depending on what that level is. These levels can be grouped into several types:

- Severity Levels 0 through 10 are informational only. They don't really affect what happens to whatever process gets the error message. Level 0 (success) errors are generally ignored.

- Severity Levels 11 through 16 indicate an error that can be corrected by the user. These are generally syntax errors. Whether they are really correctable depends entirely on what the client is. If it is a programmer using the Query Analyzer (QA) to test his TSQL statement, then it's correctable. If it's a programmed client accessing the database then whether the error can be corrected depends entirely on the programmer's error handling routine.

- Severity Level 17 indicates that the server has run out of some resource. This error occurs when a runaway database has eaten up all of your disk space and asks for more.

- Severity Level 18 indicates that some error occurred internal to SQL Server's software.

- Severity Level 19 is similar to 17 because it indicates that the server has run out of some resource, but Severity Level 19 messages are reserved for resources you can't configure.

- Severity Levels 20 through 25 indicate that something major has gone wrong within the SQL Server system. If you generate a Severity Level 20 or above error, you will stop the current request from finishing, sever the connection between the server and the client, and generally cause DBAs to complain about some major work time coming up. These are the types of errors that cause you to be glad you've got that database backed up.

Choosing the right severity will help you in creating meaningful errors. If you were creating a security system that operated outside of SQL Server's security model, you could create an error that would check for a login's authority and reject access with a Severity Level of 14 (Insufficient Permission) and the program could trap the error and handle it appropriately.

NOTE *Why would anyone want to set up a security system that bypassed the security model built into SQL Server? Well, there are several reasons, most of which are related to setting up a simple user table with logins and passwords to avoid the overhead of creating accounts on the SQL Server or within NT. Granted, it means that the application needs to maintain all of the security, but it can be more flexible than adding users to SQL Server or Windows 2000.*

Now comes the fun part, the message text. In the message text you can define dynamic messages by using placeholders. A placeholder is just that. It is designed to be replaced by a variable that is passed when the error is called. If you have programmed in C or a derivative, then the format of the string should look familiar. It is a percent sign (%) followed by the type of data that should be passed (see Table 10-1).

Table 10-1. Placeholder Formats for Error Messages

PLACEHOLDER	REPLACE WITH	EXAMPLE
%d, %ld or %D	Decimal Integer	10
%x	Hexadecimal Number	x1F
%ls or %.*ls	Character String	'test'
%S_type	SQL Server defined structure. Used by the server to handle messages related to table errors, key errors, and so on.	N/A
%c	A single character	'C'
%lf	Double floating-point number	3.14159265358979

The last thing to consider about adding an error is whether it should automatically generate an entry in the NT event log. Errors related to security should be. Any error that uses a severity level of 16 or above should be. Anything else you'll need to think about. Although the event log can be a handy place to store data, it does no good storing scads of events (ever opened an event log with millions of rows? Not a pretty picture). If you do, you'll find it more difficult to find events when something goes wrong. One alternative is to force the log entry when you use the RAISERROR command. Figure 10-5 shows a completed user-defined message, ready to be raised.

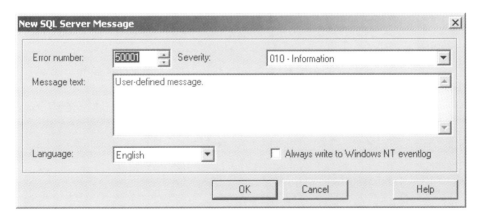

Figure 10-5. Creating user-defined messages is easiest through the Manage SQL Server Messages dialog boxes, once you get the dialog boxes opened.

How Do I Raise My Newly Created Error (or Any Error)?

Raising an error in SQL Server is as easy as using the RAISERROR command. (Note the one "e.") RAISERROR is a versatile command. You can use it to raise an existing error for testing a program, or you can use it to raise errors that you create on the fly.

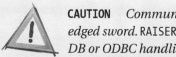 **CAUTION** *Communicating back to the client can be a double-edged sword.* RAISERROR *is an ugly subject when it comes to OLE DB or ODBC handling. ActiveX Data Objects (ADO) often kills the command in progress when it hits a* RAISERROR *return code. Be sure to set the correct severity level and experiment with how ADO or whatever programming interface you're using behaves when it encounters the error.*

We're going to start by raising a simple error. If you open up the QA, type in **RAISERROR (14109,10,1)**, and execute it, you'll get a message that says, "The @security_mode parameter value must be 0 (SQL Server Authentication) or 1 (Windows Authentication)." It's not very exciting; all it does is display an informational message. If you modify the severity level parameter from 10 to 16 and execute the statement again then you get a true error message in the results pane.

Let's look at formatting data in the message. Error number 20567 is an informational error related to cleaning up the SQL Server Agent history. If you substitute that error number for 14109 in the RAISERROR statement, you can easily generate error 2757 while trying to raise 14109 (see Figure 10-6). That's because we forgot to pass it the parameter that it needs for the string. The correct format to raise that error should be: RAISERROR(20567,10,1, 'Test RDBA'). That correctly returns an informational message that reads "Agent history clean up: Test RDBA."

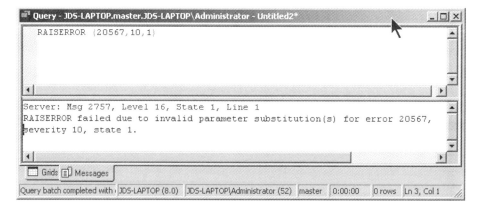

Figure 10-6. Forgetting to pass an argument for a placeholder results in an error.

Putting It All Together

> *Goto, n.: A programming tool that exists to allow structured program-*
> *mers to complain about unstructured programmers.* —Ray Simard

OK, now that we've covered how to handle errors that SQL Server raises and how
to raise errors when we need to communicate back to the client, let's take a look
at how to handle errors when the constraints are violated and how to raise errors
when the stored procedure doesn't work.

The first thing to notice in Listing 10-11 is that after each attempted update,
@@Error and @@RowCount are stored in variables (@ErrorCode and @RowsAffected
respectively). Then, if @ErrorCode is not equal to 0 or if @RowsAffected is equal to
0, execution of the stored procedure is being shifted to the ErrorHandler code at
the end of the stored procedure. This is handled through the use of the GOTO command. Although there have been some arguments against using GOTO, this is
probably the most efficient way to handle putting your error code in one place.

Listing 10-11. This version of TransferAcctTrx **handles errors and raises**
errors when invalid accounts are used. (Transaction4.sql)

```
CREATE PROCEDURE TransferAcctTrx @AccountIDFrom nvarchar(50), @AccountIDTo
nvarchar(50), @Amount money
AS
DECLARE @ErrorCode int
DECLARE @RowsAffected int
BEGIN TRANSACTION
UPDATE TrxAccounts set Balance = Balance - @Amount WHERE AccountID =
@AccountIDFrom
SELECT @ErrorCode = @@Error, @RowsAffected = @@RowCount
IF @ErrorCode <> 0 OR @RowsAffected = 0
GOTO ErrorHandler
ELSE
BEGIN
UPDATE TrxAccounts set Balance = Balance + @Amount WHERE AccountID = @AccountIDTo
SELECT @ErrorCode = @@Error, @RowsAffected = @@RowCount
IF @ErrorCode <> 0 OR @RowsAffected = 0
GOTO ErrorHandler
ELSE
COMMIT TRANSACTION
END
RETURN
ErrorHandler:
IF @ErrorCode <> 0
BEGIN
```

```
ROLLBACK TRANSACTION
RETURN
END
ELSE
BEGIN
RAISERROR ('%d: Invalid Account Provided',10, 1, 30000)
ROLLBACK TRANSACTION
END
```

A Final Word on Transactions

Many databases won't require explicit transactions—or at least require very few of them. That's because most of the business logic is wrapped in other tiers. If you use transactions regularly, you can learn more about them and error handling from the resources at the end of the chapter. Even if you're using autocommit for everything, there's another good reason for understanding transactions.

Whenever you start a transaction, SQL Server takes steps to ensure that your transaction won't affect anyone else until it has completed the transaction or rolled it back. Let's say that our TransferAcctTrx procedure performed its updates backward, adding money to the savings account before removing it from the checking account. If steps weren't taken to prevent it, the following scenario could occur:

1. Process A starts to transfer $100 from checking to savings and, as the first step, updates the savings account to display +$100.

2. Process B queries the savings account to get a balance and shows the +$100.

3. Process A attempts to debit $100 from the checking account and fails.

4. Process A rolls the transaction back, removing the +$100 from the savings account.

If this happened, then Process B would have erroneous data about the state of the savings account. To prevent such occurrences, SQL Server implements locking. Locks can have quite an impact on database performance and are closely tied to transactions in that Reluctant DBAs need to have a basic understanding of both to find where the two might be impacting database performance.

What Is Locking?

> *Reluctant DBA* definition of *locking*:
> Locking is making a row, rows, or even a whole table unavailable for
> updating or possibly even for viewing. Locking can be established at the
> row, page, and table level.

When SQL Server processes any TSQL statement that manipulates data, it
will need to create, manage, and release locks as a part of the server-side processing. Understanding how this locking process works will help you create more
efficient processing. Generally, the fewer rows affected, the fewer locks and the
more efficient the processing.

Although there are legitimate reasons to do so, the number of times when
you want all of the rows in a table to come back to you should be the exception
rather than the rule. Pulling all of the rows from a table of valid state names to
populate a drop-down ListBox control, for example. Most of the time, however,
you want to limit the data you are looking at. New programmers may opt to open
a table, pull back all of the rows, and then filter only what they wanted once they
got the data back on the client side. That's an inefficient way of doing things
when you're using SQL Server for multiple reasons. Yes, this is how it was often
done in Access and in many of the examples you see in the documentation and
in magazine articles. But if you want your application to scale beyond a couple of
users, you'll have to break yourself of this habit.

First, you can have the server do all of your filtering for you, returning only
the data you need. This reduces network traffic, making the application faster
and more efficient because the extra rows won't be in memory on the client. Second, and more importantly, letting SQL Server filter the data reduces locking.
Locking is a necessary function of a multi-user database. The down side of having
the server filter data is that any extra processing on the server also hurts server
performance. However, extra filtering is designed into the architecture of SQL
Server's query engine so it's usually cheaper to filter on the server as the rows are
chosen than on the client. Keep in mind that once your filtered rowset arrives at
the client, you can re-filter using ADO to provide a more limited subset of the
rows. Let's take a look at how locking works in the physical world of our Veterinary Office.

During any given day, pets will be coming in for normally scheduled
appointments. After each pet arrives at the office, the chart for that pet is pulled
from the filing cabinets so it is available for the veterinarian to review. Only one
chart exists for each animal; therefore, when that chart is pulled from the filing
cabinet, it is no longer available to be updated by anyone except the person who
has the chart. Once the vet is finished with the appointment, the chart is
returned to the file. That's the definition of locking: making a row unavailable for
updating or maybe even for reviewing. This type of locking (row lock) is the best

possible lock because it only affects that row, and the odds of more than one user (or everyone) hitting the same row at the same time are slim.

Now, to take this locking example a step further, what if, in the name of efficiency, the office staff removed the charts from the filing cabinet in the morning for all pets that have appointments during the day and then didn't file them until the end of the day? If a pet owner brings their pet in for an early morning appointment and then calls in later in the day to verify the vet's instructions, the receptionist will have to hunt to find the chart because it's not filed where one reasonably expects it to be. This would be an example of having locked too many rows.

Now, to take this example to an absurd extreme, let's say the office staff removed *all* of the charts at the beginning of the day, just in case an unscheduled patient comes in. Now the receptionist is really up a creek if he needs to reference a chart. I can hear you saying, "Wait a minute, that's ridiculous!" I'll agree, it is ridiculous, but that's what can happen when you retrieve all of the rows from a table. Every row can be locked until the rowset is finished being used.

How Do Locks Affect Performance?

The most noticeable way locks affect performance is by blocking another process from accomplishing something. If someone called about his or her pet and that pet's chart wasn't filed away, then there would be a certain amount of time spent finding the chart and being able to respond to the owner's questions. When a situation like that happens, we would say that access to the data was blocked.

The same thing applies with locks in the database. A well-written stored procedure can help by making sure that the fewest number of rows are affected (locked). Not only that, but using stored procedures means that if a locking problem is identified (see Chapter 16 to learn how to identify locking problems) then you can fix it in one place.

But there is another form of stored procedure that can cause locking issues, and it is one of the least understood form of database programming to those getting started: triggers.

What Are Triggers?

Reluctant DBA definition of *triggers*:
Triggers are to a SQL Server database what events are to Windows Forms. They are stored procedures that are executed in response to an event on a table such as inserting a new row or updating/deleting existing data. Triggers are executed as part of a transaction and can affect a transaction.

Triggers can be set to run when data is added (INSERT), removed (DELETE), or changed (UPDATE). One thing that confuses many people when they encounter triggers for the first time is that triggers are based on transactions, not rows. If you have a stored procedure that updates a table with an update trigger defined on it, then that trigger will fire once. If you modify the stored procedure to update that table three times then the trigger will fire three times.

What Should Triggers Be Used For?

Triggers may be to SQL Server what events are to Windows Forms, but the primary purpose of triggers is to support Referential Integrity (RI) and rules. As discussed in Chapter 5 in the "How Do I Relate Tables Together in the Diagramming Tool?" section, RI was originally done through triggers. Triggers should be lightweight TSQL that performs a simple task. Since RI can be taken care of through Declarative Referential Integrity, most triggers *should* be designed to enforce rules.

You *could* do any number of things in a trigger since triggers are made up of TSQL statements. There are many things you *shouldn't* do in a trigger though. You shouldn't:

- Execute a stored procedure

- Create a cursor and cycle through it

Executing stored procedures in a trigger is a great way to slow your database down, and cursors in a trigger can slow it down even more. If you find yourself putting a lot of logic into a trigger, you should really consider writing it as a stored procedure that is called from code rather than something that reacts to data changes.

> *Reluctant DBA* definition of an *update*:
> An update doesn't just change data. It is actually a delete followed by an insert. Unless you are dealing with triggers, however, you can consider an update to just modify data.

Because a trigger may deal with multiple rows of data, they have two special "tables" that you can use to look up data. These two tables, Deleted and Inserted, are actually virtual tables. They don't exist on disk anywhere, but you can access them from within a trigger. For normal triggers (also known as After Triggers), these are populated once the modification to the data is finished.[2] Table 10-2 lists

---

[2] There are two types of triggers, *After* triggers and *Instead of* triggers. If you don't specify which is which when you create it, the default is an After Trigger. We'll cover After Triggers first, then Instead of Triggers.

the type of modification and what you will find in each of the tables. Perhaps the easiest way to get your feet wet is to dive into triggers with both feet and create a couple of examples.

Table 10-2. What the Inserted and Deleted Tables Contain

MODIFICATION	INSERTED	DELETED
Insert	All columns for the inserted record	Empty
Delete	Empty	All of the columns for each row that was deleted
Update	All of the columns for the affected rows *after* the update (non-updated columns have the data they contained before the update)	All of the columns for the affected rows *before* the update

How Do I Build a Trigger?

Before you build a trigger, you need to answer two fundamental questions: Which table will the trigger be on, and what type of modification will execute the trigger? We're going to start with the "You can't delete me" trigger—a trigger whose sole purpose is to prevent people from deleting data from a table.

To begin with, open the EM and drill down to the Appointments table. Once you're there, right-click on Appointments and then select All Tasks ➢ Manage Triggers. This will bring you to the screen that you see in Figure 10-7. Just like functions and stored procedures, you'll have to write your triggers through TSQL code. Listing 10-12 shows the basic format of a trigger, but it really is simpler than it seems.

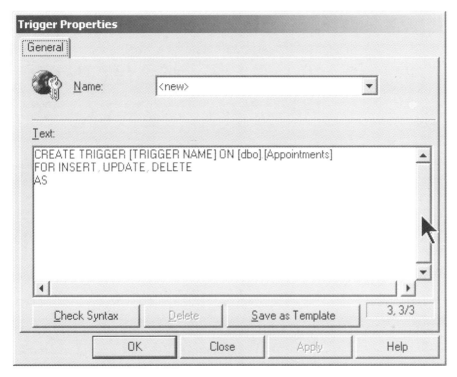

Figure 10-7. When managing triggers through the EM, you will need to use TSQL.

Listing 10-12. The basic format of a trigger
```
CREATE TRIGGER [TRIGGER NAME] ON [dbo].[Appointments]
FOR INSERT, UPDATE, DELETE
AS
```

As with any other object in SQL Server, you'll need to give your trigger a unique name; let's call this one trgAppointmentsDel. Next, you need to specify whether the trigger runs on an INSERT, UPDATE, DELETE, or all or any combination of the three. Finally, you put the code that the trigger will execute. Listing 10-13 shows the trigger. As you can see, all this trigger does is roll back the transaction in process when a DELETE command is issued against the Appointments table.

Listing 10-13. The you-can't-delete-me trigger (Triggers1.sql)
```
CREATE TRIGGER trgAppointmentsDEL ON [dbo].[Appointments]
FOR DELETE
AS
ROLLBACK TRANSACTION
```

This trigger is easy enough to test. Just select some data from the Appointments table for a known PetID (say, 5967) and then attempt to delete that PetID from the Appointments table. Then execute your SELECT statement again. You'll see that you didn't delete the rows. In fact, you'll find that you can't delete any rows from this table unless you remove the trigger first! Of course, there's also no indication that the delete didn't actually occur, but you can issue a RAISERROR command easily enough.

Why Use Triggers?

Well, there are a number of reasons to use triggers. Sometimes you want to take an action based on the data being modified. One use for triggers is to keep a record of all of the changes that have been made to the data in a table. Let's add another trigger to the Appointments table, this one designed to execute on every update of the table and to put a copy of the data into the AppointmentsArchive table.

First we'll create the trigger, trgAppointmentsUpd. You can follow along in Listing 10-14, but it is a simple process. Remember that an After Trigger populates the virtual tables, Deleted and Inserted, depending on the modification. UPDATE populates both, with Deleted holding the before data and Inserted holding the after. To populate an archive table all we need to do is INSERT into the archive table using a SELECT from the Deleted virtual table.

Listing 10-14. Archiving data on an update is an easy task through a trigger.

```
CREATE TRIGGER trgAppointmentsUpd ON [dbo].[Appointments]
FOR UPDATE
AS
INSERT INTO AppointmentsArchive
(AppointmentID, PetID, OfficeID, VeterinarianID, AppointmentDate)
SELECT * FROM DELETED
```

To test this trigger out, you check out the data in the AppointmentsArchive before an update, then execute a simple, one row update against Appointments and check out what exists in the database afterwards. As you can see in Figure 10-8, before the UPDATE there were no rows in the table. After the update, there was one.

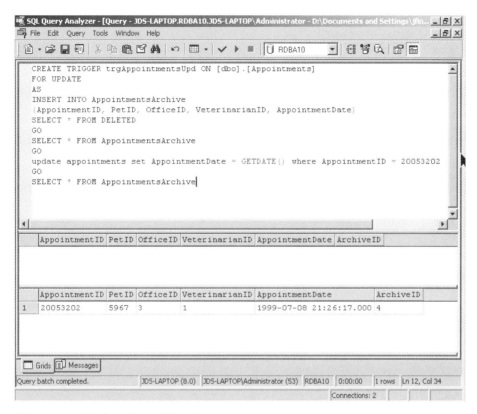

Figure 10-8. Testing the archive trigger

And now that we've got a trigger that archives data, it's time to return to locks and blocking. Let's try a little experiment. The Appointments table has 32719 rows of data, so begin by typing SELECT * FROM Appointments into the QA and seeing how long it takes to execute. It should take about two seconds. Now open a new window in the QA and execute UPDATE Appointments SET AppointmentDate = GETDATE(). While that's executing, go back to the window where you did the SELECT and try executing it again. Then wait for the results. And wait some more.

On my machine, the second SELECT took 42 seconds! Why? Well, because of locks and blocking. You see, the UPDATE statement is updating those 32719 rows of data as one transaction, but it's really processing three times that number. To understand why, let me break out what's happening in this transaction:

1.   The UPDATE command is selecting 32719 rows to be updated and locking them until the transaction is finished.

2.   In addition, that UPDATE command is inserting 32719 rows of data into the Deleted virtual table.

3. Finally, the trigger on the Appointments update is inserting those 32719 rows of data into the archive table.

So, as you can see, SQL Server has to deal with more than 98,000 rows before it can finish the transaction (not to mention that all of this is being logged at the same time)! And, until the transaction finishes and releases the locks, the SELECT statement has no data to work with. A classic case of blocking and, you say, easy enough to spot but that's only because we just finished working with setting up the database. If you hadn't then it would be harder to track down because triggers don't show up in execution plans. Of course, that's not the only form of blocking that can happen. There are other, more devious problems that can occur with triggers.

Can Triggers Trigger Triggers?

The short answer is yes. Triggers can trigger other triggers. Fortunately, however, there is a limit of 32 levels deep that triggers can nest. And this can be both good and bad. Take the two triggers in Listing 10-15. You can find these in the **RDBA10** database. When you attempt to delete a row from TestMe1, the trigger will INSERT it back into the table, triggering the InsertTrigger that will delete the row that was just inserted triggering the insert row that . . . you get the idea. In this case, attempting an INSERT or DELETE will go through 32 iterations and generate an error saying it's reached the maximum allowed limit. But that's not always the case.

Listing 10-15. Recursive triggers aren't always a good thing.
```
CREATE TRIGGER TestMeDel ON [dbo].[TestMe1]
FOR DELETE
AS
INSERT INTO TestMe1 SELECT * FROM deleted
GO
CREATE TRIGGER TestMeIns ON [dbo].[TestMe1]
FOR INSERT
AS
DELETE FROM TestMe1 WHERE TestMe1 in (select TestMe1 from Inserted)
```

I once worked on a sales automation system that implemented a number of rules through triggers. When a piece of work on an order was marked complete, it would start a process of marking other parts of the process complete and eventually, if it were the last outstanding part of an order, the whole order would be marked complete. The only trouble was, not everything was getting marked complete and there appeared to be no rhyme or reason to the few that were having problems. It took tracking an order by hand and walking through each update, delete, and insert statement before we finally saw where the error was. The order wasn't being completed because the completion routine would have been in the thirty-third trigger call. In the end, a master stored procedure that was responsible for acting as a clearing house was built and that took care of getting all of the orders through.

Can I Have More Than One Trigger of the Same Type on a Table?

Yes, but you have almost no control over what trigger executes when. You can specify which trigger is executed first and which is executed last, but if you have more than two triggers it's Murphy who decides which trigger is executed in which order.

OK, so maybe it's SQL Server and not Murphy that determines the order in which to run the triggers, but there is no guarantee that the triggers will run in the same sequence every time, or more importantly, in the desired order. If you have reached the point that you are putting multiple UPDATE triggers on a table, then it's time to rethink your database design. That doesn't mean that multiple UPDATE triggers won't be what you end up with, but you should be sure that you need them before you open that can of worms.

What Is an Instead Of Trigger?

Instead Of triggers are new in SQL Server 2000, and they are designed to run instead of the data modification just as an After Trigger is designed to run after the data modification. Perhaps the easiest way to explain is to rewrite trgAppointmentsDEL as an Instead Of Trigger.

Prior to SQL Server 2000, if you wanted to prevent deleting data from a table (and didn't want to implement security to prevent deleting data), you would implement a trigger like the one back in Listing 10-13. Of course, there are down sides to that. If the DELETE were a part of a transaction instead of the whole transaction, then issuing a ROLLBACK could lead to other problems. With SQL Server 2000, you can use an Instead Of Trigger to execute a totally different command. In trgAppointmentsDelInstead, shown in Listing 10-16, we're raising an informational-only message and then just letting the transaction complete.

Listing 10-16. An Instead of Trigger doesn't have to cancel the transaction to prevent deletions.

```
CREATE TRIGGER itrgAppointmentsDelete ON [dbo].[Appointments]
INSTEAD OF DELETE
AS
RAISERROR('Please do not delete Appointments, cancel them instead.',1,1)
```

Now, if we go back to execute the SELECT/DELETE/SELECT statements that we used for testing trgAppointmentsDel, we get something totally different (Figure 10-9). When the After Trigger executed its rollback, we only saw the results of the first SELECT statement. With the Instead Of Trigger, we see both results because the transaction doesn't get cancelled. In addition, even though the original trigger is still in place, it doesn't get executed because the actual delete statement is never executed. The Instead Of Trigger is executed instead.

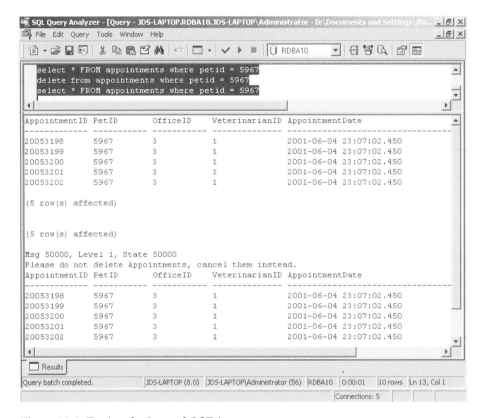

Figure 10-9. Testing the Instead Of Trigger

How do Triggers, Foreign Keys, and Cascades Fit Together?

In older versions of SQL Server, modifying or deleting data with foreign keys defined was painful. If you wanted to delete a row from Pets, for instance, you would first need to delete a row from Appointments, because it has data that depends on Pets. So does Charts.

To simplify life in the older versions, cascading deletes were often implemented using Delete Trigger. When you went to delete a row from Pets, the Delete Trigger would automatically see if there were any rows in the Appointments or

Charts tables that referenced the primary key value being deleted. If rows existed, they would be deleted (triggering any Delete Triggers on those tables). Finally, when all of that was finished, the rows could be deleted from Pets.

 You couldn't perform cascading deletes through triggers after SQL Server 6 if you defined foreign key constraints. The constraint would prevent the trigger from firing. This left you with the choice of the preferred method of performing cascades from stored procedures or, less desirable, not implementing constraints.

You no longer need to do this in SQL Server 2000. Please *don't* handle this through triggers. SQL Server 2000 will handle this better than you will. Not only that, you can run into problems with triggers and cascades as well.

Cascading changes and Instead Of Triggers are mutually exclusive. After all, if there is an Instead Of Trigger, then it will run and the DELETE will not. So you can have one or the other. If you've been following along on your system throughout this chapter, however, you have another problem. You could, if you wanted, delete the itrgAppointmentsDel and then modify the foreign key relationship between Pets and Appointments to allow cascading deletes. The problem is, you still couldn't delete any data from Pets.

That's because we created an After Trigger on Appointments several pages ago that rolls back any transaction that attempts to delete an Appointment. Did you remember that? If you didn't, don't feel bad. On more than one occasion I've had a perfectly crafted stored procedure fail because a Trigger did just what it was designed to do and I had forgotten to take it into account.

I'm not trying to scare you off triggers, mind you. But they need to be treated with respect and used correctly otherwise they will cause you no end of trouble.

System Stored Procedures and Functions

Many people hear the word *system* and cringe. System stored procedures and functions are not to be feared. You can learn a lot from them, in fact. We're not about to cover all of them in this chapter, but we'll cover a couple of handy ones that you should probably know.

You already know a couple of system functions: ISNULL, SUM, and MAX. You didn't think of them as system functions? Well, they come as part of the system and they are functions, so they are system functions. But you thought system functions were something scarier?

OK, how about @@Error and @@RowCount? They don't look like functions, but that's really what they are. They take no parameter, and you don't need to use (), but they really are best described as parameterless system functions that return a value.

Ready for something that looks scary? How about sp_helptext? When most people think of system stored procedures they think of these sp_ procedures. Of all the System system stored procedures, that's probably the most useful. What sp_helptext does is return the TSQL commands that make up whatever object you are looking at. For instance, in the **RDBA10** database, you could execute sp_helptext MentorList and you would see the SELECT statement that makes up this view.

Perhaps the handiest place to use sp_helptext, however, is on the stored procedures that Microsoft has written. All of the sp_ stored procedures can be found in the **master** database. If you switch the QA to that database and then issue sp_helptext sp_tables, you'll see the TSQL code behind the stored procedure that will give you information about tables in the database. Table 10-4 lists some of the system-stored procedures you might find useful.

Table 10-4. Handy System Stored Procedures

PROCEDURE	DESCRIPTION
sp_helptext	Prints out the TSQL commands that make up views, functions, and stored procedures.
sp_spaceused	When used without a parameter, displays disk usage for a database. When used with a table for the parameter, displays the amount of space in use, the number of rows, and how much space the indices are taking up.
sp_attach_db	Adds a database to the server based on the physical file.
sp_detach_db	Removes a database from the server by disconnecting the server from the physical files that make up the database.
sp_help_index	Lists indices and statistics on a table.

Last Words

Programming your database is the key to making it efficient. Stored procedures, triggers, and functions help you provide better management of the database in terms of efficiency and security. Not only that, but by freezing your stored procedure and function interfaces like a COM component, you can make programming to the database easier. In the next chapter you're going to learn how stored procedures can help you secure your data easily and efficiently.

Resources

If you think that the resources for this chapter look remarkably like those for the last chapter, you're correct. But they are all good resources for programming the database:

- Not necessarily the best resource for learning TSQL, but the original reference for all of the TSQL commands: SQL Server Books On Line.

- Once you've got the basics of TSQL down, get this book and work through it. One advantage of this book is that it starts with TSQL statements that look a lot like the ones I'm used to writing and demonstrates how to change them so they are much more efficient: *Advanced Transact SQL for SQL Server 2000* by Ben-Gan and Moreau (Apress).

- Another one of those books recommended for your bookshelf: *SQL For Smarties: Advanced SQL Programming, 2nd Edition* by Joe Celko (Morgan Kaufman).

CHAPTER 11

How Do I Secure My Data?

"Several large, artificial constructions are approaching us," ZORAC announced after a short pause. "The designs are not familiar, but they are obviously the products of intelligence. Implications: we have been intercepted deliberately by a means unknown, for a purpose unknown, and transferred to a place unknown by a form of intelligence unknown. Apart from the unknowns, everything is obvious."
— James P. Hogan, *Giants Star*

MAYBE YOU WON'T HAVE SECURITY problems on that scale, but security is an issue that everyone needs to deal with in today's interconnected world. Security in SQL Server has never been a glamorous subject. In fact, before SQL Server 2000, it was a running joke at demonstrations that logging into SQL Server as sa (System Administrator) with no password was Microsoft's "standard" security model. The sad truth of the matter is, however, that many SQL Server sites run with no password on the sa account and allow all data access through the sa account. This practice of not placing a password on the sa account was caused by a combination of developers not understanding how the security model worked and the fact that SQL Server installed with a default of no password on the sa account. It's also because too many books, articles, and documentation use this "security" strategy—or lack thereof.

 NOTE *Examples in this chapter use the **RDBA11** database. You'll find instructions for installing it in Appendix A, "How Do I Load the Examples?"*

Non-SQL Server Security

Although the focus of this chapter is the security used for accessing data on SQL Server, other levels of security are always involved, as with any part of an NT Domain. There is the physical security (where the box is actually located). If it is sitting in an empty cubical in the middle of an office of cubicles and the administrator happens to be logged in, then your server (and consequently your data) is not what anyone would call "secure." Worse yet, in the case of the server sitting in an unsecure area with the administrator account logged in, anyone can gain access to the operating system and potentially resources on the network.

Another point to consider is that the SQL Server works within the hierarchy of NT Security. The lowest maintenance way to set up the box is to use that security model to your advantage because it surrounds SQL Server.

SQL Server's Security Hierarchies

There are two ways to "connect" to SQL Server:

- Windows Authentication, which is managed by NT

- SQL Server Authentication, which requires creating a login and password information stored in SQL Server

More people are beginning to use NT's domain security, which can be a handy way to manage SQL Server Security, particularly when used with NT Groups and SQL Server roles, as you'll see shortly. This chapter will use SQL Security for its examples. Table 11-1 lists the security hierarchy of SQL Server objects.

Table 11-1. SQL Server Objects Security Hierarchy

LEVEL	DESCRIPTION
Server	It is entirely possible to have a login that has access to the server but no access to any of the objects on the server.
Databases	It's important to remember, when creating logins that they need access to a default database instead of the default database that SQL Server chooses. This is because SQL Server will assign every new user the **master** database. Because this database contains all of the data related to the other databases, it's dangerous to make this the default for any user.
Stored procedures	These interact with views and tables, which can be useful because you can give a user permission to run a stored procedure even though that user doesn't have access to the tables the procedure accesses. This will be explained when we start working through the security examples.
Views	A view is one way to present selected columns from a table or the product of a join or multiple tables so as to restrict which columns the user can see.
Tables	Access can be granted to tables; however, this is not recommended for several reasons. The best reason is that most end users don't like to deal with a properly normalized database.[1]
Columns	The lowest level of security in SQL Server 2000 is on columns. You could, for instance, grant access to several columns in a table and let someone either select or update just those columns, but again this is probably best handled through stored procedures and views.

In addition to the hierarchy of objects, there is another hierarchy, this one of logins. Logins do not exist in a vacuum but must be a part of a database or server group. SQL Server calls these groups *roles*, which makes sense because each group has a certain role to play in the database or server. Roles make it much easier to maintain security because access to data can be done at the role level, meaning new users simply need to be a member of the correct role to have everything working properly. In addition, when a new view or stored procedure is added, you only need add permission for it to the appropriate roles instead of large number of individual logins. The best way to explain how security works in SQL Server is by demonstration, so let's create some logins.

---

[1] I've had more than one fellow programmer tell me that they don't mind accessing the data as long as I give them views that present the data as they expect it to look.

A login is used to gain access to SQL Server. Once in SQL Server, a login is added to a database as a user or is aliased to a user. An example would be sa. Although this is the highest level account on the system, it is aliased to the dbo user for each database. Roles were introduced in SQL Server 7.0. In prior versions of SQL Server you could belong to only one group *in a database. That group was assigned permissions to objects. Inheritance works the same regardless of the version of SQL Server, however. The most important difference between roles and groups is that you can belong to multiple roles, which allows a user to inherit different permissions. Now you can add users to specific roles to achieve specific permissions without having to customize every user and object combination. This is a dramatic improvement, I must say.*

Should You Set Permissions on Tables?

In general, tables should be off limits to all users and most developers. A well-designed database will use stored procedures and views to provide access to data. That's not because users generally aren't to be trusted. It's actually to make life easier for developers (and the users who own the data) as well as to help minimize or prevent accidents—for example, when developers make mistakes by forgetting to put a WHERE clause on the DELETE statement before running it against something unimportant like all the Accounts Receivable.

If the development staff writes all of their database access routines as ad-hoc SELECT statements against a table and that table has to change, they will then need to change all of their programs to reflect those changes. If, on the other hand, they have written their programs to take advantage of stored procedures or views and you freeze these interfaces and what is being returned, then these can be kept consistent through almost any changes made to the underlying data structures. It only becomes necessary to change the application when the stored procedure changes its "interface," or when the input/output parameters change. Even then it's possible to add new parameters with default values to the end of a stored procedure and not break the existing code using the procedure.

Therefore, as a general rule, don't give permission to tables to anyone other than the database owner.

How Do I Create a Login?

Before we get into the details of how to create a login, this is a good time to talk about the differences between a user and a login. Although the two are used interchangeably, they are quite different. When we hear someone speak about a user, we generally associate that term with an individual. As a database administrator, however, we really don't want to get bogged down in the maintenance of every single employee who might need to be accessing the data. Not only is that time consuming, an n-tier system generally won't know the name of the user. Having said all that . . . SQL Server uses the term *user* to mean login, *arghhhhh.* In this chapter, we'll use the terms that SQL Server uses; however, try to remember that a user in the database may not be the person sitting next to you.

A login, on the other hand, has only one purpose, to connect to SQL Server. From there, a login is added to a database as a user of that database or aliased to an existing database user. Some examples of valid logins could be receptionist, veterinarian, officemanager, and reportgenerator. Each of these logins has a specific set of rights associated with it and, when set up as roles or NT Groups, the burden of administration falls back to the domain admins, where it belongs.

Logins are created at the server level. Open the Enterprise Manager (EM) and then one of the servers. Under the server is a Security folder. Double-click on that folder to open it up and you'll find that it contains four objects: Logins, Server Roles, Linked Servers, and Remote Servers. As you can see in Figure 11-1, there are two logins already defined, sa and Builtin\Administrators. Both of these are created and added automatically at installation time, with the latter belonging to the NT Administrators group. Thus, any login that is in the administrator's group on the box that SQL Server is installed is automatically granted sa rights to SQL Server.[2]

---

[2]   Except Windows 9x boxes, which don't support NT Login Security for SQL Server.

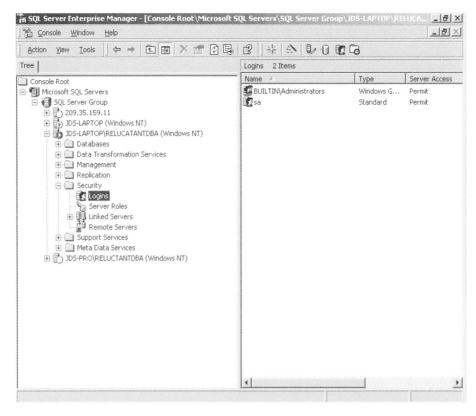

Figure 11-1. The Security folder for SQL Server

We're going to right-click on the Logins folder in the EM explorer and select New Login. That will bring up the SQL Server Login Properties dialog box (see Figure 11-2). This dialog box has three tabs and we'll cover each in turn, starting with the General tab.

Linked Servers and Remote Servers

Linked Servers provide a way to access data on other servers. Remote Servers exist solely for backward compatibility and should be replaced by Linked Servers. Although Linked Servers are an interesting facet of the security in SQL Server 2000, they really don't fit into this book. Books On Line (BOL) has some excellent information on how and why to use Linked Servers.

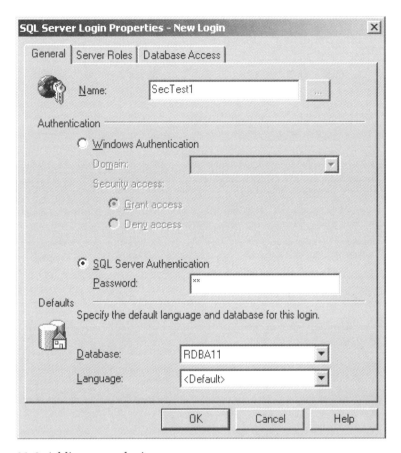

Figure 11-2. Adding a new login

What Is in a Name?

The answer to that all depends on whether you are using Windows Authentication. If you are, then you can click on the ellipses (. . .) in the button to the right of the name box. This brings up a list of the domain logins and domain groups for the default domain of the server. From the list you can choose the one(s) you want to grant access to the server, and where applicable, grant access and permissions to a database. Being able to select a predefined login, selecting the domain and then determining whether to grant or deny access are the only differences between NT Security and SQL Security. To keep these examples simple, we're going to be using SQL Security.

Keep two things in mind about logins. The first is that NT logins on the domain are managed by whomever is in charge of your network. SQL Server accounts, on the other hand, are managed by the administrators of SQL Server. When adding NT Accounts, you are effectively granting access by adding the account to SQL Server, where SQL Authentication means literally creating the account in SQL Server. The second point is "function." With SQL Server Authentication, disabling a login may involve dropping the login, depending, of course, on the situation. With Windows Authentication you can select Deny, effectively disabling a login. But even better still, if information technology should have to disable a user's domain account (and you may not be informed of this right away), that account is automatically disabled on all SQL Servers. This feature is truly awesome! So, the real differences are how logins are created and how they can be disabled, with Windows Authentication being the better and more flexible of the two.

We're going to create a login called SecTest1, click on the SQL Server Authentication, and enter a password. You can, if you want, leave the password blank, but that's not very good security, so all of these logins will have a password.

NOTE *If you look in the Transact SQL script that we've included for creating these logins, you'll discover that I'm using a password of np (short for no password). For this particular test, that's fine, but you would usually make my password something much more difficult. Generally you'll go to a word of the day site, replace letters like i, o, and e with !, 0, and 3 (or something like that) and have it be at least eight characters long.*

At the bottom of the tab we can set a couple of defaults for this new login. The most important default setting is the default database. SQL Server defaults to the **master** database if a database is not selected. Make sure you set the default database to be whatever database this login is going to be accessing most often.

CAUTION *It really is important, particularly in n-tier applications, that you don't allow programs to change the database on the fly. The reason for this is quite simple. If a middleware component has two processes, it shares the database connection. When one of the processes changes the database, the second process doesn't know that it has been changed and attempts to use it. In the best-case scenario, the middleware component starts to get errors because the stored procedures it is attempting to execute don't exist in the database. In a worst-case scenario, the middleware component could be modifying data on the wrong database, creating quite a headache for you to sort out later.*

The reason that a Login shouldn't default to the **master** database is quite simple. The **master** database contains all of the objects necessary for the other databases on the server to operate.[3] If the default database is not set for the correct database, then somewhere down the line someone will connect to SQL Server using this login and will forget to set the database correctly and then they could be making changes to tables in the **master** database that you don't want made. You should get into the habit of changing the sa login to point to a different database (**msdb** is a good one) so that if you need to use that login you won't be causing problems.

What Are Server Roles?

Server roles are best served hot with a little butter and perhaps some grated cheese . . . no, sorry, wrong book. Server roles are like predefined groups that have unique permissions that cannot be granted to individual logins. The Security Server role, for instance, has permission to create new logins. You cannot, however, give these types of permissions to an individual login directly. Instead, that login needs to be made a part of the Security Server role. Table 11-2 lists the roles and explains what each one does. As you can see from Figure 11-3, each role is listed with a checkbox that you can use to assign the login to a role.

---

[3]   That is why you are backing it up daily. You *are* backing it up daily, right?

Table 11-2. Fixed Server Roles Define Special, Broad Rights for a Login

ROLE	EXPLANATION
System Administrators	Has complete access to anything and everything in the server; all rights belong to this role. When using NT Security, the Administrators group on the server is defined as having system administrator rights.
Security Administrators	This role can create and manage logins, passwords, and rights.
Server Administrators	This role can configure settings relating to the server and how it operates. A login would need this permission to change options such as the default language on the server.
Setup Administrators	This role can add/remove linked servers and executes some system stored procedures related to linked servers. It can also determine what processes will automatically run when the server is started. Handy when you want a stored procedure's execution plan to exist in the cache for quicker access.
Process Administrators	This role can manage and kill processes running under SQL Server. This is especially handy for dealing with runaway queries.
Disk Administrators	This role can manage and create disk files. Disk files are the physical files that SQL Server stores database information in.
Bulk Insert Administrators	This role can perform bulk inserts. See the Chapter 14, "What Are the Data Transformation Services (DTS)?" for more information.
Database Creators	This role can create and change databases, including objects within the database. Although you can create a database and make an existing login the database owner, that login won't be able to create other databases unless they are assigned to this server role.

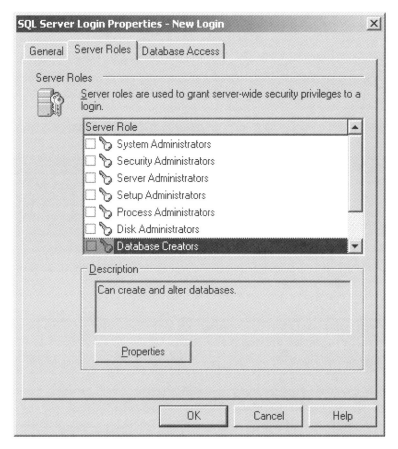

Figure 11-3. Setting server roles for the login determines what system-wide functions a login can perform.

You cannot add, delete, or change the server roles—what you see is what you get. Because this login is strictly for testing access to data, it doesn't need any server roles assigned, so we'll leave all of the boxes unchecked.

 CAUTION   *A login that is assigned to a server role can also assign other accounts to that role. That means a database creator could assign someone else to the role of database creator.*

How Do I Grant Access to Databases for a Login?

The third tab on the SQL Server Login Properties dialog box relates to database access. At a minimum, you will want to permit the login access to its default database. SQL Server won't do this automatically when you set the default database, so you'll need to make sure you do that here. When you go to save a login that hasn't been granted access to its default database, the EM will point out to you that the login won't be able to connect to the server. Fortunately, you can tell the EM that you don't want to continue. Then you can correct this oversight and save the login.

Once you click on the checkbox to permit the login to access a database, the database roles will appear in the lower half of the window where you then have the opportunity to add the login to one or more database roles (see Figure 11-4). Database roles serve a function similar to that of server roles but within the more limited scope of the database. Table 11-3 lists the database roles and their descriptions.

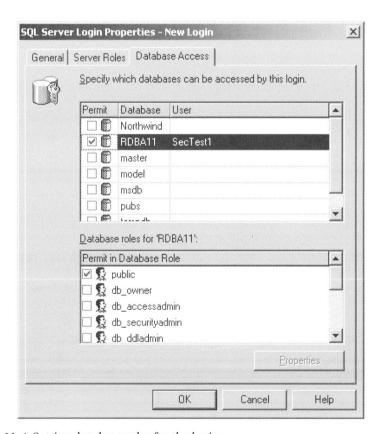

Figure 11-4. Setting database roles for the login

Table 11-3. Database Roles

ROLE	EXPLANATION
Public	Everyone is assigned to the public role and nobody can be removed from this role. This is the default role for access; however, it can be overridden by other groups or permissions granted to the login itself. In general, any user or developer will be accessing the data through this role unless another role is specifically needed.
db_owner	The login in this role (database owner or dbo) has access to any and all tables and can do anything in the database, including dropping the database entirely. By default, db_owner has all of the rights associated with any of the other db_ roles. This is the role that needs to be assigned to whomever will be maintaining the stored procedures, views, and such, generally the administrator for the database, probably you.
db_accessadmin	A member of this role can add logins as users to the database. This role, however, cannot determine what access those logins can have. That is saved for db_securityadmin.
db_securityadmin	This role manages the permissions for users granted access by the db_accessadmin role. These two roles have different functions. db_securityadmin determines what a user or role has access to, whether the user or role can run a stored procedure or access a view. db_accessadmin, on the other hand, adds SQL or Windows NT logins to the roles that db_security admin has set up. In many cases this will be one and the same person performing both of these roles, probably you.
db_ddladmin	This role can run any of the Data Definition Language (DDL) statements, meaning that logins in this role can create, drop, and modify all of the objects in the database. Typically this role is used when there is going to be a program that will handle any and all of the scripted changes to a database.
db_backupoperator	This role has permission to back up the database but cannot restore it. Logins need dbo or system admin rights to do that. This login is great for automated backup programs.
db_datareader	This login can read data from all user tables in the database that it hasn't explicitly been denied access to. Good for read-only access to the database when you don't want a login to be able to update anything.
db_datawriter	This login can add, change, or delete data from all user tables in the database. In other words, it can do anything to the data but cannot change the underlying structure. Handy if you have a program that is strictly feeding data into a database from a collection point.

(continued)

Table 11-3. Database Roles (continued)

ROLE	EXPLANATION
db_denydatareader	This login cannot read any data in the database. This is a handy way of setting a login so it cannot execute SELECT * FROM. Setting it as db_denydatareader automatically prevents it from accessing the tables and views, but not from executing stored procedures to which it has access.
db_denydatawriter	This login cannot change any data in the database. This is a handy way of setting a login so it cannot execute INSERT or UPDATE statements. Setting it as db_denydatawriter automatically prevents it from writing to the tables and views, but not from executing stored procedures to do the writing for it.

Some of these roles make sense. A login that was in db_backupoperator, for instance, would be handy to back up all of the databases on the server without actually being able to access any of the data. Other database roles, however, don't seem to make much sense. Why would you want to have a login that couldn't read any data from the database? If there were a program that was tied to a measuring device and whose sole job was to write data to the database, then it makes sense to set it up as a db_denydatareader. That way it can write but not read data.

When dealing with security, one must keep in mind the many ways in which you can access or connect to SQL Server, such as Access, Excel, or Word. With that in mind, a savvy user could connect to SQL Server with any one of these applications and thus access any or all data. In some operations data-entry clerks are responsible for simply entering data and nothing more. If one of these people were to attempt to connect to SQL Server directly with deny read, they wouldn't be able to access anything. However, by using the same account with the approved application, they would be able to enter data.

What Do You Mean the Login Already Exists?

What happens when you try to add a user who already exists? It's generally best to manage security through NT Groups, especially because it cuts down on the amount of maintenance work that needs to be done on the SQL Server. However, it isn't always possible to do that and sometimes you'll end up with a long list of logins who have been granted access to the database. When this happens, you may find yourself trying to add a user to either the server or a specific database where they already exist. As you can imagine, SQL Server won't let you do that.

When you attempt to add an existing user to the server, you'll get an "Error 21008: [SQL-DMO]Login already exists." This is similar to the error you'll get if you try to add a user to a database they already exist in, the only difference is that it is a 21002 error.

For now, we're just going to grant SecTest1 access to **RDBA11** and leave it in the public group. When we press the OK button, SQL Server will ask us to confirm the password we've given it (if it is a SQL Authentication) and then create the account. We're going to add four more logins (SecTest2, SecTest3, SecTest4, and SecTest5) and set them up exactly the same way.

How Do I Set Up Roles for a Database?

Although server roles and database roles are predefined and cannot be changed, you can create your own database roles. In the EM, expand a database in the explorer and you will find the Roles collection. Open up the Roles and you'll see a list of all of the roles we listed in Table 11-3. Double-clicking on the role brings up a window that you can use for adding users to a role (see Figure 11-5).

Creating a new role is as easy as right-clicking on Roles and selecting New Database Role. This will bring up a simple dialog box that will ask for the name of the new role and will allow you to set the role type. There are two types of roles: standard and application.

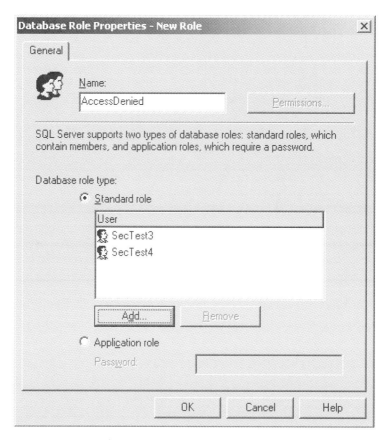

Figure 11-5. Creating a role

How does all this security affect my programming? The basic thing to remember about SQL Server Security is that any valid login that is a user in a database will be able to connect to that database. However, it's when that login tries to do something that you start to get errors because the permissions aren't set correctly.

What Is an Application Role?

An application role works like a login with a password. You can set all of the access or deny rights for the application role just as you would a login or standard role. The big difference between an application role and a standard role is that you can't add users to the application role (although you can add the application role to a group). You can also change the application role once a login is connected to the server.

There are really only two differences between an application role and a login:

- The login can get by without a password whereas the application role must have a login.

- The application role is specific to a database and, as a general rule, can't access other databases unless the NT guest user ID is enabled. Enabling the guest account is almost as good as putting a welcome mat out for unwelcome guests and is not recommended.

That means that the application role is better than a login when you need to restrict access to one database, but a login is better if the user or application will need to access more than one database. Take a look at BOL to find more information on application roles and how you can use them.

How Do I Set Security on an Object in the Database?

Setting security in the database is really a simple task. You can do it one of two ways:

- You can set security on an object for multiple logins.

- You can set security for a login on multiple objects.

Let's set security on an object for multiple logins. We're going to do that mainly so we can set the different securities for each login at the same time. To do this, we highlight the object in the EM and then right-click on it, selecting All Tasks ➤ Manage Permissions.

We're going to do this first on the stored procedure ListVeterinariansByOffice. This stored procedure returns a rowset of data for all vets in all offices, much like a function does in a programming language. In the EM, open up the **RDBA11** database and then go to Stored Procedures. In the right-hand window you should see ListVeterinariansByOffice. Right-click on that and select

All Tasks ➤ Manage Permissions. This will bring up a window like the one in Figure 11-6, except none of the checkboxes should be filled in.

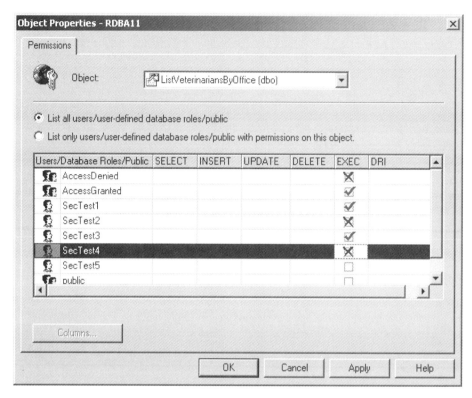

Figure 11-6. Setting security on a stored procedure

What Is the Difference between Grant, Deny, and Revoke?

SQL Server lets you specify three types of access to an object. You can grant access, deny access, and revoke access. But what do those really mean?

- Grant is used to specifically allow access to an object.

- Deny is used to specifically prevent access to an object.

- Revoke is used to remove specifically granted or denied access to an object.

The most confusing thing about these three access types is the third one, revoking access. If a login has been granted access and that access is revoked, it is not the same as having been denied. If the login SecTest1 has been granted access to Owners and we then revoke that access, it simply removes that access (similar to setting the deny or access right to NULL). If SecTest1 belongs to a role that has access, then SecTest1 would still be able to get to Owners. That's different from denying access, which prohibits access to an object.

Where the Rubber Meets the Road: Demonstrating the Security in Action

You've patiently waded through the technical aspects of SQL Server Security. Now, to see how the security model works, start up the QA and open up five connections to the server. For each connection, use a different login and then try to execute the following SQL code:

ListVeterinariansByOffice

The results are shown in Table 11-4. Access must be granted or not denied for the login and any roles to which it belongs. If we take SecTest1 and add it to the AccessDenied database role, then it won't be able to execute the stored procedure any longer. Anytime SQL Server encounters a deny on an object, even if there are fifty grants for that login, it prevents the SQL from executing and returns an error message. That error message is what your program will get if it tries to access something it either doesn't have permission to or that has permission for that login set to deny.

Table 11-4. How Grant/Deny/Revoke Affects the Logins

LOGIN	GROUP SECURITY	LOGIN SECURITY	RESULT
SecTest1	Granted	Granted	Executed Stored Procedure
SecTest2	Denied	Granted	Execute Permission Denied
SecTest3	Denied	Granted	Execute Permission Denied
SecTest4	Denied	Denied	Execute Permission Denied
SecTest5	None Specified	None Specified	Execute Permission Denied

But, you're thinking, we didn't grant access to the view that's being used in ListVeterinariansByOffice. If that's the case, how does the stored procedure access the data for the logins that are allowed to execute it? Well, that's a matter of inheritance. This stored procedure was created by the database owner (dbo), and the dbo has all rights to all objects in the database. When a login attempts to execute this stored procedure, SQL Server verifies that it has the rights to execute it. Then, if the login has the right to execute the procedure, SQL Server executes it with the permissions of the creator of the stored procedure. Table 11-5 details the different rights and how they work.

Table 11-5. Login Rights on Views and Tables

RIGHT	DESCRIPTION
SELECT	This determines whether the user has the right to select records from the table or view. On a view that is used for reporting, you can GRANT SELECT for views to the user being used for reporting but not give them rights to the underlying tables. That helps keep reports from joining tables incorrectly and displaying erroneous data.
INSERT	This determines whether the user can INSERT new records. You can almost always leave this with no specific permission (which denies everyone except the dbo) or set it to DENY.
UPDATE	This determines whether the user can UPDATE tables or views directly. You can treat this the same way as the INSERT rights and for the same reasons.
DELETE	Can you guess why we set this to either not have rights specified or to be denied? If you guessed because these should be handled through stored procedures, you're correct.
DRI	We'll talk about Data Relational Integrity (DRI) in a couple of pages in the section "What Is DRI Security?"

Actually, we usually don't DENY the rights on INSERT, UPDATE, DELETE, and DRI. By leaving them blank, you accomplish the same goal, but by marking them with those red Xs (see Figure 11-7) you should remember to think about why someone would need to be able to add data directly to the table. In most cases, access through stored procedures is the way to handle updates, inserts, and deletes.

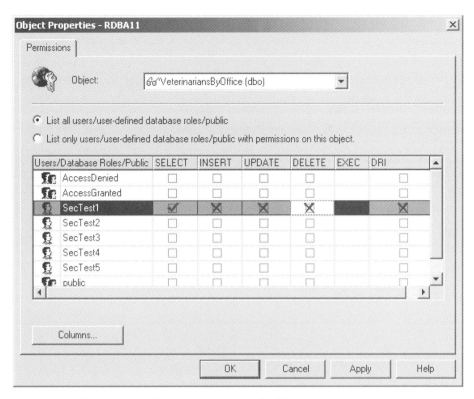

Figure 11-7. Setting permissions on views and tables

How Do I Restrict Access to Individual Columns?

Restricting access to individual columns is easy to do. If you look at Figure 11-7 again you'll see a Corners button in the lower-left corner. Pressing that button brings up the dialog box shown in Figure 11-8. Although this looks like the same dialog box used for setting permissions on the entire table, there are a couple of important exceptions.

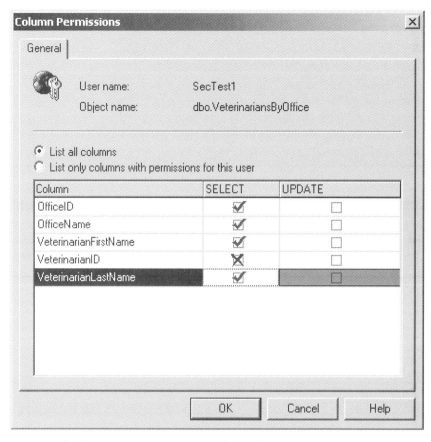

Figure 11-8. Setting permissions on individual columns

You cannot set insert rights on individual columns. When you insert a row into a table you need to insert all columns, even those that are null. Because it's impossible to insert part of a row you aren't allowed to set permissions to do so. OK, so if there are default values for the columns, it *is* possible to insert part of a row and let the default values fill in the blanks, but it would be far too much of an administrative nightmare.

There's one other detail to setting security on individual columns that makes just as much sense but may be less obvious. In Figure 11-8 we have set SecTest1 to have SELECT rights on the OfficeID, OfficeName, and VeterinarianFirstName columns. If we were to log into the QA as SecTest1 and then try to execute SELECT * FROM VeterinariansByOffice, we will suddenly get a screen full of errors. That's because SELECT * will try to return all of the columns, and SecTest1 only has access to three of them.[4]

---

[4]   Have we mentioned already that you should almost never use SELECT *. This is another
       good reason to avoid it.

What is DRI Security?

DRI Security is supposed to allow access to for verifying Data Relational Integrity (DRI). This isn't an issue for most databases. DRI Security only enters into the picture if someone other than the database owner (dbo) has permission to create permanent tables.

Now, in my history of dealing with databases I have only had one instance where I have created tables that have not been owned by dbo and that was because I was given rights to a database with table creation rights but was not marked as dbo. That meant that every table I built would show up as *databasename.ownername.tablename* instead of *databasename.dbo.tablename*. With the ability to create temporary tables and table datatypes, the need for creating tables with non-dbo owners is slight; you may encounter this in a legacy situation.

If you do have individuals creating permanent tables not belonging to dbo, it is quite possible that the individual who created the table may not have appropriate rights to a table required to establish a foreign key constraint. When you insert data into a table that has a foreign key relationship defined, the SQL Server needs to verify that the value you are using for the foreign key exists as a value in the primary key of the master table. If the login that owns the table does not have rights to read the master table to determine if the primary key exists and is valid, data can't be entered into the table. In that case, you could grant DRI rights to the login that owns the table that is being inserted/updated and that will automatically grant read rights to the master table enabling the login to insert or update data.

A better solution would be to modify the database so it doesn't use non-dbo tables, but that isn't always an option.

How Do I Set Security for a User in the Database?

OK, you've learned how to set rights for multiple users for a single object, but how about the other way around? You can assign rights to a user or role by right-clicking on the user or role and selecting All Tasks ➤ Manage Permissions. This will bring up a list of all of the objects in the database (see Figure 11-9). From this screen you can set GRANT, DENY, or REVOKE permissions on any object.

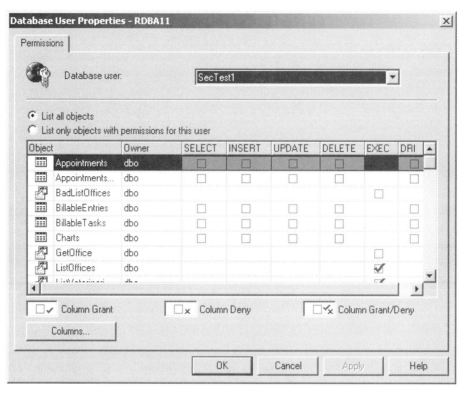

Figure 11-9. Assigning permissions for a login to multiple objects

You've probably noticed that this also displays several system stored procedures that begin with *dt*. These procedures are all related to integrating SQL Server with Visual Source Safe and are not documented. Ignore these when setting your permissions.

> **NOTE** *When you grant* UPDATE *permission, you must also grant* SELECT *permission. That's because SQL Server needs to query the database for the existing values before updating them.*

Roles or Logins, Which Is Better?

In terms of use, roles and SQL Server logins work similarly but differently. The difference lies in how they are managed. If you have a database going to be used by a lot of people (especially if they all exist as NT Logins in a Windows Domain), then it is easier to use roles assigned to distinct NT Logins. Even easier is to set up a SQL Server role for an NT Group and then assign the rights to that group as a whole. Once that is done you don't need to do anything to provide access to the server as long as the network folks set up the NT Accounts in the correct groups.

Programs, on the other hand, can't always be assumed to be running under an NT account. If you have an Active Server Page that is going to be accessing the database, odds are it needs a login and password. You don't need to assign passwords to logins, but there's really no good reason not to, particularly because data is generally the lifeblood of a company, and you don't want a hacking leech to drain your company dry.

Cascading Data and Security

Speaking of draining blood or system resources, the time has come to dig into how cascading works. We have waited to cover it until now so that we can demonstrate not only how cascading works but also how to explain security and cascades.

> *Reluctant DBA* definition of *cascading*:
> Cascading occurs when a primary key in one table that is also used as a foreign key constraint in another table is either changed or deleted. Changes to the primary key and deletions of referenced rows are not normally allowed but when cascading is turned on the rows in other tables that are dependent upon the primary key are either deleted or modified.

Now, in this sample database there really isn't any need to implement cascading. All of the primary keys are artificial identity columns, and there is little likelihood that these numbers will change. It is possible, however, that data might need to be purged. In that case, cascading will work wonders. For instance:

- The Pets table is dependent on Owners.

- Both Appointments and Charts are dependent upon Pets.

- Charts is also dependent upon Appointments.

To turn cascading on from within a diagram, simply right-click on the join and check the appropriate boxes at the bottom of the window (for more information on the Diagramming tool, see Chapter 5, "How Do I Define and Structure a Database?").

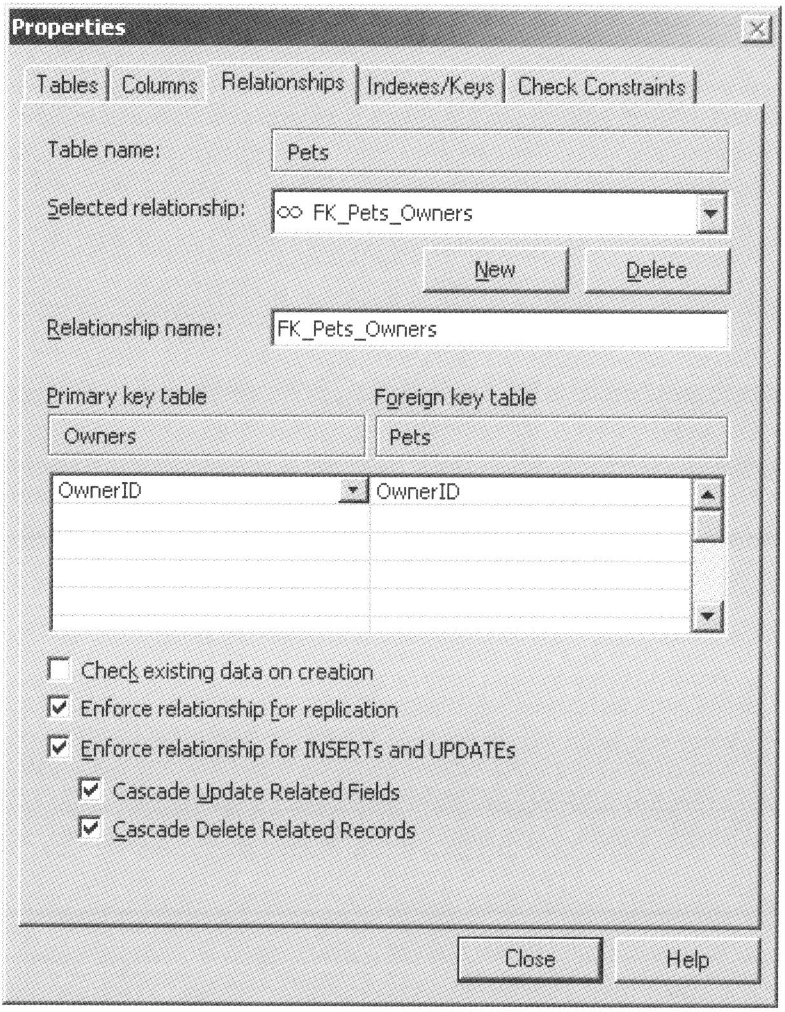

Figure 11-10. Turning cascading on and off is easy from within the Diagramming tool.

If you select Cascade Update Related Fields, then whenever you change the primary key value in the master table, the value of that column in the dependent table changes. If you select Cascade Delete Related Records, on the other hand, deleting a row in the master table deletes the rows in the dependent tables. Listing 10-1 shows an example of a Cascade Delete in action.

Listing 10-1. CascadeDelete.sql demonstrates how a cascading delete works.

```
DECLARE @MaxOwnerID int
SELECT TOP 1 @MaxOwnerID = OwnerID FROM Owners ORDER BY OwnerID DESC
PRINT @MaxOwnerID
DELETE FROM Owners WHERE OwnerID = @MaxOwnerID
```

Go ahead and run it. Did you get errors? That's because SecTest1 doesn't have rights to delete from these tables. Go ahead manually grant `DELETE` permission on the Owners table to SecTest1.

Now execute the script and it should delete a row. It should say one row(s) affected, but it really deleted a row from Owners along with any associated rows in the other tables. In fact, the execution plan is a little more complex than a simple delete (see Figure 11-11). That's because it needs to scan the cascaded tables to see what rows need to be deleted. Even with this added complexity, if you are going to delete data with dependent rows, using SQL's cascade ability is more efficient than trying to handle all the details yourself with triggers or stored procedures, something that was necessary in prior versions of SQL Server (and certainly taboo).

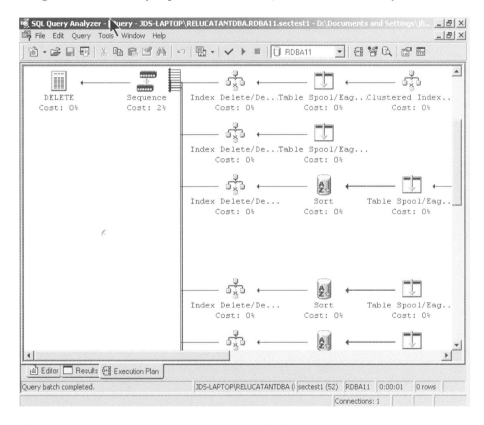

Figure 11-11. The execution plan for cascaded tables can be more complex than those that don't need cascading.

Why didn't you need to set `DELETE` permission for the other tables? Inheritance. It was the dbo who set up the cascading delete mechanism, so the deletes were handled as though the dbo were deleting the rows, once the initial delete from Owners was allowed.

Last Words

In this chapter you've learned about SQL Server's security model and you should be able to start taking advantage of it to make management of access to your data easier. In the next chapter we're going to introduce another of SQL Server's tools designed to make your job easier: the SQL Server Agent.

Resources

- Adding a linked server:
  http://msdn.microsoft.com/library/psdk/sql/prsql_6gqa.htm

- Merriam-Webster's Word of the Day site (for password inspiration):
  http://www.m-w.com/cgi-bin/mwwod.pl

- Microsoft white paper on security:
  http://www.microsoft.com/technet/sql/technote/sql2ksec.asp

How Can SQL Server Agent Make Life Easier?

Operator: What number are you calling?
Maxwell Smart: I'm calling Control, Operator. . .
Operator: You have dialed incorrectly. Give me your name and address
and your dime will be refunded.
Smart: Operator, I'm calling from my shoe!
Operator: What is the number of your shoe?"
Smart: It's an unlisted shoe, Operator!

—"Get Smart"

SQL SERVER AGENT ISN'T A SECRET AGENT like Maxwell Smart from "Get Smart." Then again, who is? Rather, SQL Server Agent will help you manage some of the chaos that surrounds the day-to-day operation of SQL Server so you'll have more C.O.N.T.R.O.L. (sorry, couldn't resist). Using SQL Server Agent you can schedule jobs (repetitive task, processes, and so forth) to run in SQL Server, and you can also set it up to notify you of problems when they occur. In fact, you can even set up SQL Server Agent to respond to an error or warning so that it not only notifies you but takes action as well. In this chapter we're going to introduce you to SQL Server Agent, explain its scheduling capability, and explain how it can respond to errors.

First, let's find SQL Server Agent. From the left-hand pane of the Enterprise Manager (EM), open a server and then open the Management Folder. As you can see in Figure 12-1, SQL Server Agent contains three separate components: alerts, operators, and jobs. One important thing to notice about Figure 12-1 is that the SQL Server Agent item has a red square on it. That means that SQL Server Agent has not been started. To start it, right-click on SQL Server Agent and select Start.

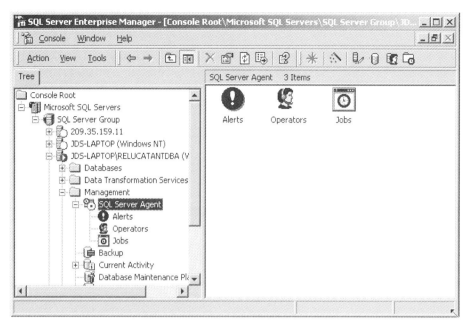

Figure 12-1. Finding SQL Server Agent in the EM

NOTE *If you right-click on the server and go to Properties you'll find a group of checkboxes at the bottom of the General properties tab, one of which automatically starts SQL Server Agent when the operating system starts.*

SQL Server Agent has a number of properties that can be set to help it in running. Right-click on SQL Server Agent and select Properties. That brings up the SQL Server Agent Properties dialog box, as shown in Figure 12-2. There are five tabs—General, Advanced, Alert System, Job System, and Connection—each with a separate set of options that can be set to configure SQL Server Agent.

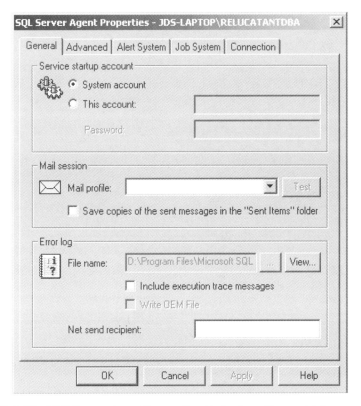

Figure 12-2. The SQL Server Agent Properties dialog box: General tab

SQL Server Agent runs as a service, so this is where you can determine which
NT account the service runs under.[1] Just like the SQL Server itself, SQL Server
Agent needs to run under an account with all of the permissions that it needs on
the box. As you can see on the General tab in Figure 12-2, you have two options
listed in the Service Startup Account section: System Account and This Account.
The first is to have it run under the local system account (this is by default unless
specified otherwise). Most services will function fine with this account; however,
you can set up a local NT account or domain account, and specify that account
for the server to run under using the second option. One problem with using
a regular NT account instead of the local system account is the problem of password synchronization. In other words, whenever that account's password
changes, it will need to be manually changed for all services that use that
account. Often jobs perform tasks that go beyond the local operating system and
therefore require a domain account, and this is why Microsoft recommends this
approach. However, such an account requires tight control over the distribution
of the password and infrequent changes to the password.

---

[1]   Under Windows 98, services aren't available. In that case, SQL Server Agent runs as a sepa-
      rate task and has the same rights as whomever is logged on while it is running.

While an in-depth explanation is beyond the scope of this book, one practice worth noting is multiple domain accounts for services. For instance, I may have SQLexec1 and SQLexec2. Why, you ask? Quite simple. There comes a time when a company faces the unfortunate event of needing to terminate access to an account quickly. Having a spare account allows for services to be quickly switched over to the alternate account (which has a new and secured password), thus protecting vital systems. Although there are many other potential reasons and uses, this does help minimize problems when an account must have its password changed.

The next section on the General tab is the Mail Session. SQL Server can email people to notify them that something is or isn't working. Getting SQLMail to work with either Exchange or a POP server can be a long process, involving security issues that go beyond the scope of this book. Check the "Resources" section to find Microsoft's answer on how to set it up. Finally, there is the Error Log section. One nice thing about this tab is that you can pull up the agent log by clicking the View button.

The Advanced tab, not surprisingly, contains the advanced options (see Figure 12-3). The two options in the Restart Services section are fairly self-explanatory. If either the SQL Server or SQL Server Agent services unexpectedly terminate, you can have them try to restart themselves. The next section, SQL Server Event Forwarding, lets you define how to send application log events to a central server. Though a handy feature, it's beyond the scope of this book. However, event forwarding means adding to the event system on the remote system; logging to the event log should be done with discretion.

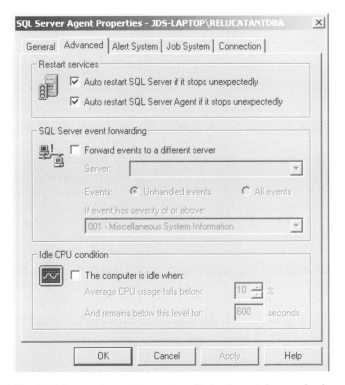

Figure 12-3. The SQL Server Agent Properties dialog box: Advanced tab

It's a well-documented fact that all computers wait at the same speed, but the third section of the Advanced Properties tab, Idle CPU Condition, lets you define when your computer can do something with those wait cycles. Jobs can be scheduled to begin whenever the computer becomes idle, but that requires the SQL Server Agent to know how you define "idle." You can use both the percentage of the processor and how long it has to remain below that threshold in order to define idle.

NOTE   *Jobs that begin when the processor has become idle run until they finish. They don't stop running just because the computer is no longer idle.*

The next tab is the Alert System tab (see Figure 12-4). Although setting up individual operators is covered later in this chapter, this is where you can set some specific ways to format alphanumeric pages. You can include a prefix and suffix to the pager name and subject. There is also a special operator called the *fail-safe* operator. The fail-safe operator is the person who gets the alerts when no one else is specified.

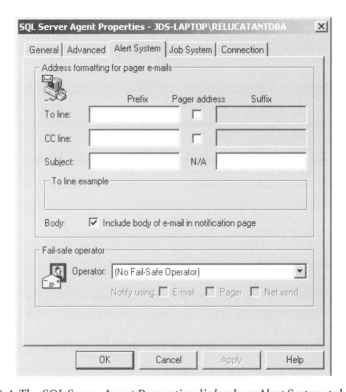

Figure 12-4. The SQL Server Agent Properties dialog box: Alert System tab

The next tab, the Job System tab (see Figure 12-5), determines how much history for jobs is kept. The Shutdown Time-out Interval option specifies how long SQL Server Agent will wait for a job to finish processing when you issue a command to shut down the server. After that time, it kills the job, rolling back any incomplete transactions.

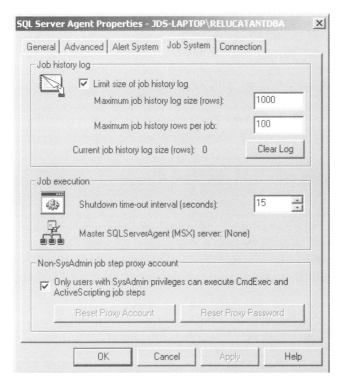

Figure 12-5. The SQL Server Agent Properties dialog box: Job System tab

The bottom section of this tab, Non-SysAdmin Job Step Proxy Account, should be marked with large bold warning symbols. This section is a way of specifying which logins can potentially wreak havoc with your operating system. Well, actually, it's for determining who can execute operating system commands from within SQL Server, but that really is the same thing. In other words, if someone tries to run FORMAT from within SQL Server, your operating system might not complain until it reboots! It is recommended that the checkbox for Only Users with SysAdmin privileges. . . be checked. If it is, then only people with SysAdmin rights can run CmdExec commands or ActiveX script commands.

> **CAUTION**   *A CmdExec command is one that executes operating system commands. You can run* DIR *and* COPY *commands, not to mention other commands that you probably don't want people to run. That means you need to keep the ability to use this limited to system administrators. Because sa is a member of system administrators, this is another good reason why folks shouldn't be allowed to login as sa.*

The Reset Proxy Account button re-creates the local system account. Reset Proxy Password does pretty much what you would think it does; it resets the password for that account.

The final tab, Connection, has to do with how SQL Server Agent connects to SQL Server (see Figure 12-6). By default it connects to SQL Server using the account set up when SQL Server was installed, but you can select to use a SQL Server user ID and password instead.

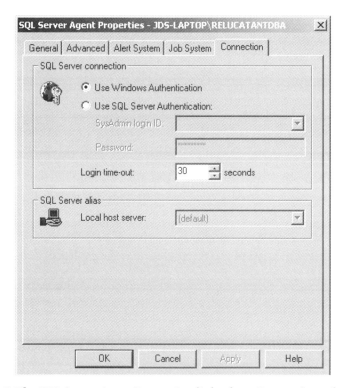

Figure 12-6. The SQL Server Agent Properties dialog box: Connection tab

What Is a Job?

At the heart of SQL Server Agent is the concept of a *job*. A job is a set of one or more steps that perform tasks in a predefined order and can have rudimentary error handling and flow control. If you have followed the steps for creating a maintenance plan, you'll find there are already jobs in the system. Figure 12-7 shows the jobs created for the maintenance plan when the **RDBA** database was first set up. If you haven't yet created a maintenance plan for your database, see Chapter 3, "How Do I Visually Manage Objects?"

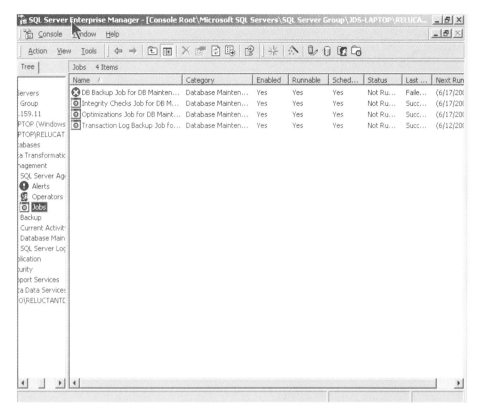

Figure 12-7. Scheduled jobs

> *Reluctant DBA* definition of a SQL Server Agent *job*:
> A set of Transact SQL (TSQL) statements that have a predefined order to achieve a purpose. Jobs are not limited to just TSQL statements though.

Let's run through the columns of information in the EM's Jobs screen, starting with the icon in the left part of the Name column. The first job has a red circle with a white X through it, signifying that the job didn't run correctly. The blue bull's-eye means the job last ran without an error. The next column is the Category for the job. These are all Database Maintenance jobs. Table 12-1 lists and defines some of the default job categories, but you can add your own to the list.[2]

---

[2] More than half of the job categories provided by SQL Server are related to replication, a topic that I'm not going to touch on in this book, so those categories are excluded from Table 12-1. If you want the full list you can run sp_help_category in the Query Analyzer. Make sure your database is **msdb** to see the categories.

Table 12-1. Default Job Categories

CATEGORY	DESCRIPTION
[Uncategorized (Local)]	This is for jobs that will run only on this server.
[Uncategorized (Multi-Server)]	If you have multiple servers running jobs under one master server, this allows you to categorize a job so it runs on multiple servers.
Database Maintenance	Jobs in this category generally run the SQLMaint utility and are part of a maintenance plan.
Full-Text	This category is for jobs related to creating and maintaining full text indexing capabilities.
Jobs from MSX	Jobs from a master server.
Web Assistant	Jobs that create HTML output from standard queries and stored procedures.

The Enabled column determines whether a job will be run from SQL Server Agent. It's possible to create jobs that are not enabled but rather run on demand. A good example of this might be backing up the **model** database because it is something that is routine in nature, but can't or shouldn't actually be scheduled. If you change it you will want to back it up, and it makes sense to have a job to take care of that for you, but because it rarely changes you don't need to back it up nightly. Therefore, you can create a job that isn't enabled and doesn't run on a schedule but can be run as necessary.

The Runnable column indicates just that, whether the job can be run. A job can be non-runnable for a number of reasons. If the server that the job is supposed to run on doesn't exist, for example, it will not be runnable. If the system tables have had rows indiscriminately removed, they may render the job non-runnable as well. If the job can't be run, however, you will have a message here telling you why you can't run the job.

The next four columns all have to do with when the job either is running, has run, or will run again. Every job can be either scheduled to run at a set time or not. The next column shows whether the job was running the last time this screen was refreshed. This is an important distinction because the EM doesn't dynamically update the screen when the status of a job changes. If you start a job running, you won't know whether it is running or not unless you refresh this pane by right-clicking on Jobs in the left-hand pane and selecting refresh.

The next column shows you at a glance, just like the icon on the far left of the job, whether the job ran successfully the last time. Finally, the last column shows the last time the job ran.

How Do I Create a Job?

To create a new job, right-click on Jobs and select New Job. This brings up the New Job Properties window, as shown in Figure 12-8. You fill in the pertinent information to describe what the job does. Every job has a unique identifier in the form of a 36-character string, which should be unique among computers in time and space, and a name. The Name is how is the job will be referenced throughout the system, so give it a descriptive and intuitive name so it's easy to find the job when we're looking for it. The next option to fill in is the Category of the job. For now select Uncategorized [Local]; we'll go through how to add new job categories shortly. The Owner option defaults to being whomever is logged into the EM, though the drop-down list will show all of the users defined on the server. Finally, describe the job in the Description box. Because we haven't defined any master or target servers, this job will default to being run on the local server.

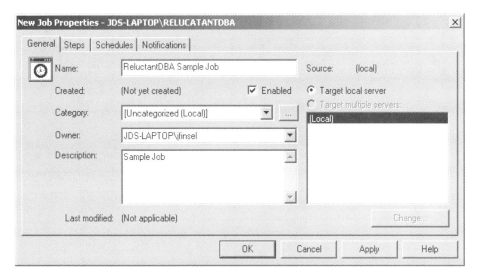

Figure 12-8. The New Job Properties window

NOTE *You might think that the ellipses (. . .) next to Category would take you to a dialog box that would let you edit jobs or possibly even create new ones. Nope. That button brings up the category's Property box, which is a list of all of the jobs in the category.*

How Do I Define What a Job Does?

Now that we have created a job, it's time to give it something to do. Clicking on the Steps tab brings up the section where we can define what a job actually does. These steps are like an early BASIC program, complete with line numbers and GOTO statements. Each step can have any TSQL statement, stored procedure, operating system command, ActiveX script, and so on. Each step can either finish successfully or fail to finish. There is also some basic level of flow control for what happens next based on those two possibilities. We're going to create a simple, three-step job to demonstrate the flexibility inherent in the steps.

When we click on the New button we get the New Job Step screen to fill in (see Figure 12-9). Each step requires a name in the Step Name box that should be fairly descriptive. If this job is going to be made up of several steps, you'll be referring back to that name when working on the flow control. The step name is also what shows up in the job history detail. It is always far easier to remember that you want to go to "Notify Me of an Error" than to try to remember step 32. You also need to specify what type of command this is in the Type box. It could be a TSQL script, an operating system command, one of several replication job types, or an ActiveX script.[3] We can specify which database this step is for in the Database box, meaning we can change databases for different steps within a job. Last, but certainly not least, we can specify the actual SQL code we want to use in the Command box. As you can see in this example, we are using a simple row count.

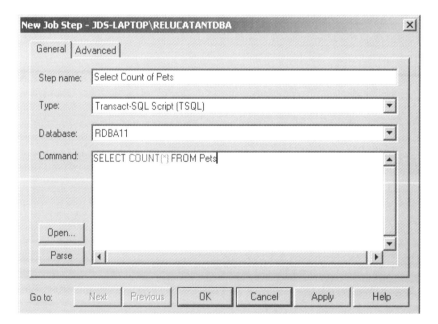

Figure 12-9. Filling in a job step

---

[3] For more information on ActiveX scripts, see the Chapter 14, "What Are the Data Transformation Services (DTS)?"

Take a look to the left of the Command box, and you'll see two buttons. The first button, Open, lets you load the commands from a saved file. It's important to note that the file will be loaded into the database only once. If you make changes to the file, you'll need to reload it into a step for the job to change; the file isn't dynamically linked to the step. The second button, Parse, checks your SQL code and makes sure that it is valid. If you were to make a mistake and type "Petss" instead of "Pets" and press the Parse button, SQL Server will tell you that it has detected an error.

Strangely enough, if we don't parse the incorrect SQL code but try to accept the step with the error, SQL Server will point the error out and ask if we want to continue on nonetheless. That isn't a mistake on SQL Server's part because it is possible that the SQL statement is referencing a table that doesn't exist now but will be created by an earlier step when the job runs.

On the Advanced tab of the New Job Step dialog box (see Figure 12-10), we can set some limited flow control. On success (or failure) we can:

- Quit the job reporting success in the job log history

- Quit the job reporting failure in the job log history

- Go to the next step

- Go to step [x] Step Name

This tab also provides access to a tool that you'll find invaluable when you need to do some debugging. Under the Transact-SQL Script (TSQL) section, you will find the Output File option followed by a text box and ellipses. You can type in a path and filename (or select the ellipses to browse for a file or path to use) for the output of the step selected. When you view a job's history, only a small portion of the output is recorded, which means you may not have all the information you need to diagnose a complex step—for example, a stored procedure that performs some housekeeping task. You can use this feature when implementing a new step or job in general, disable it when you're satisfied everything is functioning correctly, and then re-enable it when problems arise.

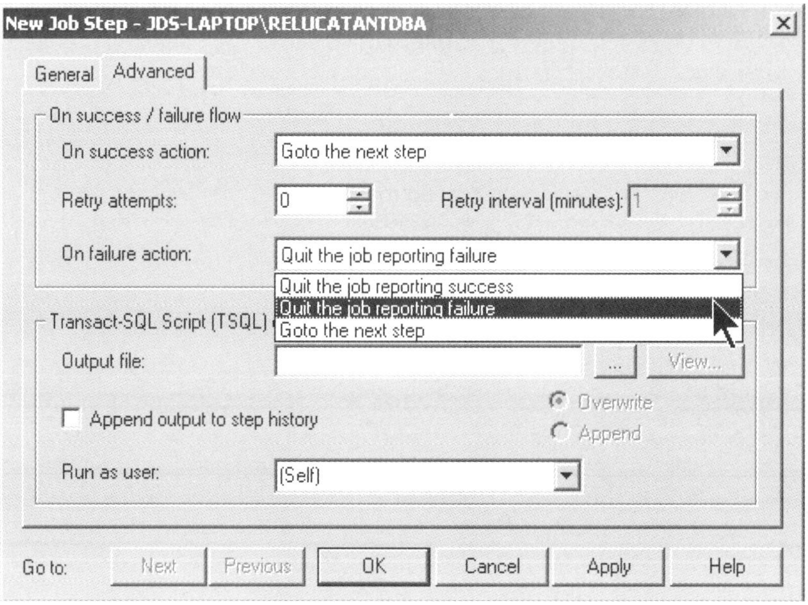

Figure 12-10. Error-parsing SQL statement

For this first step, we only have the first three options. For now, we want to accept the default of Go to the Next Step on success and Quit the Job Reporting Failure on failure. Now we are going to add two more steps. The third one will be just like the first except that it will count Owners instead of Pets. The second one, however, will purposefully raise an error so that we can see the flow control:

```
RAISERROR ('Forcing an error for testing purposes.',  16, 1)
```

If we make no modifications and run the job, it will run step 1, run step 2, and then end with a failure because step 2 raised a failure and it was defaulted to Quit with Failure for step 2. If we go back to the Advanced tab we can reset step 2 so it will continue on failure. Now all three steps will run. This job is on the CD in "\Chapter12\TestJob.SQL." Feel free to create it on your system and play with this error handling functionality. One interesting variation to try is to set step 2 so it has both quit on failure and quit on success. If you do that, you'll get a nice message from SQL Server questioning whether you really want to do this because you can't reach step 3.

Another useful feature is that you can have SQL Server retry a job step. You have the option of having it retry *x* number of times every *y* number of minutes. If you look carefully at the two retry settings, they both have an upper limit of 9,999. If that doesn't sound like a lot, let me put those limits into a bit of perspective for you. If you set a job to retry again in 9,999 minutes, then this one job step won't retry for a little more than an hour shy of a week. If, on the other hand, you set the job to retry 9,999 times at intervals of 9,999 minutes, the step could theoretically be running for *more than 27 years!*

How Do I Schedule the Job to Run?

Now that we have defined a job, we need to define how often we want it to run. Figure 12-11 shows that we have set up two scheduled times for this job to run. The first one is set to run once a week, the other runs every day. You can tell all of that from this window. You can also see a schedule's ID and whether it is enabled to run. The screens that are used for adding a job schedule are the same ones we covered in setting up a maintenance plan in Chapter 2, "How Do I Install SQL Server?" The RDBA Schedule Daily doesn't have an ID. That's because it isn't stored in the database until we press either Apply or OK.

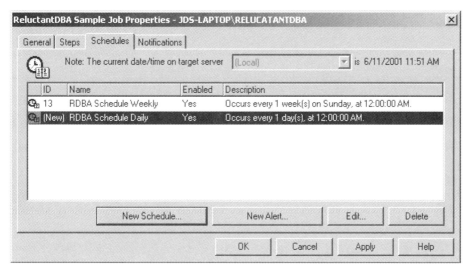

Figure 12-11. An existing job schedule

> **NOTE** *Not every job needs to be scheduled. Some tasks that have to run on a periodic basis are just plain handy to have already coded and ready to run. By creating a job to store them in, we could quickly run a series of TSQL statements to take care of that task all by running one job. With a job, we're assured of consistency, and it is always available whenever you need it, as long as you can get to the server. It's also handy to have a job ready to run in response to an error.*

There are two more things you can do with a job. One is to set up alerts for a job and the other is to set up notifications. We will cover both of those in the upcoming section, "What Is an Alert?"

How Do I Add/Delete/Modify a Category?

This is a straightforward task. Simply right-click on Jobs in the EM to get the drop-down menu and then select All Tasks, Manage Job Categories. This brings up the Job Categories window, as shown in Figure 12-12. It displays all of the job categories in tree format and, under each category, you can find the jobs assigned to that category. You can do three things from this window:

- Add a job category

- Delete a job category

- Show the properties of the job category

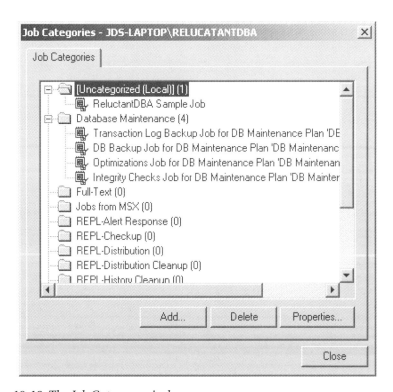

Figure 12-12. The Job Category window

We are going to add a job category, RDBA Test. There is little to configure for a job category. Just click on the Add button and the EM brings up a blank screen asking for a name. Type in "RDBA Test" and then check Show All Jobs. Now, with all of the jobs in the system listed, check the ones you want to add to this new category and you end up with the screen in Figure 12-13. This is the same screen you get when you select the Properties button. That's because the only property of a category are the jobs assigned to it.

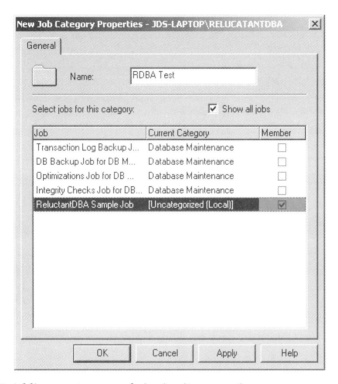

Figure 2-13. Adding a category and viewing its properties

What Happens to Jobs When I Delete a Category?

SQL Server allows you to delete a job category, even if it has jobs in it. SQL Server just moves those jobs to the Uncategorized (Local) category, after asking you if that's what you really want to do. You cannot, however, delete any of the "permanent" categories that are there when you install SQL Server. Uncategorized (Local) is one of those permanent categories.

How Can I Tell What My Job Has Done?

A job's history tells you all about when the job was run, what happened when it ran, and any number of other exciting things. To view a job's history, right-click on the job and select View Job History from the menu.

As you can see from Figure 12-14, this job has been run three times and failed twice. We can also tell which step caused the job to fail by looking in the box at the bottom of the window. There we see that this was the weekly job and that the last step to run was step 2, not surprising because that step raises an error on purpose. This screen also lists the date and time the job was run and how long it took the job to run. Also, it will tell you who was notified, if notification is turned on (see "What Is an Operator?" later in this chapter). But we can get more information with the click of the mouse. When we check Show Step Details, we can see the success and failure for each step, as well as the outcome of the job (see Figure 12-15).

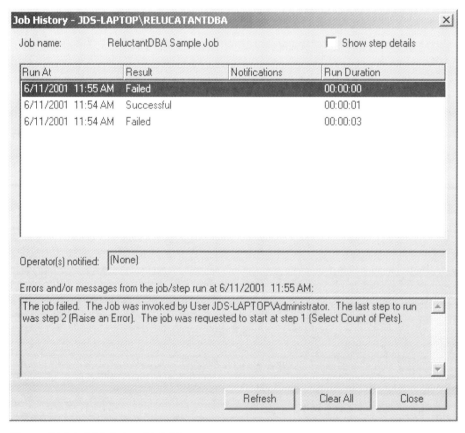

Figure 12-14. A high-level job history

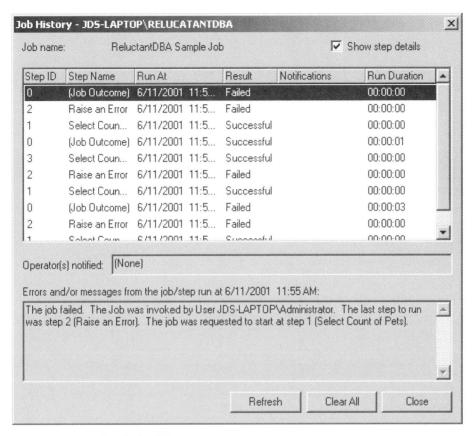

Figure 12-15. A detailed job history

When we look at the step detail for a job, we can see what errors were raised and how long each individual step took to run. It takes a little bit of working with this job history to get used to the format because SQL Server counts 1, 2, 3, and then 0, with 0 being the job outcome. That means the first three lines in Figure 12-15 (0,2,1) are one job and the next four lines (0,3,2,1) are another.

Just as with any other programming you may do, the key to setting up a successful job is to test it, step by step, outside of SQL Server Agent and then test it inside once you've set the job up. When you are sure that the job is running correctly, press the Clear All button to clear the job history for that job so you have a clean slate for your production job history.

How Do I Generate a Script to Create a Job on Another Server?

If you have a job that needs to run on multiple servers, you can easily have SQL Server script out the job for you. This capability is handy when you are building

a database to be deployed as part of a software application that requires scheduled tasks. Right-click on the job and select All Tasks ≻ Generate SQL Scripts.
This selection brings up a window slightly different than the one used in generating script for tables and such. You can either select a filename or you can select
Preview and copy and paste the code into the QA. This is how the SQL for the test
job was created.

What Is an Operator?

In this section, we're talking about human operators who can take action to
address problems, not operators such as AND, LIKE, and NOT found in TSQL. Operators and alerts combine to proactively care for your system, reducing the risk of
running out of disk space, for instance.

Right-click on Operator in the EM and select New Operator. This will bring
up a window to fill in. Figure 12-16 shows what a filled-in screen looks like. First,
put in an operator's name. This name is how you will see that operator throughout the system, so it's best to make the name appropriate. Then there are three
ways to send a message to an operator: email, pager, or a NET SEND message.

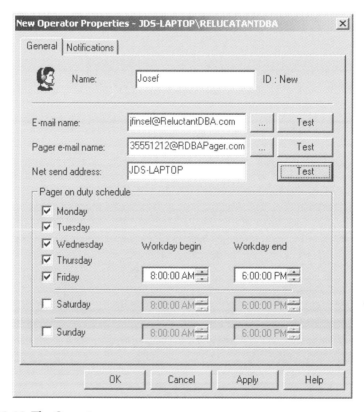

Figure 12-16. The Operator screen

Email is handled entirely through MAPI, which means you need to have an Exchange Server sitting somewhere on the network to make this work correctly. Clicking on the ellipses next to the email name will bring up your Exchange client and let you select from the address book. Pager email is handled the same way.[4]

NET SEND will send a message via the NT network, similar to typing "NET SEND *computername message*" at the command prompt. If you select this option a pop-up message will be sent to the recipient wherever they are logged in. The good thing about NET SEND is that it's almost instant, but the bad thing is that the message disappears with the click of a button.

As you can see, emails and NET SEND are sent all day long, but pager messages are time sensitive. SQL Server won't send a page if it believes the operator is not working. You can set it to recognize a Monday through Friday time and a time on weekends to contact you.

Once you have set up the operator, you can go to the Notifications tab for that operator and set the alerts that will contact the operator (see Figure 12-17). Each alert can contact an operator by email, page, NET SEND, or any combination of the three. Unfortunately, you can't set an escalation list so that it will send a NET SEND and wait. If the NET SEND isn't responded to, then it generates an email. Finally, if the email isn't responded to, it pages you directly. If all three are set then all three will happen at the same time. If you attempt to set up a notification to an operator for a method they don't have (sending a pager to someone that doesn't have paging set up, for instance), SQL Server gives you a friendly warning and ask if you really want to do that.

---

[4]   See the "Resources" section for more information on SQL Mail.

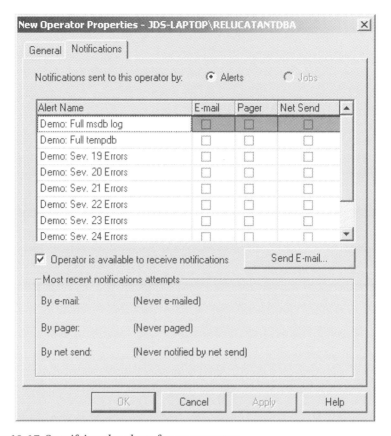

Figure 12-17. Specifying the alerts for an operator

What Is an Alert?

An alert, as all of you know, varies in intensity from a Red Alert for Klingons off the starboard bow to a Yellow Alert for either Q or Deanna Troi's mother showing up on the bridge (though both of them together rate a Red Alert). Oops, wrong book, but the idea is close. An alert defines an action to take when a specific event or error occurs. When SQL Server Agent is started, SQL Server takes any events and passes them to the SQL Server Agent to be processed. What kind of events?

There's a whole list of them in SQL Server Books On Line, but some of the more common ones are:

- Query timeouts

- Server running low on memory

- Server running low on disk space

- Server running low on processor capacity

- Tempdb is running out of space

- Transaction log running out of space

- The coffee machine running low on coffee beans

 NOTE   *OK, so that last event isn't really a SQL task, but SQL Server is flexible enough that you could rig up a sensor to the coffee grinder and link it back to the server and have an extended stored procedure check the sensor every 10 minutes and alert you when the supply is getting low. Isn't technology wonderful?*

Because we don't have a coffee sensor attached to SQL Server, we're going to set an alert to tell us when the transaction log is full on the **RDBA11** database. We start creating a new alert by right-clicking on the alerts in the EM and selecting New Alert. This brings up a dialog box like the one shown in Figure 12-18. We give the alert a name (Full Transaction Log in **RDBA11**) and then decide whether we want to set the alert by the severity level of the SQL Server event or by a specific error number. Because we want this alert to be used specifically when the transaction log is full, we enter error number 9002. If we don't know the error number, we can always search for it from here. Earlier we covered user-defined error messages. Using custom error messages you can proactively take action on events that would otherwise require a warm (and awake) body to take action on.

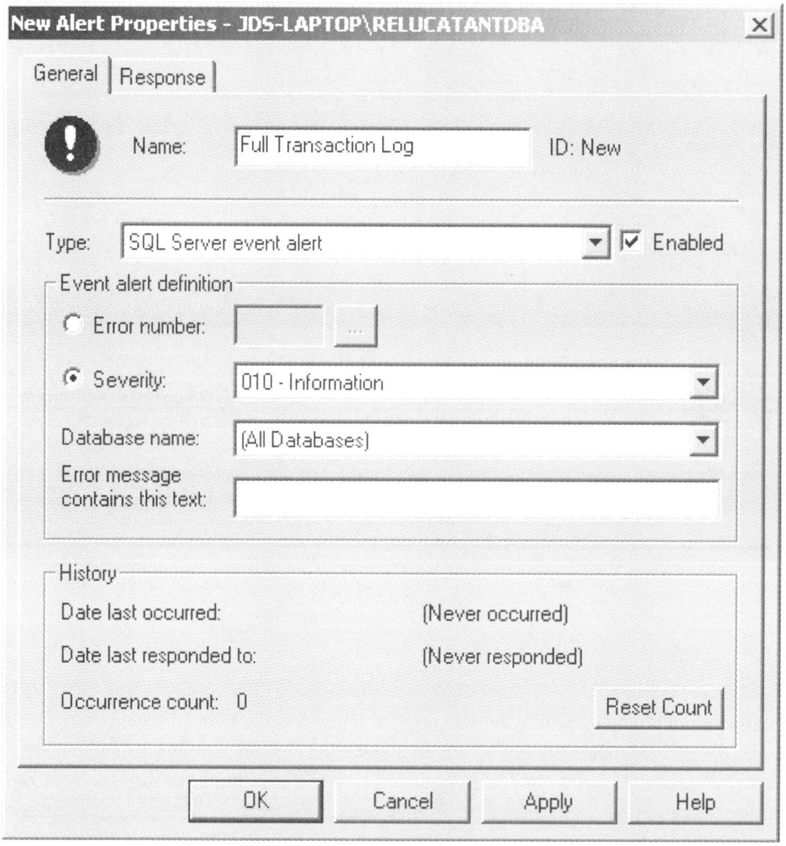

Figure 12-18. The Alert Properties window

Of course, it would be better if SQL Server could warn us *before* the transaction log filled up and brought the database to a crashing halt, wouldn't it? We'll talk about how to handle that in Chapters 15 and 16, "Should I Bother to Learn SQL Profiler?" and "What Are System Monitor and Performance Monitor?" respectively.

How Do I Set an Alert for a Specific Error?

If you're like most Reluctant DBAs, you probably aren't going to memorize all of SQL Server's errors by heart. And you don't have to. Just select Error Number and then press the Properties button (. . .) next to that. That will bring up the handy Search for SQL Server Error Messages screen, covered in Chapter 10, "Working with Data: Beyond the Basics." This is also where you can create you own error messages. See the section "How Do I Tell the Client Something Is Wrong?" in Chapter 10 for more information on creating your own errors.

How Do I Set an Alert to Respond to an Error?

Now that we have defined the error this alert needs to respond to, what responses can the alert take? Well, it can take a couple of different responses. It can notify an operator or operators or execute a job.

When we click on the Response tab of the Alert dialog box, we get a list of all of the operators that have been defined. We can have any operator receive an email, page, or NET SEND message by clicking in the appropriate box. We can also create a new operator by clicking the New Operator button. The New Operator button will take you directly to the screens covered in the previous section, "What Is an Operator?" You can also add additional text (up to 256 characters) to be displayed for this particular alert.

Alternately, you can tell SQL to run a job in response to an error. As previously mentioned, there are jobs you might create that you wouldn't want to schedule. This is another case where you might want such a job. For instance, you might want to set up a job that would notify you, expand the transaction log, and then back it up. This job could be run whenever the transaction log runs out of space. You wouldn't want that to run every day, but you would want it to run when the log is full. This capability makes for a handy safety net, buying you time to determine what caused the problem in the first place.

To execute a job in response to an error, check the Execute Job box. This fills in the drop-down box with all of the jobs defined on the server. Errors defined would include not only the ones that come standard with SQL Server, but any that have been defined as custom errors (see Chapter 10, "Working with Data: Beyond the Basics," for more information on creating your own errors). You can also modify the job by clicking on the . . . button. You cannot, however, add a new job from here, you can only select from an existing job.

Last Words

Now that you've been introduced to SQL Server Agent, you'll probably dream up all kinds of ways to make it useful for more than just running your maintenance plans. I've used it to handle automating all kinds of tasks, from loading data in and pushing data out to having reports auto-generated and mailed to various people. But some of that pushing of data out the door may be going away, something we'll explore in the next chapter as we look at XML and SQL Server 2000.

Resources

- Learn how to configure SQLMail:
  `http://support.microsoft.com/support/kb/articles/q263/5/56.ASP`

- Find more information on "Get Smart": `http://www.wouldyoubelieve.com`

CHAPTER 13

If SQL Server 2000 Is a .NET Server, Where's the XML?

This is like déjà vu all over again. —Yogi Berra

THERE IS ENOUGH MATERIAL about SQL Server and XML to write an entire book on the topic. Because this is only one chapter, we're not going to cover everything. Instead, we'll cover the basics of what XML is and how you can interact with it in SQL Server 2000. Use the "Resources" section at the end of this chapter to find more information about using XML and about using SQL Server and XML together. You'll also find out where you can download the latest Microsoft XML parser. (The samples in this chapter use the version 3.0 parser.)

 NOTE   *This chapter relies heavily on the **RDBA13** database. You'll find instructions for installing it in Appendix A, "How Do I Load the Examples?" In addition to setting up the database as outlined in the appendix, you'll need to use some supplemental files designed for this chapter. In the CD's "\Chapter13" directory you will find a "RDBAXML" directory, which contains the files and directory structure used later in this chapter. You need to copy this over to one of your local drives to follow along with the examples.*

What Is XML, and Can I Skip This Section?

If you know what XML is, please feel free to skip this section and move directly to "How Does SQL Server 2000 Use XML?" If you aren't familiar with XML, then let's begin. XML stands for eXtensible Markup Language. But what does that mean? Well, let's take a quick tour of markup languages and how they work before getting into the extensible ones.

HyperText Markup Language (HTML) is another markup language and, for the purposes of learning about markup languages in general, it is probably the one with which most people are familiar. Markup languages use text-based files with special processing instructions called *markup tags*. These tags are contained within less-than and greater-than brackets ($<$ $>$). A *parser* processes these tags. In the case of HTML, the processor is usually an Internet browser such as Internet Explorer (IE) or Netscape. The processor interprets each tag and displays it properly on the screen.[1]

Each tag has a specific meaning. For instance, `<I>` is the HTML tag for italics. Each HTML tag also has a closing tag so that the parser knows when to stop using that markup format. That tag is the same as the beginning tag except it includes a slash (`</I>`). Let's take a quick look at an HTML example:

```
This line of text needs <I>more</I> emphasis.
```

When viewed through a Web browser, this line would look like this:

This line of text needs *more* emphasis.

If this were all tags could do, there wouldn't be much excitement, but tags can also have attributes to help further define them. Take one of the most popular tags in HTML, the anchor tag, for instance. Even if you've never built an HTML page or looked at the source for one, you've probably used an anchor tag because this is the tag that provides the links in the World Wide Web. The anchor tag is a simple `<A>`. It's not much to look at, and it won't do much unless you add properties to it, but add one simple `HREF` property, and it becomes a quite powerful tag: `Visit <A HREF="http://www.apress.com">Apress</A> and see our new books!` With that one simple attribute defined, the anchor will take you to an entirely different page on the Web.

> *Reluctant DBA* definition of a markup language *attribute*:
> An attribute is another term for *property*. Although this chapter uses *attribute* when discussing XML, you may freely substitute the word *property* if it helps you remember its meaning.

The previous example also illustrates two often-overlooked points about HTML tags. First, opening and closing tag pairs (or an empty tag that doesn't require a closing tag) are grouped together as *elements*. Second, HTML tags

---

[1] I use the word *properly* loosely. Just as with every other technology, HTML has rapidly evolved to include new tags, and keeping up in the browser wars is still a daunting task. The good news is that browsers just ignore tags they don't understand. So, older, text-based browser ignore `<BLINK>` tags, for example, because that is a new feature they don't support. The flip side is that the cool new feature you just implemented in your pages will be ignored by anyone who doesn't have the latest and greatest version of whichever browser you're using.

include values as well as properties. In the example, the property HREF (defined as http://www.apress.com) has the value Apress. This value is often overlooked when using HTML, but it becomes important in XML.

> *Reluctant DBA* definition of an *element*:
> An element is defined as all of the attributes of a tag and anything between the opening and closing of that tag, including the opening and closing tags themselves.

> *Reluctant DBA* definition of an element's *value*:
> The value of a tag or element is the content found between the opening and closing tags.

HTML was based on another markup language, Standard General Markup Language (SGML). The International Organization for Standardization (ISO)[2] defined SGML in 1986 as a way to create documents not dependent on the application that created them or on the system for which they were built. Theoretically, an SGML document could be taken from an Apple to a Windows machine and appear the same. When you want to format text, either SGML or HTML will do a fine job, but for formatting data they both fall short.

The World Wide Web Consortium (W3C), the same folks who brought you the World Wide Web, recognized this fact. They brought together a group of vendors to help define XML. It's still a work in progress, but it's one that has already delivered a stable platform to be used in business today.

NOTE *What's the W3C, and where do I found out more about it? W3C is the short form for World Wide Web Consortium. It is the organization that attempts to maintain order on the Web. If you want to go to the W3C Web site, you can do so in several different ways. You can go to* http://www.w3c.org, *but that's the most obvious choice. If you touch type and want to work out your ring finger, go to* http://www.www.org. *Or, if you want the most direct route, try* http://www.w3.org, *the page the other two URLs redirect you to anyway.*

---

2   If you're wondering why the International Organization for Standardization is not the IOS, you're not alone. For years I thought it was because it was headquartered in France, but I was wrong. It's actually derived from the Greek *isos*, meaning equal, a term you may remember from learning about isometric triangles in Geometry class. This is also a way to prevent each country referring to the organization by whatever the translated name would be in their language, for example, IOS in English or OIN in French.

Although XML stands for eXtensible Markup Language, it really isn't a language *per se.* It is probably easier to think of XML as the alphabet of a language, one in which you can put the parts together to form your own dialect (data definition). For instance, you can create your own Math Markup Language so that `<minus>` would indicate subtraction. This ability to function as a building block is important because a standard for data representation will expand the Internet in much the same way that the HTML standard did for displaying information. By providing a simple, flexible means of transferring data, it opens a new level of programmability through the Web. At least, that's what Microsoft's .NET espouses. But it does have potential.

 NOTE *Electronic Data Interchange (EDI) was, until recently, the* de facto *method for moving data between disparate organizations. All of the data was turned into* messages *and sent from one company to another. Is EDI dead? I doubt it. I'm not even sure that XML will really deal it a mortal blow, but that's because there is a large embedded base of hardware and customer-written software that is EDI specific. Now that XML exists, a number of folks are working to bridge the gap between XML and EDI. Microsoft's BizTalk server supports both EDI and XML, so Microsoft believes EDI will be around for a while, and they aren't the only ones. ebXML (`http://www.ebXML.org`) is another source of information concerning XML and EDI.*

Do I Need to Know XML?

This is really the $64,000 question. Microsoft's .NET technology uses XML extensively—it's based on MSXML 4.0, but you don't need to know XML in depth to build or use .NET technology.

You need to understand what XML is and be familiar with the basic terminology so you can understand what someone is talking about when you are presented with XML. You need to be knowledgeable enough to read an XML document, to know how to have one created for you, and to know what options you have. That's what every good programmer probably should need to know about XML, and that's what we're going to cover in this section. The last part of this chapter ("How Does SQL Server 2000 Use XML?") deals with how SQL Server actually uses XML and what you can do with it.

How Do I Define an XML Document?

An XML document is a text file, either ANSI or Unicode that follows certain rules. The first rule it follows is that the first line must be an XML declaration. If you have built any Web pages you know that you *should* start Web pages with an `<HTML>` tag but, if you don't, it's not the end of the world. That `<HTML>` tag declares your text file to be an HTML file, but the browser assumes that what it is opening is HTML. This is not the case with XML.

XML documents must start with `<?xml version="1.0"?>`. This signifies to the parser that it has an XML document to work with or to open. Once the parser knows it is working with an XML document, then it will start to expect things to be formatted in a certain way. For one thing, it expects the document to be *well formed*.

What Is a Well-Formed XML Document?

A well-formed XML document is one that obeys *all* of the rules—not just some of them as with HTML. In fact, an XML parser will not parse and display a document that is not well formed. So, what does it mean to be well formed? Well, it means that the XML file must follow these rules:

- There must be one unique root element.

- Elements in the root occur sequentially, nested, or a combination thereof.

- Elements must not overlap.

- Attributes of an element must be in quotes.

- All elements must have a starting tag and an ending tag.

- Case matters (all element and attribute names are case sensitive).

- Elements that contain data start with an element name tag such as `<Element_Name>` and end with an element name tag such as `</Element_Name>`.

- Empty elements start and end with empty element name tags such as `<Element_Name/>`. Although that is the preferred way to display empty elements, you can also use `<Element_Name></Element_Name>`.

The easiest way to explain a well-formed document is to look at one. As each rule is explained, we'll show how a row from the Owners table must be formatted to be considered well formed. Figure 13-1 shows the results of following the rules, but you could open the file Example13-01.XML from the "\Chapter13" directory on your CD as well.

 NOTE *If your XML document violates any of these rules and is not well formed, it will not display in your parser. Instead, you will get an error message telling you which of these rules you have violated.*

```
<?xml version="1.0" ?>
- <rdba11.dbo.Owners>
    <OwnerID>1</OwnerID>
    <OwnerLastName>Apsel</OwnerLastName>
    <OwnerFirstName>Robert</OwnerFirstName>
    <OwnerAddress1>7430 Fish Ranch Road</OwnerAddress1>
    <OwnerAddress2>Apt. 2</OwnerAddress2>
    <OwnerCity>Orinda</OwnerCity>
    <OwnerState>CA</OwnerState>
    <OwnerPostalCode>94563</OwnerPostalCode>
    <OwnerPhoneNumber>9255551212</OwnerPhoneNumber>
  </rdba11.dbo.Owners>
```

Figure 13-1. A well-formed XML document displaying a row of data from the Owners table

There Must Be One Unique Root Element

XML works on a hierarchical system, much the way SQL Server does. Although SQL Server does a better job of defining its hierarchy (for instance, columns belong to rows, rows belong to tables, and tables belong to databases), XML has greater flexibility in letting you define your own hierarchy. Although one element can have multiple elements underneath it, there can be only one root element because XML is a hierarchy.

> *Reluctant DBA* definition of XML *root element*:
> The element that contains all other data in the XML file. There can be only one root element.

This can be a minor problem if you aren't watching out for it because SQL Server assumes you will follow this rule. Does that mean SQL Server will *automagically* create XML for you? The "Splicing Data" section tells you how to do it, but don't skip there quite yet or you'll become frustrated when it doesn't work the way you think it should. Listing 13-1 shows how SQL Server will create XML *automagically*, even though it's not well formed.

Listing 13-1. SQL Server *automagically* created this XML, but it isn't well formed because there is neither a single root element nor the <?xml version="1.0"?> declaration.

```
<Owners>
<OwnerId>1</OwnerId>
<OwnerLastName>Apsel</OwnerLastName>
</Owners>
<Owners>
<OwnerId>2</OwnerId>
<OwnerLastName>Sclarenco</OwnerLastName>
</Owners>
```

This is the result of *automagically* generated XML by SQL Server; however, it's been reformatted from a single string with no breaks into something easier to read. Although there are several reasons why a parser would not display this, the one we'll focus on is the duplicate root elements. The Owners elements have been emphasized in the code because they are at the top of the hierarchy and would logically be interpreted as the root elements, which they cannot be. The only way to get around this is to put a new element before and after the generated XML to encompass all of the elements into one root element, but we'll cover how to do that in "What Is a Valid XML Document?"

Elements in the Root Occur Sequentially, Nested, or a Combination Thereof

This rule is a mouthful, but it can be boiled down easily enough. Look at the data in Figure 13-1. The root element is Owners. Then, between the opening and closing tag for the root elements are nine more elements. Between the opening and closing tags of each element are the values of those elements. Thus, you can see that the element OwnerLastName has the value Apsel. But an element is not restricted to having data for its value; it can also have other elements. Why would you want to do that? Well, you can do this to handle joined tables.

Take a joined table where you might have several rows in one table for each one in another, such as an owner having several pets. Instead of having to repeat the one row each time, it is possible to nest the Right table into the elements of the Left (for more information on Right and Left tables in joins, see Chapter 6, "What Is a View?"). A join like the one that follows could easily be represented by the XML in Figure 13-2, which would be generated by the code in Listing 13-2.

```
<?xml version="1.0" encoding="utf-8" ?>
- <root>
  - <Owners>
      <OwnerID>1</OwnerID>
      <OwnerLastName>Apsel</OwnerLastName>
      <OwnerFirstName>Robert</OwnerFirstName>
    - <Pets>
        <PetName>Thunderbolt</PetName>
      </Pets>
    - <Pets>
        <PetName>Greased Lightning</PetName>
      </Pets>
    - <Pets>
        <PetName>Avoiding the Glue Factory</PetName>
      </Pets>
  </Owners>
</root>
```

Figure 13-2. Subelements in XML are indented when viewed in IE.
(Example13-02.xml)

Listing 13-2. Joining two tables
```
SELECT Owners.OwnerID, Owners.OwnerLastName,
Owners.OwnerFirstName, Pets.PetName FROM Owners
JOIN Pets ON Owners.OwnerID = Pets.OwnerID WHERE Owners.OwnerID = 1
```

If you look closely, you can see there are three levels of elements: root,
Owners, and Pets. The easiest way to tell how the elements are nested is to load it
into a parser such as IE 4.0 or higher. IE does two things to make it easy to see the
nesting of elements: It indents the subelements, and it marks them with a minus
sign next to the top of the nested element. You can click on the minus sign to hide
lower levels of data, as shown in Figure 13-3. The data for two of the pets is hidden while the subelement for the middle pet is expanded.

```
<?xml version="1.0" encoding="utf-8" ?>
  - <root>
    - <Owners>
        <OwnerID>1</OwnerID>
        <OwnerLastName>Apsel</OwnerLastName>
        <OwnerFirstName>Robert</OwnerFirstName>
      + <Pets>
      - <Pets>
          <PetName>Greased Lightning</PetName>
        </Pets>
      + <Pets>
      </Owners>
    </root>
```

Figure 13-3. Hiding subelements in XML is easy with IE.

The element `Owners` consists of four child elements: `OwnerID`, `OwnerLastName`, `OwnerFirstName`, and `Pets`. It just happens that `Pets` is repeated three times and is made up of a child element itself: in this case, the child element `PetName`, though it could also have multiple child elements. Child elements themselves can also be parent elements to other child elements.

Elements Must Not Overlap

Some of these rules, like this one, are more applicable to HTML pages that need to have XML added to them, but because we will be talking about generating Web pages with XML and SQL Server, it doesn't hurt to cover them here. The HTML parser is a forgiving piece of software, and it overlooks a lot of sloppy coding. If you needed a word to be bold and italicized, you could use the following code:

`<B><I>Hello World!</B>` and the browser would go on.

That would indeed print ***Hello World!*** *and the browser would go on.* (Oops, sorry, I forgot my close italics tag, `</I>`). The XML parser is much stricter, and for good reason. The XML parser is dealing with the values and structure of data, not how it appears on the screen. Because data has a specific format and any data that doesn't fit into that format is potentially garbage, the XML parser forces you to follow some strict rules. You *must* close what you open in the reverse order it was opened. The HTML parser had a random order stack, but the XML has a LIFO stack: Last In, First Out. If you open an element (`<B>`, for instance) and then open another element (`<I>`), you need to close the `<I>` before the `<B>`. This is required because the XML parser is treating HTML elements by passing them through the XML parser first.

Attributes of an Element Must Be in Quotes

This strict rule is *enclose attributes in quotes*. HTML would let you put `<FONT size=1>` and doesn't care whether the value of the size attribute is in quotes. XML requires that you put the quotes around the 1 so that it knows that 1 is the value of that attribute. So make sure you use `<FONT size="1">`.

All Elements Must Have a Starting Tag and an Ending Tag

This rule causes more grief when trying to convert standard HTML to XML than any of the others. HTML has a number of opening or empty tags that don't require using closing tags. Take `<IMG>`, for instance. How many pages have you seen that read: `<IMG Name="someimg.jpg">` without an ending tag? In fact, no one used the closing `</IMG>` tags prior to XML. It just wasn't done, though there was no reason not to use them. What this means is that if you are planning on converting a static page to be dynamically driven with XML from SQL Server, it will probably take you several passes before you have issues like this one cleaned up. There is, however, a simple fix for this; see "Empty Elements Start and End with <Element_Name/>" for more information.

Case Matters (Element and Attribute Names Are Case Sensitive)

This is my own personal bugaboo; you can't mix case. As far as the XML parser is concerned, `<B>` and `<b>` are two different elements. So, `<B>Hi</b>` will cause an error. If you look at a lot of Web pages, you'll frequently find mixed cases, probably because you have to use the Shift key to get a < symbol but not to get a / symbol.

Elements That Contain a Value Start with <Element_Name> and End with </Element_Name>

As mentioned, the value of an element is whatever is placed between the tags. In `<B><I>Hello World!</I></B>`, you can break it down as seen in Table 13-1.

Table 13-1. Breaking Down the Data in `<B><I>Hello World!</I></B>`

ELEMENT TAG	VALUE
`<B>`	`<I>Hello World!</I>`
`<I>`	`Hello World!`

Empty Elements Start and End with `<Element_Name/>`

Empty elements are elements that do not have a value associated with them; that is, they have no data between the opening tag and the ending tag. These empty tags don't have to have a `</TAG>` at the end; instead, they can end with a slash (/). Look at the `<IMG>` tag, as shown in Listing 13-3.

Listing 13-3. Example of using an empty element

```
<IMG Name="someimg.jpg"></IMG>
<IMG Name="someimg.jpg"/>
```

Closing the `<IMG>` tag by using `/>` accomplishes two things:

- It cuts down on the size of the file being parsed. File size is important because XML is essentially an interpreter, which means it needs to read the whole file to get it to work.

- It means that translating old HTML (HTML that doesn't follow the strict rules of XML) into a format that does is slightly easier because you can just add one character to the existing tags to create empty elements.

OK, we've defined a well-formed XML document as one that follows all of these rules, but we can also validate an XML document to make it even more consistent.

What Is a Valid XML Document?

A valid XML document is well-formed XML "plus." The plus is that the XML conforms to the definition contained in a schema or Document Type Definition (DTD). Both the DTD and the schema let you define the structure of your data, but the schema uses XML to define the XML document, making it somewhat easier to use.

Are DTDs Going Away?

The short answer to this question is "no." DTDs are a part of the SGML definition, so they will stay around. Whether they are applicable for XML documents—now that's a whole different story. Let me quote from the W3's XML Schema Working Group's Activity Statement:

> *While XML 1.0 supplies a mechanism, the Document Type Definition (DTD) for declaring constraints on the use of markup, automated processing of XML documents requires more rigorous and comprehensive facilities in this area. Requirements are for constraints on how the component parts of an application fit together, the document structure, attributes, data typing, and so on. The XML Schema Working Group is addressing means for defining the structure, content and semantics of XML documents.*

DTDs will be sticking around, and it is quite possible you will encounter them, so you should have an idea of how they work. However, schemas will be of more value to XML for the reasons outlined previously.

In many ways, it is easiest to think of the validation of an XML document like a contract. The contract lays out everything the XML must have as well as whatever options it is allowed to have. Using our example of pet owners and pets, a pet owner may have one or more pets, making the number of pets optional. If the XML breaks the contract in any way, it is not valid and the parser will not display the XML.

Document Type Definition Documents

The biggest difference between DTDs and schemas is that schemas define the structure using XML, and DTDs define elements and attributes using `<!ELEMENT>` and `<!ATTRIBUTE>`. Perhaps the best way to introduce DTDs is by looking at one. Figure 13-4 shows the DTD that could be used with the XML join of Owners and Pets.

```
<?xml version="1.0" ?>
<!ELEMENT       root (Owners+)>
<!ELEMENT       Owners (OwnerID, OwnerLastName, OwnerFirstName, Pets+)>
<!ELEMENT       OwnerID (#PCDATA)>
        <!ATTLIST OwnerID
                NAME CDATA #FIXED "OwnerID"
                TYPE_NAME CDATA #FIXED "int identity"
                COL_SIZE CDATA #FIXED "11"
                SCALE CDATA #FIXED "0"
                AUTO_INCREMENT (true|false) #FIXED "true"
                NULLABLE (true|false) #FIXED "false"
        >
<!ELEMENT       LastName (#PCDATA)>
        <!ATTLIST OwnerLastName
                NAME CDATA #FIXED "OwnerLastName"
                TYPE_NAME CDATA #FIXED "varchar"
                COL_SIZE CDATA #FIXED "30"
                NULLABLE (true|false) #FIXED "false"
        >
<!ELEMENT       OwnerFirstName (#PCDATA)>
        <!ATTLIST OwnerFirstName
                NAME CDATA #FIXED "OwnerFirstName"
                TYPE_NAME CDATA #FIXED "varchar"
                COL_SIZE CDATA #FIXED "25"
                NULLABLE (true|false) #FIXED "false"
        >
<!ELEMENT       Pets (PetName+)>
<!ELEMENT       PetName (#PCDATA)>
        <!ATTLIST PetName
                NAME CDATA #FIXED "PetName"
                TYPE_NAME CDATA #FIXED "varchar"
                COL_SIZE CDATA #FIXED "25"
                NULLABLE (true|false) #FIXED "false"
        >
```

Figure 13-4. Example of DTD for joining Owners and Pets (Example13-03.dtd)

The DTD language was designed specifically to mark up SGML. Because XML is a subset of SGML, you can use a DTD to validate an XML document as well, but, as you can see, the DTD syntax is somewhat different from XML and HTML, filled with !s and #s. The nice thing about using a DTD is that it can work with SGML, which can be useful sometimes. For instance, a publisher could turn a reference manual into a database by taking the SGML and turning it into XML without having to change the DTDs. Let's take a closer look.

The <!ELEMENT> tag defines the elements that make up the XML document. As you can see, an element can contain either data or other elements. The <root> element, for instance, contains Owners elements. What's the plus sign for after Owners? Glad you noticed that. A plus means there can be multiple elements. You'll notice the same plus after Pets. That's because we can have zero, one, or many Pets elements within each Owners element, all indicated by the plus at the end of the element name. The other thing to notice is that each element has attributes that help define it. OwnerID is defined as an integer that auto increments.

Although it is different from XML, the DTD is still easy enough to read, though creating it is really something you might want to use a tool to do because tools are more likely to get it right. The "Resources" section at the end of this chapter has more information on XML tools you can use.

Applying the DTD to an XML file is fairly simple. All you need to do is add one line of code, as shown in Listing 13-4.

Listing 13-4. One line of code is all that is required to add a DTD to an XML file.

```
<!DOCTYPE Data SYSTEM "Example13-03.DTD">
```

This one line tells the parser to load the DTD and use it when parsing the XML file. That makes a valid and well-formed document of your data, but it does more than that. Although we haven't modified the data contained in the elements from Figure 13-3, you can see that a lot more data appears in Figure 13-5. Each of the elements now contains the attributes listed in the DTD. As you can see, DTDs are readable, but they are not as intuitive as they would be if you could write the validation in XML format. To solve that, schemas were created.

```
<?xml version="1.0" encoding="utf-8" ?>
<!DOCTYPE Data (View Source for full doctype...)>
- <root>
  - <Owners>
      <OwnerID NAME="OwnerID" TYPE_NAME="int identity" COL_SIZE="11" SCALE="0"
        AUTO_INCREMENT="true" NULLABLE="false">1</OwnerID>
      <OwnerLastName>Apsel</OwnerLastName>
      <OwnerFirstName NAME="OwnerFirstName" TYPE_NAME="varchar" COL_SIZE="25"
        NULLABLE="false">Robert</OwnerFirstName>
    - <Pets>
        <PetName NAME="PetName" TYPE_NAME="varchar" COL_SIZE="25"
          NULLABLE="false">Thunderbolt</PetName>
      </Pets>
    - <Pets>
        <PetName NAME="PetName" TYPE_NAME="varchar" COL_SIZE="25"
          NULLABLE="false">Greased Lightning</PetName>
      </Pets>
    - <Pets>
        <PetName NAME="PetName" TYPE_NAME="varchar" COL_SIZE="25"
          NULLABLE="false">Avoiding the Glue Factory</PetName>
      </Pets>
  </Owners>
</root>
```

Figure 13-5. Applying a DTD to XML better defines the elements. (Example13-03.xml)

Internal or External Definitions?

DTDs and schemas can be either internal or external. Which is better? Well, that depends on what you are doing with them. If you need a flexible and valid XML document, then you might want to consider building the DTD or schema into the body of the XML document.

If, on the other hand, you are going to have a large number of XML documents referencing the same definitions, it makes sense to put the definition in an external file so you don't have to keep rebuilding it. Most parsers will also cache these files, eliminating network overhead. Not only that, but you can also reuse DTDs, including an existing DTD into the current DTD.

Finally, you can publish your DTDs on a Web server and make them available to anyone who wants to use them. A good example of this would be an industry standard like the HR-XML (`http://www.hr-xml.org`).

Schemas

Using a schema offers many advantages over using a DTD. For starters, a schema must be a well-formed XML document, so the parser doesn't need to be able to interpret both XML and DTD documents. Come to think of it, neither do the developers. The main difference between a schema and a typical XML document is that the schema tags are all predefined (see Table 13-2) while XML tags can be whatever you create. Another advantage is that SQL Server will create the schema for you. The down side to using schemas, however, is that the XML parser has to be able to interpret them. The XML parser that comes with IE 5 can, but there are no guarantees for other parsers.[3]

> *Reluctant DBA* definition of an XML *schema*:
> A document type definition written in XML (by SQL Server). It can be found either in the same document as the data or in a separate document referenced by the data document.

---

[3] Schemas have far more potential than what we are covering in this book. I highly recommend you take a look at the XML SDK that Microsoft provides (see the "Resources" section at the end of this chapter). I am only covering the parts of schemas that are incorporated into SQL Server 2000.

Table 13-2. Schema Tags Are Predefined

TAG	DEFINITION
Schema	The top-most elements it can contain are `AttributeType`, `ElementType`, and `description` tags.
description	The `description` element is available for all other elements and has nothing to do with the parser's evaluation of the data. It exists to give a description to whatever tag it is in. Limited to one per tag but can have many description elements within a schema (in other words, one for the schema itself, one for each element, and so on).
AttributeType	Defines a type of attribute. Within SQL-generated schemas, this generally represents and defines a column. Can belong to either a `Schema` or an `ElementType`.
ElementType	Defines a type of `Element`. `ElementTypes` can contain `element`, `Attribute`, `AttributeType`, `description`, and `group` tags. In SQL Server this represents a table.
element	No, that's not a misprint. The `element` tag is for a specific `ElementType` and defines how many copies of the `element` may exist in the parent of the `element` tag. The `ElementType` and `AttributeType` tags function to define the `element`/`Attribute` and the actual `element` and `Attribute` tags serve to instantiate them.
Attribute	Like the `element` tag, this further defines the `AttributeType`.
group	This tag defines elements into specific sequences.

Let's take a look at a schema for `Owners` listed in Listing 13-1. Although it was created by SQL Server, it has been formatted with indentations so it is easier to read (see Listing 13-5). The first thing to note is that this schema has a name and a definition. The `xmlns` attributes in the `Schema` tag define a namespace for Microsoft's data types.

Listing 13-5. An XML schema for Owners

```
<Schema name="Schema3" xmlns="urn:schemas-microsoft-com:xml-data"
   xmlns:dt="urn:schemas-microsoft-com:datatypes">
<ElementType name="Owners" content="empty" model="closed">
<AttributeType name="OwnerID" dt:type="i4"/>
<AttributeType name="OwnerLastName" dt:type="string"/>
<AttributeType name="OwnerFirstName" dt:type="string"/>
<AttributeType name="OwnerAddress1" dt:type="string"/>
<AttributeType name="OwnerAddress2" dt:type="string"/>
<AttributeType name="OwnerCity" dt:type="string"/>
```

```
<AttributeType name="OwnerState" dt:type="string"/>
<AttributeType name="OwnerPostalCode" dt:type="string"/>
<AttributeType name="OwnerPostal4" dt:type="string"/>
<AttributeType name="OwnerPhoneNumber" dt:type="number"/>
<AttributeType name="OwnerEmailAddress" dt:type="string"/>
<attribute type="OwnerID"/>
<attribute type="OwnerLastName"/>
<attribute type="OwnerFirstName"/>
<attribute type="OwnerAddress1"/>
<attribute type="OwnerAddress2"/>
<attribute type="OwnerCity"/>
<attribute type="OwnerState"/>
<attribute type="OwnerPostalCode"/>
<attribute type="OwnerPostal4"/>
<attribute type="OwnerPhoneNumber"/>
<attribute type="OwnerEmailAddress"/>
</ElementType>
</Schema>
```

Namespaces: A Way to Uniquely Identify Duplicate Definition Names

Namespaces help set a definition within a context by providing a unique place to look for the definition. For instance, if the word *muffler* appeared in an automobile book, it would have to do with the exhaust system used on cars. If the same word appeared in a book by Charles Dickens, it would mean a scarf. Each book uses the same word differently. When the word is out of context, it is hard to say what it really means.

In XML, namespaces help clear up that confusion. You could have an XML document that has an `auto` namespace and a `dickens` namespace. Then the word *muffler* would be used in context as either `auto:muffler` or `dickens:muffler`.

Of course, XML isn't the only technology that uses namespaces. Visual Studio .NET also embodies namespaces to separate similarly named objects. You might have two grid objects from different companies, both named `Grid`. Namespaces allow for correctly referencing the objects by using references and dots to refer to the correct grid: `CompanyA.Grid.Row.Value = CompanyB.Grid.Row.Value`.

After the schema comes the `ElementType` definition. In this case the `Element-Type` being defined is the table `Owners`, so the `ElementType` is named `Owners`.[4] The next attribute of the `ElementType` is the content, listed as `empty`. Every element can be empty, contain a value only, contain only the specified elements, or contain a mixture of elements and free text. Because this `ElementType` is storing only attributes and won't have any child elements, it is defined as empty. When joining tables together, this will show up as element only. The last part of the `ElementType` tag is the model type. SQL Server defines the model as being `closed`. This means that additional elements or attributes can't be added to the `ElementType`; it can only contain what has been defined.

Now that the `ElementType` has been defined, it is time to define the attributes that make it up.[5] We do this through the use of a combination of `AttributeType` and `Attribute` elements. The `AttributeType` defines the `Attributes` of the element. SQL Server defines the name of the attribute based on the name used in the `SELECT` statement (defaulting to the column name if an alias isn't used). In addition, the data type of the element is defined based on the data type namespace defined in the schema element. For each `AttributeType` element, there is a corresponding `Attribute` element. Although the `AttributeType` defines default values, data types, a name, and whether the `Attribute` is required, the `Attribute` tag instantiates and orders them.

This has been a whirlwind tour of XML. It's highly recommended that you review the XML Software Development Kit (SDK) or any of the other resources listed in "Resources" section. In the meantime, let's see how SQL Server 2000 uses XML.

How Does SQL Server 2000 Use XML?

SQL Server 2000 uses XML in two ways: for *splicing* data and for *shredding* data. We're going to look at splicing data first because it is easier to understand. Then we'll walk through shredding data. XML isn't the only functionality that lets Microsoft proclaim SQL Server 2000 to be a .NET server. The other part of the .NET puzzle is Web access, so we will finish the chapter by looking at how SQL Server 2000 integrates with the Web to provide you another way to access your data.

---

[4]   Something to keep in mind is that SQL Server generates the `ElementType` name based on the SQL statement, and XML is case sensitive where SQL is not. This means that, even if the table is really named `Owners`, you can create an `ElementType` named `OWNers` just by referencing the table with a different capitalization in your TSQL command. This means it is important to be consistent in how you capitalize in your SQL statements.

[5]   The default for SQL Server's XML is to return the fields of data as attributes of an element. It is also possible to have them returned as elements, in which case there would be element tags for the `ElementType` tags instead of `AttributeType` and attribute tags.

Splicing Data

One of the many things I enjoyed learning about in Boy Scouts was all you can do with ropes—not the cotton ropes you get at the local mega-store but the old-fashioned manila ropes made from multiple, smaller strands. When I first began working with ropes, I learned to tie all kinds of knots. And each of those knots had a different purpose. The problem with a knot is that it won't go through pulleys easily. If you want to join two ropes together so they work like one, you separate the ends of the rope and weave them together in a splice. And that is exactly what SQL Server 2000 does when it splices data together into XML.

> *Reluctant DBA* definition of *data splicing*:
> Taking data from one or more tables and rendering it into XML format.

First, let's look at how easy it is to have SQL Server generate XML. All you need to do is use FOR XML at the end of the SELECT statement. Well, OK, there are some options used with FOR XML, but let's take a look at what adding FOR XML AUTO to a SQL statement does. FOR XML tells SQL Server to render XML, and AUTO tells it to use the basic format, transforming each row into an element and each column into an attribute, as shown in Listing 13-6.

Listing 13-6. Creating XML from one table

```
SELECT VeterinarianLastName, VeterinarianFirstName  FROM Veterinarians
FOR XML AUTO

<Veterinarians VeterinarianLastName="Bairn" VeterinarianFirstName="Dennis"/>
<Veterinarians VeterinarianLastName="Forrest" VeterinarianFirstName="Gerald"/>
<Veterinarians VeterinarianLastName="Grannis" VeterinarianFirstName="Linda"/>
<Veterinarians VeterinarianLastName="Stovall" VeterinarianFirstName="Jerome"/>
<Veterinarians VeterinarianLastName="Charles" VeterinarianFirstName="Pippin"/>
```

Now, that XML code is *not* valid. For one thing, it has no root element or header. To understand why that is, you need to take a look at the bigger picture of how SQL Server 2000 fits into Microsoft's .NET architecture.

Not Designed to Stand Alone

XML, although it is much easier to read than binary, isn't really designed for human beings. It's designed to be the lowest common denominator between many different platforms. It just so happens that the format that meets that criterion is also fairly easy for us to understand as well. SQL Server's XML support is designed to operate within that framework.

Before XML was all the rage it is today, I wrote a simple program to create XML from a database table, shown in Listing 13-7. It was mostly an exercise to teach me how to do it, but it's worth revisiting here. It was a simple task. All I did was walk the recordset and print brackets around the field name, then print the value of the field, and then put a closing tag for the field. Oh, and I needed a tag for the row. And did I forget the root element? Actually, once I had finished, it was a useful tool that I could have used to create XML from any single table. But what if I had two tables?

Listing 13-7. A join creates redundant data within a normal rowset.

```
SELECT Owners.OwnerID as OwnerID, OwnerLastName, PetID, PetName FROM Owners
 INNER JOIN Pets ON Owners.OwnerID = Pets.OwnerID WHERE Owners.OwnerID < 4
```

OwnerID	OwnerLastName	PetID	PetName
1	Apsel	2	Thunderbolt
1	Apsel	3	Greased Lightning
1	Apsel	4	Avoiding the Glue Factory
2	Sclarenco	7	QT
3	Brock	8	Cuddles
3	Brock	9	Killer

Look at the simple query of `Owners` and `Pets` in Listing 13-7 and the rowset it returns. That rowset has a lot of duplicate data, however. Although there are only three distinct owners, there are six rows of owner data. Although we could easily pass this recordset to the program just outlined, it wouldn't create a hierarchical representation of the data. To create a hierarchical representation it would need to parse the SQL code, figure out which columns came from which table, and then come up with something like Listing 13-8.

Listing 13-8. This heirarchical view of the data doesn't contain redundant data.

```
<Owners>
<OwnerID>1</OwnerID><OwnerLastName>Apsel</OwnerLastName>
<Pets><PetID>2</PetID><PetName>Thunderbolt</PetName></Pets>
<Pets><PetID>3</PetID><PetName>Greased Lightning</PetName></Pets>
<Pets><PetID>4</PetID><PetName>Avoiding the Glue Factory</PetName></Pets>
</Owners>
<Owners>
<OwnerID>2</OwnerID><OwnerLastName>Sclarenco</OwnerLastName>
<Pets><PetID>7</PetID><PetName>QT</PetName></Pets>
</Owners>
<Owners>
<OwnerID>3</OwnerID><OwnerLastName>Brock</OwnerLastName>
<Pets><PetID>8</PetID><PetName>Cuddles</PetName></Pets>
<Pets><PetID>9</PetID><PetName>Killer</PetName></Pets>
</Owners>
```

In this XML, the owner information is only repeated once for each set of pets. This not only shows the relational aspect of the data more clearly, it is more efficient in terms of the size of the data. And the best part is that we don't need to create our own component or perform any string manipulation. SQL Server does it for us, as long as it knows about the other tables.

 CAUTION *If the join is hidden in a view instead of specified in the SQL statement, it will not parse the data as effectively. That's because a view functions like a virtual table and the XML processor will treat it like one table. That means that the owner data would be included for every row even if it were duplicate data.*

OK, so SQL Server will format the data to XML for me, but it's still not valid XML, so what good is it? Well, to answer that question we need to go slightly off-topic and delve into programming.

If you have installed SQL Server 2000 to your development machine, you've also installed another fun tool, ActiveX Data Objects (ADO) 2.6.[6] Now, in ADO 2.5, you could easily create XML. It was as simple as taking an `ADODB.Stream`, saving an existing recordset to it, and selecting the `ReadText` method of the stream. In 2.6, however, you can skip a whole section of that process and open the recordset directly in the stream. What happens is that the `SELECT . . . FOR XML AUTO` statement is actually passed as part of the `ADODB` command stream. The command stream needs to contain the root elements that SQL Server doesn't supply. Although Microsoft's Knowledge Base examples all use `SELECT` statements, there is no reason you couldn't have a stored procedure returning XML in the correct format. Listing 13-9 demonstrates how to build a string that can be executed within the `ADOStream`.

Listing 13-9. Building a string to run within an `ADOStream`
```
sQuery = '<ROOT xmlns:sql="urn:schemas-microsoft-com:xml-sql">'
sQuery = sQuery & '<sql:query>EXEC ListOfficesXML</sql:query>'
sQuery = sQuery & '</ROOT>'
```

But Microsoft didn't stop with ADO 2.6. If you have installed Microsoft's Visual Studio .NET, then your machine is up to ADO 2.7 (or .NET or ADO Plus). In .NET, populating and processing an XML stream is even easier. Listing 13-10 shows how to connect to the server, populate an XML stream with data, and then

---

[6]   Some of what I am going to say will work with earlier versions of ADO, but you're best bet is to stick with 2.6 or higher, especially if you've already installed it. And, if you have installed SQL Server Service Pack 1 you'll have ADO 2.61, and if you've installed Visual Studio.NET you've got ADO 2.7!

walk through the elements. No longer is it necessary to define the root element, and you can walk the elements just like you can a recordset.[7]

Listing 13-10. Processing XML in ADO.NET is even easier than in ADO 2.6.

```
Option Strict On
Option Explicit On

Imports System
Imports System.IO
Imports System.Xml
Imports System.Data.SqlClient
Module RDBASample
Sub Main()
  Dim connection As New SqlConnection("Initial Catalog=RDBA11;Data
Source=JDS-LAPTOP\RELUCATANTDBA;Integrated Security=SSPI;")
  connection.Open()
  Dim command As New SqlCommand("exec ListOfficesXML", connection)
  Dim reader As XmlReader = command.ExecuteXmlReader()
  Try
      'Parse the XML and display the text content of each of the elements.
      While reader.Read()
      'Loop through the elements
    If reader.IsStartElement() Then
      ' The first element
        If reader.IsEmptyElement Then
         Console.WriteLine("<{0}/>", reader.Name)
        Else
         Console.Write("<{0}>" + " ", reader.Name)
         reader.Read() 'Read the start tag.
        If (reader.IsStartElement()) Then 'Handle nested elements.
          Console.WriteLine()
          Console.Write("<{0}>", reader.Name)
        End If
        'Read the text content of the element.
        Console.WriteLine(reader.ReadString())
      End If
    End If
  End While
  Finally
```

---

7   This was done with Visual Studio .NET Beta 2 and Bill Vaughn's ADO.NET book wasn't available at the time, so please pardon the code. It *should* work with the final release of Visual Studio.NET but betas are not final, released products.

```
        If Not (reader Is Nothing) Then
            reader.Close()
        End If
    End Try
End Sub 'Main
```

The key to remember in this instance is that your stored procedure would need to have `FOR XML AUTO` added to the `SELECT` statement.

Why Can't I Directly Manipulate the XML the SQL Server Generates?

When you generate XML through SQL Server, it creates a recordset of data with one column that is 4,066-bytes long, storing 2033 Unicode characters. Given the fact that you can load tables from XML, it seems like it would be an excellent mechanism for transferring data back and forth between tables. However, you can't do that.

Although you can easily create a recordset using `FOR XML`, you cannot store that recordset to a temporary table, use it as the basis of a cursor, or in any other way manipulate the data in the recordset from within SQL Server or Query Analyzer (QA). If you take a moment to think about that, it makes sense. Because the XML that SQL Server generates isn't designed to stand alone, it doesn't make sense to let you manipulate it within SQL Server. Not only that, but XML was designed to facilitate *cross-platform* data transfer and manipulation. Although SQL Server 2000 can process XML, as we're about to demonstrate, it has much better mechanisms for manipulating data internally through TSQL.

Shredding Data

Just as SQL Server can create XML by splicing the various tables together, it can also shred XML apart to load new and update existing data. We're going to demonstrate how to do this in QA, but everything we're going to cover can be done by a client program as well.

SQL Server has two system stored procedures used in processing XML. They are `sp_xml_preparedocument` and `sp_xml_removedocument`. `sp_xml_preparedocument` takes a valid XML string and creates an internal SQL Server object that can be used like any valid recordset. Because the stored procedure can handle an `NTEXT` data type, it should be able to handle any size XML file that gets thrown to it. It's important to note, however, that this object will take up memory for as long as it exists, and it exists until the connection is broken or it is removed from memory with `sp_xml_removedocument`.

Once the document is prepared, you access it through the OPENXML function. OPENXML takes a prepared XML document and transforms it into a SQL recordset, but not one like any you've probably seen before. Let's take a look at the data it creates. The code in Listing 13-11 can be found in ShowOpenXMLStructure.sql in the "Chapter13" directory on the CD. It uses two of OPENXML's three parameters. The first one is the Document ID that is created through sp_xml_preparedocument. The second one tells OPENXML which part of the XML tree to return. In this case we have asked only for the Pets data that exists under Owners that exists under ROOT (and don't forget that XML is case sensitive).

Listing 13-11. How to display what a real XML rowset looks like in SQL Server

```
DECLARE @h int
DECLARE @xmldoc varchar(1000)
set @xmldoc =
'<?xml version="1.0" ?>
<ROOT>
 <Owners OwnerID="3" OwnerLastName="Brock">
  <Pets PetID="8" PetName="Cuddles" />
  <Pets PetID="9" PetName="Killer" />
  </Owners>
  </ROOT>'

EXEC sp_xml_preparedocument @h OUTPUT, @xmldoc
SELECT *
FROM OpenXML(@h,'/ROOT/Owners/Pets')
EXEC sp_xml_removedocument @h
```

The table shown in Figure 13-6 is the output of the OPENXML. The XML has been parsed into a linked list of data, where id and parentid create the links. The nodetype defines the type of data being stored in the record: 1 for an element, 2 for an attribute name, and 3 for the attribute value. The far right column, text, shows the value of the attribute. Of course, it wouldn't be any use if this were the only way to look at the data. You can also force it to show up like a normal recordset by using the WITH parameters. Listing 13-12 demonstrates how to use the WITH parameters (see the ShowOpenXMLNormal.sql file in the "Chapter13" directory on the CD).

	id	parentid	nodetype	localname	prefix	namespaceuri	datatype	prev	text
1	8	5	1	Pets	NULL	NULL	NULL	NULL	NULL
2	9	8	2	PetID	NULL	NULL	NULL	NULL	NULL
3	14	9	3	#text	NULL	NULL	NULL	NULL	8
4	10	8	2	PetName	NULL	NULL	NULL	NULL	NULL
5	15	10	3	#text	NULL	NULL	NULL	NULL	Cuddles
6	11	5	1	Pets	NULL	NULL	NULL	8	NULL
7	12	11	2	PetID	NULL	NULL	NULL	NULL	NULL
8	16	12	3	#text	NULL	NULL	NULL	NULL	9
9	13	11	2	PetName	NULL	NULL	NULL	NULL	NULL
10	17	13	3	#text	NULL	NULL	NULL	NULL	Killer

Figure 13-6. Sample output from OPENXML *recordset*

Listing 13-12. A partial listing showing how to view XML as a normal rowset

```
. . .
SELECT * FROM OpenXML(@h,'/ROOT/Owners/Pets') WITH (PetID INT,
   PetName \ VARCHAR(50))
. . .
```

If you add WITH and then define the column names and their data types, you end up with the data in a normal format. And, once the data looks like any other table, you can use it like any other table.

Using XML with INSERT/UPDATE Statements

OK, now that we've pulled the curtain aside to reveal some of what SQL Server is doing, we're going to look at how to use this to insert new records and update existing ones. Let's begin with the update.

Bulk updates are fairly simple, provided that the table providing the bulk update has the primary key in it. The basic syntax for such a bulk update is shown in Listing 13-13. For every row that matches, the data in tblA.colName will be updated to reflect the values in tblB.colName.

Listing 13-13. How a bulk update statement works in TSQL

```
Update tblA SET tblA.colName = tblB.colName FROM tblB
   where tblA.IDCol = tblB.IDCol
```

The premise is the same when using XML data, but it takes a little more work to get there (see Listing 13-14). First the XML needs to be defined, then loaded into an XML document, and finally opened via OPENXML. When this is run it will update two records in Pets with new names. This code can be found in XMLUpdate.sql in the "Chapter13" directory on the CD.

Listing 13-14. How to shred XML to update data

```
—Set the Variables to use
DECLARE @h int
DECLARE @xmldoc varchar(1000)
— Create the Valid XML Document String
set @xmldoc ='<?xml version="1.0" ?>
<ROOT>
        <Owners OwnerID="3" OwnerLastName="Brock">
                <Pets PetID="8" PetName="XMLCuddles" />
                <Pets PetID="9" PetName="KillerXML" />
        </Owners>
</ROOT>'
—Prepare the document
EXEC sp_xml_preparedocument @h OUTPUT, @xmldoc
— Select the data from the table
Update Pets SET Pets.PetName = X.Petname
FROM OpenXML(@h,'/ROOT/Owners/Pets')
      WITH (PetID INT, PetName VARCHAR(50)) X
WHERE Pets.PetID = X.PetID
— Free up memory by removing the document
EXEC sp_xml_removedocument @h
SELECT * FROM Pets where OwnerID = 3
```

Inserting records works along the same general principles, except that all of the fields must be present at the same level. The XML in the previous example wouldn't work for inserting new records into Pets because the OwnerID, although it exists, isn't on the same level as the information for Pets. This means that you need to think ahead about the structure of your XML. Another advantage of using the whole table is that we no longer need to identify the columns individually. Instead we can use the table name in the WITH statement to have SQL Server load the correct data types (see Listing 13-15).

Listing 13-15. How to shred XML to insert new data

```
—Set the Variables to use
DECLARE @h int
DECLARE @xmldoc varchar(1000)
— Create the Valid XML Document String
set @xmldoc ='<ROOT>
<row OwnerID="3" OwnerLastName="Brock" PetID="8" PetName="Cuddles" OfficeID="2"
VeterinarianID="1" />
<row OwnerID="3" OwnerLastName="Brock" PetID="9" PetName="Killer" OfficeID="2"
VeterinarianID="1" />
  </ROOT>'
```

```
—Prepare the document
EXEC sp_xml_preparedocument @h OUTPUT, @xmldoc
— Select the data from the table
INSERT INTO Pets (PetName, OwnerID, OfficeID, VeterinarianID)
SELECT PetName, OwnerID, OfficeID, VeterinarianID
FROM OpenXML(@h,'/ROOT/row') WITH Pets
— Free up memory by removing the document
EXEC sp_xml_removedocument @h
SELECT * FROM Pets where OwnerID = 3
```

As handy as this feature is, you still need to connect to the SQL Server to use any of this. If XML is supposed to be a way to work between platforms, how do you connect other platforms to SQL Server 2000? Well, if SQL Server is a .NET server, then the answer is with HTTP, of course.

How Do I Integrate XML, SQL Server, and IIS?

HTTP is the abbreviation that stands for the ubiquitous HyperText Transport Protocol that was instrumental in creating what we now call the World Wide Web. It has been implemented in everything from computers to toasters to cell phones.[8] The premise is simple. You open up port 80 on a TCP/IP address and use some basic text commands to communicate back and forth. That's all there is to HTTP. All of the rest of it (formatted Web pages, for instance) are the result of what is sent over the HTTP. The protocol itself doesn't really care what is sent. And, with a very little work, SQL Server 2000 can open up a door via HTTP to communicate with the world.

Now, we won't go into all of the details behind setting up Microsoft's Internet Information Server (IIS) on your server. The short version is that it is an optional part of the operating system under Windows 2000. If you're not running Windows 2000, then you can still find plenty of references on how to install either IIS or, for Windows 98, Personal Web Server. Once IIS is installed, you're ready to install the hooks into SQL Server 2000.

What Do I Need to Do First?

Although you can follow along with these examples, it's recommended that you step back for a moment and think about what you are going to do and why. It

---

[8]   OK, OK. At the time that I am writing this, Web-enabled toasters don't exist, and I can't think of one good reason why anyone would want to use one, but you know that somewhere, in the bowels of some big toaster manufacturer, the marketing gurus are pleading for their engineers to design one.

never hurts to have a plan in place, and it is a good idea to answer (or at least think about) the following questions:

- Why do I need to open up my data to the Web? Does it need to be accessible to different platforms or does it just sound cool?

- Who needs access to this data? Do I need to secure it with NT Security? SQL Server 2000 Security? A combination?

- What data should I make accessible on the Web?

There is cool technology and then there is cool technology that fills a need. If you are planning on putting an HTTP interface to SQL Server in place just because it's cool, then you should stop and think carefully about the implications of what you are doing. Do you really want to make your company's vital data available through the Web? Now, there are many reasons to do so as long as the data you make available is the right data and is secured correctly. One example of Web-enabling SQL Server could be to provide a way for your business partners to access critical data when they need it instead of forcing them to wait for someone to manually provide that data. When they need the data, their program opens an HTTP connection to your Web server and downloads the data in a standard format (XML) and can manipulate the data immediately without having to convert it.

And there are multiple levels of security to consider. There is the security built into IIS, which we will touch upon briefly. Then there is the security built into SQL Server 2000, which was covered in Chapter 11, "How Do I Secure My Data?" That being said, however, it is easier to think through what should be opened up and what shouldn't *before* you create the access. So, having set up a list of questions to answer, let's proceed to build a Web connection to the database.

How Do I Configure SQL XML Support in IIS?

This is really straightforward. Just like many things in SQL Server 2000, Microsoft has supplied the reluctant DBA with a wizard to walk us through the configuration. Under the Microsoft SQL Server section in your Start menu you'll find the Configure SQL XML Support in IIS option. When you click it, it will begin a version of the Microsoft Management Console designed to manage SQL Server Web connections.

SQL Server will create a virtual directory on the Web site. A virtual directory is one that appears to exist but really exists somewhere else. For instance, we are going to create the virtual directory RDBA. When we point the browser to the directory it will be pointed to `http://localserver/RDBA`. The actual RDBA directory will exist somewhere other than directly under the root directory for the Web server. To begin the process, right-click on the Default Web Site and select the New Virtual Directory option.

As you can see in Figure 13-7, there are a number of tabs for this wizard, and we'll deal with each in turn. The General tab is where you define both the virtual directory and the location of the physical directory. For simplicity's sake, we're creating the physical directory as C:\RDBAXML and the Virtual Directory as RDBA. The physical folder has to exist to be used, but you can create the folder from here. When you click on the Browse button, it will bring up a listing of all of the drives and directories on your system. To create a new directory, you first must open where the directory will reside. In this example, we're putting this on the "C:" drive, so we'll drill down to open "C:\." Then press the New Folder button, and name the folder "RDBAXML."

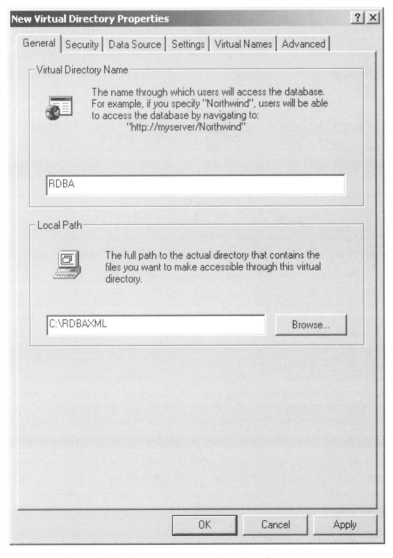

Figure 13-7. Configure SQL XML support in IIS wizard

The security tab has three options for handling the security (see Figure 13.8). You can set the login to be permanently set to either a SQL Login or an NT Login, you can use Windows Integrated Authentication, or you can use Basic Authentication directly to the SQL Account. Table 13-3 outlines the differences between these authentication methods. For more information on security, see Chapter 11, "How Do I Secure My Data?" We're going to use the Basic Authentication to SQL Server; it will ask for the login and password.

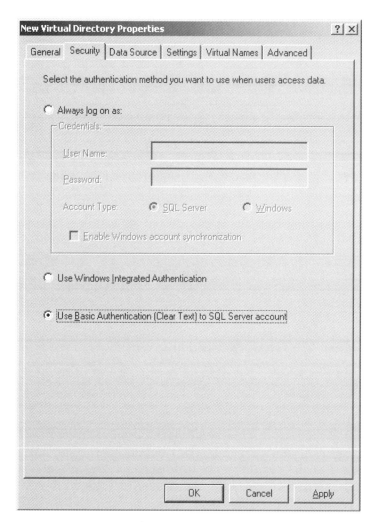

Figure 13-8. Security options in the IIS Virtual Directory

Table 13-3. IIS SQL Authentication Methods

METHOD	WEB SECURITY	SQL SECURITY
Always Log On As	This option sets the Web security to allow anonymous logins (by default, IUSR_servername on the server).	A specific Windows or SQL login/password combination is used for access to the data. This is the least secure of all because anyone who can get to the virtual directory can get to any of the data that this login/password is allowed to access. This is a very good reason not to use the sa account.
Windows Authenticated Integration	This option forces the Web browser to authenticate with the NT account the user is currently logged in under. If the user is not logged in to the server's domain, then a box comes up prompting for authentication.	The valid Windows login/password used by the browser is used to connect to the SQL Server.
Use Basic Authentication to SQL Server	This option uses anonymous access to the Web site.	A login box prompts for a SQL Server login and password.

The Data Source tab is where we set the data source. The text box in the top half is for listing the SQL Server. If you are not on a Windows 98 machine, you should be able to press the button to the right of the text box to open a list of servers from which to pick. Once you have selected the server, you can either type in the database name or select it from the drop-down list. If you select it from the drop-down list, the first thing that happens is the wizard will attempt to connect using the parameters set in the Security tab. For that reason, it's always good to try to open the drop-down list when you change something, even if you have no plans to change the database.

Because we have selected the Basic Authentication, we're prompted for a SQL Server login and password. Once we enter them, we get the complete list so we can choose the one we need. If, on the other hand, there's a problem with the data entered on the Security tab, then we will get a message saying the wizard is unable to display a list of databases on the server and the drop-down box will be empty (see Figure 13-9).

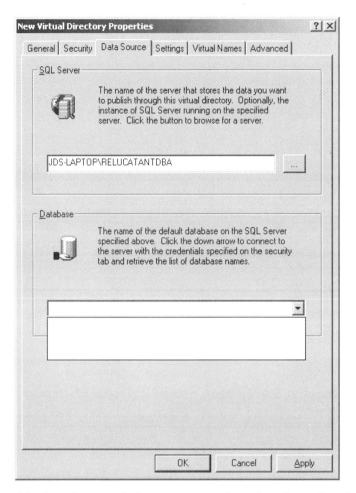

Figure 13-9. The Data Source tab shows an empty drop-down box when there's an error in the Security tab.

The Settings tab is for setting options related to Web page access (see Figure 13-10). Although there are several options, we are only going to go into two of them: Allow URL Queries and Allow Template Queries. The others are outside the scope of this book; however, you can easily find them by looking up Xpath and Allow Post in Books On Line (BOL).

BOL has this to say about URL queries: "For security reasons, it is recommended that you not use this option." Regardless, URL queries provide the easiest means of demonstrating how the Web access works, and we'll demonstrate the security problem graphically.

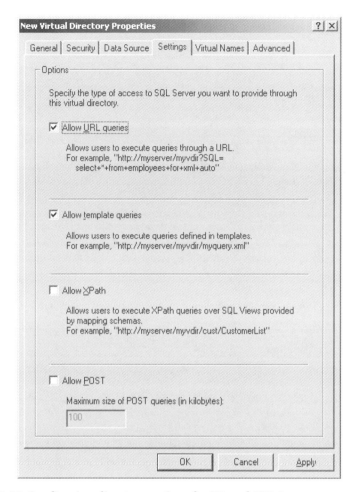

Figure 13-10. Configuring directory options for IIS and SQL Server

What Is a URL Query?

URL queries take an HTTP address and create a query from them. The format used is `http://servername/virtualdir?SQL=sqlstring`. The `sqlstring` needs to be properly separated with + to replace spaces, just like any URL. To get a list of the first two records in Owners, we just need to use the string shown in Listing 13-16 (see Figure 13-11 for the sample output).

Listing 13-16. A URL query
```
http://jds-laptop/RDBA?SQL=SELECT+*+FROM+Owners+WHERE+OwnerID<3+
FOR+XML+AUTO &ROOT=ROOT
```

```
<?xml version="1.0" encoding="utf-8" ?>
- <ROOT>
    <Owners OwnerID="1" OwnerLastName="Apsel" OwnerFirstName="Robert"
      OwnerAddress1="7430 Fish Ranch Road" OwnerAddress2="Apt. 2" OwnerCity="Orinda"
      OwnerState="CA" OwnerPostalCode="94563" OwnerPhoneNumber="9255551212" />
    <Owners OwnerID="2" OwnerLastName="Sclarenco" OwnerFirstName="Clarence"
      OwnerAddress1="901 Grayson St." OwnerAddress2="Apt. 2" OwnerCity="Berkeley"
      OwnerState="CA" OwnerPostalCode="94710" OwnerPhoneNumber="5105495930" />
  </ROOT>
```

Figure 13-11. Output from a URL query

Let's take a look at the parts that make up this URL. The first thing to notice is that the URL directory name is immediately followed by a question mark (?). That question mark signifies that the rest of the URL can be separated in to parameters. Each parameter is followed by the equal sign (=) and then the value of the parameter. This URL has two parameters, SQL and ROOT.

The SQL parameter is, not surprisingly, the SQL command to be executed. It functions just as though QA was up and running. The security to run the command is based on the Security settings in the wizard. Can you see why you don't want sa even with a password being used here? If someone were to use SQL=DROP+DATABASE+dbname while logged in as sa, then that database would be gone and you'd have to resort to restoring the most recent maintenance backup (for more information on automating backups, see Chapter 12, "How Can SQL Server Agent Make Life Easier?").

The next parameter is ROOT. Valid XML must have a root element of some sort and this is where you can specify what that root element is. For this example, we are using ROOT, but we could just as easily use a unique identifier such as the name of the table. The important thing to remember is not to use the table name when you are using FOR XML AUTO. That's because the table name is used for the element name. Instead use a unique prefix for the table name, like X.

Now that we've gone through the basics, let's take it a step further by adding multiple tables to the SQL. The code in Listing 13-17 will return a well-formed XML document like the one shown in Listing 13-18.

Listing 13-17. A more advanced URL query

```
http://jds-laptop/RDBA/?sql=SELECT+Owners.OwnerID,OwnerLastName,PetID,PetName+
FROM+Owners+INNER+JOIN+Pets+ON+Owners.OwnerID=Pets.OwnerID+
WHERE+PetID+<+10+AND+Owners.OwnerID=3+FOR+XML+AUTO+&ROOT=ROOT
```

Listing 13-18. A well-formed XML document

```
<?xml version="1.0" encoding="utf-8" ?>
 <ROOT>
 <Owners OwnerID="3" OwnerLastName="Brock">
  <Pets PetID="8" PetName="XMLCuddles" />
  <Pets PetID="9" PetName="KillerXML" />
 </Owners>
 </ROOT>
```

This is all handy for creating XML on the fly, but it seems cumbersome to have to put the SQL command in the URL, not to mention that the URL has a limit on how long it can be. If you think that there has to be an easier way to accomplish this, you're right.

How Do I Use XML Templates?

XML templates provide a means for storing frequently used SQL statements in files. This makes referencing them easier by using a shorter filename in the URL instead of the cumbersome SQL command. In addition, you have greater control over the formatting of the XML, and using templates means you do not have to allow SQL statements in the URL, preventing people from attempting to hack into your system or inadvertently creating problems by entering a SQL command that joins two huge tables together in a query that consumes system resources. But what, exactly, is a template?

> *Reluctant DBA* definition of an XML *template*:
> An XML file containing special tags that can execute SQL commands.

A template is an XML file that contains special tags. Template files are stored in a directory defined through the Configure SQL XML Support in IIS wizard. Open the wizard and double-click on the RDBA directory created earlier. Select the Virtual Names tab. This tab is where virtual directories are made for both templates and schemas. These virtual directories will reside under the main virtual directory, although the physical directory can be placed anywhere.

Let's take a look at a template file (see Listing 13-19). The following template file is the simplest type. It has a root element named ROOT that references the XML-SQL namespace. Next comes the sql:query element. This element will attempt to process whatever it contains as a SQL command, in this case selecting data from Owners and returning it in XML format. Now that you see what a template file looks like, let's step through setting the Web page up to use templates.

Listing 13-19. An XML template

```
<ROOT xmlns:sql="urn:schemas-microsoft-com:xml-sql">
<sql:query>
SELECT *
FROM   Owners
WHERE OwnerID = 2
FOR XML AUTO
</sql:query>
</ROOT>
```

Setting up templates is a straightforward task. Pull up the Configure SQL XML Support in IIS and double-click on the RDBA directory created earlier. Click on the Virtual Names tab, select New, and you'll get a pop-up window like the one in Figure 13-12. Virtual directories can be created for dbobjects, schemas, and templates. The dialog box is fairly simple, taking the name of the virtual directory, the type of directory it will be, and, for schemas and templates, the path of the actual directory. This virtual directory (templates) will exist underneath the virtual directory RDBA although the physical directories could be on different disks.

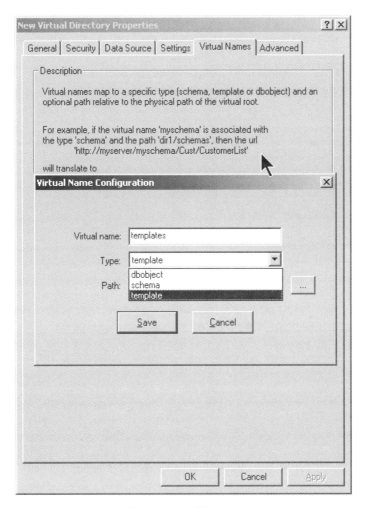

Figure 13-12. Setting up a template virtual directory

Now that the virtual directory is set up, copy the template file Owner1.xml over to it (if you haven't already copied it, it's in the "Chapter13\RDBA\Templates" directory). Now open it up in Internet Explorer by using `http://servername/RDBA/templates/Owner1.xml`. That's it. It should look much like all of the other examples in this chapter. Now that we've introduced templates, let's make them far more useful by passing parameters to them.

Passing parameters to a template requires two new XML elements: `sql:header` and `sql:param`. The `sql:header` element is designed to hold any SQL-related elements, though at the moment all it can contain are `sql:param` elements. There is a limit of one `sql:header` element in a template. The `sql:param` element defines a single parameter to be passed in to the `sql:query` element. Although each `sql:parameter` defines only one parameter, multiple parameters are allowed as long as each one is named differently. Let's modify our template so that it takes the OwnerID as a parameter and see what it looks like (see Listing 13-20).

Listing 13-20. An XML template that takes a parameter

```
<ROOT xmlns:sql="urn:schemas-microsoft-com:xml-sql">
<sql:header>
<sql:param name="OwnerID" />
</sql:header>
<sql:query>
SELECT * FROM   Owners
WHERE OwnerID = @OwnerID
FOR XML AUTO
</sql:query>
</ROOT>
```

The first thing to notice is that `sql:param` has one attribute, the name. Because we're not adding anything else to this, we are closing the element with a / at the end. The next change is in the `sql:query` section where we use the parameter, replacing 3 with `@OwnerID`. Now it's time to try out the new template, as soon as we mention one quirky detail. XML is case sensitive and that applies here but not the way we expect. The parameter in the URL must match the case for the parameter as defined in the `sql:param` element, but the parameter in the `sql:query` doesn't need to match case with the `sql:param`. That's because SQL Server, by default, is not case sensitive. If you are not getting data when you attempt to use this template, make sure that the `OwnerID` parameter in the URL matches the case of the `sql:param`. If you did get data, it should look like Figure 13-13.

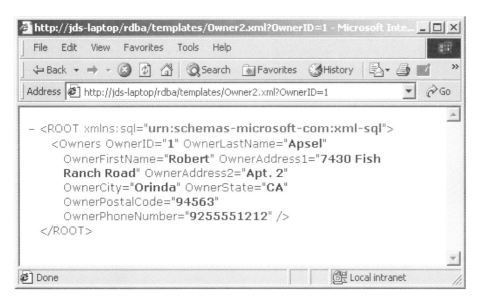

Figure 13-13. Paramaterized templates give you more control over what SQL is run from your Web server.

Although using templates to cut down on the amount of SQL you need to put in the Web address is impressive, you can also set up templates to call stored procedures with parameters. Once the template is set up, any program that can access a Web page can interact with the database to add, update, and retrieve data, returning the data in XML format so that any program that can read text can process the data. As mentioned, this topic really deserves a book of its own, but this basic explanation should be enough to get you started in seeing the possibilities that XML offers you.

The Future of XML and SQL Server 2000

Even as this book is being written, XML and how SQL Server implements it are evolving. Microsoft recently released XML for SQL Server Web Release 2 (http://msdn.microsoft.com/sqlserver) with Web Release 3 due out in mid-2002. (If you're wondering, Web Release 1 was built into SQL Server 2000.) Some of the functionality in these packages includes:

- UpdateGrams are used to modify SQL data within an XML document.

- XML Bulk Loader. A high-performance engine for inserting large amounts of XML data into SQL Server.

- MSXML 4.0 parser, providing better performance.

There is, however, a caveat that goes with the XML for SQL Server Web Releases. They are not necessarily backward compatible with the existing server. Microsoft is saying they will release two versions of the Web Releases, one dependent upon the version of SQL Server you have and one that is not. If you should install the non-version dependent Web Release on SQL Server 2000, you may find functionality different from what exists natively in SQL Server 2000. In other words, you could break your programs if you install the wrong version, so test thoroughly before implementing.

Last Words

We've taken a whirlwind tour of some of the features that make SQL Server 2000 a .NET server. No longer do client programs need to have ODBC connections built. Instead, they can use HTTP to connect to a Web server that delivers up XML data. Next we'll look at another way of getting data into and out of SQL Server. Data Transformation Services (DTS) are especially handy when there's lots of data involved.

Resources

- Microsoft's XML page lets you download all kinds of information about XML, get the latest XML parser, and read about how Microsoft is implementing XML: `http://msdn.microsoft.com/xml/default.asp`

- Microsoft's Web and Application Services page tells you where to find more information about IIS:
  `http://www.microsoft.com/windows2000/technologies/web/default.asp`

- BizTalk.org is a place to find out how companies are using XML, to share your templates, or to find a template that meets your company's needs:
  `http://www.biztalk.org/home/default.asp`

- SQL Server XML View Mapper 1.0 enables you to produce an XML View schema file that relates an XDR schema to a SQL Server schema, making life easier on you than having to do this manually:
  `http://msdn.microsoft.com/downloads/default.asp?URL=/code`
  `/sample.asp?url=/MSDN-FILES/027/001/443/msdncompositedoc.xml`

What Are the Data Transformation Services (DTS)?

All butterflies go through four life stages. The first is the egg, which is laid on a host plant leaf by a gravid (pregnant) female butterfly. The female will only lay her eggs on plants that the resulting caterpillar can eat. Once the caterpillar has hatched from the egg, it will eat and grow until it reaches its full size. At that point, it enters the third or pupae stage. The caterpillar forms a structure called a chrysalis in which it will transform into an adult—a butterfly. (There's no such thing as a baby butterfly!) This is the fourth and final stage. The adult will most likely seek a mate after emerging from its chrysalis and the cycle of life will continue. —Milkweed Café Advertisement

LIFE BEFORE THE Data Transformation Services (DTS) was much like that of the butterfly. It was a time-consuming process of writing programs to read data from text files or another source and then to write the data to a database. Utilities like the Bulk Copy Program (bcp) can pump data into or out of SQL Server, but mastering the arcane parameters of bcp could take a long time. Fortunately, in SQL Server 7, Microsoft introduced DTS. Suddenly, getting data into or out of SQL Server became a lot easier.

DTS clearly makes getting data into or out of SQL Server easier, but it isn't necessarily more efficient. When performance is an issue, use Bulk Insert *to load data and* bcp *to extract data.*

DTS makes it easier to do many things, and this is a subject deserving of its own book (see "Resources" at the end of the chapter), but we will cover the basics of importing and exporting data, then we'll look at the DTS Designer and how to modify and create a package through it. Finally, we'll look at DTSRun, a great little utility to use with DTS packages to get syntax correct.

How Do I Import/Export Data?

Before DTS, this was no easy task, especially if we needed to put the data in an Excel spreadsheet or had a spreadsheet of data to load into a database. One way was to run a query in the Query Analyzer (QA) and then cut and paste the data into Excel. One of my favorite ways to load data from an Excel spreadsheet from way back was to create a long formula in the column to the right of the data that contained the Transact SQL (TSQL) that I'd need to execute in the QA. Then I'd cut and paste that column into the QA and run it.

Fortunately, neither of those methods is required any longer. We can use DTS to do all of the dirty work for us.

NOTE   *This chapter relies heavily on the **RDBA14** database. You'll find instructions for installing that database in Appendix A, "How Do I Load the Examples?"*

How Do I Import or Export Data?

To get started with DTS, select the Data Export wizard from within the Enterprise Manager (EM) by opening up the server and selecting Tools ➤ Wizards.[1] Then, from within the Select Wizard window, open the DTS and select DTS Export Wizard (see Figure 14-1). The wizard starts with a screen informing us that it is the DTS Import/Export wizard and that it will help us to import or export data easily to many popular formats, including spreadsheets and other databases.

---

[1]   You need to have selected a database from within the EM. Otherwise, the DTS wizards might not be available.

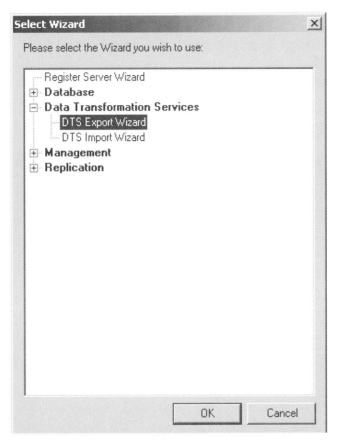

Figure 14-1. The easiest way to dive into creating a DTS package is to select either the DTS Export wizard or the DTS Import wizard, which really are the same thing.

What's the Difference between Importing and Exporting?

When we talk of importing or exporting data, we are really talking about the same task from different viewpoints. If we are importing data into a database, then the data destination is our database, and the data source is something other than our database. When we speak of exporting data, the source and destination are reversed. With that in mind, Microsoft provided us with one wizard and two entry points.

Press Next and we're taken to the first screen of any value, Choose a Data Source. From this screen we are able to select the source of our data. For this demonstration we're going to select Microsoft OLE DB Provider for SQL Server (see Figure 14-2). We can choose whether to use a SQL Login or Windows Authentication, and we're going to use Windows Authentication for now. The last thing we're going to do is select **RDBA14** for the database and then press the Next button.

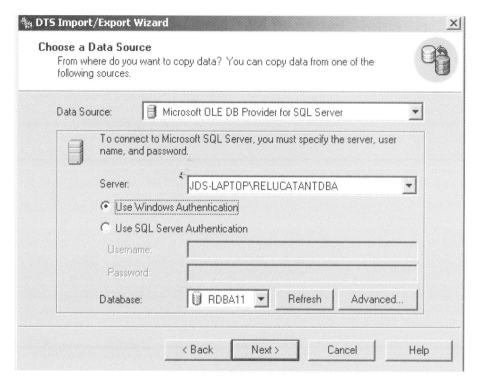

Figure 14-2. Choosing the data source for importing and exporting data is as easy as selecting options from a dialog box.

If you think the next screen is *déjà vu* all over again, you're almost correct. Because the only difference between importing and exporting is the direction, the same screens are used for defining the source and defining the destination, differentiated only by the captions. But these are dynamic windows. When we change the destination, it changes the options that appear in the frame below it. For this example we'll choose Microsoft Excel 97-2000; we then get a prompt to select the name of the text file (see Figure 14-3). We're going to name the spreadsheet Owners because we're going to export the Owners table.

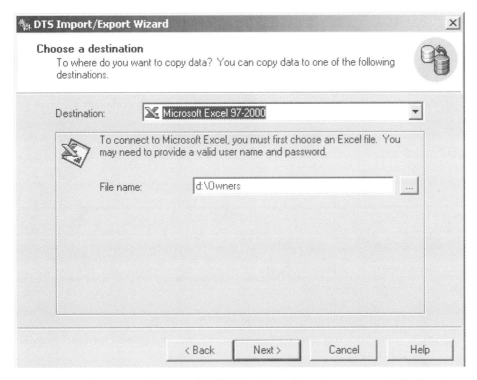

Figure 14-3. The options that can be filled in depend on the source and destination.

After pressing the Next button, we get a screen with three options (see Figure 14-4):

- Copy Table(s) and View(s) from the Source Database

- Use a Query to Specify the Data to Transfer

- Copy Objects and Data between SQL Server Databases[2]

---

[2]   This is only enabled when both the source and the destination are SQL Server.

These are fairly straightforward options. We can select the table or view to use for the copy, and we will get the equivalent of a SELECT * from the table. If we want to change the order of the columns or to filter the data we are retrieving, we can use a TSQL command, either a SELECT or a stored procedure that returns data. For this example, we're going to stick with copying a table and go on to the next screen.

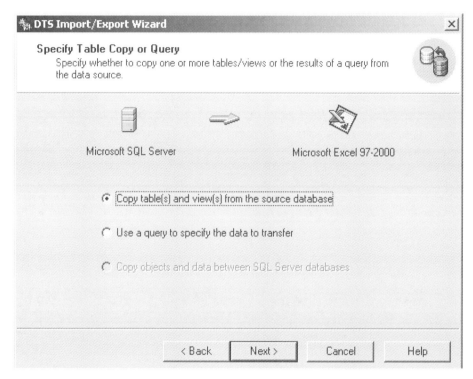

Figure 14-4. It's easy to specify whether we are copying an entire table or the results of a TSQL command.

Now we get to define what table or tables we are going to copy and where we want them put in the Excel spreadsheet (see Figure 14-5). We're going to select Owners, and the wizard automatically fills in the table name for the Destination sheet in the spreadsheet. There's a third column, Transform, and it contains a button (marked with ellipses) to press, so let's do that and see how we can transform data.[3]

---

[3]   I did say this is the Data *Transformation* Services.

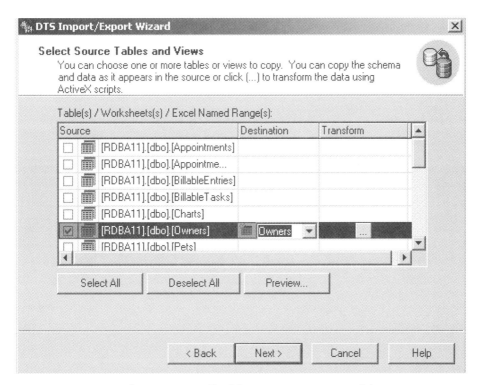

Figure 14-5. We can choose any or all tables to export to a spreadsheet.

How Do I Transform Data While Importing/Exporting It?

When we click the Transform button during the Import/Export Data Wizard, we're opening the Column Mappings and Transformations window (see Figure 14-6). Excel doesn't actually recognize the integer data type, so the window automatically translates that into a long data type for Excel (same for Access).

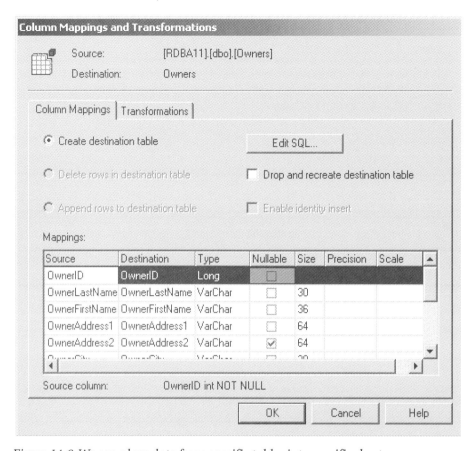

Figure 14-6. We can place data from specific tables into specific sheets.

This window is where we get our first opportunity to change the data. The Source column contains the list of columns being exported. It is possible to modify the order of the columns by modifying which columns show up. It's *possible,* but that doesn't mean it's desirable. It would be far easier to change the order by using a SELECT statement.

Instead, leave everything just as it is here and go to the second tab in this window, Transformations (see Figure 14-7). If you think the code in the bottom of that screen looks like VBScript, you're correct. Data transformation is handled through either VBScript or Jscript. This book's examples all use VBScript.

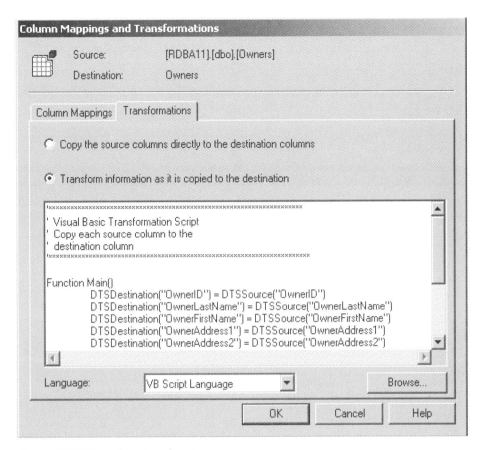

Figure 14-7. Transforming data is easy.

Do I *Have* to Transform Data?

The short answer is "no." In fact, if all you are doing is funneling data from one place to another, it is quicker to select the option of copying the source columns directly to the destination columns. When you transform data, you force SQL Server to run either VBScript or Jscript, and both of them are interpreters, meaning they run s-l-o-w-l-y. However, if you need to modify your data on the fly, transformations are fast.

Let's take a closer look at the code being used in the transformation. Listing 14-1 shows the code as it was generated by the wizard. It creates a `Main` function that is called *once for each row*! That means you really want to keep your transformations as simple as they can be. ActiveX scripts and transformations are covered in the section "What Are ActiveX Script Transformations?"

Listing 14-1. Simple transformation of the Owners table

```
'***********************************************************************
'  Visual Basic Transformation Script
'  Copy each source column to the destination column
'***********************************************************************
Function Main()
  DTSDestination("OwnerID") = DTSSource("OwnerID")
  DTSDestination("OwnerLastName") = DTSSource("OwnerLastName")
  DTSDestination("OwnerFirstName") = DTSSource("OwnerFirstName")
  DTSDestination("OwnerAddress1") = DTSSource("OwnerAddress1")
  DTSDestination("OwnerAddress2") = DTSSource("OwnerAddress2")
  DTSDestination("OwnerCity") = DTSSource("OwnerCity")
  DTSDestination("OwnerState") = DTSSource("OwnerState")
  DTSDestination("OwnerPostalCode") = DTSSource("OwnerPostalCode")
  DTSDestination("OwnerPostal4") = DTSSource("OwnerPostal4")
  DTSDestination("OwnerPhoneNumber") = DTSSource("OwnerPhoneNumber")
  DTSDestination("OwnerEmailAddress") = DTSSource("OwnerEmailAddress")
  Main = DTSTransformStat_OK
End Function
```

From the Column Mappings and Transformations dialog box, click OK or Cancel, and then click Next. This brings us to Save, Schedule, and Replicate Package. The Save, Schedule, and Replicate Package screen is almost the last one (see Figure 14-8). The default of Run Immediately is checked, letting us create our output, but we also want to check the Save DTS Package so that we can play with this package some more. We have four options for how we can save the package, detailed next.

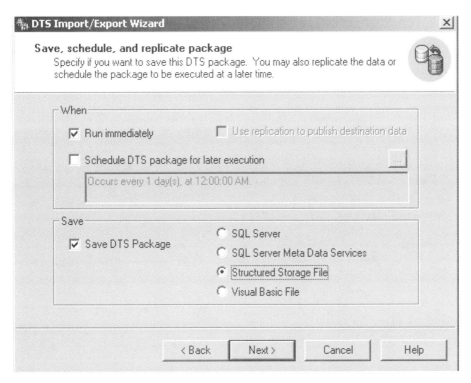

Figure 14-8. There are four ways to save a DTS package.

- SQL Server: This saves the package on the SQL Server under the Data Transformation Services folder for a server. Each package saved to a server must have a unique name and can be password protected.

- SQL Server Meta Data Services: This option is for storing the package within Microsoft's Data Repository, which is beyond the scope of this book.

- Structured Storage File: The package, and all of its components, is stored in a Structured Storage File, which is something like a file system within a file. See "Resources" at the end of the chapter to find out more information about Structured Storage Files.

- Visual Basic File: This is new in SQL Server 2000, and it saves the package as a .bas file that will create and run a package programmatically using the DTS object model.

For now, let's run the program immediately *and* save it as Structured Storage File. This brings up the Save DTS Package screen shown in Figure 14-9. From here we'll name our DTS package, which will be appended to the text in the File Name text box. A single file can contain many packages and revisions of packages, but the default is to keep the file and package names in sync. We can also enter a description and, if we want, a password. There's an Owner password and a User password. If an Owner password is assigned, then it will be required before changes can be made to the package where a User password, if assigned, would be required before running the package. This package is on the CD ("\Chapter14\Packages\Owners2Excel.dts") and is not password protected.

TIP *Consider changing the path for the file if there's a preferred location for storage and distribution of such files.*

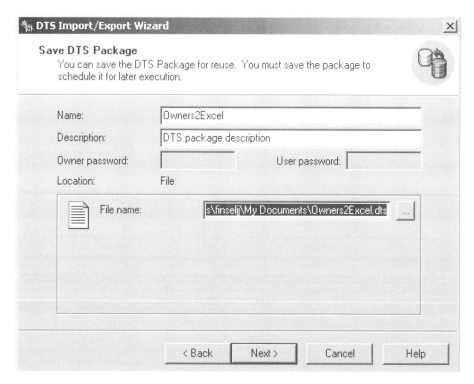

Figure 14-9. There are two levels of password protection available for a package.

Press Next to save the file and to have the wizard bring up a summary screen, detailing everything it is about to do. Press Finish, and the wizard starts. As it runs through the assigned tasks, it displays a window that details how far it has gotten (see Figure 14-10). Once it has finished, we'll have to close a few status windows but now we've got a package we can explore.

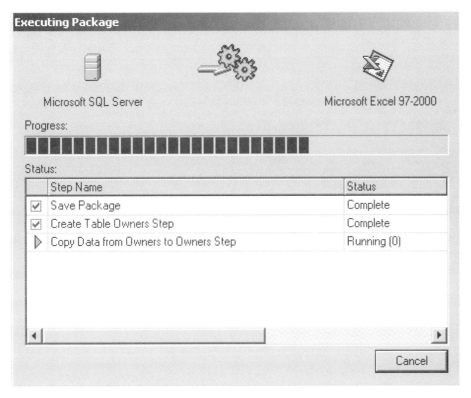

Figure 14-10. DTS keeps us informed of what it's doing.

What Is the DTS Designer?

The DTS Designer is a Rapid Application Development (RAD) tool for DTS packages. But what are DTS packages?

> *Reluctant DBA* definition of DTS *package*:
> The framework for storing all of the component parts required to accomplish a related set of data transformations. It can include connections, steps, and tasks.

Let's open up the package we just saved (if you didn't save it, it's on the CD). To open a package that has been saved as a file, right-click on the Data Transformation Services in the EM and select Open Package. If the package is saved as either a local package or a metadata services package, then it will be in the appropriate collection under the Data Transformation Services folder. If the package was saved as a Visual Basic file, it'll be where the folder was saved and must be opened with Visual Basic.

When we go to open a package, it is possible there are multiple revisions within the package (see Figure 14-11). If we open the package, save the package without changing anything and then open it again; we'll find a new revision. If we double-click on Owners2Excel or highlight Owners2Excel and not a dated revision below it, we'll open the most current revision. Another interesting fact is that we can have multiple packages with multiple revisions stored within one file, making it easy to store related packages.

Another plus, of course, is troubleshooting. You can run comparisons of the final output or of performance by storing and running variations of the DTS package. Pretty slick.

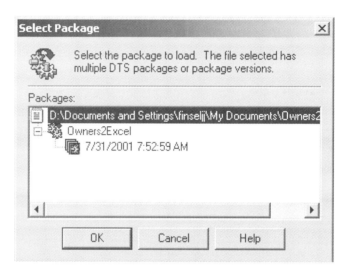

Figure 14-11. We can store multiple revisions of a package.

Once we've opened the package in the DTS Designer, we'll see a graphical representation of the contents of the package. As shown in Figure 14-12, there are three parts to this package: Connection1, Connection2, and an arrow joining the two of them together. Before we cover the details of the package, let's cover the basics of working with a package in the Designer.

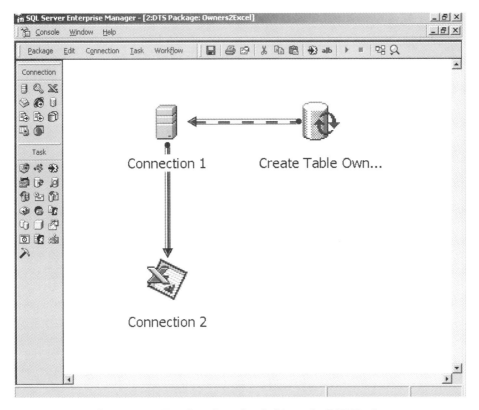

Figure 14-12. The Owners2Excel package loaded into the DTS Designer

The toolbar across the top looks very much like the one in the QA. The functionality of all of those buttons was covered in Chapter 8, "Introduction to Query Analyzer," so they won't be covered here. Instead, we're going to start with the toolbox along the left side, the one split into Connections on the top and Tasks on the bottom.

What Are DTS Connections?

> *Reluctant DBA* definition of DTS *connection:*
> A connection is a link to a data source. The data source can be a relational database, a text file, an XML file, a spreadsheet, or any other ODBC-compliant data source.

The Owners2Excel package has two connections, Connection1 and Connection2. These aren't the friendliest names, but the wizard never claimed to be perfect. One of the major drawbacks of creating packages through the wizard is that connections can't be renamed within the DTS. We can create new ones, giving them more intuitive names, that are configured exactly like the old ones and use the new connection(s) instead, but we can't just rename a connection.[4]

Naming tasks and connections intuitively helps by making it easier to understand the DTS diagram and, when the DTS package is run, we'll see the name of the step being executed rather than some meaningless cryptic name give by the wizard. This makes it much easier to debug. To edit the properties of a connection, double-click on the connection in the Designer (or right-click and select Properties, or select the connection and then press the Properties button on the toolbar). This brings up the Connection Properties window shown in Figure 14-13. Although we can't change the name of the connection, we can change everything else, including where the connection is pointing. This is a good thing because your server probably has a different name than shown here.

Changing the server isn't all we can do. We can also change the *type* of connection. However, if we change from `Microsoft OLE DB Provider for SQL Server` to `Text File (Source)`, we could end up with some problems, but SQL Server will let us do it and ask us to reconcile the differences between the two connections as they relate to the rest of the package.

> **CAUTION** *It is easy to "lose" a connection if you aren't paying attention. If you double-click on Connection1 to bring up the Connection Properties window and then select Connection2 as the Existing Connection instead of Connection1, the diagram changes and Connection1 seems to disappear. It's still there and you can still access it from the Connection Properties window, but you won't see it until you add it to a task. So if you do suddenly find a connection "missing," don't panic! Just create a new task and link the missing connection to it.*

---

[4] Actually, this isn't exactly true. You can go into Package ➢ Disconnected Edit. . . and from there modify *anything* about the package. Be warned, however, that there are no checks that what you are editing is correct, and you can really screw up a package this way if you don't know what you're doing.

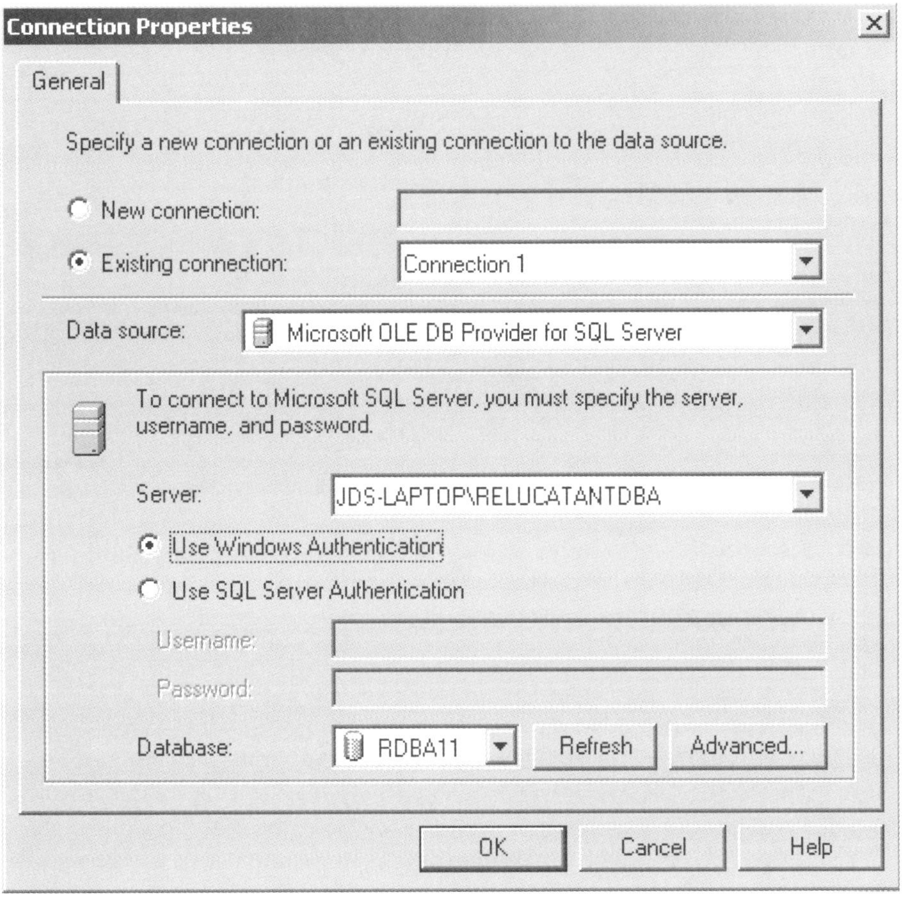

Figure 14-13. Modifying the properties of a connection is easy.

We can add a new connection by clicking on the connection in the toolbar to the left. As the mouse lingers over a connection, a pop-up tool tip tells us what type of connection it is. Once we've established your connection, we can start adding tasks.

What Are DTS Tasks?

> *Reluctant DBA* definition of DTS *task*:
> A DTS task is an action to be taken to move or manipulate data.

Actually, there are two types of tasks, but the Designer hides them as one task. The first type of task is a DTS task, which is really nothing more than a place-holder for a custom task.

> *Reluctant DBA* definition of DTS *custom task*:
> A DTS custom task is what is actually executed within the placeholder task. That's because there are many different types of custom tasks (ActiveX scripts, TSQL commands, operating system commands) and hiding those different types of custom tasks within the generic DTS task makes it easier to manipulate the tasks in the Designer.

When we are creating and manipulating packages within the Designer, the Designer takes care of creating the generic task and then adding the custom task to it. If we are working with tasks programmatically (in Visual Basic for instance), then we'll need to remember to do this ourselves. If we double-click on the arrow joining the two connections, we'll see that it is a Transform Data Task, which is the custom task. Some of the more common tasks include:

- Transform Data: This task moves and manipulates data between two connections.

- Execute Process: This task executes any executable file as part of the DTS package.

- Execute SQL: This task executes a TSQL statement.

- Bulk Insert: This task quickly and efficiently loads data into the database.

- Data Driven Query: This task lets us perform different actions depending on the values in the source table.

- Execute Package: This task executes a completely separate package.

What Is a Data Transformation Task?

For now, however, we're going to concentrate on the existing data transformation task and open it up by double-clicking on it (see Figure 14-14). It has five tabs across the top: Source, Destination, Transformations, Lookups, and Options. We'll cover all five in turn, starting with Source. Source is where the data to be transformed is coming from—in this case, from a table in a database. Even though we selected to copy a table in the wizard, our request was translated into a SELECT statement that contains all of the column names.[5]

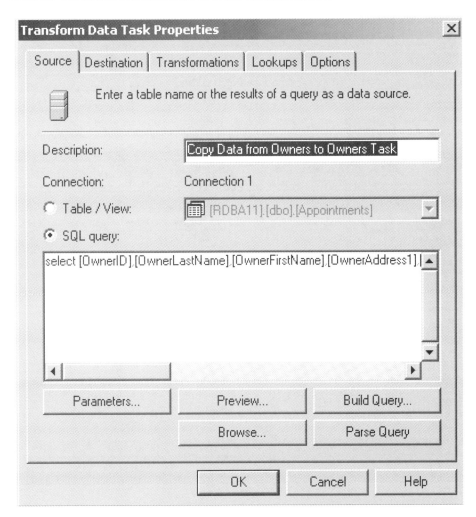

Figure 14-14. Modifying the properties of a data transformation task

---

[5]   What, you're expecting me to make a point that SELECT * is so bad that even the SQL Server Wizard doesn't use it? Naw. . . You are already well aware of the dangers, and it would just be redundant and repetitious to drive the point home here.

There are a series of buttons along the bottom of the Source tab that should look familiar:

- Preview opens a grid with the results of the TSQL command.

- Build Query opens a window similar to the View Designer for creating a TSQL statement.

- Browse lets us load a file of TSQL commands from disk.

- Parse Query verifies that the TSQL is syntactically correct (though if column name is misspelled, it won't get caught until the code is executed).

How Do I Parameterize TSQL in a Data Transformation Task?

Parameters, however, is a new button for a concept initially covered in Chapter 9, "Working with Data: Basic Stored Procedures." To use parameters for TSQL within DTS, we need to use a question mark (?) where we want to put your parameter. The ? indicates to SQL Server that we are going to replace it with a value at some point in time. To make the Owners2Excel package more flexible, we might want to be able to pull out just those owners in a specific zip code. To handle that, we could add a WHERE condition to the SQL query that has a parameter, like this:

```
WHERE [OwnerPostalCode] = ?
```

Now that we've defined a parameter, we can press the Parameters button. This opens up the Parameter Mapping window, as shown in Figure 14-15. This window has a grid with two columns, one for the parameter and one for the input global variable that will be used to replace the parameter in the query. We cannot just enter a value for the parameter; we have to map it to a global variable. If we wanted to just put a value in, we could skip the parameters altogether.

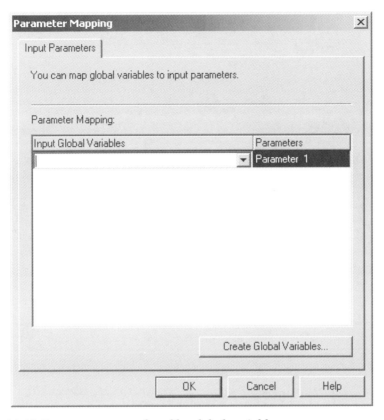

Figure 14-15. Parameters are replaced by global variables.

> *Reluctant DBA* definition of DTS *global variable*:
> A global variable within DTS is a named bucket that stores a value. That
> value can be referenced by name within a DTS package.

You might point out to me that we don't have any global variables defined
yet, and you would be correct. Fortunately, however, we can overcome that by
clicking on the Create Global Variables button at the bottom of the screen. This
brings up the Global Variables window, which will allow us to create, delete, or
modify global variables at will (see Figure 14-16). As you can see, a variable called
TestParameter has already been created, defined as an unsigned int, and given it

a value of 1. Once we click on the OK button, we'll be taken back to the Parameter Mapping window and will be able to select TestParameter as the global variable to which to map Parameter 1.

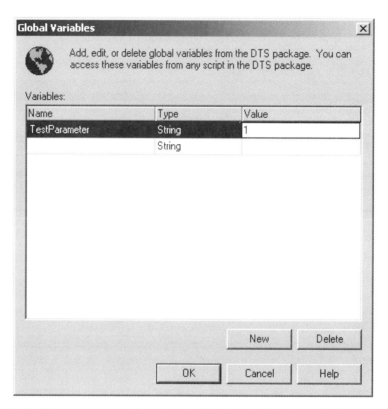

Figure 14-16. We can create and maintain global variables through the Global Variables window.

OK, now that we've created a parameterized query and given the parameter a value, let's finish up with the tabs in the Transform Data Task Properties window. Then we'll cover how to modify the global variables in "How Do I Run a DTS Package?"

How Do I Define the Destination for the Task?

The Destination tab of the Transform Data Task Properties dialog box is where we define the table/columns that will receive the information being transformed. This is a fairly straightforward, fill-in-the-blanks (FITB) type of window (see Figure 14-17). This window is very much like the one we used in the wizard. We can modify the column names and data types, and we can choose which sheet will be the destination for the data.

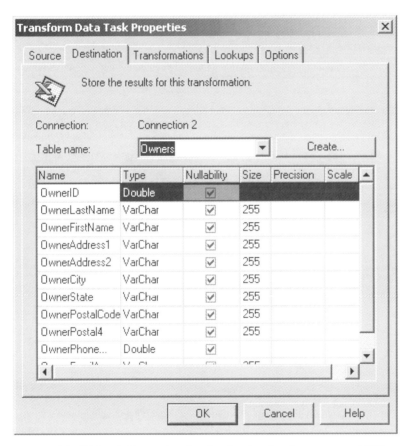

Figure 14-17. Modifying information for the destination is a matter of filling in the blanks.

A Closer Look at Transformations

Now let's take a closer look at the Transformations tab (see Figure 14-18). This tab is the heart of the data transformation task, and it looks slightly different than it did in the Import/Export Wizard. All of the source columns point to a destination column, but they all bunch up in the middle. This is a good thing because it means there is only one transformation to run for each row.

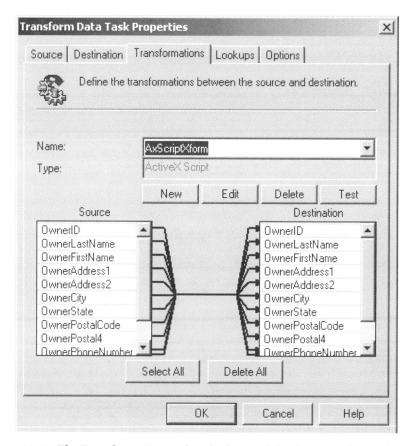

Figure 14-18. The Transformations tab is the heart of the data transformation task.

This is, however, a simple transformation, but we could make it more complex. The Postal Service prefers that all addresses be in uppercase, so let's rebuild our transformation from scratch by pressing the Delete All button to remove all existing transformations. Now that we have a clean slate, we can start building a new transformation.

The easiest way to create a transformation is to select the columns in the source grid and then select the matching columns in the destination grid. Once we've selected the columns, press the New button and we'll be presented with a list of transformation options. This is a nice feature of SQL Server 2000. Microsoft took the most commonly created ActiveX script tasks and turned them into optimized transformations. Now, instead of having to write a bunch of `DTSDestination(colname)` = `DTSSource(colname)` we can now have all of that done behind the scenes. Table 14-1 details the types of tasks that Microsoft has included. For this demonstration, we'll select Uppercase String and press OK.

Table 14-1. DTS Transformations Provided by Microsoft in SQL Server 2000

TRANSFORMATION	DESCRIPTION
Copy Column	Moves data from source to destination with no change
Date Time String	Creates a formatted string from a `DATETIME` or `SMALLDATETIME` data type
Lowercase String	Changes all letters to lowercase
Middle of String	Helps to remove spaces or to upper/lowercase a portion of the string
Read File	Puts the contents of a file into a destination column (handy for moving image files into a database, which isn't recommended)
Trim String	Trims excess spaces from the beginning, end, or both sides of a string
Uppercase String	Changes all letters to uppercase
Write File	Writes the contents of a column to either a new file or appends the data into another file (file's name is found in another column in the source)

First thing we'll do is an uppercase conversion. Select OwnerLastName, OwnerFirstName, OwnerAddress1, OwnerAddress2, OwnerCity, and OwnerState from both the Source and Destination grids, then click New. We can use Ctrl and Shift to select multiple columns, but be careful because any type mismatches (selecting to perform a uppercase conversion on a numeric field, for instance) will generate an error so make sure you've selected the correct columns. Now we are faced with the Transformation Options window open to the General tab (see Figure 14-19). From here we can further modify this transformation, including giving the transformation a more descriptive name like UpperCaseForPostalService.

If we press the Properties button, we'll be given a grid of the source and destination columns previously selected, so you can match them up correctly. That's pretty much all we can do from here. Now click OK or Cancel.

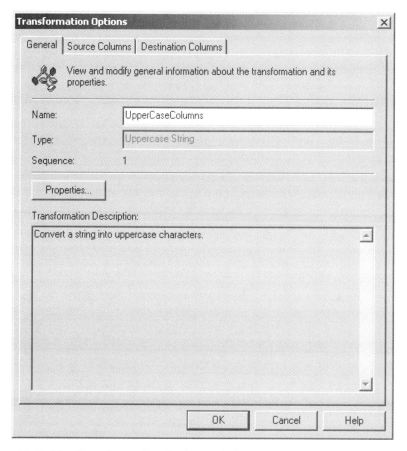

Figure 14-19. The Transformation Options window

What Are ActiveX Script Transformations?

ActiveX Script Transformations are snippets of VBScript or Jscript, similar to what we created through the Import/Export Wizard. When SQL Server 7 came out, many people used these scripts to perform the tasks that are now built-in transformations, such as uppercasing or trimming strings. It is better to use Microsoft's built-in transformations for these because they are optimized to run better than an interpreted script. That having been said, there are times when we need something beyond what Microsoft has provided. That's when we turn to ActiveX scripts.

One example that comes to mind is fixing the PostalCode and Postal4 columns. Although this should be done on the front end before data actually gets into the database, it is possible that data could have slipped past and been entered without the correct number of digits. The United States Postal Service would like to have five digits of a zip code with leading zeros if necessary. That way they don't need to figure out if 1302 is the first four or last four digits of the zip code. To accommodate them, we're going to create an ActiveX transformation that will zero fill any zip code that isn't five digits long.

To begin, select the OwnerPostalCode column for both the source and the destination from the Transform Data Task Properties window, press New and select ActiveX Script. That will take us to the Transformation Options window, just as it did when we were converting all of the address columns to uppercase characters. Rename it PostalCodeCleanup and then click on the Properties button. If you've followed along, your screen should look like Figure 14-20.

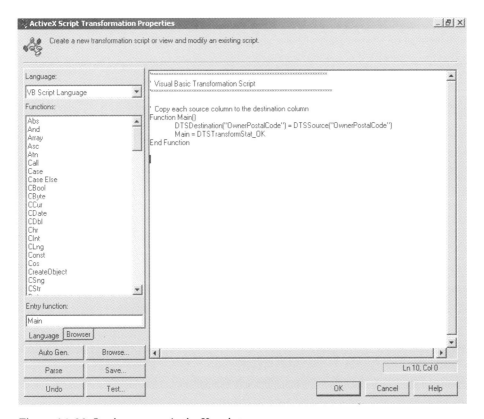

Figure 14-20. Setting up an ActiveX script

Along the left side of the screen we'll see a list of functions we can use and, below them, six buttons. Using these buttons we can load a saved script (Browse), save the script for future reference (Save), parse the script to test that it is syntactically correct (Parse), undo a change (Undo), or make sure the script actually works (Test). Perhaps the most interesting one is Auto Gen, however.

Auto Gen stands for *automagically* generated code. What it will do is create the `DTSDestination(colname) = DTSSource(colname)` lines of code. This button can be handy if we have added a lot of new source or destination columns. But, like many other helpful features, it doesn't play well with the script. It assumes that it owns all of the code and will erase any code in the function before it puts the *automagically* generated code out there. That means you should save your work frequently.

We're not going to get into all of the nuances of programming a VBScript within DTS, but let's look at the code used for this example (see Listing 14-2). All it does is determine the number of zeros it needs to prepend based on the length of the trimmed column.

Listing 14-2. ActiveX VB Script for padding OwnerPostalCodes with zeros

```
'***********************************************************************
'  Visual Basic Transformation Script
'***********************************************************************


'  Copy each source column to the destination column
Function Main()
  DTSDestination("OwnerPostalCode") = _
 String(5- len(trim(DTSSource("OwnerPostalCode"))),"0") _
 & trim(DTSSource("OwnerPostalCode"))
  Main = DTSTransformStat_OK
End Function
```

One way to improve performance would be to replace the column names with the column number. Whenever the interpreter encounters a column name, it is required to resolve that column name to the column number, so by replacing OwnerPostalCode with 7 (column counting begins with 0) we could improve performance. On a small table like this it might not matter, but on a large project it could save a lot of processing time. But this is not without its own unique problem. If columns are added or removed from the middle of a table, or columns are re-arranged (certainly not a good practice), then the column numbers will be incorrect. And, because such changes are rarely well documented, you will suddenly find yourself scrambling to fix a package that is suddenly broken because the database changed. This is another good reason to make sure you add columns to the end of tables or views or the results being returned from a stored procedure. It makes life easier on all involved.

The last step will be to click on the remaining columns, click New one more time and select Copy column. Then click OK. As with the previous steps, name the transformation and "be done with it."

How Many Transformations at a Time?

When we create transformations we could create a separate transformation for each column. The only problem with this is that each transformation runs separately. If we create two transformations, one to change the data for text columns to uppercase and one to copy the remaining columns, then SQL Server runs two transformations for each row of data, taking longer than if we can process one. With our final package (Owners2ExcelFinal.dts), we have three transformations (as shown in Figure 14-21):

- One to change the address information to uppercase letters

- One to prepend missing zeros to the zip code

- One to copy all of the rest of the columns

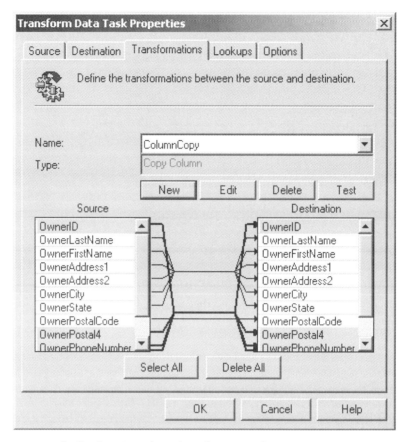

Figure 14-21. The final DTS package has three transformations.

Whenever possible, you want to make sure you are executing the fewest possible transformations. In this instance, the TSQL being used to pull data back could have been modified to perform all three of these actions and then a straight bulk insert task could have been used. The moral of the story? Always evaluate whether you're using the right tool for the job.

How Do I Run a DTS Package?

There are several ways to run a DTS package. These include:

- Opening the package in the DTS Designer and then selecting Package ➢Execute

- Creating all of the parameters for DTSRun and executing from the command prompt or a command script

- Running the DTSRunUI utility, which helps create all of the parameters for DTSRun

Let's take a look at DTSRun and DTSRunUI, starting with DTSRun. DTSRun takes several parameters that it uses for determining which package to run, which server to run it against, what security model and login to use for SQL Server, and the values of any global variables. To execute Owners2ExcelParameters, for instance, requires a simple command:

```
DTSRun /N "Owners2ExcelParameters" /V "{E92342BF-30DD-4B1B-88FD-167F9B8BFC30}"
    /F "D:\ReluctantDBA2\Packages\Owners2ExcelParameters.dts"
    /A "OwnerPostalCode":"8"="94563" /W "0"
```

Let's take a closer look at those parameters.

- /N is the name of the package—in this case, Owners2ExcelParameters. This is the name given when we saved the package.

- /V is the Package Version Global Universal IDentifier (GUID) String. Every time we revise and save the package, it saves a new version with a different GUID. This is how DTS actually tells which revision for which we are looking.

- /F is the name of the file in which the package is stored. If the package had been in a SQL Server then the server name, login, and password would be required.

- /A sets the value of a global variable—in this case, the variable OwnerPostalCode and the value 94563.

- /W determines whether the completion status is written to the event log.

If you've used DTS in SQL Server 7, then you know that creating these command strings can be a royal pain. (I will be the first to admit, however, that I cheated and used DTSRunUI, one of those really nice utilities included with SQL Server 2000.)

> **TIP**   *To put* DTSRunUI *at your fingertips, go into the EM and then select Tools* ➤ *External Tools. . . . From the window that comes up you can add* DTSRunUI *as a new external tool, and it will appear on the Tools menu. If SQL Server installed correctly you should be able to run* DTSRunUI *without providing the path for the program.*

To start DTSRunUI, go to a command prompt, type in DTSRunUI and hit the Enter key, or select it from the Tools menu after adding it. Once we've got DTSRunUI running, it's as easy as filling in the blanks. As shown in Figure 14-22, DTSRunUI is a FITB application. The most confusing part of the interface is that we need to select how the package is stored (SQL Server, Meta Data, or Structured Storage File), then go down to the bottom panel and actually find the package's storage location and finally open the actual package in the middle prompt. Once we get around that minor inconvenience, we're ready to set up a package to run.

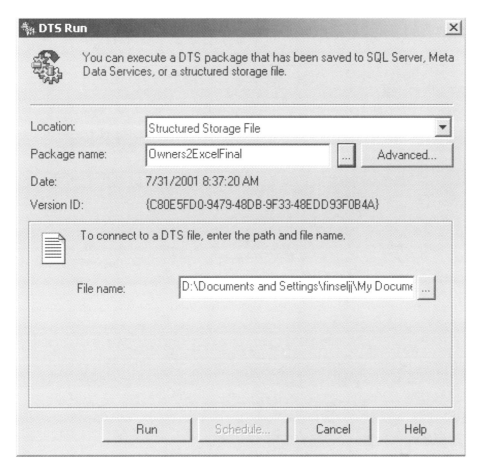

Figure 14-22. DTSRunUI *makes it easy to run DTS packages.*

Click on the Advanced button to bring up the Advanced DTS Run window. Here is where life gets a whole lot easier than it was in SQL Server 7. To begin with, all of the global variables are listed in a drop-down box in the top grid. Select the variable you want to give a value to and then type in the value. DTSRunUI already has the package's GUID, package name, package location, and all of the other pieces of information it needs to be able to run. All we need to do is press the Generate button at the bottom of the screen. That creates a string that can be embedded in a program or run at a command prompt (see Figure 14-23). All we need to do is highlight the code and copy it to the clipboard.

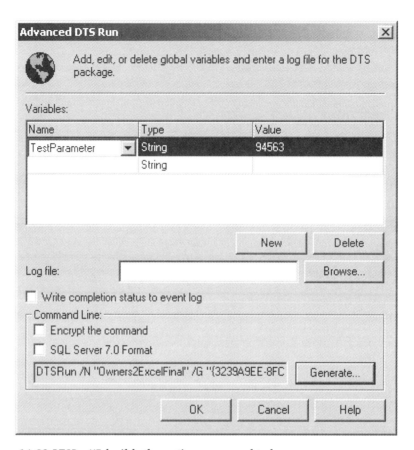

Figure 14-23. `DTSRunUI` *builds the entire command to be run.*

There's one last part of `DTSRunUI` we should cover and that's the how and why of encrypting the `DTSRun` command. If the package had been stored inside SQL Server, then it might be necessary to have a SQL login and password in the command prompt. If you have password protected your package, then that information would be in the command prompt. Having passwords in clear text that anyone can read is never a good idea, so SQL Server allows you to encrypt the command. It's actually an option on the `DTSRun` program to return all of your parameters as encoded parameters (/!Y). This is what the encrypted DTSRun command looks like:

```
DTSRun
/~Z0xE6F6B6255FA141AEB9E1F07F01678EE08387D4E8C676B0ADF0004B979CD54BFDD2065E6B7EFC
5D7F16022C986B929AF9F711EF825E2948B274ABA932CCFD2506564F3A36AF075C0DF88D90E062C32
AF8A8DB8E3D7201C917E1DC02B6D2EA8A270367B47F2F62F618729E102A1EF3C3D5855C8E7B0B0E2D
AE619C7AD1EDE215364E152EF9B430E865184891E6B89758436A397EB87CB0056DBE03E2D3952E7DE
C7932C35ADB08386085F87F00A9FDE51837039579D3DD759CDCA82E6537721995522713A609152FC9
A96CC33C6E420BC2504A554FD52A0AB2528B11940CA78A03F8EC28DAEFF8F13FA384B17DED389779D
CDD99127D3288EEADC487E5C4DB7692E4066016080908BF8717FA907CBE53920A6AB6CE29EFACA508
79653BE04FD27B3A1B3DA6B3DF9746421CE6DFB1A65CA20986220CFAB945FA54D2724D21732CCAFA4
6BC0036FA262ED7C1323A7B29B5629FD5FC263F4B4B779F449D6CFDA915E573B6C11EFC63981A2428
1434860934A7C617EFE52CEBE61B570221EAF83DB73D46CD514A4948778542DA9A0C3B77A20CF4754
02D249A26BB6AC630328F3ED9E06532265EA9D0098689440447042BB9D3E53FAE2C4C00242FFE29F8
143E35177E7E7E5E3000686B9F51264F4E9AF0CFC3957EADFF8B9B59AB183E77
```

 When you schedule a DTS package, you'll find that SQL Server encrypts the command by default. If you need to determine what DTS is being run (due to a cryptic name, for example), simply use the DTSRun *command to "un-crypt" the command.*

Last Words

SQL Server's Data Transformation Services are a powerful tool that can make many projects easier. I would recommend you invest some time in exploring this tool and in checking out the available books and online resources. Also, I recommend you take the examples presented in this chapter and see what you can do to improve them. Much of the work done in the ActiveX script could have been done through TSQL, especially if the data manipulation is simple (parsing columns, concatenating data, or just changing case). But transformations can be useful and powerful especially when dealing with "conditional" issues or disparate data/data types.

Resources

- When I first needed to use DTS, I wasn't getting far in doing what I wanted with Books On Line, so I hit the bookstores, only to find there weren't really any books on the subject. To my utter delight, however, one book was chock full of the information necessary to help me do my job and to go further than I thought possible with DTS. Although there are a couple of new DTS books out, I haven't found one I like better than this one: *Microsoft SQL Server 2000 DTS* by Timothy Peterson (Sams).

- This book came out about the same time but wasn't in the bookstore when I went looking for DTS books, and it is as good as Peterson's book: *Professional SQL Server 2000 DTS (Data Transformation Service)* by Mark Chaffin, Brian Knight, and Todd Robinson (Wrox Press).

- Microsoft's online documentation and DTS overview:
  `http://msdn.microsoft.com/library/en-us/dtssql`
  `/dts_tools_des_07xh.asp`

- This article demonstrates how to program within the DTS object model: "DTS and SQL DMO" by Josef Finsel, *Visual Studio Magazine*, September 2001.

- For more from Microsoft on structured storage files:
  `http://msdn.microsoft.com/library/en-us/mapi/html/_mapi1book_`
  `structured_storage.asp`

CHAPTER 15

Should I Bother to Learn SQL Profiler?

*Wanting people to listen, you can't just tap them on the shoulder any-
more. You have to hit them with a sledgehammer, and then you'll
notice you've got their strict attention.* —John Doe, *Se7en*

RELUCTANT DATABASE ADMINISTRATORS (DBAs) often feel like they're on the receiving
end of that "sledgehammer." Performance issues can come back to haunt us,
almost with a vengeance, and all too often it's not for lack of proper planning.
After all, we frequently build databases based on unrealistic or even nonexistent
specifications. Still, we try to simulate what we believe the load characteristics
will be like, such as the quantity of data to expect, the type and diversity of
queries, and so forth. But human nature is unpredictable, and when we're working with an Internet audience, the diversity is exponential.

   In this chapter we're going to explore Profiler, a tool that helps us survive,
and maybe even avoid, some of those sledgehammers.

What Is SQL Profiler?

SQL Profiler can help you to build a better database or application, and it can
help you troubleshoot an existing database or application. Up until SQL Server
6.5, determining query performance problems was rather challenging. Your best
option was to use Query Analyzer (QA) in an attempt to expose the problem and
then determine what part of the application may have been running at that time.
Early on, this procedure was a little easier because you would get feedback from
end users who, while performing a given operation in an application, would
notice a performance change or other abnormality. Based on their feedback, you
would do a little digging, run some tests, and—with some effort and patience—
find the troubling code. Sometimes it was a "prepared statement" and sometimes
a stored procedure, but often it could be as simple as needing an index where you
hadn't anticipated needing one.

   Today, databases have become far more complex as their usage becomes
more diverse and as many Relational DataBase Management Systems (RDBMSs)

such as SQL Server begin to co-mingle and, in some cases, replace legacy systems. Databases have also become far more widespread—thanks in part to companies such as Microsoft putting these products within financial reach of small- to medium-sized businesses and in part to the prolific expansion of Web-based business. Further, many company departments now want to "share" the data that has been collecting over time and finally begin to prove its worth. One such example is Knowledge Base applications. Initially these databases were created as a means of collecting consumer complaints, problems, suggestions, and so forth to aid technical support staff. Now sales, marketing, and manufacturing departments depend on access to these systems to make decisions that dictate current and future products.

Sharing a database has its benefits. The benefits, obviously, are uniformity, centralization of information, availability, and so on. But these benefits can at times lead to problems. For example, the uniformity of the information may be such that determining demographics is difficult or impossible, and the centralization of data may place restrictions on what is collected and how it's recorded (tight control of design could hamper or delay change). However, a lack of uniformity can also cause problems. For example, with differing methods of design and recording, one design may have a full_name column in a table, and another part of the same system may have first_name and last_name, which would force parsing data for the prior and concatenating for the latter, not an ideal situation for reporting. Another problem is duplicity, where the same type of information, such as an address, is maintained in multiple tables (a customer address showing up in a [customer] table and an [invoice] table), leaving one wondering which version is accurate.

So what, if anything, do these problems have to do with SQL Profiler? Well, Profiler helps determine where problems exist. For example, it can weed out problems that stem from poor indices, from applications that have too many connections open, or from applications that don't close connections no longer used. Profiler can also help you find security issues, such as someone using an unauthorized application to access SQL Server. Problems don't have to be related or limited to performance and security.

Prior to SQL Server 6.5, uncovering problems could be a cumbersome proposition requiring monitoring processes using sp_who, performing selects out of sysprocesses, or using DataBase Consistence Checks (DBCCs). Using these methods separated the "wannabes" from the true practitioners. After all, you had to be either a hard-core DBA or a seriously unstable individual to take on such a challenge.

So, with version 6.5, Microsoft introduced the SQL Trace Utility. This allowed the monitoring of transactions in real time, thus adding a new tool to a DBA's arsenal. With SQL Server 7.0, Trace Utility evolved and became Profiler. But Microsoft didn't stop there: With SQL Server 2000, it enhanced Profiler even more. Profiler is a tool that goes well beyond simply tracing the activity on a server, so much so that you can target a host, login, application, Server Process ID (SPID), and on and on. Its functions and filters are almost limitless.

Books On Line (BOL) says it best: "SQL Profiler provides a graphical user interface to a set of stored procedures that can be used to monitor an instance of SQL Server." Yes, Profiler uses stored procedures; in fact, these same stored procedures can be accessed directly. The problem is that learning all the switches and syntax makes this method impractical. On the other hand, it does allow you to leverage a particular stored procedure, maybe for an in-house troubleshooting tool if you so desire. Let's take a quick look at Profiler, but first we should be aware of the following:

- Profiler requires at least 10 megabytes of free space to operate.

- To run SQL Profiler, you must be a member of the sysadmin server role.

Using SQL Profiler to Work with Traces

To start SQL Profiler, click Start and select Programs ➤ Microsoft SQL Server ➤ Profiler. You can also start Profiler from the Enterprise Manager (EM) by choosing Tools ➤ SQL Profiler. This brings up Profiler, as shown in Figure 15-1.

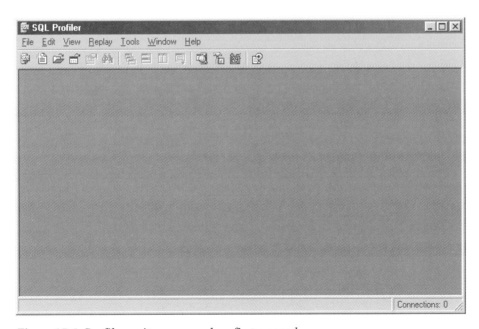

Figure 15-1. Profiler as it appears when first opened

Before we get into the standard menu items in Profiler, we'll create a new trace. This procedure activates most of the options under the various menus. There are three ways to create a new trace:

- Click on the New Trace button.

- Use the shortcut keys Ctrl+N.

- Select File ➢ New ➢ Trace.

Performing any of these three actions brings up a familiar dialog box, Connect to SQL Server (see Figure 15-2).

Figure 15-2. A dot (.) appears where the server name would be. This is permissible when connecting to a local installation, but a better practice is to use the name of the server because it is displayed in the window's title.

This dialog box looks like the QA logon dialog box. We'll select the SQL Server we want to connect to and optionally start it, if it's not currently running. This is also where we choose the method to connect to SQL Server with, either Windows Authentication or SQL Server Authentication, with the latter requiring a login and password. For this example, we'll choose the server we have the **RDBA11** database installed on and select the method of connection using an account or login that has sa privileges. Then we'll click OK. This brings up the Trace Properties dialog box, as shown in Figure 15-3. It contains four tabs: General, Events, Data Columns, and Filters. We'll talk about each in turn.

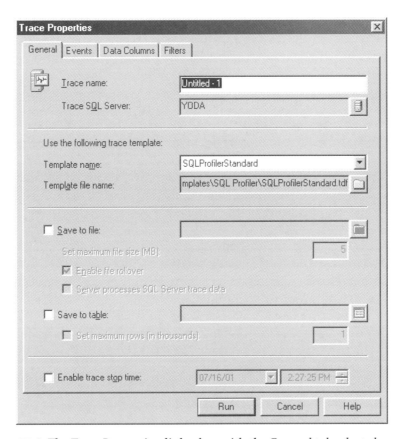

Figure 15-3. The Trace Properties dialog box with the General tab selected

The General Tab

On the General tab, the Trace Name option is where we name our trace. Users of 7.0 should note that the Shared and Private options are no longer supported. If, for some reason, we didn't select the correct server at logon, we can change our selection by typing the server name or clicking on the button to the right, which opens the Connect to SQL Server dialog box again.

The next section on this tab is for naming and/or selecting a template. The Template Name is where we define the objects, events, and filters we want to use for this trace. Both traces and templates must have unique names and are saved in files local to the machine. As with objects such as tables, stored procedures, and views, it's good practice to use meaningful and intuitive names (initially the trace comes up "Untitled - 1," and the template name is "SQLProfilerStandard"). Note that the default location for the file is "My Documents," the path of which varies with the user that is logged in and the operating system being used. For example, in Win2k would be "C:\Documents and Settings\[login name]\My Documents." Although this is convenient, we could also save templates in the "Templates" folder, which can be found in the following path: "\Program Files\Microsoft SQL Server\80\Tools\Templates." We could also create a folder for our trace files.

The next section is where we select the Save to File option. When we click on this checkbox we get the standard Save As dialog box, with the File Name box already populated (with the name we gave the trace and once again using the default path for our files). Note the .trc extension for the file; this is helpful in case we need to perform a search for a trace file on our own system, someone else's system, or maybe even a server. If we don't choose to save our trace, none of the events we monitor are saved to file. (We'll cover using the trace file in the "Using SQL Profiler's Menus" section.)

Once we check the Save to File option, three options are enabled: Set Maximum File Size (MB), Enable File Rollover, and Server Processes SQL Sever Trace Data. The first of these options is pretty self explanatory; however, it should be pointed out that not only would it be prudent to set a value for Set Maximum File Size (MB), but the default maximum is 1GB, so this could render a server useless if the drive used is also used by the operating system and there is less than 1GB free. When Enable File Rollover is selected (which it is by default), Profiler automatically generates a new file when the current running file hits the maximum size limit. The new file carries the same name except that a numerical extension is added; in other words, rdba_trace.trc would become rdba_trace_1.trc. The Server Processes. . . option is a little more complicated. BOL explains it best:

> *Specify that the server running the trace should process the trace data. If selected, no events will be skipped under stress conditions; however, performance of the server may be affected, depending on the number of events being traced. If this check box is cleared, then the processing is performed by the client application, and there is a possibility that some events will not be traced under stress conditions.*

The next option in this section is to Save to Table. When you check this option, the Destination Table dialog box comes up, as shown in Figure 15-4.

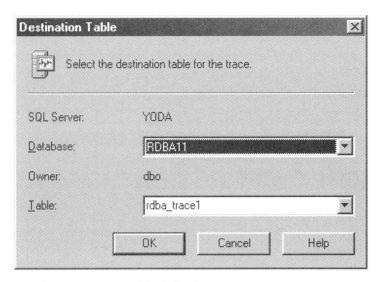

Figure 15-4. The Destination Table dialog box

Note the server listed is the server to which we're connected. First, we'll select the database and the table into which we will capture the trace data.

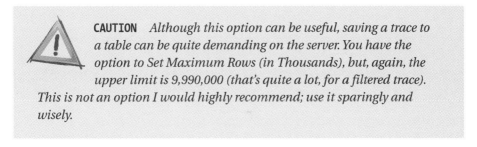

CAUTION *Although this option can be useful, saving a trace to a table can be quite demanding on the server. You have the option to Set Maximum Rows (in Thousands), but, again, the upper limit is 9,990,000 (that's quite a lot, for a filtered trace). This is not an option I would highly recommend; use it sparingly and wisely.*

Click Cancel to return to the Trace Properties dialog box and deselect Save to Table. The last option for this tab is Enable Trace Stop Time. When we select this option, we can set the date and time we want Profiler to stop and automatically close. This feature can be handy if we need to capture data during a specific time frame and stop at a designated time. The start time may be a time when suspected processes kick off, thus avoiding processes that may skew the results in the trace, or a time frame that avoids undesirable activity. One possible scenario would be to say, "I don't want to stay until 'Oh dark thirty' to stop the trace." In other words, we may have a need to start a trace, or it needs to start late in the evening and then complete later that evening or maybe the next day. In any case, we don't want to stay at work until it's time to start and stop the trace. Scheduling obviously is preferable in such a case.

The Events Tab

We'll now move on to the Events tab, as shown in Figure 15-5. Events are activities such as a connection to SQL Server, an execution of a stored procedure, and so on.

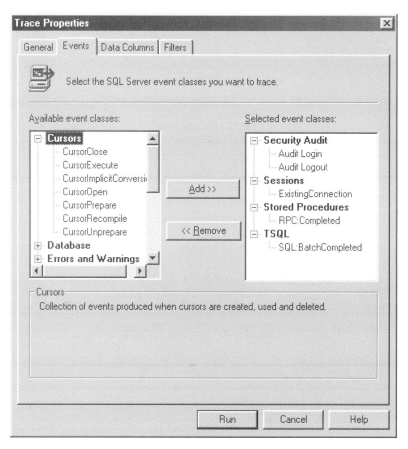

Figure 15-5. The Events tab for the Trace Properties dialog box

This tab is what Profiler is all about. This is where we select the events (SQL Server connect/disconnect, execution of stored procedures, SQL code passed by an application, and so on). The left pane, Available Event Classes, lists events grouped in event classes. One such class is Cursors. Next to an event class is a plus (+) symbol. When clicked, this displays all the events available for that class. For example, the following appear under Cursors: CursorClose, CursorExecute, CursorImplicitConversion, and so on. When we click on an event class such as Cursor, we see a description of that class in the text area below the list. If we choose a template, event classes and events appear in the right pane,

Selected Event Classes. Between the two panes are the Add and Remove buttons (for adding or removing events and or event classes), but we can simply double-click on an event or an event class to add or remove the event, event class, or all a class's event. Type in "rdba_trace" for the trace name, select the Save to File option, accept the default name, and then click OK. You should now see a screen like the one shown in Figure 15-6.

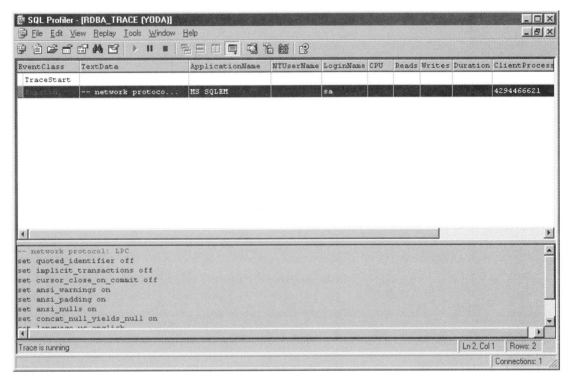

Figure 15-6. SQL Profiler just after a trace session is started

Most of the buttons are now enabled. You can get a description of each button by moving your cursor over it. The icon that looks like a new document is the New Template button. The next eleven buttons should look familiar, including the Play, Pause, and Stop buttons, common on CD players and debuggers. Following the group of eleven buttons is one that may not be familiar: Auto Scroll Window. This button turns scrolling on or off, and only those speed-readers who are monitoring a lot of traffic will want the Auto Scroll on. The last four buttons should look familiar: SQL Server Query Analyzer, SQL Server Enterprise Manager, Performance Monitor (covered in Chapter 16, "What Are System Monitor and Performance Monitor?"), and Help.

Earlier on when we were on the General Tab, we chose to use the default template that has all the columns in Figure 15-6, plus the following columns to the right that are not visible: SPID and Start Time. When we select a row in the window, we get details for the TextData column appearing in the bottom pane. Notice that in Figure 15-6 there are a number of SET commands that took place when we created the trace. The screen provides the following information:

- ApplicationName: This is the name of the application used to connect to SQL Server (in this figure it's Microsoft SQL Enterprise Manager).

- NTUserName: We're not using Windows Authentication in this example, but had we been we would see the NT Account for this row/entry.

- LoginName: This is the login used to connect to SQL Server. If the NTUserName had an entry, and that user belonged to the NT Administrators group, this entry would still be sa.

- CPU: This is the processor cycles in milliseconds.

- Reads: This is the number of "logical" reads performed by the server on behalf of the event.

- Writes: This is the number of writes performed by the server on behalf of the event.

- Duration: This is the amount of time taken by the event.

- ClientProcessID: This is provided by the client and is the process ID assigned by the host (not the SQL Server).

- SPID: This is the process assigned by SQL Server.

- Start Time: This is the time the transaction began.

Right away the value of trace information becomes apparent, for example, the duration and CPU cycles. These alone can be invaluable when trying to determine how efficient or inefficient a query is. The Duration field tells us how long the SQL ran, and the CPU field tells just how many CPU cycles have been used.

 TIP *Measures like CPU are cumulative, meaning that this is the total amount of CPU utilization for this session, so an idle connection will still show CPU cycles but will only grow with activity.*

The status line at the bottom indicates if the trace is running, paused, or stopped. To the right is the line number that is selected, the column that the cursor is in for the selected row, and the number of rows in the trace. In the lower-right corner is the number of connections, which is the number of traces that are running.

People often don't realize just how busy SQL Server is, so we're going to simply fire up a session of the QA. Figure 15-7 shows what happens when we do.

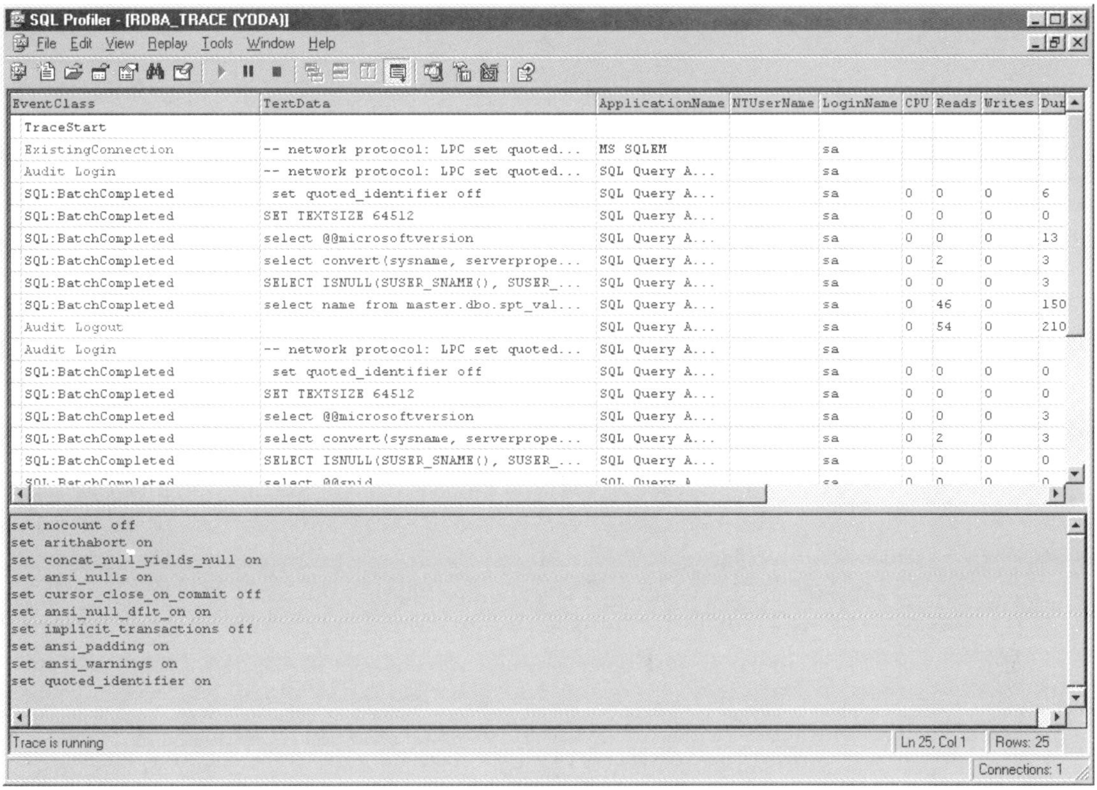

Figure 15-7. Example of trace information resulting from launching the QA

There are now twenty-five lines in the Profiler trace, and all we did was connect to SQL Server using the QA! Once again, the wealth of information and value of Profiler is apparent. Imagine connect information being sent by the application. Then, assume that SET commands (like in Figure 15-7) are being issued; these of course are not immediately apparent unless you're intimately familiar with the application. SET commands, of course, can change the behavior of SQL Server for the connection that issued the command(s). There are many such options, but without a Profiler Trace, they become stealth objects, so you'll never know they've occurred. Take, for example, `set ansi_nulls` on from the sample set in Figure 15-7. This instructs SQL Server to treat any comparison with `NULL` as unknown. If the application was written to recognize only `TRUE` or `FALSE` answers, an error may not necessarily be generated, but the application certainly will be affected. Although this is merely an example, the point is that the trace will capture detailed information that you won't catch in `sp_who`, the sysprocesses system table, or using DBCC.

Take a second to launch the QA and then examine what happens in your trace, following these steps:

1. In the QA, use the Database drop-down list to pick the **RDBA11** database (if it isn't already selected) and then choose Examine Trace.

2. Now, run the following SQL statement in the QA: `SELECT * from MentorList`. Notice only one line was entered, showing the difference between executing a simple `SELECT` statement in the QA and the many rows that show up when simply connecting to the server.

3. Now, copy the code for the MentorList view (using the EM), paste it into the QA, run it, and then go back to your trace. We'll see the code has been run, but in addition to this we see the entire SQL statement!

Just imagine a complex join and then imagine a stored procedure! Now we'll be able to see what was executed, how long it took, and so on. This information was also available using DBCC, but unfortunately it truncated the SQL (which has a limit of 255 characters), severely limiting its usefulness.

Now we'll bring up the properties (the fifth button from the left), so we can go into a little more detail on the event classes. Leave the current trace running, and then click the Properties button. The first thing to notice is that every option on every tab is disabled, and there are no classes listed in the Available Event Classes list on the Events tab! How did that happen? Profiler won't allow us to edit a trace that is running, so we need to exit this dialog box, stop the trace, and then bring the properties back up.

Now, let's make some simple changes. First, let's remove Security Audit, which will remove all the events in that class. Normally we would do this for a trace where we're not interested in security (for the moment). This will help keep traffic down. We can remove it by selecting Security Audit and clicking the Remove button or simply double-clicking on Security Audit in the right-hand pane. Now, go to Stored Procedures under Available Event Classes and click on the + symbol so we can display all the events. Now add RPC by either selecting it and clicking Add or just double-clicking on the event.

The Data Columns Tab

Now, let's move on to the Data Columns tab, which is shown in Figure 15-8. We have two panes to work with, Unselected Data and Selected Data, as well as a text area that provides a description of the selected column. The Data Columns tab allows us to tailor the display so that we only see the information that assists us in troubleshooting the server. We won't discuss the columns in detail because the descriptions are easy to understand. The right pane not only lists the columns that have been selected, but it displays them in the order they were initially selected or last saved. To change the order in which the columns are displayed, simply click on the column and then click on the Up or Down buttons to move it. When we select a column on the right side, its description appears in the text area labeled "Columns."

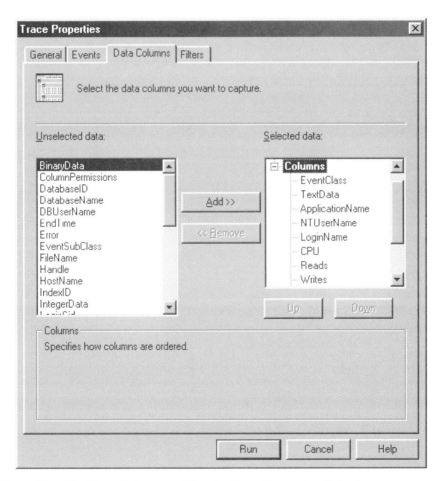

Figure 15-8. The Data Columns tab for the Trace Properties dialog box

The Filters Tab

The next tab we'll look at is the Filters tab, shown in Figure 15-9. The two most important tabs are Events and Filters. Unlike Events, which allows you to identify what types of events you're interested in, Filters allows you to eliminate extraneous information and focus on select users, SPIDs, databases, and so on. There is so much we can filter on; it's incredible. We could, for example, concentrate on an application and, more specifically, a host. Why? Let's say we have multiple Web servers connecting to our SQL Server, but only one seems to be having problems. We can select the events we think are appropriate, then use filters to eliminate hosts we're not interested in monitoring while at the same time capturing only processes by a specific application. Think of filters as a way of controlling the number of rows returned, such as in a WHERE clause in SQL statements.

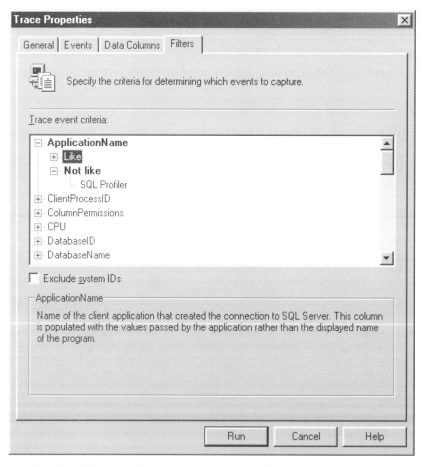

Figure 15-9. The Filters tab for the Trace Properties dialog box

The Trace Events Criteria pane displays the criteria for the default template or, if this is a customized trace or template, the criteria last saved. At this point, we should see Application Name highlighted and two subcriteria: Like and Not Like. Notice that the syntax is just like SQL Server queries: EQUAL, LIKE, NOT LIKE, and so on. Spelling and punctuation matter, so when we're filtering on an application such as Internet Information Server, we won't use "IIS" to find the application. If we're not sure what the application name is, we use the QA and execute sp_who. As long as we can identify the login or host, we should be able to identify the application.

Let's take a look at CPU. Click on CPU, and notice the description. If we have an application that is "chewing up" CPU cycles, we can use this filter to look at only processes using CPU cycles in four possible combinations (Equal, Not Equal To, Greater Than, Less Than). Let's say, for example, an application is perceived to be a "hog"; we'll likely want to use Greater Than, so click the plus sign next to CPU. Now, open Greater Than by clicking on the + symbol. We now have a place to put in a value. Type in the value "abc" and press Enter or click on another filter option. Notice we get an error telling us that only numeric values can be entered. Just like SQL Server queries, data types play a role in the filtering. Logically, if the criterion being filtered were numeric only, like an SPID or client process ID, we would be permitted to enter only a numeric value.

How do we know for what value we're looking? If we're monitoring Profiler on a busy system, it may not be an easy thing to watch for the specific ID, so click on the QA button (the fourth button from the right). Once in QA, we can run a simple sp_who to determine what ID or IDs we're interested in monitoring or ignoring. We could do this from the EM (which can also be launched from Profiler) as well by simply opening the SQL Server we're interested in, then opening Management, then opening Current Activity, and then clicking on Process Info. This procedure takes longer than just running a query, so if you get familiar with the QA, you'll often find that as you become more comfortable with writing SQL, you'll be able to work more efficiently in the QA than drilling through layers of objects in the EM.

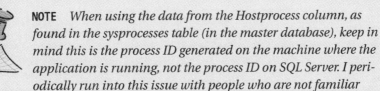

NOTE *When using the data from the Hostprocess column, as found in the sysprocesses table (in the master database), keep in mind this is the process ID generated on the machine where the application is running, not the process ID on SQL Server. I periodically run into this issue with people who are not familiar with from where the process ID actually comes. This information will come in handy should you locate a bad process and need to kill that process, because you will have to kill the process at the source (often using* KILL *in SQL Server won't do the job). Some people resort to rebooting the server running the application or SQL Server, but this is often* not *necessary when you know the process ID.*

TIP *The Hostprocess is a Hex value, so depending on what tool you use, you may have to convert this value to decimal to locate the process in the tool of your choosing. Calculator comes with a great scientific calculator that will, among other things, convert Hex to Dec or vice versa.*

Using SQL Profiler's Menus

Now that we've covered the basics of how to set up a trace, including picking events and setting filters, we're going to step through Profiler's menus. The File menu is pretty self-explanatory, so we'll just talk about one option that may not be intuitive: File ➢ Save As ➢ SQL Script. By choosing the SQL Script option, we create a file that we can run and rerun for testing purposes, such as for testing an artificial load or for testing index modifications (we'll cover this in "Profiler and the Index Tuning Wizard"). With this file we can test servers that are configured differently to see what kind of performance we get running the exact same load and queries on different configurations. Maybe we're talking hardware, maybe we're talking operating system configuration, but whatever the scenario, we now have something with which to work. If you collected this information from your production environment, you have a script that truly simulates a "real-world" load and scenario. Pretty cool, huh? For now let's accept the default path, enter the name "rdba_trace" and click Save.

The other option under the File menu that we want to talk about is Script Trace. When selected, this displays a submenu with two options: For SQL Server 2000 and For SQL Server 7.0. Script Trace is not the same thing as Save As ➢ SQL Script; instead, this lets you script the trace itself, thus allowing you to transport this trace to other machines or to send it to a remote site for testing a similar server. This feature is beyond the scope of this book, but be aware that it's available.

Now that we have a SQL script saved, how do we use it? Let's go back to File ➢ Open ➢ SQL Script and select the file we just saved. You should now see a screen that looks like Figure 15-10.

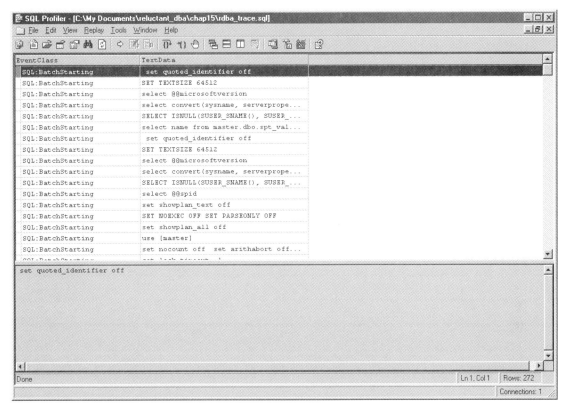

Figure 15-10. A SQL script file opened for replay. Notice all the standard SQL commands collected using trace.

Note that this is a new window, and your last trace should still be open. (To confirm this, click on the Window menu, and you should see the trace listed.) This is what BOL has to say:

> *When you create or edit a trace, you can save the trace to replay it later. SQL Profiler features a multithreaded playback engine that can simulate user connections and SQL Server Authentication, allowing the user to reproduce the activity captured in the trace. Therefore, replay is useful when troubleshooting an application or process problem. When you have identified the problem and implemented corrections, run the trace that found the potential problem against the corrected application or process, then replay the original trace to compare results.*

This screen should have some familiar buttons such as Executing One Step at a Time, Run to Cursor, Toggle Breakpoint, and so on. So, we have a number of really cool tools and options for debugging. These features can be useful for refinements in our application or database. To run the script, we click on the Play button (the yellow arrow) and get the familiar Connect to SQL Server dialog box. Profiler doesn't assume the script will be run against the server that the script was created on or the server that we are currently connected to with your trace. This is a good thing; after all, if we were connected to a production server, would we really want to rerun these scripts against that production server? Once we've filled in the dialog box options and clicked OK, we get the screen shown in Figure 15-11.

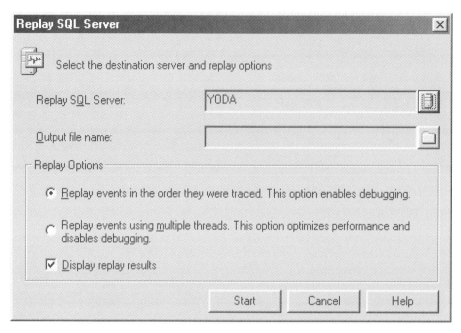

Figure 15-11. The Replay SQL Server dialog box is where you pick the server to execute the SQL script and the replay options to use

We'll see the server listed in the Replay SQL Server box; if this is wrong click the Server icon and enter the correct server. Next is the Output File Name option. Use this option to save the output of the test script for later review. Sometimes searching through a file for a specific error can be easier than scrolling through a live trace. To create the file, simply click on the folder icon to the right, pick a path, type in a name for the file, and click Save.

Next is the Replay Options section. The first option, Replay Events in the Order They Were Traced, plays the events in sequence. The second option, Replay Events Using Multiple Threads, uses multiple threads, but when we select this option, debugging is disabled. If the script you've chosen to run is rather large, we might consider deselecting Display Replay Results. Having it enabled adds load to the process, and, besides, we won't likely be able to read everything that goes by. Now we can click Start and let it rip. Depending on the speed of the machine and the SQL Server we're running against, we may actually see the cursor scrolling through the script executing each step. In theory, we could rerun this procedure a bunch of times to create an even larger test script, but it won't be realistic because we'll be repeating the same events over and over.

The Tools menu allows us to launch the Index Tuning wizard, the QA, the EM, Client Network Utility, and Performance Monitor. The remaining two menus are pretty straightforward. Just about everything in the main menus is represented by a toolbar button with the exception of a couple of options under the File menu: Toggle Bookmark and Next Bookmark, used when debugging the SQL script file.

Profiler and the Index Tuning Wizard

Ah, but wait, there is one more thing we need to discuss, something hinted at earlier: indexing! So many SQL Server tools are intertwined in such a way that the tools now work together in ways we could only imagine (thank you, Microsoft!). One such integration is between Profiler and the Index Tuning wizard. We've covered the Index Tuning wizard in Chapter 7, "The Power of Indexing," but we'll go through it again for a special reason. Start by opening the Index Tuning wizard (Tools ➤ Index Tuning Wizard), which brings up the Welcome screen. Select Next and, once again, we get the Connect to SQL. . . dialog box. Complete this screen and click OK. The next screen looks like Figure 15-12.

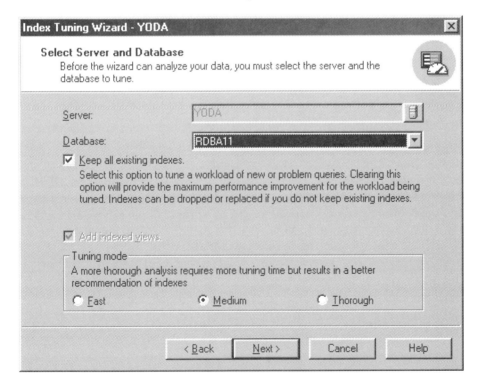

Figure 15-12. The Index Tuning Wizard dialog box. Note the Tuning Mode options. These options have a significant impact on the index tests and final recommendations.

In the figure, the **RDBA11** database has already been selected. Remember to check Keep All Existing Indexes; otherwise, they will be replaced with the new ones created through this process (unless, of course, that is wanted). Note the option Add Indexed Views is not available. We can create indexed views only if we install Microsoft SQL Server 2000 Enterprise Edition or Microsoft SQL Server 2000 Developer Edition.

As for the tuning mode, that's each DBA's own call, but heed this advice provided in the Tuning Mode section: "A more thorough analysis requires more tuning time but results in a better recommendation of indexes." Although thorough is the best choice, it would be best to perform this on a test server. After completing this dialog box, click Next. Now we come to the good stuff. Remember the SQL Script file we created earlier in this chapter? We should now have a screen like the one shown in Figure 15-13.

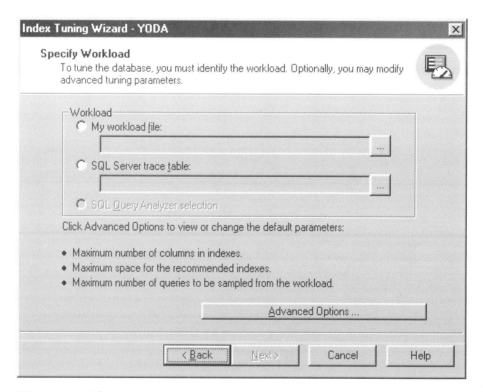

Figure 15-13. The next step for the Index Tuning wizard, which is the Specify Workload dialog box. Here we specify the source for the workload.

Notice the Workload options? When we created the trace log, we had a choice between creating a file and writing the information to a table. From here we can choose to use the script we saved or a table (if that's where we chose to save the script). Let's assume that the file option was selected and click on My Workload

File, then select the Script file that was saved, and click Open. The next option we have is Advanced Options (see Figure 15-14).

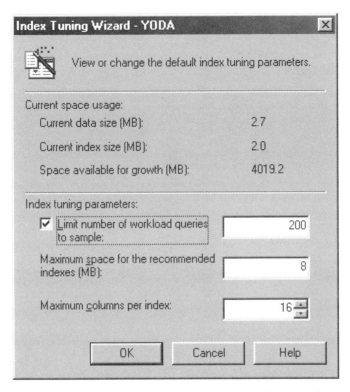

Figure 15-14. The next step for the Index Tuning wizard, which are the tuning parameters. From here we configure the degree of index testing that will be performed.

We want to make sure we have enough space in the Space Available for Growth option. This is, after all, the space on the disk drive, not the database! Under the Index Tuning Parameters section, we have a couple of options:

- Limit Number of Workload Queries to Sample: This is where we set the number of workload queries that we want to sample (the default is 200). If we enter a value higher than the number of queries we have, then all the queries are tuned.

- Maximum Space for the Recommended Indexes (MB): This is where we set the maximum space consumed by the recommended index set. The default space is three times the current data size or the maximum available space on all attached disk drives, whichever is the smaller number.

- Maximum Columns per Index: This is where we set the maximum number of columns in indices (the default, and maximum, is 16).

> **TIP** *Although SQL Server is not likely to use the maximum of sixteen columns for an index, it doesn't mean it won't, as this decision is based on the queries captured in your trace. If you have queries that routinely search sixteen or more columns, SQL Server may treat that as normal and recommend an index accordingly. In addition, if such a scenario applies, you may want to review the design of your database, as it's possible it may not be properly normalized.*

Once we've completed adjusting the parameters, we click OK. This will return us to the Index Tuning wizard. Now click Next. This brings us to the screen shown in Figure 15-15.

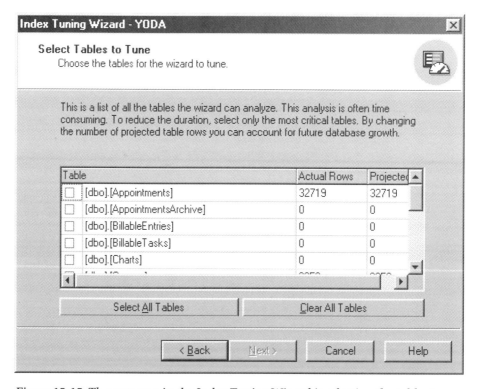

Figure 15-15. The next step in the Index Tuning Wizard is selecting the tables to be tuned

Although this whole operation has the potential of improving performance, it's only as good as the data or, more importantly, the quantity of data. It's not a simple task predicting how big a database will grow or, more specifically, what tables will grow and to what extent. The closer we come to real numbers, the better a job the Index Tuning wizard can do. So dummy up the data as best you can for a "new" database, or if available "borrow" data from production. Select only tables in the Index Tuning wizard that have data in them because selecting tables without data may not prove to be very useful—and may in fact add overhead with no benefit. As mentioned earlier, it's sometimes easier to simply click Select All and then deselect the tables we don't need. Once done, click on Next. That brings up the message shown in Figure 15-16.

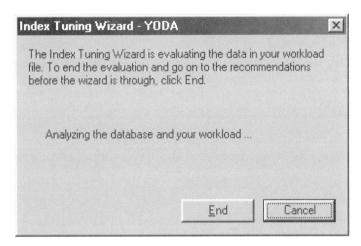

Figure 15-16. The Index Tuning wizard notifying us the wizard is ". . . evaluating the data in your workload. . . ."

This message lets us know the wizard is working. We only click Cancel at this point if we want to start over or the process has been running too long for our liking. In the case of the latter, we can start again and select fewer tables or use a more conservative setting for the interrogation. The next screen that comes up is the Index Recommendations screen, as shown in Figure 15-17.

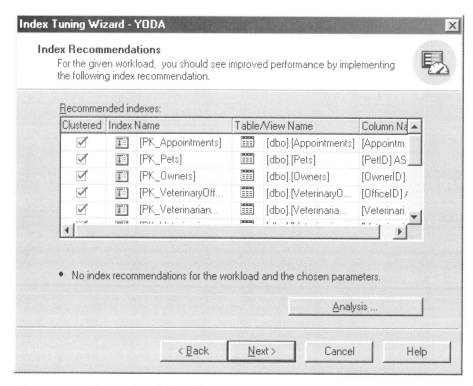

Figure 15-17. The results of the evaluation. Here we will see the recommended indices as proposed by the wizard based on the workload script used. The recommendations can vary depending on the size of the workload and the amount of data present in the tables.

To get the results shown in Figure 15-17, we removed all the indices from all the tables (except those created on the primary keys) so that we could see what the listing would look like. Otherwise it would have been empty (for a scenario where there in fact may be no need for changes). If we click on Analysis we'll get the screen shown in Figure 15-18.

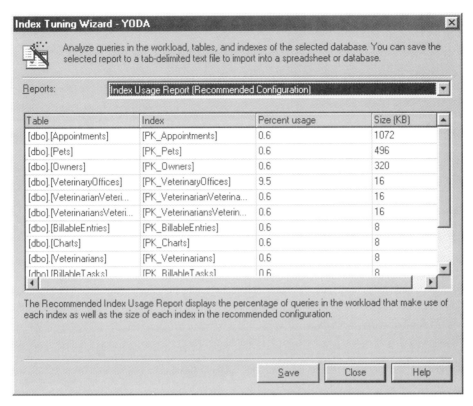

Figure 15-18. The reports available for the Index Tuning wizard. There are a number of valuable reports, all of which can be saved to file for further examination or for future reference.

Notice the Percent Usage column. In Figure 15-18, most of the tables show a 0.6 percent usage, in other words, ". . .the percentage of queries that make use of each index. . .." The exception is VeterinaryOffices, which shows 9.5. The wizard believes, correctly of course, that this table would benefit from indices, but note that this table is *not* one of the larger ones. In fact, it's less than a third the size of the largest. So, although the rule that the largest table is certainly a strong candidate for an index, never dismiss the smaller tables because indexing has a lot to do with how the tables are accessed and how often, not just how big they are.

The Index Tuning wizard offers several reports. One cool one is the Table Analysis Report, which shows the top 100 tables most heavily used by the workload. Keep in mind that the closer to "reality" your sample script is, the more accurate the results from the wizard will be. If we take some time to check each of the reports, we will find not only the data impressive, but that the report description is both meaningful and helpful. You also have the option to save the reports for reference. When you're done, select Close to return to the list of tables. When you click Next, you will be given an explanation of what can be done next, as shown in Figure 15-19.

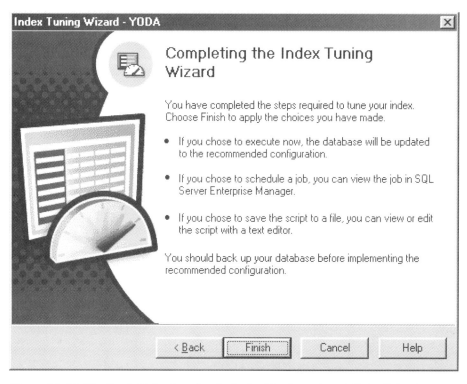

Figure 15-19. The final dialog box for the Index Tuning wizard. This dialog box simply notifies us of what will take place when we click Finish.

We have the option of implementing the recommended indices now, scheduling them to run at a specific time, or saving the script to a file. The typical inclination would be to run the scripts now or schedule them for off-peak hours, but keep in mind the potential load placed on the server, especially if we're working with tables containing millions of row of data. We may want to edit the script and possibly break it up into multiple jobs and schedule those separately to reduce the load on the server. We may want to consider testing it on a "staging" server to measure the impact of running the entire script at once. Whatever method we choose, make certain to consider impact; there's no point frustrating end-users with horrible performance, building indices to help improve performance and reliability, and so on.

Last Words

Profiler is a tool that can be used to help improve the quality and reliability of our applications, both the front end and the back end. When used in conjunction with other tools in Windows NT/2000 and SQL Server, it helps us build applications that will scale well and provide long and reliable service.

Resources

- See "Administering SQL Server," "Monitoring Server Performance and Activity," "Monitoring with SQL Profiler," and "Viewing and Analyzing Traces" in BOL for more information on these topics.

- On the BOL Index tab, type in "trace" and then double-click Replaying for more information about replaying traces saved as SQL scripts.

What Are System Monitor and Performance Monitor?

Well, boys, we got three engines out, we got more holes in us than
a horse trader's mule, the radio is gone, and we're leaking fuel, and if
we was flying any lower why we'd need sleigh bells on this thing . . .
but we got one little budge on those Roosskies. At this height why
thy might harpoon us but they dang sure ain't gonna spot us on no
radar screen!

—Major T. J. "King" Kong, *Dr. Strangelove*

THERE ARE TIMES BEING A database administrator (DBA) feels something like Major T. J. Kong did in *Dr. Strangelove.* Your processors are maxed, memory is running out, the hard drive where Windows Page File is located has only 10 megabytes free, the Backup Power System is reporting problems, the Company Backup Generator is being serviced, and your company just started a major advertising campaign. It's all just a day in the life of a DBA.

So we get hit from every possible angle, with problems that tell us something is just not right with the system. Is there a tool we can use to assist us in determining what exactly is up? Performance Monitor? PerfMon? System Monitor? What do these mean? PerfMon is short for Performance Monitor; in other words, PerfMon and Performance Monitor are synonymous. The System Monitor is what Windows 2000 now calls PerfMon; hence, we'll refer to it as System Monitor in this chapter. Arguably, this name is right to the point—the tool monitors the "system." By contrast, Performance Monitor tends to sound as if it has more to do with speed than the "health" of the system.

In this chapter we're going to spend some time with System Monitor in Windows 2000 so that we can optimize our applications and databases. Keep in mind that much of what we'll go over is also applicable to Performance Monitor, with the difference being primarily the dialog boxes and menu options.

Life before NT

Perhaps this section should be called "Back When Dinosaurs Ruled the Earth." In the days before NT 3.1 (or as some people would say, "In the days before New Technology"), Microsoft was talking about "enterprise" operating systems. That concept meant employing tools that not only allowed for the administration of the system but provided a means of monitoring its health as well. The question was not simply, "Is the system running?" but, "How well is the system running?" For example, is memory underused or overused, are processors underused or overused, and where are the bottlenecks in the system? Typically, the only people remotely interested in Performance Monitor were system administrators. But this situation changed quickly when SQL Server 4.21a came on the scene. Any DBA worth anything knew the operating system and knew SQL Server; after all, they were joined at the hip. The integration between NT and SQL Server was so tight that if you didn't understand both well, you would never be able to fully optimize your server.

The need to monitor a system's health hasn't changed, but the number of ways we can monitor our system, and the detail and depth in which we can monitor it, has changed. To be at all serious about the performance of our system, we need a grasp of SQL Profiler (discussed in Chapter 15) and System Monitor. Is the system slow? Are there four processors, but it feels as if only three are running? Maybe one or more are being dogged by an application or a service; we'll be able to pinpoint this and other abnormalities using the correct tools. System Monitor is more than up to the task.

What Does the System Monitor Do?

The System Monitor uses what are called *counters* to measure parts of the system. All counters are grouped as *objects*. For example, under the Processor object is the counter % of Processor Time. This counter is then broken out (not all counters have this granularity) into instances such as _Total for all processors. For a system with four CPUs, we would see the values 0 to 3, listed one after the other.

 NOTE *CPU 0 is not necessarily the first physical CPU in the system—this is determined at bootup. We won't go into detail on this point because it's beyond the scope of this book.*

Let's take a look at System Monitor. Click on Start ➤ Programs ➤ Administrative Tools ➤ Performance. We should see a screen like the one shown in Figure 16-1.

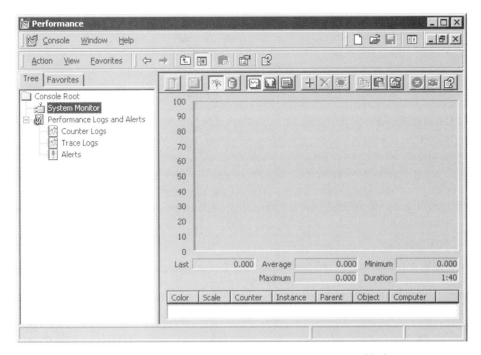

Figure 16-1. The System Monitor screen without any counters added

The System Monitor will look different from Performance Monitor, which was used in earlier versions of NT, but not so much so that we couldn't find our way around. Notice that System Monitor is a Microsoft Management Console (MMC), the same interface used for the Enterprise Manager (EM) and many other tools in recent versions of Microsoft operating systems and applications. If we're familiar with MMC, we're already familiar with the Tree and Favorites tabs. But if not, don't worry, because we'll only be focusing on System Monitor functionality, under the Tree tab and using the menus. For a server, we'll probably want to avoid customizing System Monitor just in case a recovery should have to be performed, so the fewer things that need to be restored, the faster the server can be back up and running again. It's up to each DBA, of course.

The Tree tab has a standard tree with a Console Root folder. Below Console Root is System Monitor. When selected, this displays a graph showing all the activity for the objects and counters selected. Below System Monitor are Performance Logs and Alerts, which has three objects:

- Counter Logs is where all monitored activity can be written.

- Trace Logs contains the data that is part of a monitored event.

- Alerts contains actions based on thresholds set for counters.

We'll cover all of these in more detail in the section, "How Do I Add a Counter?" Because this is an MMC, we can customize the view as well as add and remove plug-ins. Those who are not hardcore users should probably leave these settings alone; those with more experience will go to town with modifications.

By default System Monitor should be selected, and we should see the graph taking up the better part of the console. Above the graph are several buttons, some of which are not activated because we have no counters presently, but we'll remedy that issue soon enough. Below the graph area are the *value bars*, five self-explanatory boxes: Last, Average, Minimum, Maximum, and Duration. When we have a counter selected, we'll see the corresponding data displayed in these value bars. Keep in mind that the values are for the displayed information and are not historical. So when Maximum displays a value, the value is for a peak that is currently displayed only, likewise for the others. To see the Maximum and Minimum for an entire session, we would have to view logs, covered in the section "How Do I Create a Log?"

What Is the Legend?

Below the value bar is the *legend*, which is where all the counters are listed. As in previous versions of Performance Monitor, the graph and counters share the same pane. The upper portion has the graph, and the lower portion has the counters. One advantage to this configuration is we can easily identify what a line on a graph represents by simply looking at the counters below it, matching the color and style of the line with the counters in the legend. The obvious negative side is that if we had, say, twenty or more counters (which is certainly possible), we'd have to scroll through the list to find the counter in which we're interested. Ah, but wait a minute—in previous versions we would have had to scroll because double-clicking the graph changed the display of the window, hiding features in favor of a larger display for the graph. But now we can double-click a line on the graph and System Monitor will highlight the corresponding counter!

 TIP   *If you're lucky and have a machine that can be dedicated to running System Monitor, you might want to consider opening multiple sessions for different objects or servers.*

How Do I Add a Counter?

We'll now add a counter to System Monitor. (I have to install a new one of these in our main bathroom, but that's a horse of a different color.) Directly above the graph is a row of buttons, the menu bar. One of the buttons is marked with a large plus (+) symbol. Click on this button and we get the Add Counters dialog box, as shown in Figure 16-2.

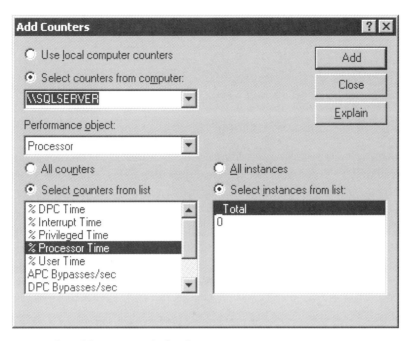

Figure 16-2. The Add Counters dialog box

The first items in this dialog box are two radio buttons, one marked Use Local Computer Counters, which is not checked, and Select Counters from Computer, which has a drop-down list directly below it. By default the current machine will be selected. Because we can monitor more than one computer, this drop-down permits us to pick a server and add counters for that server. So, picking a server displays objects and counters available on that server.

Below the server drop-down list is the Performance Object option with a drop-down list below. By default (for the template we chose), Processor is selected. Below this are two more radio buttons: All Counters and Select Counters from List. When we choose Select Counters from List and highlight a counter, we can click the Explain button in the upper-right to bring up a floating text box that explains the counter's purpose. Figure 16-3 shows the explanation for % Processor Time. The Explain button can prove to be handy as it's quick, it's informative, and we don't have to load Books On Line (BOL) and search for this information. Cool? Yes, but what's really nice is that it floats, instead of being part of the Add Counters dialog box.

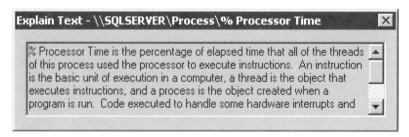

Figure 16-3. The Explain Text text box for % Processor Time

By default the Select Counters from List is selected and below it is a listing of all the counters for Processor. As in many Windows dialog boxes of this type, we can hold down the Ctrl key and perform multiselects. If we randomly picked counters and then clicked the Add button, we would only get the _Total counter for each of the selected counters. This is because of the radio buttons just to the right: All Instances and Select Instances from List. By default the Select Instances from List option is chosen, and in the Instance list, _Total is selected. If we clicked on All Instances, all instances for a counter or counters would be added to the graph. By now the logic should be pretty straightforward. Add Counters is not much different from most similar Windows dialog boxes.

Moving on, we're going to add some basic counters, and although these aren't necessarily the best for any or all given situations, most are relatively easy to understand and intuitively relate to what is happening in SQL Server. Let's start with the Processor object: Select the counter % of Processor Time for all the processors (if there's only one, choose just that one). Now let's go back to the Performance Object drop-down list and scroll down to SQL Server Access Methods and select it. By default we'll get Full Scans/sec. This counter tracks full table or index scans and gives us a clue into performance issues related to poor indexing or lack of indexing. We want the full scans to remain low; if they're peaking out a lot or remain constant (holding 40 percent or higher, for example) then we know where we can begin looking.

Note there are no instances listed. Just imagine if we had every table and index listed. That would be ugly, not to mention murder on the system. Some things lend themselves to more granularity, and other things are best tracked at a "higher" point or level. If we scan through the remaining counters, we'll see the common tie between the counters and their respective object.

What Are SQL Server Objects?

Because the remaining counter objects we're going to focus on all begin with "SQL Server," we'll just reference the description that follows that name. Next up is Buffer Manager. We skipped over the object Backup Device, but that's because we're not focusing on issues related to backups; however, having this counter gives us an idea of just how "targeted" we can get with monitoring. The Buffer Manager helps us determine if we're short on memory or loading too much data into memory, either because of poor indices, queries lacking WHERE clauses, or poorly written WHERE clauses (clauses that don't filter the data down to more realistic or manageable levels). Please be sure to add these objects as we go along, except of course Backup Device.

Now we're going to skip down to Cache Manager. This object has similar counters to the Buffer Manager, but here we'll have fewer counters from which to choose and more instances from which to select. This capability permits us to dig really deep into Cache, which is the single fastest place to hit for data. If all is working well, and queries, indices, and general activities are balanced, the Cache will be the most active counter. Cache is one of the few counters we want to see climb and stay there. It's a pretty good bet that if Cache Hits are low, our scans will be high. After all, if SQL is not able to find what it's looking for in Cache, it's going to have to hit the hard drive(s), and this will lead, with a high degree of certainty, to a bottleneck. Let's just add the counter Cache Hit Ratio and the instance _Total.

The next object we're going to go to is Database. Here we'll find a large number of counters available, but note that, along with the counter _Total for all databases, is a list of all the databases installed on the server. One of the more common counters here is Transactions/sec. If you've been following Microsoft Press Releases you know this to be one of the key areas of focus in the TPC races (see "Resources" at the end of this chapter). This counter is a great way to measure how busy the SQL Server "really" is. Rather than measuring a server based purely on how "busy" the processors are, this counter measures how many transactions are taking place.

 TIP *The more SQL Server objects and counters we add, the more load we put onto our server. A greater load could distort the information we're looking for and possibly hide or distract us from the information that could help in the quest to improve performance.*

What Do You Mean I've Exceeded My Licenses?

One counter that can prove to be of particular value is under the object General Statistics. How many times have you had entries in the Windows event logs that tell you that you're running out of licenses for your current configuration? Many of us know we can check the number of connections by using the stored procedure sp_who, or checking Process Info under Current Activity in the EM, or even performing a select from sysprocesses (not a recommended practice as these tables change). If you've followed me so far, you know that while using any one of these methods will give you a clue how many connections there may be to SQL Server, the number will only be accurate at the moment when you run the procedure. So what? I ran into a situation where an application was using more than one connection at a time—in fact, it was using numerous connections. It was a Web application, and it wasn't closing unused connections, so they would stay open until they timed out. You may not know which application is guilty, either because of the time of day it's used or it could be due to a user running multiple sessions of the same application, whatever the case with an alert you can identify this situation the moment it happens!

What Is Dynamic SQL?

We're going to cover one more object and then move on. The object is SQL Statistics, and the counter is SQL Compilations/sec. I had to use this object recently to determine what was causing a lot of CPU activity. I conducted a number of performance checks/tests using Profiler and a bunch of ad-hoc queries, but nothing seemed to stand out. Not "knowing" the internals of the application that was accessing the server, I had to go to something that would at least help me determine the behavior of the application; SQL Compilations/sec and SQL Re-Compilations/sec were just the ticket. The latter can be helpful, but the prior was the one that exposed something not obvious. It turns out that the Compilations/sec was not only abnormally high (20 to 50 percent, depending on the number of connections), but it would remain constant for extended periods of time.

Why should this behavior be of concern? Earlier on we discussed the various methods of querying objects in SQL Server and concluded that as a general rule stored procedures are the best bet. If stored procedures are a good thing, how about dynamic stored procedures? How about dynamic views and other dynamically created objects? Guess what? If the plans are not reusable, SQL Server will be forced to compile the SQL code for every occurrence in every connection. There was so much dynamic SQL being performed that optimization of tables in the form of indices and views and stored procedures made little impact because so much processor time was being used to compile all the dynamic code that was being submitted. If we want to choke our server, dynamic SQL (while cool and leaving quite a bit of leeway for creative flexibility) is one sure way to accomplish that goal. Just be judicious about it. OK, click the Cancel button, and this should return us to the System Monitor (see Figure 16-4).

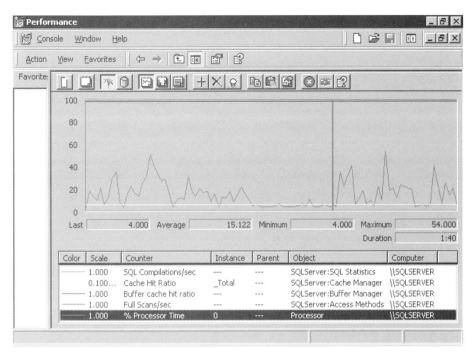

Figure 16-4. The System Monitor screen with counters and sample activity

System Monitor, like Performance Monitor, allows us to tailor the collection of information as well as customize the display of information. In previous versions if we wanted to change the appearance of the graph we would click on the Properties button. There we could add horizontal or vertical lines (grid) to the graph, change the values displayed on the "Y" axis of the graph, and so forth. To change the properties of the counters we double-click the counter and adjust the properties. To bring up the properties in System Monitor, we can click on the Properties button just above the graph (the standard image of the pointing finger over a page), or we can right-click anywhere on the graph and select Properties from the menu, or click Action and select Properties.

Figure 16-5. The System Monitor Properties dialog box with the General tab selected

The General Tab

We have six tabs from which to choose. All settings having to do with the graph, including counters, will be set using this dialog box. This screen is reminiscent of earlier versions of PerfMon, except that we can perform just about everything from one dialog box. The General tab comes up by default, so we'll start there. The first set of radio buttons determine the view, however, we have buttons just above the graph that allow us to do this. The next set, Display Elements, turn on and off the legend (all the counters), the value bar (Minimum, Maximum, and so forth), and the toolbar (just above the Graph itself). The Report and Histogram Data options dictate what type of sample will be represented for the Report and Histogram displays.

We're going to skip to an important setting: the Update Automatically Every and its corresponding text box Seconds. When this option is checked, System Monitor "polls" the target server based on the interval in the Seconds box. So, if we were to leave the setting at 1 (the default), the polling would occur every second. Changing this setting is recommended. However, if we're working on a test box, bash away; after all, how else will we be able to learn? Have some fun. Go ahead, and use System Monitor to bring the server to its knees. All right, just kidding.

The Source Tab

Now we'll move onto the next tab, Source (see Figure 16-6). In the Source tab we have two radio buttons, Current Activity and Log File. The Log File option is without a doubt one of my favorite features of System Monitor and PerfMon. By default Current Activity is selected, which means we're looking at real-time information. Assuming we're "logging" our monitor sessions—and we'll discuss how to do that in the "How Do I Create a Log?" section—we have an opportunity to open a log file from an earlier session, maybe a different day, week, or even a month ago. We can open that file, optionally pick a point in time, and do some real honest to goodness sleuthing. If for example we suspect some "scheduled" activity is causing problems, the counter log is the place to find the proof. Telling people we suspect something is a problem is one thing, but showing the hard evidence (accumulated logs with the same activity) is hard to knock down. We'll come back to this feature after creating a log, so we can open it and check it out.

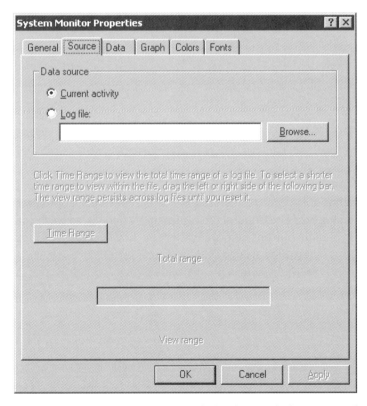

Figure 16-6. The System Monitor Properties dialog box with the Source tab selected

The Data Tab

The next tab is Data, shown in Figure 16-7. The first thing we'll notice is a list box labeled Counters. Here we can add, remove, or edit counters. There are only four options to set here: Color, Scale, Width, and Style. Color is self-explanatory. Scale, on the other hand, can be confusing. One of the easiest examples to use often is Connections. Let's add this counter, click on the plus (+) sign, and, from the objects, select SQL Server: General Statistics. Then select User Connections from the counters, click Add, and then click Close. Depending on the number of current connections, we may have a "flatline," or we may have a line that climbs to a point and then levels out and stays there. We may see fluctuations depending on activity.

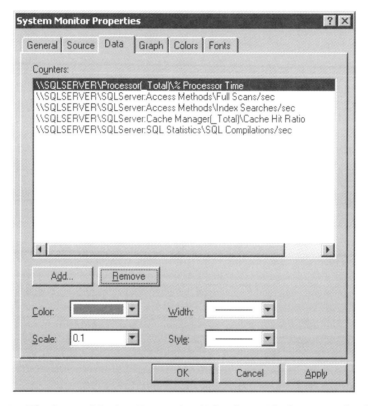

Figure 16-7. The System Monitor Properties dialog box with the Data tab selected

The graph is labeled 0 to 100. We could think of this as a count of 0 to 100 or as a percentage. In the case of connections, the default Scale is 1, so if we have twenty connections, we'll see your line on the graph at 20, but if you have a server with 200 connections you'll have a line that is "pegged." Not very useful, right? By adjusting the scale, as shown in Figure 16-8, and using the % Processor counter, we can "scale" the line up or down.

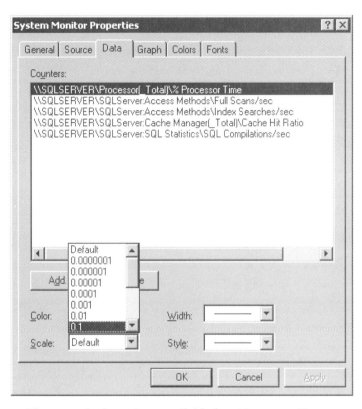

Figure 16-8. The many Scale settings available for % Processor Time counter

By selecting 0.1 as the scale for the Connections counter, and assuming we have those same 200 users connected, the line on the graph would appear at 20 (10 percent of 200). If connections should climb, it would be easier to detect visually, and as long as the number of connections remains between 100 and 1,000, we won't often have to guess or look at the value bar to determine how many connections there are. This ability exists with all the counters, so we can tailor them based on the normal load for our server. When the first Width is selected, we can change the Style to a broken line, a dotted line, and so forth. When any of the other Widths are chosen, the line is always solid. Given the variety of Color and Style combinations, we may not often run into a problem requiring the use of Width.

The Graph Tab

The next tab is Graph, shown in Figure 16-9. In the Graph tab we can give our graph a title and label the vertical axis. This is also where we apply our grid, which can be useful if we start monkeying around with scale on the counters and vertical scale here on the Graph tab. This is another area that can be useful, as sometimes a scale of 0 to 100 can be too broad to distinguish subtle differences or changes. We have to experiment with settings for a while to get a feel for this feature, but trust me, it really can be useful. Figure 16-10 shows the horizontal grid turned on. Sometimes the grid is useful in determining how close counters are or if a counter keeps hitting the same level or levels.

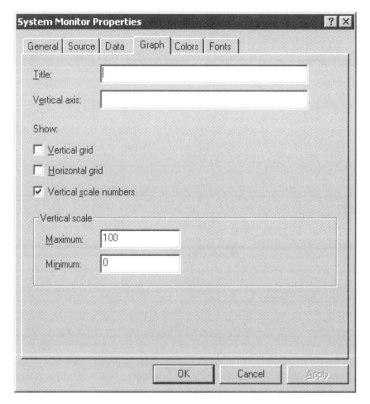

Figure 16-9. The System Monitor Properties dialog box with the Graph tab selected

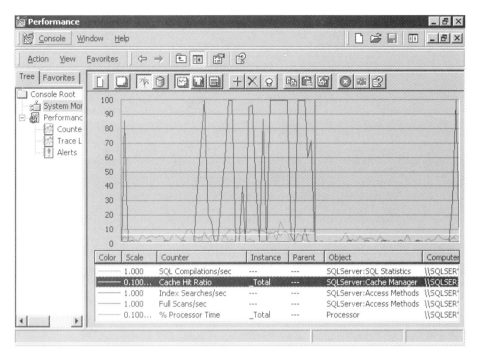

Figure 16-10. System Monitor with a horizontal grid

The Colors Tab

Now we move on to the next tab, Colors, shown in Figure 16-11. It almost seems a waste of a tab because the options are rather limited, although they are still functional. This tab allows us to adjust the colors for the user interface, including the controls, buttons, and so on.

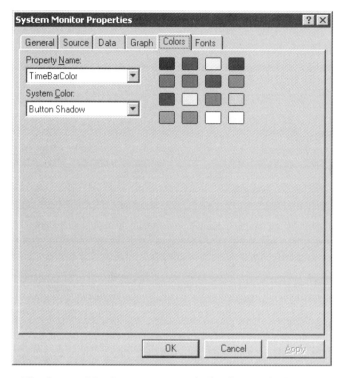

Figure 16-11. The System Monitor Properties dialog box with the Colors tab selected

Changing fonts at first may not seem to make sense. We would change fonts in a word processor or spreadsheet, but why change fonts in System Monitor? The reason may be a matter of preference, we may have trouble reading certain fonts, or we may like smaller type to see more detail or larger type for easier reading.

The Fonts Tab

Figure 16-12 shows the Fonts tab where we'll find plenty of flexibility for changing fonts.

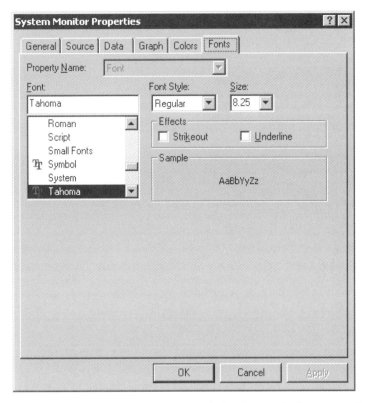

Figure 16-12. The System Monitor Properties dialog box with the Fonts tab selected

How Do I Create a Log?

We can create a log by right-clicking on Counter Logs and selecting New Log Settings or New Log Settings From, the latter being a file that we've saved from an earlier session or maybe from another system. We're doing this for the first time, so we'll select New Log Settings. That brings up the screen shown in Figure 16-13.

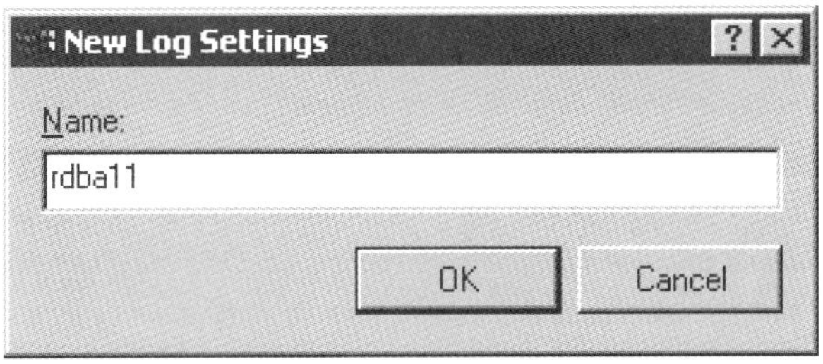

Figure 16-13. The New Log Settings dialog box

Note that all we put in is **RDBA11** for the name of the database. We can name it anything we like, but use **RDBA11** for now. After we enter a name for the settings, we're brought to the dialog box shown in Figure 16-14.

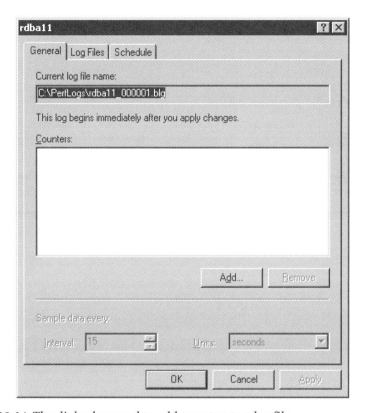

Figure 16-14. The dialog box used to add counters to a log file

This dialog box provides three tabs: General, "Log Files, and Schedule. Note the name of the file that will be created in the Current Log File Name text box. It starts off with the name we gave it followed by an underscore and numbers (six digits) and then the extension BLG. We'll get to what the extension means on the next tab. Let's add some counters. I've selected the counters shown in Figure 16-15, which we optionally can do as well.

NOTE *Although you can't pick the instances here, they are recorded as part of the counter and are available for review when you look at the log later.*

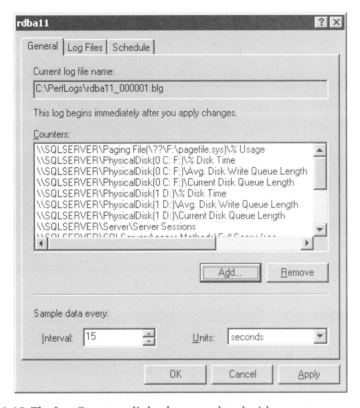

Figure 16-15. The Log Counters dialog box populated with counters

What we don't see are the counters Access Methods: Full scans/sec, Buffer Manager\Cache Hit Ratio, Buffer Manager\Free Pages, Buffer Manager\Page Reads /sec, Cache Manager (Prepared SQL Plans)\Cache Hit Ratio, Cache Manager (Procedure Plans)\Cache Hit Ratio, General Statistics\User Connections, and SQL Statistics\SQL Compilations/sec. The next setting is going to make a difference not only in the performance of System Monitor, but the target system as well. I've set Sample Data Every to 15 seconds. On my box that's no big deal as it's almost always inactive. When we click the Units drop-down list we'll see Seconds, Minutes, Hours, and Days. Nothing comes to mind as to why we would use Days, but certainly there is a good reason or it wouldn't be there. Right? Let's move on.

The Log Files Tab

The next tab is Log Files, as shown in Figure 16-16. The first section has to do with the file location and its suffix, here called End File Names With. Note that we see nnnnnn (that's six *n*s), which matches the physical name we saw on the General tab. We even have the option of setting the seed value in the Start Numbering At option. If we click on the drop-down list next to End File Names With we'll see a pretty good selection from which to choose. We can choose "mmddhh" (month/day/hour), so that the filenames are consistent and the suffix is a clear indication when the file was created. Now when we sort on names in Explorer we'll see file names grouped together in date-time order, rather than having to sort on the date column and then trying to find the correct filename. Note also that the Start Number At is grayed out. Just below that we'll see an example of what the filename will look like. What have we here? Log File Type—that's interesting (see Figure 16-17).

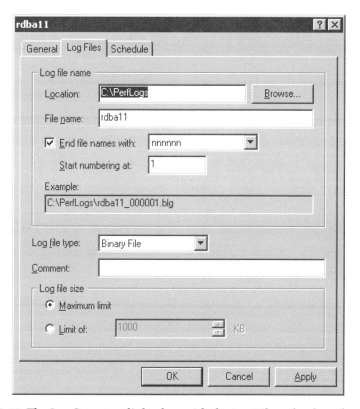

Figure 16-16. The Log Counters dialog box with the Log Files tab selected

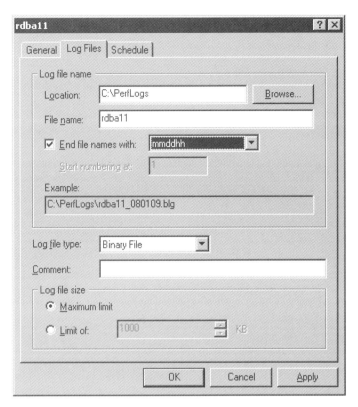

Figure 16-17. The Log Counters dialog box with the Log Files tab selected. Note that End File Names With has been checked and a format selected.

By default the file type is binary, but we can choose from three other file formats, two of them we can see their respective extensions in the drop-down list (see Figure 16-18).

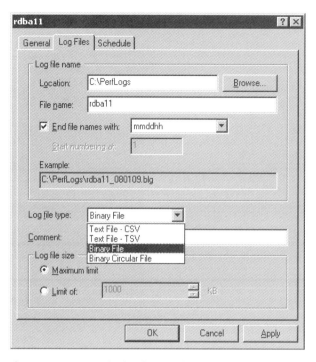

Figure 16-18. The Log Counters dialog box with the Log Files tab selected. Note the Log File Type drop-down list.

Table 16-1 explains each of the four options.

Table 16-1. File Type Options

Text File CSV	This option defines a comma-delimited log file (with a CSV extension). Use this format to export the log data to a spreadsheet program.
Text File TSV	This option defines a tab-delimited log file (with a TSV extension). Use this format to export the log data to a spreadsheet program.
Binary File	This option defines a sequential, binary-format log file (with a BLG extension). Use this file format if we want to be able to record data instances that are intermittent—that is, stopping and resuming after the log has begun running. Nonbinary file formats cannot accommodate instances that are not persistent throughout the duration of the log.
Binary Circular File	This option defines a circular, binary-format log file (with a BLG extension). Use this file format to record data continuously to the same log file, overwriting previous records with new data.

The choice of a file type obviously opens doors to many analytical possibilities, so choose wisely. The last option could have the most fatal ramifications. We want, of course, to collect as much data as is necessary to make an informed decision or at a minimum some educated conclusion, but at what cost? The cost may be drive space, and because we're saving this log to the "C" drive, the last thing we want to do is fill up the default drive for the operating system and bring the entire server to a screeching halt. Some may have terrabytes of storage, but many more of us do feel these limitations. Either set the log file size to something realistic or change the path where the files are created to a more expansive drive.

That about covers it for creating counter logs. Let's return to the Log Files tab for a moment in reference to the extensions. By default Binary is used, but should we want to do more intense analyzing, we can save the file with CSV or TSV so that we can open the file with other applications, such as Excel, Word, Access, or Crystal Reports. Choosing the desired file type will be dictated by whom will be using the output and how they will use it.

The Schedule Tab

Moving on we come to Schedule, shown in Figure 16-19. The Start option is pretty obvious—the choices are Manual or At a Specified Date and Time. Stopping, however, is another matter. Here we have quite a bit of flexibility. We can stop Manually, or we can select After with a value and Units, which are Seconds, Minutes, Hours, or Days. This feature is handy if we only need logging to run for a specified time, like when we suspect something is amiss, but most importantly it allows us to "set it and forget it." The last option, When the Log File Is Full (which is grayed out), works in conjunction with Limit Of in the Log File Size section of the Log Files tab. When Limit Of is set, this option becomes activated. We can simply have the logging stop as soon as the file is full. The next section, "When a Log File Closes," permits us to choose what actions to take when a log closes based on one of the Stop options picked earlier. The first, "Start a New Log File," is only available when After has been chosen. The option Run This Command can be used to run an application (like a Visual Basic program) or maybe a batch file. Why? Maybe we'd like a copy of the log moved to a central system that is used to examine, analyze, or process the logs. At one of my employers the logs would be moved to a Web server where decision-makers had quick easy access to the data collected. The scheduling feature offers many possibilities.

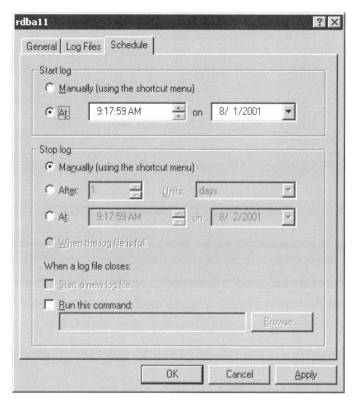

Figure 16-19. The Log Counters dialog box with the Schedule tab selected

Returning to System Monitor, select the Counter Logs object from the tree. We'll see two logs, one the default that comes with our operating system installation, System Overview, and the one we just created. When the icon for the log is red it is stopped, when it is Green it is running. When starting a log manually we can either use the Play button on the menu bar or right-click the log we want to start and select Start.

I've Created a Log, but How Do I View It?

The first thing to do to view a log is to stop the log. Use the Stop button or right-click the log and select Stop. Now click on the System Monitor object. Next we're going to bring up the properties. Once we have the Properties dialog box open, select the Source tab. We should see the screen shown earlier in Figure 16-6.

Select the Log File radio button. Now, if we click on the Browse button, it should bring us to the folder where the log is saved. Select the log and open it. When we return to the Properties dialog box, the Time Range button becomes activated, as shown in Figure 16-20.

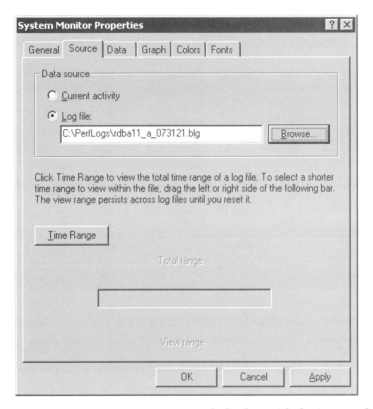

Figure 16-20. The System Monitor Properties dialog box with the Source tab selected. Note the Time Range button is now active.

Now click the Apply button. You'll notice that System Monitor has changed and you should see a graph, but without the scan line going across. You now have a snapshot of activity from a specific point in time. Now click on the Time Range button. This will fill the text box Total Range as well as activate the label. The box should look something like Figure 16-21 (the dates and times may vary).

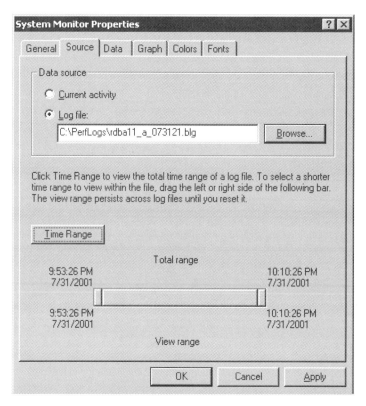

Figure 16-21. The System Monitor Properties dialog box with the Source tab selected. Note the lower portion of the screen displays a range bar with beginning and ending dates and times.

Because this is a floating dialog box, and because we can apply changes and see them take affect without having to close it, we'll now get to play with something pretty cool. On both sides of the Range box are vertical bars. These bars can be grabbed, like a volume control, and moved right or left. While we do this a gray vertical line appears from the left (when moving the left bar) or from the right (when moving the right bar). Using both bars we can "frame" the range we're interested in, select Apply, close the dialog box, and view just the information for that range. This feature won't be as impressive with a short sample, but when collecting a day's worth of activity with varying spikes, peaks, and valleys, it will become quite clear how this feature helps. Imagine looking at a Database Model with 200 objects, and you're zoomed all the way out. It's hard to distinguish one object from another, let alone all the intersecting lines. Adjusting the time range is like the zoom feature in the Modeling tool. Suddenly you see details that you couldn't before.

Intruder Alert, Intruder Alert...

Although we aren't talking about aliens or such, we do consider abnormalities in our system to be just as threatening. So, the last thing we'll touch on in this chapter is alerts.

Creating an alert is just like creating a counter log. First right-click on Alerts and then select New Alert Settings. Type in a name for the alert and click OK. The dialog box for Alert Properties looks just like Counters, so we're going to cruise through this (see Figure 16-22).

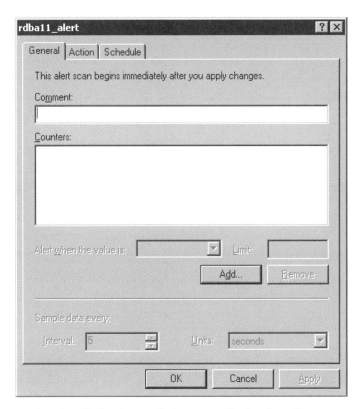

Figure 16-22. The Alert dialog box with the General tab selected

We have only three tabs here: General, Action, and Schedule. Put whatever you like in the Comments box, and we'll then add a counter. Adding a counter is just like the counters log, so let's add the Processor: % Processor time. Once added you'll notice all the options are now activated, as shown in Figure 16-23.

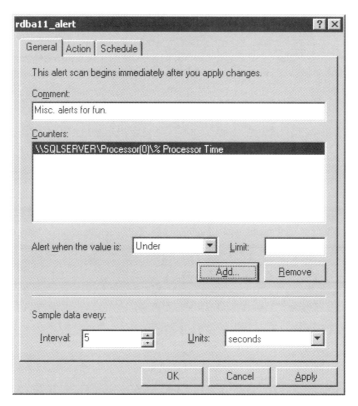

Figure 16-23. The General tab of the Alert dialog box with a counter added

An alert is configured to respond to an event, and this alert will monitor how busy our processor is. Because we don't like to see our processor too busy, we're going to set a threshold for our alert, and we do that by selecting an option from the Alert When the Value Is drop-down list. This list has only two options: Over and Under. We're going to use Over, and that's where Limit comes into play. The rule of thumb has always been to keep your processors under 80-percent utilization for SQL Server. Remember, this is just a rule of thumb; some people don't like them above 20 to 30 percent.

So we've decided the value is over and the limit is 80. Now comes the tricky part: Sample Data Every and Units. It's not uncommon for one or more processors to hit 80 percent or more for brief moments, so do we want these firing off *every* time we exceed 80 percent? Not likely. We know that we don't want to see sustained rates, so the logic is simple. First, what is too high? We've decided 80 percent. So now, what is too long? That's a little tougher. For this test we'll be using a smaller value, but if we had a busy server we may want to extend it some. If we've got Interval set to 5 and Units set to Seconds, this alert will fire off if the processor is running over 80 percent *and* it's sustained for more than five seconds. How do we know this? Well that's a little tricky. Because the "poll" won't necessarily take place the moment the processor exceeds 80, the processor would have to sustain that 80 percent long enough for the next poll to take place. So, if you were to monitor your system and you see that your processor sustains more than 80 percent for what appears to be longer than five seconds and alerts don't fire off or rarely fire off, it's timing, not a problem. All this means is you have to consider all the variables involved and think this through before jumping in and arbitrarily changing intervals and units. Let's move onto the Action tab, shown in Figure 16-24.

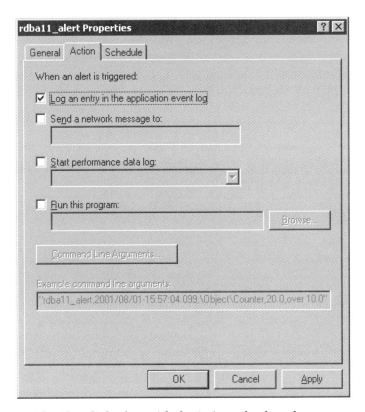

Figure 16-24. The Alert dialog box with the Action tab selected

By default the Log and Entry in the Application Event Viewer option is checked. Normally this setting can be left alone. However, depending on the nature of the counter, you may not want or need to log it there, especially because adding entries to the event log can make it grow quite fast. Ask any system administrator about that, particularly for servers that have been running for months without a reboot. Sending a network message would be useful when something absolutely requires the attention of a "warm body." Maybe you're monitoring disk space because of a runaway application, but in any case you need to take action before the problem gets out of hand. This is generally something you can't automate. Whenever I have scripts that permit the server to "heal itself," I don't often require a Net message.

The Performance Data Log can be useful for situations where there may be a data-related issue. Arguably, you could use Profiler in the same manner; however, to use Profiler you would have to leave it running continuously until the event manifests itself or the event would have to be predictable. If only this were the case more often, but alas it's not, so we use these tools just to ferret out these things. The option Run This Program can be useful when you want to automate your system. The sign of a truly competent DBA (even if reluctant) is the ability to build a system that is proactive—one that heals itself. Doing so may not give you more free time, but certainly it may allow you to focus on other outstanding issues. Things you can run include batch scripts, Visual Basic applications, or just about any other executables. In addition to Run Program are the command-line arguments. This is where you put switches or parameter values. When Run This Program is selected and you click on the Command Line Parameters button, you get the dialog box shown in Figure 16-25.

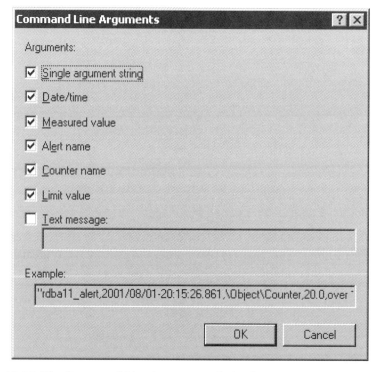

Figure 16-25. The Command Line Arguments dialog box

If you look closely you'll note that the values in the example are reflective of the Options checked. The option Single Argument String treats the command line as one string, which requires all arguments to be separated by a comma. The leading value in the string (`rdba11_alert`) is just an example, however, because everything else that follows reflects the checkboxes exactly. For example, the next value you see is the date and time, which is the option following Single Argument String, the option Measured Value is represented by the placeholder `\object\counter`, and so on. Any applications or scripts you build must be written to accept these parameters and must be in the correct sequence. The option Text Message is the only argument that enables you to type in what you want passed to the command-line application. The Schedule tab looks and functions just like the Schedule tab on counter logs with the only exception being that the latter has the Run Command option.

Last Words

Although we've only touched the surface, it's not the purpose of this book to make you a Performance Monitor guru. I hope you have found some things that you can make use of in your daily challenges, something that may help you beat back those daunting problems and help you in automating what up to now required a warm body standing by to interact with the system. Unfortunately, the way BOL is organized on this topic, it can sometimes be challenging to find the answers for which you're looking. By using the Search function in BOL I often can find what I need more quickly than by using the index or drilling through the tree. I hope this chapter helped and will allow you to be more comfortable using PerfMon or System Monitor.

Resources

- BOL: "Monitoring with System Monitor"

- Search the Knowledge Base for "Performance Monitor," "SQL Server Performance Tuning," and "SQL Server Counters." There are many great articles with excellent examples and hints: `http://www.msdn.microsoft.com`

- This site provides a great deal of performance related information, but not just hard numbers and "standings": `http://www.tpc.org`

What a Reluctant DBA Needs to Know about .NET

Dot NET, or not dot NET: That is the question.

THAT SLIGHT TUG in the earth's gravitational pull you feel is William Shakespeare spinning in his grave from this mangling of Hamlet (the complete .NET version of the soliloquy is on the CD in the "Whitepapers" directory), but the question is actually more complicated than it might appear. .NET *is* the way to go but with its introduction comes a whole host of questions related to how .NET relates to data, what means of data access is best, and what new tools are available for interacting with your data. This chapter will try to answer some of your questions but comes with a large warning.

 CAUTION *This chapter is being written and tested with Visual Studio.NET beta 2. Beta software is different from production software. If you are using either a different beta or the production version, then you may find things that are different from what this chapter states.*

To clarify that warning, beta software and *production* software have three major differences:

- Beta software contains a great deal of debugging code that means it is slower than the same code would be if it were in production.

- Beta software may contain features that do not make it into the production code, or it may not contain features added to the production code.[1]

---

[1] Actually, this happens between betas as well. The version of ADO.NET released in Beta 1 was different from the one shipped with Beta 2, meaning major code rewrites for those who were running on the bleeding edge of technology.

- The Visual Studio.NET Beta 2 is the Professional Edition. It is different from the Enterprise Edition, which will contain some of the additional tools that Microsoft is touting. Some of these will be mentioned in this chapter based on Microsoft's comments and writings.

For these reasons, this chapter is not going to contain code but will concentrate on the concepts in ActiveX Data Objects.NET (ADO.NET) of which you should be aware. Once Visual Studio .NET is released, you can go to `http://www.reluctantdba.com` for code samples and updates on anything that has since changed.

Let's look at what you need to know about .NET.

ADO.NET Is Not ADO

ActiveX Data Objects (ADO) should not be confused with ADO.NET. ADO.NET was designed from the ground up for the Web by incorporating scalability, statelessness, and eXtensible Markup Language (XML). To make ADO.NET more scalable, stateless, and more supportive of XML, there have been several fundamental changes in the objects and how they work. But the basic question that everyone is asking is, "Do I need to upgrade to ADO.NET?" The answer is both "yes" and "no," but to understand that seemingly contradictory answer we need to take a closer look at what ADO.NET is.

The first difference between ADO and ADO.NET is the fact that there is a unique provider for SQL Server. Just like with ADO, you start building your objects with a connection; but unlike ADO, there are different types of connections from which to choose. If you are connecting to SQL Server you can use SQLConnection (`System.Data.SqlClient`), which provides a direct connection to the server. If, on the other hand, you are connecting to a non-SQL Server data source, you can use an ADOConnection (`System.Data.OleDb`). From what the manuals say, this is not a Microsoft-centric view, and there will be other connections available as vendors write them, so you should be able to use `System.Data.Oracle` at some point.

NOTE *Of course, just because there's a* SQLConnection *doesn't mean you can't use an* ADOConnection *to connect to SQL Server. However, that's not recommended because by going through* ADOConnection, *you are adding another level the program has to go through, which makes your program less efficient.*

What Are the ADO.NET Objects?

Like ADO, ADO.NET has several objects for connecting to and communicating with the database. Let's take a quick look at them and how they relate to their ADO counterparts:

- Connection: This is similar to the ADO connection object; its purpose is to connect to a data source. There is a SQL Server–specific version.

- Command: Again, this is similar to the ADO command object; it executes commands against a data source. These commands can be stored procedures, SELECT statements, or anything else the data source allows. There is a SQL Specific–version of the command.

- DataReader: The DataReader is similar to the ADO recordset, but it isn't the same. The DataReader most closely resembles ADO's read-only (fire hose) cursor.

- DataSet: The DataSet is also similar to the ADO recordset, but it is data. And where the DataReader is read-only, the DataSet can be gone through forward, backward, and sideways, and you can modify the data at will.

- DataAdapter: The DataAdapter is used for pushing data into a DataSet as well as for putting data back into the database through UPDATE, INSERT, and DELETE.

Although the Connection and Command objects are similar to what existed in ADO, the other objects in ADO.NET require more explanation. Let's start with the simplest, the DataReader. This object opens up a set of data and lets you walk through it from first to last. Once you've read a record and moved on to the next one, you can't go back. You also can't modify the data; it is read-only. This is handy for dumping lists to the screen or processing through a set of records when you are only going through them once.

Can I Use ADO in VS.NET?

Well, yes, you can, but the question is whether you should. ADO 2.6 can be accessed through VS.NET, but it requires that you register ADO 2.6 through the Common Language Runtime (CLR) for your project. This effectively adds another layer between your program and the database. The differences between using ADO.NET with the SQLConnection and ADO 2.6 are probably best explained by showing the layers that each one uses.

ADO.NET with SQLConnection directly accesses the Tabular Data Stream (TDS) that is SQL Server's native tongue, so to speak, so the layers your program goes through look like this:

```
SQLConnection / TDS / SQL Server
```

With ADO 2.6, on the other hand, you get:

```
CLR / OLE DB / TDS / SQL Server
```

In addition, there is overhead in converting from the CLR to the old, COM-type environment in which ADO 2.6 exists. That means you should see dramatic time differences if you were writing a .NET program using ADO 2.6 compared with ADO.NET. Once the final version is out and the debug code is gone, you can go to http://www.reluctantdba.com for details on the performance differences between these.

Perhaps one of the most noticeable things about ADO.NET to experienced ADO programmers is the lack of cursors. In ADO, you can specify whether you want the server to create a record set and only give it to you in small batches (a server-side cursor) or whether you want to dump the whole thing down to the client (client-side cursor). This could be a big deal because dumping a couple hundred–megabyte table to the client could take a lot of time, memory, and disk space, especially if the program was waiting to get the whole table before it did anything else. If you were able to use a server-side cursor to assemble the data and then just page through it on the client side as you wanted, the program would move much faster as far as the user was concerned.

But TANSTAAFL[2] still rules, and running a server-side cursor ties up resources on the server and requires keeping the connection between client and server up for the entire time the table is being accessed.

---

[2]   There Ain't No Such Thing As A Free Lunch.

Given that ADO.NET is stateless, you can see that server-side cursors can't be allowed.[3] The good news is that ADO.NET makes stateless recordsets much easier to deal with. In ADO, you could create a client-side cursor of a recordset and disconnect it from the database. In this disconnected state you could manipulate the data, adding new records, deleting records, and modifying records. Once you were finished you could execute a single method and have the recordset reconnect to the database and attempt to enact all of your changes.

Unfortunately, the disconnected recordset was limited in what it could do. It would execute INSERT, UPDATE, or DELETE. This totally bypassed any logic built into the database through stored procedures and required that the table's security be set up for allowing direct manipulation of the table. In ADO.NET, however, that has changed.

Instead of opening up a record set, you create a DataSet. That DataSet is filled through the use of the DataAdapter and gives you a whole new set of functionality. When you set up the DataAdapter you can define what it should be using for the SELECT, INSERT, UPDATE, and DELETE. That means you can define stored procedures and implement proper security even while using disconnected record sets.

Another problem with disconnected record sets relates to building foreign key relationships. If you have two disconnected DataSets that should be related, say a subset of Owners and Pets, you need to keep the two sets of data in sync with each other. Before ADO.NET you had to write code within your program to ensure that anytime the data was modified in one grid, the foreign key/primary key relationship would be kept intact. In ADO.NET it is possible to join two DataSets together in a relationship and avoid all of the overhead of managing the relationship.

ADO.NET: It Isn't Just for Databases Anymore

Another point to make, and to clarify for those who are reading closely, is that ADO.NET is designed to work with data *sources* more than with data*bases*. That may sound like we're bandying semantics, but the difference between a data source and a database can be huge (although a data source can *be* a database). Instead of focusing on getting data out of the data source, ADO.NET is designed for generic data handling.

For instance, you could query your Exchange Server to get an employee list and join that together with the phone log you've downloaded from your phone system to generate a list of who has been handling the most customer calls in your tech-support department. Then, by joining those two disconnected DataSets with a list of area codes and exchanges that you keep in your SQL

---

[3]   On the bright side, that means programmers need to be more discriminating about the data they return to the client. So I can hope there will be fewer SELECT * FROM tablename with no WHERE filters.

Server, you can see what areas of the country are calling the most. You can define how each DataSet relates to the other and then spit out an XML report that is viewable on your Web server.

That's All Very Interesting, but Do I Need to Move to ADO.NET?

OK, let's further explain the "yes" and "no" answers to the question of whether you should upgrade to ADO.NET. Yes, you need to move to ADO.NET for all of your *new* development. That's because ADO.NET is designed to work more efficiently in the stateless, scaleable world that some have called the *third generation of the Internet*, or the programmable Web—that's the "yes" answer. But it will take work. Programmers will need to relearn what they think they know about interacting with the database.

ADO, on the other hand, won't disappear for quite a while. There are a number of ADO applications, they work fine, and there is no real need to port them to ADO.NET—that's the "no" answer.

From the point of view of the database administrator (DBA), however, it may seem to be a whole lot of fuss that has no bearing on the server side of things, but that's not quite true. Using the DataAdapter will probably lead to more folks wanting stored procedures to interface with the database, which is a good thing. Then there are all of the tools available for the database.

What New Tools Are Available for Managing Databases in Visual Studio .NET?

This is exciting news. In Visual Studio .NET (VS.NET), there's a new project type, the database project. From within the database project you can design databases, views, stored procedures, triggers, user-defined functions, and all the other parts of a database. Unfortunately, these features are part of the VS.NET Enterprise Edition, which isn't available for the beta. It is, however, documented in the VS.NET online books, and Microsoft has been showing off the Enterprise version at VS.NET demonstrations, so we'll share some insights.

First, in many cases you'll be able to leverage your knowledge from this book because it *appears*[4] that many of the database design tools have been lifted from SQL Server. The tool for designing views looks much like the View Designer outlined in Chapter 6, "What Is a View?" The database designer included in VS.NET looks a great deal like the Diagramming tool introduced in Chapter 5, "How Do

---

[4] Beta software may differ from production software.

I Define and Structure a Database?" Bear in mind, however, that these may change before the final release.

One of the reasons these tools haven't been included in the beta, according to Microsoft, has been a timing issue. The Enterprise Edition is also slated to include a version of Visio, the flowcharting/modeling/diagramming tool that Microsoft bought a couple of years ago. Visio would provide a more flexible and powerful tool for database diagramming and documentation but, even with Visio, that's not the most exciting news for VS.NET.

The most exciting thing about VS.NET is source control. Yep, full integration with Source Safe for database development *done through VS.NET*. And many of the options that can be handled through the Enterprise Manager are supposed to be doable through VS.NET. When you modify a table through the tools in VS.NET, you'll be able to save a "change" script and have that script placed into Source Safe *automagically*. Even if you are a DBA and do no other programming, you could use VS.NET to handle that because Source Safe and SQL scripts currently require manual processing that makes it a hassle to maintain.

Last Words

.NET is an exciting concept and much of what I have seen shows excellent promise of making the programmable Web easier and faster. Dealing with the ADO.NET should make our lives as DBAs easier because programmers will be required to get just the data they need rather than browsing and locking an entire table. In addition, the tools that are supposed to ship with VS.NET will make our jobs as DBAs fit more tightly with the rest of the programming staff and, for the many of us who are both programmers and DBAs, we'll have one environment to use for all of our development.

If you haven't gotten a VB.NET beta 2, get one. Microsoft has promised to make the CDs so plentiful that AOL CDs will seem rare. Install it on your personal system and start getting familiar with the .NET framework, ADO.NET, and how it all ties together. If you're not already subscribed to *MSDN Magazine* or *Visual Studio Magazine*, you probably should either sign up or start perusing the online versions to bring you up to speed. And as things change, remember to check out `http://www.reluctantdba.com` to see the latest information on VS.NET and how it relates to SQL Server.

Resources

- For Microsoft's definitive take on .NET, visit the .NET home page:
  `http://www.microsoft.com/net/default.asp`

- For information about VS.NET, visit the Visual Studio.NET Next Generation
  page: `http://msdn.microsoft.com/vstudio/nextgen/`

- For developer resources on .NET:
  `http://msdn.microsoft.com/vstudio/nextgen/`

- *MSDN Magazine*: `http://msdn.microsoft.com/msdnmag`

- *Visual Studio Magazine*: `http://www.devx.com`

Does Reading This Book Make Me a DBA?

It is a task, like the landing of an aeroplane, of choosing the right moment between two opposite sets of dangers. —Winston Churchill

IT MAY SEEM LIKE this question should really be the introduction to this book rather than the conclusion. However, I know this is the question most people will ask, so I thought it best to cover it at the conclusion.

If you really want to be a database administrator (DBA), then you'll have to pass Microsoft's Certification Exams to become a Microsoft Certified Database Administrator (MCDBA). These exams cover more topics and more topics in-depth than this book does, and I'll be the first to admit that Transcender puts out a great series of books to help you to earn Microsoft's certifications.

This book's goal never was to make you a DBA. Only Microsoft (or Oracle or Sybase or IBM or . . . well, you get the idea) can certify you and turn you into a DBA. This book's goal is to help programmers understand database design, administration, and programming so that they can better perform their jobs. Recent surveys have shown that SQL Server is the most commonly used tool by Visual Basic programmers, and I know from personal experience that more and more programmers are being called upon to handle the chores traditionally assigned to a DBA. The only problem is, most books (and many articles) related to database design, administration, and programming require you to know all of the terms and concepts first, where this book is written from the perspective of a programmer for programmers.

So, although this book may not make you a DBA, it *will* help you to understand the terms and concepts that the certification preparation books use. And, although knowing all of the tips and tricks outlined in this book may not make you a DBA, it sure will make your job easier. I know when I started to design and implement databases, I frequently felt like I was choosing between "two opposite sets of dangers," but as I have gained experience those dangers become less and less dangerous. The same will happen to you as you continue to hone your skills with Microsoft SQL Server.

Consider this book a first step into the process of transforming yourself from a programmer to a programmer with DBA skills.

APPENDIX A

How Do I Load
the Examples?

*Any sufficiently advanced technology is indistinguishable from a
rigged demo.*

YOU HAVE MANY WAYS to distribute databases for SQL Server. One way is to back up
the data and then distribute the backup file to be restored. For this book, however, I am distributing the actual database device files.

For each chapter of the book that has sample data, you will find a directory
on the accompanying CD. That directory contains a self-extracting zip file that
you can execute to unzip the database files. There are two files, an .MDF and an
.LDF. These are the database and log files, respectively. In addition, there is a SQL
script entitled "RestoreExample" followed by the chapter number. The following
is a sample of what one of those scripts looks like:

```
-**************************************************
- Reluctant DBA Database Restore Script for Chapter x
-**************************************************
DECLARE @RestoreDirectory varchar(2048)
- Change the following value to the directory where you unzipped
- the files and then execute the script
SET @RestoreDirectory =
'C:\Program Files\Microsoft SQL Server\MSSQL$RELUCTANTDBA\Data'
- WARNING: Do not change anything below this line or the script may break
DECLARE @RestoreDBFile varchar(3096)      - Name of database file
DECLARE @RestoreLogFile varchar(3096)     - Name of log file
DECLARE @DatabaseName varchar(256)        - Name of database
- Check to see if the directory path ends with a \ and add one if necessary
IF right(@RestoreDirectory,1) <> '\'
    SET @RestoreDirectory = @RestoreDirectory + '\'
SET @RestoreDBFile = @RestoreDirectory + 'PetDB.mdf'
SET @RestoreLogFile = @RestoreDirectory + 'PetDB_Log.ldf'
SET @DatabaseName = 'PetDB'
exec sp_attach_db @DatabaseName, @RestoreDBFile, @RestoreLogFile
```

For the script to execute correctly, you may need to modify the line in bold. This needs to be the directory where the unzipped files are. The default is the "C:\Program Files\Microsoft SQL Server\MSSQL$RELUCTANTDBA\Data" directory. If you have put the files anywhere else, then you will need to change this variable.

My Database Didn't Restore

This script could fail to work for a few reasons. Some error codes and ways around them are listed next.

Database Already Exists

Error: Server: Msg 1801, Level 16, State 3, Line 1
   Database *databasename* already exists.
   Problem: The database already exists. Because each chapter has a uniquely named database in these scripts, you have probably already run this script.
   Solution: To fix this problem, go into the Enterprise Manager and drop the database. Then run the script again.

Device Activation Error

Error: Server: Msg 5105, Level 16, State 4, Line 1
   Device activation error. The physical filename *filename* may be incorrect.
   Problem: The device file does not exist.
   Solution: Check to see if you modified the @RestoreDirectory variable to have the correct value. If it does, verify the files are really in the directory.

Header Error

Error: Server: Msg 5172, Level 16, State 15, Line 1
   The header for file *filename* is not a valid database file header. The FILE SIZE property is incorrect.
   Problem: The file is corrupt.
   Solution: Delete the files and then unzip again. Verify you have enough disk space for this operation.

How Can I Find Information More Efficiently?

When confronted by a difficult problem, you can solve it more easily by reducing it to the question, "How would the Lone Ranger have handled this?" —Brady's First Law of Problem Solving

FOR BETTER OR WORSE, the Lone Ranger seems to have lived and worked in simpler times. When a reluctant database administrator (DBA) encounters a new problem, she generally needs to find out what the problem is and how to solve it quickly. Fortunately, a number of resources are available to help resolve problems.

Reading Books On Line

Books On Line (BOL) is SQL's online help documentation. You can get to BOL from your Start menu by using Start ➤ Programs ➤ Microsoft SQL Server ➤ Books On Line. There are a number of options for working with BOL (see Figure B-1). If you are seeking general information, you can expand the book titles in the left-hand panel. Once you find a topic, you can right-click on it and print out that page, or you can print out all of the subtopics underneath that topic. I've printed out entire books when I'm encountering a new process, but that's because I like paper.

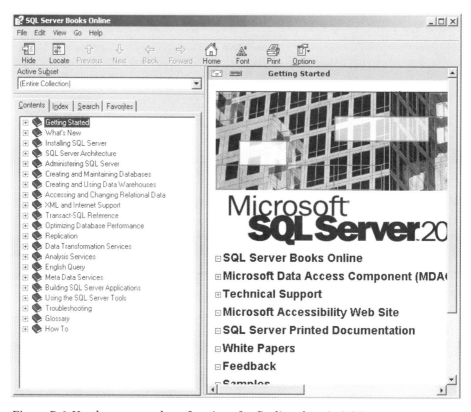

Figure B-1. You have a number of options for finding data in BOL

Another option is to select the Index tab and start typing in a topic. As you type, SQL Server will attempt to match your request to an index entry. As you can see in Figure B-2, I've started to type *transactions*, and BOL has started to match entries. Almost every major topic has an Overview section that introduces the topic.

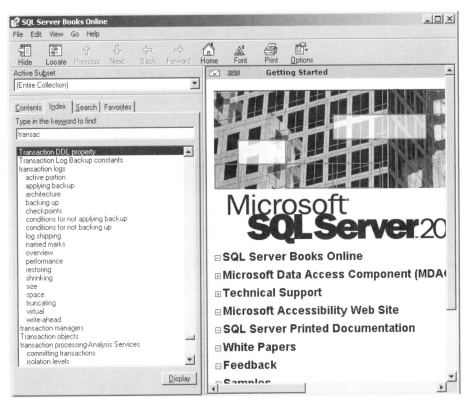

Figure B-2. As you begin to type in the index section, SQL Server takes you to matching entries

Once you've found the topic you need information on, you can double-click on the index entry to bring up the related page in right-hand panel. Once you've gotten that far, you have several options for finding more information. You can press the Locate button in the toolbar across the top of the screen. That will open up the Contents tab and drills down to where that page is located. For instance, if you open the Transaction Log topic, highlight the Overview section, and then press the Locate button, you'll see the Contents tab at the top of the book on transaction logs (see Figure B-3). At the bottom of most pages you'll also find a couple of related links, which take you to other BOL topics.

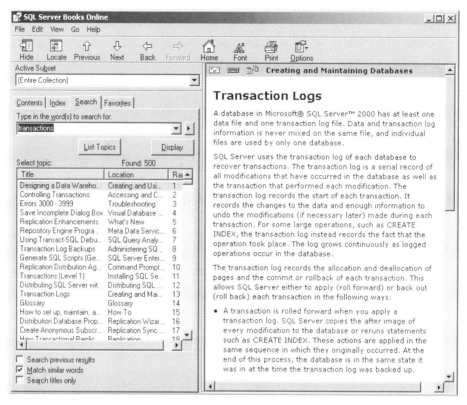

Figure B-3. The Locate button makes it easy to find your place in the table of contents once you've located a page that helps you

Another way to find information is to use the Search tab. Unlike the Index tab, the Search tab searches all of the pages for the topic you want to find. Once you've entered the topic, and your search returns a list of all of the pages that contain your data, you can scroll through the titles of the pages in the left tab. The tab lists the page's title and location as well as your request's relevance; however, the relevance isn't very useful when you're searching for only one word.

 CAUTION *Using a non-specific word such as "a" or "the" in your search request results in almost every page being returned.*

If you want to search on more than one word, you need to be aware of a couple of things. If, for instance, you want to search with a multiple word phrase, you'll probably not get the results you want. Searching on the words *SELECT* and *INTO* returns any page that contains both *SELECT* and *INTO*. If you place the words between quotes, however, they are interpreted as a single phrase. That means *"SELECT INTO"* returns a first page with the syntax for using that Transact SQL command where *SELECT INTO* displays the DTS Import/Export wizard.

The second thing to be aware of is that you can nest your searches. Rather than searching for *"SELECT INTO"* you could search for *SELECT*. Once you get your results, you could check the Search Previous Results box at the bottom of the page and then search for *INTO*. Another option that will cut down on results being returned is to search only the titles.

Going to the Microsoft Developer Network

BOL, although a good reference, has a couple of strikes against it. First, it's a collection of technical manuals, and sometimes those manuals assume you understand what they are trying to explain. Second, it's only updated when you install SQL Server or a Service Pack.

Microsoft Developer Network (MSDN), on the other hand, is dynamic data that contains not only all of the technical manuals from BOL but also from a number of other periodicals and online forums. The starting point for MSDN is `http://msdn.microsoft.com`. From here you have access to the same information that Microsoft Tech Support has. Every Knowledge Base article is listed, and links to any patches are easy to find. Searching through MSDN is painless: Just enter the words you want to search for in the search box at the upper left of the screen. The search will return a list of links that match you criteria as well as give you a chance to determine what should be searched (see Figure B-4).

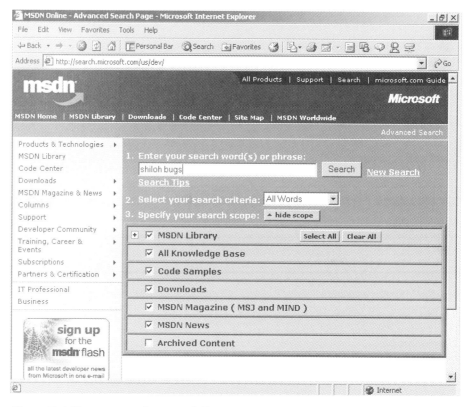

Figure B-4. You can search many different areas on MSDN

TIP *If you are searching for what you think might be a bug, you should use the keyword* shiloh_bug. *For some reason, Microsoft keeps track of the bugs by the prerelease code name for SQL Server 2000. If, on the other hand, you are looking for something that isn't a bug, include* SQL2000.

MSDN also sells a DVD (or several CDs) with all of the MSDN content on it. This comes as a quarterly update and, although it isn't as up-to-date as the online version, it can be handy for searching locally when you don't have an Internet connection.

Other Online Resources

These online resources will help you find more information about SQL Server and database administration:

- Pinnacle Publishing's free bi-weekly SQL Newsletter (`http://www.pinnaclepublishing.com/sql`): Every issue offers interesting tidbits and explores a new system stored procedure.

- Microsoft's SQL Server home (`http://www.microsoft.com/sql`): What can I say? This is *the* source for finding out new information straight from Microsoft's Web servers. It also contains links to service packs, technical resources, and information about all of the versions of SQL Server and the related products.

- Microsoft SQL Server on MSDN (`http://msdn.microsoft.com/sql`): This contains all of the SQL documentation along with links to new information, downloads for service packs, and more.

Calling on a Friend

Another good source of help is the folks you know. If there is a SQL Server User's Group in your area, then it may be a good place to learn new things and network with other DBAs. Rarely are any of the problems you'll encounter new; generally they are only new to you. Knowing folks you can email or call to help walk you through a problem frequently speeds up solving that problem.

With the Internet, your neighborhood spreads much farther than it used to spread. Communities with forums for trading information and news abound, and those communities and accompanying email lists are good places to get help as well. There are two online communities that I pay close attention to, one is at `http://www.reluctantdba.com` and the other is my local SQL Server Users Group at `http://communities.msn.com/CincinnatiSQLServerUserGroup`. If you're interested, visit the Cincinnati community, and you'll find information on how to start your own local user's group.

Other Reading Material

Now that I've covered the online material, Appendix C, "Recommended for the Bookshelf," lists some of the paper-bound products you might find helpful.

APPENDIX C

Recommended for the Bookshelf

The best book on programming for the layman is Alice in Wonderland; *but that's because it's the best book on anything for the layman.*
—Anonymous

OK, AS SOMEONE WHO BEGAN life as a programmer and has needed to learn on the job, I have winnowed through many different books and magazines. This appendix contains what has made it onto the bookshelf that I reference most often. I'll also add an explanation of *why* the magazine or book has made it onto my bookshelf.

Magazines

I recommend these magazines:

- *SQL Server Magazine* (`http://www.sqlmag.com`): This magazine is all SQL Server, all the time, or, as they put it: "The independent source of technical, how-to information for SQL Server developers and administrators." Once a month, when this shows up in my mailbox, I read it from cover to cover and always learn something new.

- *SQL Server Professional* (`http://www.pinnaclepublishing.com/sql`): Although pricier than *SQL Server Magazine*, *SQL Server Professional* publishes some of the top authors focusing on real-life problems, and the online archive is filled with wonderful gems like Dr. Tom's articles that help you solve real problems.

SQL Server Books

SQL Server books fall into several broad categories. Some books, such as this one, are general-reference books that cover many things. Others focus in on specific areas such as Transact SQL (TSQL) or Data Transformation Services (DTS). With that in mind, I've broken these books out by category.

General Reference

These are good general-reference books:

- *Inside Microsoft SQL Server 2000* by Kalen Delaney (Microsoft Press). This is *the* ultimate reference for SQL Server. It covers everything in depth. It's not a book I've read cover to cover but an invaluable resource for turning to when you need to understand the way SQL Server works. That the entire book is on CD makes it a handy reference resource for searching.

- *Microsoft SQL Server 2000 Administrator's Companion* by Garcia, Reding, Whalen, and DeLuca (Microsoft Press). This is another good reference book that focuses on what administrators need to know.

Transact SQL Language

Both of the general-reference books cover TSQL, but once you think you know TSQL, pick up the following two books for more information:

- *Advanced Transact SQL for SQL Server 2000* by Ben-Gan and Moreau (Apress). When I first picked this book up, I thought I was pretty good with SQL. One of the nice features of this book is that Ben-Gan and Moreau start out with the type of SQL code that I would usually write and then they do a nice job of explaining how to make it better.

- *SQL For Smarties: Advanced SQL Programming, 2nd Edition* by Joe Celko (Morgan Kaufman). This is another advanced book but well worth the read. Celko is a recognized speaker and author who does a good job of explaining frequently encountered problems and offering tested solutions for solving them without having to reinvent the wheel.

From the Programming Side

Even if you are a full-time DBA and don't get involved with coding at all, I recommend you pick up one or both of these books to help your programmers when they encounter road blocks not related to the server. And if you are programming both the server and client, these books are must haves:

- *Hitchhiker's Guide to Visual Basic and SQL Server* by William Vaughn (Microsoft Press). I once rewrote a program four or five times as I worked my way through this book, but at the book's end, my program sang. This book is the bible for writing Visual Basic code to interface with SQL Server. Vaughn's writing style makes the book easy to read, and it's filled with great examples.

- *ADO Examples and Best Practices* by William Vaughn (Apress). The second edition should be available and packed with ADO.NET information. This is a good explanation of ADO, how it works, and the best way to incorporate it into programs.

Data Transformation Services

This is a good book to learn more about DTS:

- *Microsoft SQL Server 2000 DTS* by Timothy Peterson (Sams). When I first needed to use DTS, I wasn't getting far in doing what I wanted with Books On Line, so I hit the bookstores, only to find there weren't really any books on the subject, just this one. To my utter delight, however, I found it to be chocked full of the information necessary to help me do my job and to go further than I thought possible with DTS. Although there are a couple of new DTS books out, I haven't found one I like better than this one.

Non-Programming Books

You may be wondering about this section, but it is a fact of life that you can learn things anywhere that apply to programming. To that end I want to recommend a couple books that have helped me immensely in programming and they are related, although they don't look it.

- *Alice's Adventures in Wonderland and Through the Looking Glass* by Lewis Carroll. Perhaps it's not the best book on *anything* for the layman, but Charles Dodgson (a.k.a. Lewis Carroll) was a logician who also wrote stories and filled them with puzzles that both entertain and educate. Working your way through the illogical logic that populates the worlds Alice finds herself in makes for good practice in deciphering what users are asking for.

- *Godel, Escher, Bach: An Eternal Golden Braid* by Douglas R. Hofstadter (Basic Books). A Pulitzer Prize-winning book, this book is for anyone who has ever encountered recursion in programming. Walking through the artwork of Escher, the music of Bach, and the mathematics of Godel, Hofstadter gives you a lot to think about and does it in a way that will entertain along the way.

APPENDIX D

Bulk Copy Program

For those who like this sort of thing, this is the sort of thing they like.
—Abraham Lincoln

THE BULK COPY PROGRAM (bcp) utility is designed to load data into SQL Server from files. In reality, bcp provides a command-line interface to special functionality built into Open DataBase Connectivity (ODBC). Before SQL Server 7 came out, bcp was widely used for getting data into and out of databases when whole tables were involved. With SQL Server 7 came a new tool, Data Transformation Services (DTS), which was discussed in detail in Chapter 14, "What Are the Data Transformation Services (DTS)?" Although DTS uses bcp, there are some things it doesn't allow you to do; so, we're going to introduce bcp in this appendix.

One reason I haven't fully committed to DTS is the flexibility of bcp. What many people don't realize is that you can format data using views. If data has to be altered—data type changes, column orders changed, rows eliminated—I use views. DTS just can't compete with bcp and a view. Likewise, I use both Bulk Insert and bcp to load data, and, again, rather than use DTS, I load data directly into the destination database using a transition table to hold the data and then use queries or stored procedures to "cleanse" the data. I haven't run into a situation where DTS could do something I couldn't do by using good old-fashioned SQL, but of course I haven't experienced every possible scenario. There is no doubt in my mind DTS is a useful product, but I just prefer bcp.

To see bcp, get to a command prompt, type bcp, and hit Enter (see Figure D-1). This brings up a list of all of the parameters you can use with the utility. We're not going to go over all of the options, but we'll cover some of the basics, starting with how to create a file from a database table.

```
D:\>bcp
usage: bcp {dbtable | query} {in | out | queryout | format} datafile
  [-m maxerrors]            [-f formatfile]           [-e errfile]
  [-F firstrow]             [-L lastrow]              [-b batchsize]
  [-n native type]          [-c character type]       [-w wide character type]
  [-N keep non-text native] [-V file format version]  [-q quoted identifier]
  [-C code page specifier]  [-t field terminator]     [-r row terminator]
  [-i inputfile]            [-o outfile]              [-a packetsize]
  [-S server name]          [-U username]             [-P password]
  [-T trusted connection]   [-v version]              [-R regional enable]
  [-k keep null values]     [-E keep identity values]
  [-h "load hints"]
```

Figure D-1. bcp has a number of parameters you can use to insert or extract data

What Are bcp's Required Parameters?

BCP has three required parameters. The first parameter to discuss is (dbtable | query). The pipe character (|) indicates that either dbtable or query can be used. This is the database location that bcp will use. If a table is being used, it is best to fully qualify the name of the table with the database name, owner, and table name. For instance, rdba11.dbo.VeterinariansVeterinaryOffices would refer to the database **RDBA11** and the table VeterinariansVeterinaryOffices that was created by dbo. It's possible to eliminate the "dbo" and just use database..tablename if the table is owned by dbo. Alternately, if you didn't want an entire table, you could use a Transact SQL (TSQL) statement instead. This could be a SELECT statement or a stored procedure. The important thing to remember is that the query must be in quotes so that the command will be interpreted as a single parameter.

The second parameter is (in | out). This determines the direction that bcp processes the data. If this parameter is in, then the data moves from the data file into the database; if out, from the database to the data file.

NOTE *When you specify a query is to be used, instead of the command "out" you must use "queryout" or the command will fail.*

The third required parameter is the name of the data file you want to load data from or create. If no path is specified, the file will be created/looked for in the current directory.

What Are bcp's Security Parameters?

bcp has four security parameters: -S, -T, -U, and -P. Each of these is related to determining which SQL Server to connect to and how to connect to it.

NOTE *With bcp, case counts. If the parameter is shown with uppercase, then you can't use lowercase. All of the security parameters are uppercase.*

- -S is the server name. If this parameter isn't specified, then bcp assumes you are connecting to the default instance of SQL Server on the machine where bcp is running. If you are connecting to another server or an instance of SQL Server other than the default, then you can specify the server using -S ServerName\Instance.

- -T specifies you want to use a trusted connection. This uses the Windows Login to determine whether bcp has access to the objects on the server.

- -U specifies the SQL Server account to be used when connecting. If neither -T nor -U is used, then bcp assumes it is connecting as sa, which is a potential security breach.

- -P specifies the password for the user account specified in -U. If you have a login that has no password, then you can use -P without a value after it.[1]

How Does bcp Format Data?

When it comes to formatting data, bcp offers a wealth of options. The first two options are to use either character or native format. Native format stores information in a binary format that SQL Server can understand. Character format stores the data in a text format with tabs between columns and ends rows with carriage return/line-feed combinations. Listing D-1 shows a sample bcp command for getting data out of the database. In this case, it is creating a text file that contains all of the data from the table VeterinariansVeterinaryOffices. Figure D-2 shows the difference between the character output and native output for this table.

Listing D-1. Using bcp to extract data to a text file from a specific server using a trusted connection

```
bcp rdba11..VeterinariansVeterinaryOffices out VeterinariansVeterinaryOffices.
txt -c -T -SJDS-LAPTOP\Reluctantdba
```

---

[1] If you have a login that has no password, or worse, if your sa login has no password, please go back and read Chapter 11, "How Do I Secure My Data?" Alternately, you can post a sign on your server that says, "Open to the world, please help yourself to my data."

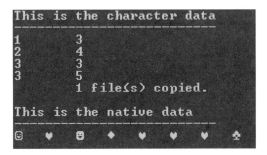

Figure D-2. bcp data can be put out in either character format that is easy for humans to read or native format that is easy for computers to read

Of course, these are the simplest ways to use bcp, but there are more options available for formatting either the data files you want to create or the files you want to import. Fortunately, bcp offers two other parameters that help in formatting your data: -t and -r.

-t lets you specify the field terminator to be used. When a field terminator isn't specified, the default value of a tab is used. In some instances, however, you might want to use another value, especially if the data contains tabs within a character or text field. One frequent field terminator is the pipe character (|). This character is rarely found in text fields, so it makes a good field terminator.

If your data contains carriage return/line feeds within some columns or the program using the file you are exporting (or that created the file you are importing) can't handle carriage returns or line feeds, then you won't be able to use carriage return/line feed for your row terminator. Instead, you can define a new row terminator using -r. For instance, you might use three pipes (|||) to define the end of a row. Using the code in Listing D-2 would result in a file that looked like this:

```
1|3|||2|4|||3|3|||3|5|||
```

Listing D-2. Using bcp to extract data to a text file using specific row and field terminators

```
bcp rdba11..VeterinariansVeterinaryOffices out
VeterinariansVeterinaryOffices.txt -c -T -SJDS-LAPTOP\Reluctantdba -r"|||"  -t"|"
```

With both -r and -t you use special characters to represent control characters such as tabs or carriage returns. Table D-1 lists the control characters and the codes to use. You can use any combination of characters, but the maximum number of characters you can specify for a row or field terminator is 10. Each control character represents a single character.

Table D-1. Control Characters for Row and Field Terminators

CONTROL CHARACTER	SPECIAL CODE
Tab	\t
Line feed	\n
Carriage return	\r
Backslash	\\
Null	\0

Is bcp Faster?

It depends. If you are loading a table that has no indices, no triggers, that isn't being replicated, and your database is set to either simple or bulk-logged recovery, then this is the fastest way to load data. Well, OK, you could use the TSQL BULK INSERT command, but that's just another interface to the same application programming interface (API) calls that bcp uses. When all of these conditions are met, this is a blazingly fast way to load data into the database.

When all of these conditions are not met, you won't get the same blazingly fast performance. Still, it is pretty good at loading data *and* much more efficient than writing separate programs to handle loading data. It is a flexible tool that is good at what it does: pushing data into or pulling data out of the database. Depending on how your database is set up, it can be fast or slow.

 CAUTION *Whether using bcp,* BULK INSERT, *or some program that shoves data in, you can fill up your transaction log quickly if you load a multimillion-row table.*

Last Words

So, why use bcp at all? That's a legitimate question. I've spent most of this book showing you how to use interfaces built into the Enterprise Manager or another tool that put a useful interface over the ugly command-line interfaces. I even spent an entire chapter—Chapter 14, "What Are the Data Transformation Services (DTS)?"—showing you how to import and export data using wizards, all so that you wouldn't have to be bothered by the messy parameters that are bcp, so why am I taking a few pages to detail how to use bcp?

Well, there are two reasons. First, I *love* bcp. I've been using it since before DTS existed. That's probably the programmer in me going back to my MS-DOS roots and remembering `DIR` and `CLS`. My second reason is probably more pragmatic. DTS is a great tool. I wouldn't get rid of DTS, but it can be a lot of overhead for a simple process. When I need a quick and dirty data dump in either direction, I turn to bcp because it is a lightweight interface designed specifically to push data into or pull data out of SQL Server.

It isn't without some problems, though, as a quick scan of Microsoft's Knowledge Base will show. Table D-2 lists some of the bugs present at the time of this writing. (If you have Internet Explorer 5, you can access Knowledge Base "Q" articles by simply typing in MSKB Qxxxxx, for example MSKB Q179657.) Even so, if all I need to do is to pull data from a table, I can have the data finished using bcp before I am halfway through the steps necessary to use DTS. And, because it never fails that someone needs a snapshot of data "just this once," I keep bcp handy and ready to use.

Table D-2. Potential bcp Problems

KNOWLEDGE BASE ARTICLE	TITLE
Q179657	BUG: BCP Fails to Parse Format File If It Has White Space in Column Name
Q180711	BUG: DMO BCP Fails When Using Mixed Security and Trusted Connection
Q182074	BUG: HDR Hangs When You Transfer Decimal Data to SQL DateTime Column Using BCP

Resources

- How to Bulk Copy Out All the Tables in a Database, Microsoft Knowledge Base article Q176818:
  `http://support.microsoft.com/support/kb/articles/Q176/8/18.ASP`

Glossary

"Would you tell me, please," said Alice, "what that means?"
—Lewis Carroll, *Through the Looking Glass*

alias:

An alias is another name given to an object. Aliases can be used for clarity when two objects of the same name are used in a Transact SQL statement (such as referencing two copies of the same table). Aliasing is often used for compatibility, to make table or column names "friendlier," or to minimize typing, such as using initials for tables with long names. Minimizing typing is probably one of the more common uses.

Boolean statement:

A Boolean statement resolves itself to either TRUE or FALSE. In SQL Server, Boolean statements will not include values that resolve to NULL. Those must be accounted for separately.

bottom:

BOTTOM, along with TOP, is a keyword used in SELECT to limit the amount of data that will be returned. This may or may not impact the amount of processing that needs to be done to return data.

cascading:

Cascading occurs when a **primary key** in one table that is also used as a **foreign key** constraint in another table is either changed or deleted. Changes to the primary key and deletions of referenced rows are not normally allowed, but when cascading is turned on, the rows in other tables that are dependent upon the primary key are either deleted or modified.

check constraint:

A check constraint works like a **foreign key** constraint except that the allowed values aren't contained in another table but defined within a Boolean statement.

clustered index:

A clustered index physically sorts the table according to the **index**. The leaves of a clustered index, instead of containing pointers to the physical location of the data in the table, *are* the physical location of the table. Including all of the data for that row in the index eliminates the need to walk through both the index and the table.

composite key:
A **foreign key** or **primary key** made up of more than one column.

constraint:
A constraint is a rule used to enforce data integrity on a SQL Server database.

covered query:
A covered query is one in which every single column referenced in the query is contained within an **index** and no reads of the physical data file need to be made to return data.

data shredding:
Taking data from an XML format and updating one or more tables.

data splicing:
Taking data from one or more tables and rendering it into XML format.

database:
A database is any system that lets you store and retrieve information.

database backup:
A backup is a *complete* copy of the database structure, including any **index, constraint** or programming that it contains at a moment in time.

Declarative Referential Integrity:
Declarative Referential Integrity is a fancy term that means, "verifying that the data being used as a **foreign key** exists in the **primary key** table."

differential database backup:
A snapshot of everything that has been changed since the last backup and up to the time the backup is executed. This requires multiple steps in restoring data to recover to a given point in time.

distribution steps:
Distribution steps indicate the number of bins that the data has been split into for the histogram.

DTS
Data Transformation Services provide an easy to use interface for importing and exporting data and modifying the data during the import/export process.

DTS connection:

A connection is a link to a data source. The data source can be a relational database, a text file, an XML file, a spreadsheet, or any other ODBC-compliant data source.

DTS custom task:

A DTS custom task is the actual task being done within the **DTS task**. For instance, an Execute SQL task is the custom task that actually executes a Transact SQL command within a task placeholder.

DTS package:

The framework for storing all of the component parts required to accomplish a related set of data transformations. Can include a **DTS connection**, **DTS step**, and **DTS task**.

DTS global variable:

A global variable within DTS is a named bucket that stores a value. That value can be referenced by name within a **DTS package**.

DTS step:

A DTS step is used for structuring the order in which DTS tasks are run.

DTS task:

A DTS task is an action to be taken to move or manipulate data.

fill factor:

The fill factor determines how much free space is created within the leaves of an **index** when it is created.

first normal form:

First normal form is a database where all repeating properties are separated into a table as rows and linked back to the original table using a **foreign key**.

foreign key:

A foreign key is a column in one table (foreign/child) that references a unique row in another table (primary/parent). The data types of the columns being related between the two tables must match, and the value must exist in the referred table. Because that value was not generated in the current table, it is called *foreign*.

fragmentation:

A table is fragmented when it has empty holes in the pages and extents that it takes up.

identity column:
An identity column is one in which SQL Server automatically generates a value (beginning with 1 by default) for an inserted row and which is incremented with each subsequently inserted row. You can define the starting number (*identity seed*) and the increment value for each subsequent number. This identity seed gets reused every time the table is either truncated or re-created. Please note that SQL Server does not reuse numbers that have been deleted. Instead you simply have gaps in your numbers, as it should be.

index:
An index is a sorted subset of the fields that make up a table and includes a pointer to where each row that makes up the rest of the row of data is located.

indices:
The proper plural of **index** though often replaced by the word *indexes*.

inline functions:
A user-defined function that returns a rowset and uses the function parameters to filter the data in the WHERE condition of the SELECT statement. Inline functions can be used in the FROM clause of a SELECT.

Inner Join:
An Inner Join matches two tables based on one or more column both tables have in common, usually a **foreign key** relationship. Both tables must have matching rows to display data. It's best to have the smallest result set as the first table listed in the view.

junction table:
A junction is a table where every column is a part of the **primary key** that is designed to relate two tables together in a many-to-many relationship.

markup language attribute:
An attribute is another term for *property*. You may freely substitute the word *property* if it helps.

optional parameters:
Optional parameters are **parameters** for a **stored procedure** that contain a default value. Specifying a default value for the parameter means that the parameter doesn't need to be provided when calling the procedure.

Outer Join:
An Outer Join displays *all* records from one table and the matching records from the other. If there is no matching row in the joined table, NULL is displayed for that table's selected columns.

output parameters:
Output parameters are **parameters** that can return data, much like using the
ByRef keyword in Visual Basic. If the value is changed within the context of
the stored procedure, the new value can be used by the client.

parameters:
Parameters are named buckets that hold data passed between a program
and a stored procedure or function. See also **output parameters** and
optional parameters.

primary key:
A primary key is a special property or group of properties of an object that
uniquely identify it from like objects. This book's ISBN number, for instance, is
unique to this specific book and could function as a primary key.

relational:
Relational databases are composed of tables where logically related pieces of
information are stored. Relational databases logically break data up so that each
table stores all of the data "related" to that information. This is different from
"relating" data in two or more tables by joining them together.

rollback:
Rolling back is not merely stopping a **transaction**; it is resetting the database to
the state it was in *before* the transaction started. Rolling back a transaction
doesn't exit a set of Transact SQL statements.

runaway database:
Any database whose combined data and transaction log size exceeds disk capacity or vastly exceeds the amount of usable data in the database.

second normal form:
Second normal form is a database where all repeating data values are put into
one separate table and linked back to the original table using a **foreign key**.

selectivity:
The amount of uniqueness in an **index**. The more unique hits per total number
of rows, the more effective the index and the higher the selectivity.

SPID:
System Process ID. This is the unique process ID generated when a user connects
to the server. This value remains constant for the life of the connection. Note:
recording the SPID in the application is not a good practice as the SPID can
change if the application needs to reconnect and uses the SPID for any process
activity.

SQL Server Agent job:
A set of Transact SQL (TSQL) statements that have a predefined order to achieve a purpose. Jobs are not limited to just TSQL statements, though.

stored procedure:
A stored procedure is a set of Transact SQL (TSQL) statements that function like a Visual Basic sub or an object's method. TSQL stored procedures allow for flow control, parameters, and output functionality.

subquery:
A subquery is a part of a SQL statement that could stand on its own as a query but is included as a filter in another query.

third normal form:
Third normal form is a database where all fields in a table are directly related to the primary key of that table.

Top:
TOP, along with BOTTOM, is a keyword used in SELECT to limit the amount of data that will be returned. This may or may not impact the amount of processing that needs to be done to return data.

Transact SQL:
SQL Server's Transact Structured Query Language (TSQL) can be used for everything you do in SQL Server, including creating new tables, putting data into them, getting data out of them, and changing the properties of the database itself. Its syntax is kind of like the English language, only not.

transaction:
A transaction is a group of commands that are either *all* completed successfully or none of them are.

transaction log backup:
A backup of all of the transactions that have occurred since the last full **database backup** or last transaction log backup, whichever is more recent, whether full, differential, or transaction log.

triggers:
Triggers are to a SQL Server database what events are to Windows Forms. They are stored procedures executed in response to an event on a table such as inserting a new row or updating/deleting existing data. Triggers are executed as part of a transaction and can affect a transaction.

update:
An update doesn't just change data. It is actually a delete followed by an insert. Unless you are dealing with **triggers**, however, you can consider an update to just modify data.

variables:
Variables are named buckets that hold data that can be manipulated by name. They are named with the DECLARE keyword and require that the data type of the variable be specified.

view:
A view is a virtual table that doesn't really exist. In more technical terms, a view is a stored Transact SQL (TSQL) statement that has a name. When that name is used, SQL Server replaces the name with the predefined TSQL statement.

XML:
Although XML stands for eXtensible Markup Language, it really isn't a language *per se*. It is probably easier to think of XML as the alphabet of a language, one in which you can put the parts together to form your own dialect (data definition).

XML element:
An *element* is defined as all of the attributes of a tag and anything between the opening and closing of that tag, including the opening and closing tags themselves.

XML element's value:
The value of a tag or element is whatever is found between the opening and closing tags.

XML root element:
The **XML element** that contains all other data in the XML file. There can be only one root element.

XML schema:
A document type definition written in XML. It can be found either in the same document as the data or in a separate document referenced by the data document.

XML template:
An XML file containing special tags that can execute SQL commands.

Index

Announcing *About VS.NET*—
the *free* Apress .NET e-newsletter with great .NET news, information, code—and attitude

We guarantee that this isn't going to be your typical boring e-newsletter with just a list of URLs (though it will have them as well).

Instead, *About VS.NET* will contain contributions from a whole slate of top .NET gurus, edited by award-winning, best-selling authors Gary Cornell and Dan Appleman. Upcoming issues will feature articles on:

- Best coding practices in ADO.NET

- The hidden "gotchas" in doing thread programming in VB.NET

- Why C# is (not) a better choice than VB.NET

- What Java can learn from C# and vice versa

About VS.NET will cover it all!

This *free* e-newsletter will be the easiest way for you to get up-to-date .NET information delivered to your Inbox every two weeks—more often if there's breaking news!

Apress Titles

ISBN	LIST PRICE	AUTHOR	TITLE
1-893115-01-1	$39.95	Appleman	Appleman's Win32 API Puzzle Book and Tutorial for Visual Basic Programmers
1-893115-23-2	$29.95	Appleman	How Computer Programming Works
1-893115-97-6	$39.95	Appleman	Moving to VB.NET: Strategies, Concepts, and Code
1-893115-09-7	$29.95	Baum	Dave Baum's Definitive Guide to LEGO MINDSTORMS
1-893115-84-4	$29.95	Baum, Gasperi, Hempel, and Villa	Extreme MINDSTORMS
1-893115-82-8	$59.95	Ben-Gan/Moreau	Advanced Transact-SQL for SQL Server 2000
1-893115-90-9	$44.95	Finsel	The Handbook for Reluctant Database Administrators
1-893115-85-2	$34.95	Gilmore	A Programmer's Introduction to PHP 4.0
1-893115-17-8	$59.95	Gross	A Programmer's Introduction to Windows DNA
1-893115-62-3	$39.95	Gunnerson	A Programmer's Introduction to C#, Second Edition
1-893115-10-0	$34.95	Holub	Taming Java Threads
1-893115-04-6	$34.95	Hyman/Vaddadi	Mike and Phani's Essential C++ Techniques
1-893115-50-X	$34.95	Knudsen	Wireless Java: Developing with Java 2, Micro Edition
1-893115-79-8	$49.95	Kofler	Definitive Guide to Excel VBA
1-893115-56-9	$39.95	Kofler	MySQL
1-893115-87-9	$39.95	Kurata	Doing Web Development: Client-Side Techniques
1-893115-75-5	$44.95	Kurniawan	Internet Programming with VB
1-893115-19-4	$49.95	Macdonald	Serious ADO: Universal Data Access with Visual Basic
1-893115-06-2	$39.95	Marquis/Smith	A Visual Basic 6.0 Programmer's Toolkit

ISBN	LIST PRICE	AUTHOR	TITLE
1-893115-22-4	$27.95	McCarter	David McCarter's VB Tips and Techniques
1-893115-76-3	$49.95	Morrison	C++ For VB Programmers
1-893115-80-1	$39.95	Newmarch	A Programmer's Guide to Jini Technology
1-893115-81-X	$39.95	Pike	SQL Server: Common Problems, Tested Solutions
1-893115-20-8	$34.95	Rischpater	Wireless Web Development
1-893115-93-3	$34.95	Rischpater	Wireless Web Development with PHP and WAP
1-893115-24-0	$49.95	Sinclair	From Access to SQL Server
1-893115-94-1	$29.95	Spolsky	User Interface Design for Programmers
1-893115-53-4	$39.95	Sweeney	Visual Basic for Testers
1-893115-29-1	$44.95	Thomsen	Database Programming with Visual Basic .NET
1-893115-65-8	$39.95	Tiffany	Pocket PC Database Development with eMbedded Visual Basic
1-893115-59-3	$59.95	Troelsen	C# and the .NET Platform
1-893115-54-2	$49.95	Trueblood/Lovett	Data Mining and Statistical Analysis Using SQL
1-893115-16-X	$49.95	Vaughn	ADO Examples and Best Practices
1-893115-83-6	$44.95	Wells	Code Centric: T-SQL Programming with Stored Procedures and Triggers
1-893115-95-X	$49.95	Welschenbach	Cryptography in C and C++
1-893115-05-4	$39.95	Williamson	Writing Cross-Browser Dynamic HTML
1-893115-78-X	$49.95	Zukowski	Definitive Guide to Swing for Java 2, Second Edition
1-893115-92-5	$49.95	Zukowski	Java Collections

Available at bookstores nationwide or from Springer Verlag New York, Inc. at 1-800-777-4643; fax 1-212-533-3503. Contact us for more information at sales@apress.com.

Apress Titles Publishing SOON!

ISBN	AUTHOR	TITLE
1-893115-73-9	Abbott	Voice Enabling Web Applications: VoiceXML and Beyond
1-893115-45-3	Anderson	Beginning Web Services for .NET
1-893115-37-2	Bock/Singer	.NET Security
1-893115-39-9	Chand/Gold	A Programmer's Guide to ADO .NET in C#
1-893115-99-2	Cornell/Morrison	Programming VB .NET: A Guide for Experienced Programmers
1-893115-72-0	Curtin	Building Trust: Online Security for Developers
1-893115-71-2	Ferguson	Mobile .NET
1-893115-42-9	Foo/Lee	XML Programming Using the Microsoft XML Parser
1-893115-55-0	Frenz	Visual Basic for Scientists
1-893115-36-4	Goodwill	Apache Jakarta-Tomcat
1-893115-96-8	Jorelid	J2EE FrontEnd Technologies: A Programmer's Guide to Servlets, JavaServer Pages, and Enterprise JavaBeans
1-893115-49-6	Kilburn	Palm Programming in Basic
1-893115-38-0	Lafler	Power AOL: A Survival Guide
1-893115-58-5	Oellermann	Architecting Web Services
1-893115-89-5	Shemitz	Kylix: The Professional Developer's Guide and Reference
1-893115-40-2	Sill	An Introduction to qmail
1-893115-26-7	Troelsen	Visual Basic .NET and the .NET Platform
1-893115-68-2	Vaughn	ADO Examples and Best Practices, Second Edition

Available at bookstores nationwide or from Springer Verlag New York, Inc. at 1-800-777-4643; fax 1-212-533-3503. Contact us for more information at sales@apress.com.

books for professionals by professionals™

apress™

About Apress

Apress, located in Berkeley, CA, is an innovative publishing company devoted to meeting the needs of existing and potential programming professionals. Simply put, the "A" in Apress stands for the "Author's Press™." Apress' unique author-centric approach to publishing grew from conversations between Dan Appleman and Gary Cornell, authors of best-selling, highly regarded computer books. In 1998, they set out to create a publishing company that emphasized quality above all else, a company with books that would be considered the best in their market. Dan and Gary's vision has resulted in over 30 widely acclaimed titles by some of the industry's leading software professionals.

Do You Have What It Takes to Write for Apress?

Apress is rapidly expanding its publishing program. If you can write and refuse to compromise on the quality of your work, if you believe in doing more then rehashing existing documentation, and if you're looking for opportunities and rewards that go far beyond those offered by traditional publishing houses, we want to hear from you!

Consider these innovations that we offer all of our authors:

- **Top royalties with *no* hidden switch statements**
  Authors typically only receive half of their normal royalty rate on foreign sales. In contrast, Apress' royalty rate remains the same for both foreign and domestic sales.

- **A mechanism for authors to obtain equity in Apress**
  Unlike the software industry, where stock options are essential to motivate and retain software professionals, the publishing industry has adhered to an outdated compensation model based on royalties alone. In the spirit of most software companies, Apress reserves a significant portion of its equity for authors.

- **Serious treatment of the technical review process**
  Each Apress book has a technical reviewing team whose remuneration depends in part on the success of the book since they too receive royalties.

Moreover, through a partnership with Springer-Verlag, one of the world's major publishing houses, Apress has significant venture capital behind it. Thus, we have the resources to produce the highest quality books *and* market them aggressively.

If you fit the model of the Apress author who can write a book that gives the "professional what he or she needs to know™," then please contact one of our Editorial Directors, Gary Cornell (gary_cornell@apress.com), Dan Appleman (dan_appleman@apress.com), Karen Watterson (karen_watterson@apress.com) or Jason Gilmore (jason_gilmore@apress.com) for more information.

Apress™

License Agreement (Single-User Products)